AF531752

EMOTIONAL INTELLIGENCE, OCCUPATIONAL STRESS AND JOB SATISFACTION OF SPECIAL EDUCATION TEACHERS

EMOTIONAL INTELLIGENCE, OCCUPATIONAL STRESS AND JOB SATISFACTION OF SPECIAL EDUCATION TEACHERS

By

R. POORNIMA

Project Fellow
Department of Education
School of Education and HRD
Dravidian University, Kuppam
A.P. State, India

D P H

DISCOVERY PUBLISHING HOUSE PVT. LTD.

NEW DELHI-110 002

Published by:
Tilak Wasan
DISCOVERY PUBLISHING HOUSE PVT. LTD.
4383/4A, Ansari Road, Darya Ganj
New Delhi-110 002 (India)
Phone : +91-11-23279245, 43596064-65
Fax : +91-11-23253475
E-mail : parul.wasan@gmail.com
discoverypublishinghouse@gmail.com
web : www.discoverypublishinggroup.com

***First Edition:* 2012**

ISBN: 978-93-5056-009-7

Emotional Intelligence, Occupational Stress and Job Satisfaction of Special Education Teachers

Printed at:
Shree Balaji Art Press
Delhi

Preface

"Anyone can become angry that is easy. But to be angry with the right person, to the right degree, at the right time, for the right purpose and in the right way is not easy.

—Aristotle

As inclusion is gaining ground throughout the world, teachers and others involved in education are working to develop positive educational experiences to all children with disabilities. Any educational system should change to better accommodate the diversity of needs that pupils have and include them in all aspects of school life, identify any barriers within and around the school that hinder learning and participation and reduce or remove these barriers. In this context, the special education teachers have to play vital roles in the organization of the class, teaching and training, guidance and counselling, intra and interpersonal relations apart from research activities. Special educators constitute the active resource of any special schools, who really determines the efficiency and utilization of all other resources in schools. Due to increased demands and changes, the special education teachers in both special schools and in regular schools have to play multiple roles and have many responsibilities.

The need for flexibility, autonomy and novelty makes their job definitions inherently ambiguous making room for more role conflicts. Also, the complexity of their roles creates stress and strain in them. As a student of Special Education in the year 2006, I had an opportunity to teach children with disabilities and interact with the special education teachers during my Internship Training Programme. During that time, I have observed that the teachers teaching children with disabilities are undergoing stress and strain because of various stressors like lack of supportive staff, inadequate resources, diversified roles and responsibilities and so on. These stress factors made them cynical towards work, colleagues, children and the school as a whole and had low self-efficacy, less organizational commitment, low job satisfaction which further deteriorated their job performance. Dissatisfied teachers may deliver poor service to the children with disabilities and affects the well-being of the teachers themselves. During teaching-learning process, most of the teachers exhibited false face towards their students. Also they felt that teaching small concept as big burden as they are not properly trained to meet the requirements of the diverse needs of children with disabilities.

The challenge of overcoming stress and performing the tasks in special school is such that they need high degree of emotional strength, flexibility of procedures and routines, freedom to act according to the student needs and co-worker's support. Emotional competence is as important, sometimes more important than academic competence in managing special needs children. The most unique feature of the special education teachers is that their contribution can enhance considerably through adoption of an effective management policy based on emotional intelligence parameters. But in India, the special education school management emphasis only the cognitive aspect of the special education teachers, whereas their emotional or affective aspect is neglected.

The present book is an effort of the investigation that aimed to identify the level of emotional intelligence, occupational stress and job satisfaction of special education teachers teaching visually impaired, hearing impaired and mentally retarded children, working in the special schools of Chennai city. For this purpose, the rating scales to assess the emotional intelligence, occupational stress, job satisfaction of special education teachers and infrastructure facilities in special education schools was developed. The survey intended to find out the effect of independent variables of the special education teachers like their age, community, educational qualification, nature of special school the teachers working in, training received in special education, level of classes handled, nature of job, years of experience and salary they receive. Also, the investigation attempted to find out the relationship between the emotional intelligence and occupational stress; emotional intelligence and job satisfaction; and occupational stress and job satisfaction of the special education teachers working in three types of special schools. Further, the investigation continued to find out the contribution of special education teachers personal variables to their emotional intelligence, occupational stress and job satisfaction. In addition, the availability of the infrastructural facilities in special schools is quantified from the perception of the special education teachers working in the special schools.

The readers of this book will find it useful in understanding the conceptual framework of emotional intelligence, stress, occupational stress and job satisfaction; components of emotional intelligence and various models of emotional intelligence; sources of occupational stress and different models of stress and occupational stress; factors influencing job satisfaction and important theories of job satisfaction; relationship between emotional intelligence, occupational stress and job satisfaction apart from the roles and responsibilities of the special education teachers in the changing society; and the need and importance of identifying the EI, OS and JS of special education teachers.

The second chapter gives a comprehensive review of literature on the headings like emotional intelligence of teachers, student teachers; occupational stress of teachers, special education teachers; antecedents/consequences of occupational stress; job satisfaction of teachers; and relationship between EI, OS and JS in teaching and other professions. The studies have been reviewed with a fresh perspective and a different focus based on a part of the data from research work of renowned scholars throughout the world. The readers will take pleasure in going through the studies as it reviews thoroughly the entire piece of work (like objectives to results) carried out in different parts of the world and provide insight into the concept of the study. The third chapter describes the statement of problem, objectives, hypotheses, scope and delimitations of the study.

The fourth chapter describes as how the research tools have been developed?; what type of method and sampling procedure adopted?; how the data have been collected ? and what type of statistical techniques was used to analyse the data ?. The fifth chapter is concerned with the analysis of data, testing of hypotheses, presentation of results and discussion both descriptively and differentially with supportive studies. The last chapter concludes with some empirical based educational implications that will be quite useful to enhance the emotional intelligence to reduce occupational stress and promote job satisfaction in teachers. The researches in this area provide better insights to create effective organizational environment, give opportunities to develop healthy intra and inter-personal relations, strengthen professional training components and equip teachers with competencies to meet the needs of the special needs children.

As the statement goes *'the apples on the top of the basket are there because a number of apples are supporting them from inside the basket'*, the persons who have helped me in completing this book have quietly supported. I am taking pride in placing on record the gratitude to my guide: *Prof. G. Lokanadha*

Reddy, Dean, School of Education and HRD, Dravidian University, Kuppam, A.P. State and my parents *Sri. V. Rajendran* and *Smt. R. Sakunthala Mani.*

I am hopeful that this book will be a valuable resource document for the students, research scholars, educationists, policy makers, principals and teachers working in the field of education, special education, integrated/inclusive education to provide barrier free environments, both physically and psychologically and to facilitate better classrooms with enhanced resources and appropriate teaching-learning technologies to promote inclusive classrooms, schools and societies.

Author

Acknowledgement

Lord Almighty is thanked from the bottom of my heart for his infinite blessings on me to complete the thesis. I wish to place on record my deep indebtedness and extreme gratitude to my revered guide *Prof. G. Lokanadha Reddy*, Dean, School of Education and HRD, Dravidian University, Kuppam for his meticulous guidance, constant encouragement, immense patience, care and concern and incessant support throughout the conduct of the study and eternal for my life too.

I express my deep heartfelt thanks to the *Dravidian University Administration* for providing Ph.D. Registration and giving all infrastructural support from time to time to carry out the present study. I am also thankful to the *Head* and the *Staff,* both teaching and non-teaching of the Department of Education, Dravidian University, Kuppam for their constant motivation and appreciation.

I am indebted to *C. Vijayaraj Kumar,* IAS, State Commissioner for the Disabled, Chennai, Tamil Nadu State and *A. Joseph Xavier,* District Disabled Rehabilitation Officer, Chennai, Tamil Nadu State for permitting me to collect the data from the special education schools in and around Chennai City. I take this opportunity to sincerely thank all *Principals* and *Teachers* of the special education schools of Chennai City who have cooperated and helped me during the data collection. Also, I thank *Dr. R. Ramar,* Headmaster, S.S. Hindu Nadar Hr. Sec. School, Muhavur for the support he has rendered for my investigation.

I acknowledge the help rendered by my cousin *Ms. R. Sudha Priya* and *Ms. Bushanamma,* Junior Assistant, Dravidian University in data entry process and *Mr. Shiva Raman* for the statistical analysis. Also, I am obliged to *all the investigators* whose findings are cited/substantially made used for the present study and also had given better insight into the problem under study.

I also express my appreciation to all my *friends, relatives, well wishers* and *co-scholars* for their motivation and encouragement given to me throughout the investigation. Above all, I convey my deep sense of gratitude to my parents *Sri V. Rajendran* and *Smt. R. Sakunthala Mani* for their blessing and support throughout my life.

R. Poornima

Contents

CHAPTER 1

Introduction

Concept, Meaning and Definitions of Emotional Intelligence

The success of any organization depends very much on the quality of its human resources. Of all the prime resources of an organization namely: man, material, method and money, the human resource is recognized as the most vital and the most valuable because it's ultimately the human being who uses and controls all other resources and determines the efficient utilization of these resources. Further, the importance of the human factor also stems from the fact that whereas all other resources depreciate in value with the passage of time and use, the human resource appreciates in value through the acquisition of knowledge and experience. Thus, human resource reflects an inherent dynamism and development potential. Thus in any educational system, the teacher is the key figure. The success of the system to a greater extent depends on the teachers working in the system whether it is primary, secondary, higher secondary, collegiate or university level.

The key objective in the management of any school should be to provide various kinds of learning experiences to its pupils with the objective of developing human beings for their advantage and harnessing their physical, mental, emotional and intellectual endowments and abilities for the growth of society. Unfortunately our management policies, be it in the educational set-up or any other organizational set-up emphasizes only the cognitive aspect of the human resource, whereas the emotional or affective aspect of human resource is neglected. Emotional competence is as important, sometimes more important than academic competence in managing the organization.

A child will not learn if he does not 'want' to learn or feel the 'need' to learn despite having good ability or intelligence, similarly, an employee will not put in his maximum effort unless his emotional needs are taken care of. Human being is not merely a cognitive man possessing various abilities and skills. He is also an emotional being which determines the effective and efficient utilization of his cognitive abilities. People constitute the active resource of any organization, who really determines the efficiency and utilization of all other resources. The most unique feature of human resources is that their contribution can enhance considerably through adoption of an effective management policy based on emotional intelligence parameters.

The concept of emotional intelligence started its journey to prominence in 1920 when Thorndike (Thorndike, 1920) formulated the concept of 'social intelligence'. Since then other forms of intelligence have been identified by scholars in the field of psychology. Three clusters of intelligences have been identified. These are: Abstract intelligence which pertains to the ability to understand and manipulate verbal and mathematical symbols; Concrete intelligence, which describes the ability to understand and manipulate objects; and Social intelligence, which describes the ability to understand and relate with people.

Thorndike (1920) conceptualized social intelligence as the ability to understand and manage men and women, boys and girls, to act wisely in human relations. Building on the work of Thorndike, Gardner (1983) developed the theory of multiple intelligences, wherein he classified social intelligence into two categories namely: interpersonal and intrapersonal intelligences. He described interpersonal intelligence as the ability to understand the intensions, motivations and desires of other. He identified teachers, politicians, salespersons, clinicians and religious leaders as individuals who are likely to have a high degree of interpersonal intelligence. Intrapersonal intelligence is the capacity to understand oneself, to appreciate one's feelings, fears and motivations.

Salovey and Mayer (1990) coined the term emotional intelligence which they conceptualized 'as the subset of social intelligence that involves the ability to monitor one's own and others' feelings and emotions, to discriminate among them and to use information to guide one's thinking and action. To clarify the concept further, Mayer and Salovey (1997) postulated that emotional intelligence involves the ability to perceive accurately, appraise and express emotion, the ability to access and/or generate emotional knowledge, and the ability to regulate emotion to promote emotional and intellectual growth. This definition succeeds not only in clearing the ambiguity inherent in the previous definition; but also in carving a distinct image for the construct of emotional intelligence.

Goleman (1995) formulated the best-known theory of emotional intelligence. Goleman's explanation of the construct was based on Salovey and Mayer's (1990) original theory. Among other claims, Goleman theorized that intelligence (IQ) accounts for only about 20 per cent of a person's success in one's professional and personal life. The balance 80 per cent can be attributed to emotional intelligence (EQ). Elaborating further on the construct, Goleman (1998) explained that an individual's emotional intelligence can affect one's work situation. He has also applied his conceptual understanding to organization as a whole.

In simple terms, emotional intelligence can be defined as knowing what feels good, what feels bad, and how to get from bad to good. A more formal academic definition refers to emotional awareness and emotional management skill which provide the ability to balance emotion and reason so as to maximize productivity and happiness.

Singh (2003) defines emotional intelligence as a way of recognizing, understanding and choosing how we think, feel and act. It shapes our interaction with others and our understanding of ourselves. It defines how and what we learn, it allows us to set priorities, it determines the majority of our daily actions. Emotional intelligence is the ability and freedom to grow from mistrust to trust, self-doubt to self-empowerment, following to leading, incompetence to competence, isolation to synergy and despair to hope (Singh, M., 2006 as cited in Singh, D., 2006).

Goleman, Boyatzis and Mckee (2002) assert that the effective use of emotion is basic to the function of successful leadership. They postulated further that leaders are emotional guides influencing not only follower emotions but also follower action through that emotional influence. Leaders exercise this influence through relationship management, motivational appeal, and goal-setting, and the leader's emotional intelligence is necessary to effectively perform these efforts.

Bar-On (2005) proposed a new model of emotional intelligence which provides a theoretical basis for the Emotional Quotient Inventory (EQ-I) which was originally designed to assess various aspects of this construct as well as to examine its conceptualization. In this model emotional-social intelligence is a cross section of inter-related emotional and social competencies, skills, and factors that determine how effectively we understand and express ourselves, understand others and relate with them and cope with daily demands. According to Bar-On (2005), the model of emotional and social intelligence has very much in common with the earlier models that have one or more of the following components: (*a*) the ability to recognize, understand, and express emotions and feelings; (*b*) the ability to understand how others feel and relate with them; (*c*) the ability to manage and control emotion; (*d*) the ability to manage change, adapt, and solve problems of a personal and interpersonal nature and the ability to generate positive effects and be self-motivated. Based on Bar-On's model, to be emotionally and socially intelligent is to effectively understand and express oneself, to understand and relate well with others, and to successfully cope with daily demands, challenges and pressures. At the intrapersonal level, it involves the ability to be aware of one self, to understand one's strengths and weaknesses and to express one's feelings and thoughts non-destructively. On the interpersonal level, being emotionally and socially intelligent encompasses the ability to be aware of other's emotions, feelings and needs and to establish and maintain cooperative, constructive and mutually satisfying relationships. Thus, to be emotionally and socially intelligent implies the ability to effectively manage personal, social and environmental changes by realistically and flexibly coping with the immediate situation, solving problems and making decisions.

Emotional intelligence has been found to have impact on psychological health particularly occupational stress (Ciarrochi, Chan and Bajgar, 2001). Ciarrochi, Chan and Caputi (2000) for example, posit that emotional intelligence may protect people from stress and lead to better adaptation. They opine that an objective measure of emotion management skill is associated with a tendency to maintain an experimentally induced positive mood which has obvious implication for preventing stress. Again, Bar-On (2003) found that there was a moderate yet significant relationship between emotional and social intelligence and psychological health. The aspects of emotional and social intelligence competencies that were found to impact on psychological health are: (*a*) the ability to manage emotion and cope with stress, (*b*) the drive to accomplish personal goals in order to actualize one's inner potential and lead a more meaningful life; and (*c*) the ability to verify feelings and thinking.

Models of Emotional Intelligence

Mayer, Caruso and Salovey (1999) outlined three criteria in conceptualising an Emotional Intelligence (EI) model. *Firstly,* the conceptualisation must reflect an ability to perform in the workplace, rather than reflecting preferred ways of behaving; *secondly*, the conceptualisation should encompass a set of related abilities that are distinct from already established psychological constructs (such as personality or general intelligence); and *thirdly*, the conceptualisation should be developmental, that is, it not only develops with age but is able to be enhanced and further developed within the individual through professional training programmes. The creation of a criterion for assessing workplace EI has the potential to assist researchers and practitioners alike in programmes of selection, assessment, training and development of employees at every level within an organisation. There are three main models of EI: (*i*) Ability-based EI Models; (*ii*) Mixed Models of EI and (*iii*) Trait EI Model. Each of these conceptions (models) draws in some way from the criteria suggested by Mayer et al. (1999) outlined above.

(i) Ability-based Model : The ability-based model views emotions as useful sources of information that help one to make sense of and navigate the social environment (Salovey and Grewal, 2005). The model proposes that individuals vary in their ability to process information of an emotional nature and in their ability to relate emotional processing to a wider cognition. This ability is seen to manifest itself in certain adaptive behaviours.

Mayer and Salovey's (1997) Model of Emotional Intelligence

Salovey and Mayer's (1990) conception of EI strives to define EI within the confines of the standard criteria for a new intelligence. Following their continuing research, their initial definition of EI was revised to 'The ability to perceive emotion, integrate emotion to facilitate thought, understand emotions and to regulate emotions to promote personal growth'. The model was revised in 1997 by Mayer and Salovey to give greater emphasis to the cognitive components of EI and to highlight the potential for emotional and intellectual growth. The revised EI model is ordered hierarchically from basic psychological processes to more psychologically integrated processes and includes the following four branches:

(*a*) *Perceiving emotions* is the ability to detect and decipher emotions in faces, pictures, voices and cultural artifacts—including the ability to identify one's own emotions. Perceiving emotions represents a basic aspect of emotional intelligence, as it makes all other processing of emotional information possible;

(*b*) *Using emotions* is an ability to harness emotions to facilitate various cognitive activities, such as thinking and problem solving. The emotionally intelligent person can capitalize fully upon his or her changing moods in order to best fit the task at hand;

(c) *Understanding emotions* is the ability to comprehend emotional language and to appreciate complicated relationships among emotions. For example, understanding emotions encompasses the ability to be sensitive to slight variations between emotions, and the ability to recognize and describe how emotions evolve over time;

(d) *Managing emotions* refers to the ability to regulate emotions in both ourselves and in others. Therefore, the emotionally intelligent person can harness emotions, even negative ones, and manage them to achieve intended goals.

Each of the stages in the model includes levels of abilities which it is hypothesized that an individual completes in sequence before progression to the next stage.

(ii) Mixed Models of EI : Models that mix together emotional intelligence qualities with other personality traits unrelated to either emotion or intelligence are often referred to as mixed models of emotional intelligence (Alternatively, they can be considered broad models of personality traits). The term 'mixed model' stems from the fact that the models mix together the core idea of emotional intelligence with a variety of other personality traits.

Goleman's (2001) Model of Emotional Intelligence

Goleman's Emotional Intelligence Model-2001 (*Source:* Goleman, 2001)

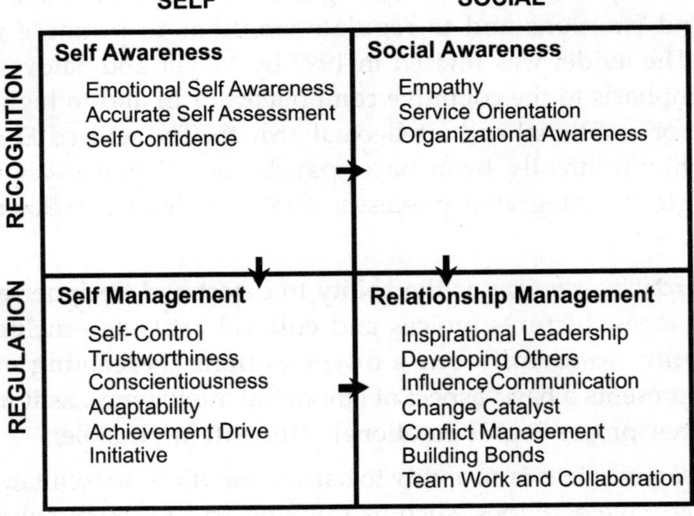

The model introduced by Goleman (1998) focuses on EI as a wide array of competencies and skills that drive leadership performance. Goleman's definition of EI, incorporates a combination of personality traits, abilities and emotional traits. Interestingly, Goldman's conceptualisation of EI closely parallels the earlier ideas of social intelligence (Thorndike, 1920) and personal intelligence (Gardner, 1983), however, it departs significantly from Salovey and Mayer's Ability Model (1997). Goleman includes a set of emotional competencies within each construct of EI. Emotional competencies are not innate talents, but rather learned capabilities that must be worked on and can be developed to achieve outstanding performance (Bradberry and Greaves, 2009). Goleman posits that individuals are born with a general emotional intelligence that determines their potential for learning emotional competencies (Boyatzis, Goleman and Rhee, 2000). Goleman's (2001) model outlines four main EI constructs and twenty competencies.

1. *Self awareness*—the ability to read one's emotions and recognize their impact while using gut feelings to guide decisions;
2. *Self management*—involves controlling one's emotions and impulses and adapting to changing circumstances;
3. *Social awareness*—the ability to sense, understand, and react to others emotions while comprehending social networks;
4. *Relationship management*—the ability to inspire, influence, and develop others while managing conflict.

Bar-On's (1997) Model of Emotional Intelligence

The Bar-on model describes EI as a cross-section of interrelated emotional and social competencies, skills and facilitators that impact intelligent behaviour. Bar-On defines emotional intelligence as being concerned with effectively understanding oneself and others, relating well to people, and adapting to and coping with the immediate surroundings to be more successful in dealing with environmental demands (Bar-On, 1997). Bar-On posits that EI develops over time and that it can be improved through training, programming, and therapy. He has hypothesized that those individuals with higher than average E.Q.'s are in general more successful in meeting environmental demands and pressures. He also notes that a deficiency in EI can mean a lack of success and the existence of emotional problems. Problems in coping with one's environment are thought, by Bar-On, to be especially common among those individuals lacking in the subscales of reality testing, problem solving, stress tolerance, and impulse control. In general, Bar-On considers emotional intelligence and cognitive intelligence to contribute equally to a person's general intelligence, which then offers an indication of one's potential to succeed in life (Bar-On, 2005).

Bar-On's Model (1997) includes the following five dimensions viz. intrapersonal skills, interpersonal skills, adaptability, stress management and general mood.

1. *Intrapersonal skills*—being aware of and understanding oneself and one's emotions, expressing one's feelings and ideas;
2. *Interpersonal skills*—being aware of, understanding and appreciating others feelings, establishing and maintaining satisfying relationship with others;
3. *Adaptability*—verifying feelings with external cues, sizing up immediate situations, being flexible in altering feelings and thoughts with changing situations and problem solving;
4. *Stress management*—coping with stress and controlling impulses;
5. *General mood*—being optimistic and being able to feel and express positive emotions.

However, doubts have been expressed about this model in the research literature (in particular about the validity of self-report as an index of emotional intelligence) and in scientific settings, it is being replaced by the trait EI model discussed below (Kluemper, 2008).

(iii) Trait EI Model : The Trait EI model of emotional intelligence focuses more on the personality framework and is defined as 'a constellation of behavioural dispositions and self-perceptions concerning one's ability to recognize, process, and utilize emotion-laden information'. In other words, in this model, emotional intelligence is regarded as a personality trait and a distinct branch from the taxonomy of human cognitive ability.

Petrides, Pita and Kokkinaki (2007) proposed a conceptual distinction between the ability based model and a trait based model of EI (Petrides and Furnham, 2000). Trait EI refers to individuals self-perceptions of their emotional abilities. Trait EI should be investigated within a personality framework (Petrides and Furnham, 2001). An alternative label for the same construct is trait emotional self-efficacy. The trait EI model is general and subsumes the Goleman and Bar-On models discussed above. The conceptualization of EI as a personality trait leads to a construct that lies outside the taxonomy of human cognitive ability. This is an important distinction in as much as it bears directly on the operationalisation of the construct and the theories and hypotheses that are formulated about it (Petrides and Furnham, 2000).

Components of Emotional Intelligence

Goleman (1998) identifies five elements as the components of emotional intelligence: Self awareness, Self regulation, Motivation, Empathy, and Social skills. There are five basic competencies that comprise the field of Emotional Intelligence. The first three are intra-personal (Self-awareness, Self-regulation, Motivation): they are invisible to others and occur inside of us. The last two are Inter-personal (Empathy and Social Skills): they occur between us and other people and are observable in our behaviour. Intra-personal skills and inter-personal skills are interdependent as the development of one skill demonstrates the other skill.

(i) Self Awareness : Knowing oneself is a key to any success. Self awareness is knowing one's internal states, preferences, resources, intuitions, etc. It indicates the ability to recognize, understand and accept one's own moods, emotions, drives, strengths and shortcomings as well as to see how these affect other people. According to Goleman, self awareness includes emotional awareness, accurate self-assessment and self-confidence.

Emotional awareness refers to the ability of recognizing one's emotions and their effects. People with this competence know which emotions they are feeling and why; realise the links between their feelings and what they think, do, and say; recognize how their feelings affect their performance; and have a guiding awareness of their values and goals. *Accurate self assessment* is knowing one's own strengths and limits. People with this competence are aware of their strengths and weaknesses; reflective, learning from experience; open to candid feedback, new perspectives, continuous learning, and self-development; and able to show a sense of humour and perspective about themselves. *Self confidence* is the sureness about one's self-worth and capabilities. People with this competence present themselves with self assurance; have presence of mind; can voice views that are unpopular and go out on a limb for what is right; and are decisive, able to make sound decisions despite uncertainties and pressures.

(ii) Self Regulation : Self regulation refers to managing and handing impulses, distressing feelings and upsets rather than denying or repressing these feelings. It implies making a choice as to how one expresses his/her feelings. Self regulation helps in staying compose, focussed, calm and helps to think clearly even under pressure. Self regulation includes self-control, trustworthiness, conscientiousness, adaptability and innovativeness.

Self Control is the ability of managing disruptive emotions and impulses. People with this competence manage their impulsive feelings and distressing emotions well; stay composed, positive, and unflappable even in trying moments; and think clearly and stay focussed under pressure. *Trustworthiness* is the ability of the person to maintain standards of honesty and integrity. People with this competence act ethically and are above reproach; build trust through their reliability and authenticity; admit their own mistakes and confront unethical actions in others; and take tough, principled stands even if they are unpopular. *Conscientiousness* is taking responsibility for personal performance. People with this competence meet commitments and keep promises; hold them accountable for meeting their objectives; and are organized and careful in their work. *Adaptability* means flexibility in handling change. People with this competence smoothly handle multiple demands, shifting priorities and rapid change; adapt their responses and tactics to fit fluid circumstances; and are flexible in how they see events. *Innovativeness* is being comfortable with and opens to novel ideas and new information. People with this competence seek out fresh ideas from a wide variety of sources; entertain original solutions to problems; generate new ideas; and take fresh perspectives and risks in their thinking.

(iii) Self Motivation : Motivation helps in the achievement of goals. Motivation is an ability to pursue goals with energy and persistence. It provides the drive and zeal to shape our thoughts and actions. Three important motivational competencies are achievement drive, commitment, optimism and initiative.

Achievement drive will make a person to strive to improve or meet a standard of excellence. People with this competence are results-oriented, with a high drive to meet their objectives and standards; set challenging goals and take calculated risks; pursue information to reduce uncertainty and find ways to do better; and learn how to improve their performance. *Commitment* is one of the competencies of motivation that make the people to align with the goals of the group or organization. People with this competence readily make personal or group sacrifices to meet a larger organizational goal; find a sense of purpose in the larger mission; use the group's core values in making decisions and clarifying choices; and actively seek out opportunities to fulfill the group's mission. *Initiative* is being ready to act on opportunities. People with this competence are ready to seize opportunities; pursue goals beyond what's required or expected of them; cut through red tape and bend the rules when necessary to get the job done; and mobilize others through unusual, enterprising efforts. *Optimism* is the persistence in pursuing goals despite obstacles and setbacks. People with this competence persist in seeking goals despite obstacles and setbacks; operate from hope of success rather than fear of failure and see setbacks as due to manageable circumstance rather than a personal flaw.

(iv) Social Awareness : Social awareness refers to be aware of the problems that different societies and communities face on a day-to-day basis; to be conscious of the difficulties and hardships of society. This includes reading people and groups accurately and encompasses five competencies viz. empathy, service orientation, developing others, leveraging diversity and political awareness.

Empathy is to sense others feelings and perspective and taking an active interest in their concerns. People with this competence are attentive to emotional cues and listen well; show sensitivity and understand others perspectives; and help out based on understanding other people's needs and feelings. *Service orientation* is anticipating, recognizing, and meeting customer's needs. People with this competence: understand customer's needs and match them to services or products; seek ways to increase customer's satisfaction and loyalty; gladly offer appropriate assistance; and grasp a customer's perspective, acting as a trusted advisor. *Developing others* make sense of what others need in order to develop and bolstering their abilities. People with this competence acknowledge and reward people's strengths, accomplishments, and development; offer useful feedback and identify people's needs for development; and mentor, give timely coaching, and offer assignments that challenge and grow a persons skill. *Leveraging Diversity* refers to the ability to recruit, develop, and retain a diverse high quality workforce in an equitable manner. This ability leads and manages an inclusive workplace that maximizes the talents of each person to achieve sound results; respects, understands, values and seeks out individual differences to achieve the vision and mission of the organization; develops and uses measures and rewards to hold self and others accountable for achieving results that embody the principles of diversity. People with this competence respect and relate well to people from varied backgrounds; understand diverse world views and are sensitive to group differences; see diversity as opportunity, create environment where diverse people can thrive; and challenge the bias and intolerance. *Political awareness* is reading a group's emotional currents and power relationships. People with this competence: accurately read key power relationships; detect crucial social networks; understand the forces that shape views and actions of clients, customers, or competitors; and accurately read situations and organizational and external realities.

(v) Social Skills : Ability to communicate, persuade, and interact with other members of the society, without undue conflict or disharmony. In other words social skill is an ability to build rapport with various sections of society and create network of people. This social skill includes eight competencies i.e. influence, communication, leadership, change catalyst, conflict management, building bonds, collaboration and cooperation and, team capabilities.

Influence refers to the ability of exercising effective tactics for persuasion. People with this competence are skilled at persuasion; fine-tune presentations to appeal to the listener; use complex strategies like indirect influence to build consensus and support; and orchestrate dramatic events to effectively make a point. *Communication* is an ability of an individual in sending clear and convincing messages. People with this competence are effective in give-and-take, registering emotional cues in attuning their message; deal with difficult issues straightforwardly; listen well, seek mutual understanding, and welcome sharing of information fully; and foster open communication and stay receptive to bad news as well as good. *Leadership* is an important competency where people involve in inspiring and guiding groups and people. People with this competence articulate and arouse enthusiasm for a shared vision and mission; step forward to lead as needed, regardless of position; guide the performance of others while holding them accountable; and lead by example. *Change catalyst* refers to initiating or managing change. People with this competence recognize the need for changing and removing barriers; challenge the status quo to acknowledge the need for change; champion the change and enlist others in its pursuit; and model the change expected of others.

Conflict management is negotiating and resolving disagreements. People with this competence handle difficult people and tense situations with diplomacy and tact; spot potential conflict, bring disagreements into the open, and help deescalate; encourage debate and open discussion; and orchestrate win-win solutions. *Building bonds* refers to nurturing instrumental relationships. People with this competence cultivate and maintain extensive informal networks; seek out relationships that are mutually beneficial; build rapport and keep others in the loop; and make and maintain personal friendships among work associates. *Collaboration and cooperation* is working with others toward shared goals. People with this competence balance a focus on task with attention to relationships; collaborate, sharing plans, information, and resources; promote a friendly, cooperative climate; and spot and nurture opportunities for collaboration. *A team capability* is an ability of creating group synergy in pursuing collective goals. People with this competence model team qualities like respect, helpfulness, and cooperation; draw all members into active and enthusiastic participation; build team identity and protect the group and its reputation; share credit.

Concept, Meaning and Definitions of Stress and Occupational Stress

In our daily life situations, human beings have many biological, psychological and social needs. When these needs are not satisfied they experience stress. Besides these needs there are many challenges in human life and they all are likely to produce both distress and eustress. The term stress is derived from the Latin word 'stringere', which means 'to draw tight', and was used in this way in the 17th century to describe a hardship or an affliction (Cartwright and Cooper, 1997). Later in the 18th century, the term stress referred primarily to an individual's 'force, pressure, strain or strong effort'. It was these early definitions used in physics and engineering that began to influence the notion that stress may affect individuals, where forces are seen to exert pressure on an individual, producing strain (Hinkle, 1977). Distress is the most commonly-referred to type of stress, having negative implications, whereas eustress is a positive form of stress, usually related to desirable events in a person's life. Both can be equally taxing on the body, and are cumulative in nature, depending on a person's way of adapting to a change that has caused it. Selye (1976) talked about how persistent stress that is not resolved through coping or adaptation, deemed distress, may lead to anxiety or withdrawal (depression) behaviour. In contrast, if the stress involved enhances function (physical or mental, such as through strength training or challenging work), it may be considered eustress. Lazarus (1974) defined eustress as a stress that is healthy, or gives one a feeling of fulfillment or other positive feelings. Eustress is a process of exploring potential gains. It is very subjective experience. What may be challenge for one will be a stressor for another.

Stress depends largely on background experiences, temperament and environmental conditions. The term stress refers to an internal state, which results from frustrating or unsatisfying conditions. Defining stress is a very complex matter, which is the subject of different analyses and continuous debate among experts. Beyond the details of this debate, a general consensus can be reached about a definition of stress, which is centered on the idea of a perceived imbalance in the interface between an individual, the environment and other individuals. When people are faced with demands from others or demands from the physical or psycho-social environment to which they feel unable to adequately respond, a reaction of the organism is activated to cope with the situation. The nature of this response depends upon a combination of different elements, including the extent of the demand, the personal characteristics and coping resources of the person, the constraints on the person in trying to cope and the support received from others. Stress is involved in an environmental situation that perceived as presenting demand which threatens to exceed the capabilities of a persons and resources for meeting it, under conditions where he or she expects a substantial differential in the rewards and costs from meeting the demand versus not meeting it (McGrath, 1976).

Stress refers both to the circumstances that place physical or psychological demands on an individual and to the emotional reactions experiences in these situations (Hazards, 1994). Although, the adverse effects of stress on physical health and emotional well-being are increasingly recognized, there is little agreement among experts on the definition of stress. According to Selye (1976), stress is caused by physiological, psychological and environmental demands. When confronted with stressors, the body creates extra energy and stress occurs because our bodies do not use up all of the extra energy that has been created. Selye (1936) first described this reaction and coined it the General Adaptation Syndrome (GAS). The GAS includes three distinct stages: (*a*) alarm reaction; (*b*) stage of resistance; and (*c*) stage of exhaustion. According to Lazarus (1976), stress occurs when there are demands on the person, which taxes or exceeds his adjustive resources. According to Spielberger (1979), the term stress is used to refer to a complex psycho-biological process that consists of three major elements. This process is initiated by a situation or stimulus that is potentially harmful or dangerous stressor. If a stressor is interpreted as dangerous or threatening, an anxiety reaction will be elicited.

According to Steinberg and Ritzmann (1990), stress was defined as 'an under load or overload of matter, energy or information input to, or output from, a living system'. Similarly, Bowman (1998) defines stress 'as the body's automatic response to any physical or mental demand placed upon it'. When pressures are threatening, the body rushes to supply protection by turning on 'the juices' and preparing to defend itself. It's the 'flight or fight' response in action.

Occupational Stress

In many countries the job of the teachers is often considered as one of the most stressful profession. Teaching profession is generally considered as a noble profession with lots of expectations from the parents towards their children's education and the development of their personalities. These expectations may also contribute as a source of stress.

Kyriacou and Sutcliffe (1978) defined teachers stress as 'a response of negative effect such as anger or depression by a teacher usually accompanied by psychological and biological changes (such as increased heart beat) resulting from aspects of teachers job and mediated by the perception of the demands made upon the teacher which constitute a threat to his self-esteem'. Kyriacou (1987) defines 'teacher stress as the experience by a teacher of unpleasant emotions such as tension, frustration, anger and depression resulting from aspects of his work as a teacher'. Okebukola and Jegede (1989) defined occupational stress as 'a condition of mental and physical exertion brought about as a result of harassing events or dissatisfying elements or general features of the working environment'.

Borg (1990) conceptualizes teacher stress as a negative and potentially harmful to teacher's health. The key element in the definition is the teacher's perception of threat based on the following three aspects of his job circumstances: (1) that demands are being made on him; (2) that he is unable to meet or has difficulty in meeting these demands; and (3) that failure to meet these demands threatens his mental/physical well-being. According to National Institute of Occupational Safety and Health, Cincinnati, (1999), Job stress can be defined as 'the harmful physical and emotional responses that occur when the requirements of the job do not match the capabilities, resources, or needs of the worker'. Job stress can lead to poor health and even injury. According to a discussion document presented by United Kingdom Health and Safety Commission, London, (1999), 'Stress is the reaction people have to, excessive pressures or other types of demand placed on them'. Likewise, Allen, (2001) points out that stress is a feeling we experience, when we loose confidence in our capability to cope with a situation.

In the context of special education teachers, occupational stress can be defined as the effect of task demands that the teacher face in the performance of their professional roles and responsibilities. According to Reddy (2007) occupational stress of special education teachers refers to the stress experienced by them due to various constituents and conditions of their job such as organizational structure of the special schools they are working in, their inter and intra personal professional interactions, professional training they received, and the instructional assignments and arrangements.

Models of Stress

Research reveals the complexity of stress phenomenon. In researchers endeavour to understand it, they have developed different models of stress. Three main models of stress have been identified.

(a) Stimulus-based Model of Stress : The stimulus-based model of stress emanates from physics, in particular the field of engineering (Cooper, Dewe and O'Driscoll, 2001; Rout and Rout, 2002). It views stress as a condition of the environment that is external to the individual and influences him or her in a disruptive way (Koslowski, 1998; Bemansour, 1998; Cooper et al., 2001; James, 1999; Rout and Rout, 2002). The perceptions of the individual are not taken into account in this approach. According to this model, the load or demand placed upon a person (known as stressor) exceeds the elastic limit of the persons ability to cope or adapt to it (Tosi, Mero and Rizzo, 2000; Wilson and Hall, 2002; Rout and Rout, 2002). Educators in this model are viewed as passive recipients rather than as actors. Situations such as working with learners with special needs or during probation may give rise to demands above their elastic limits (Wilson and Hall, 2002)

(b) Response-based Model of Stress : The response-based model emerges from the field of medicine and is explained from a physiological perspective (Cooper et al., 2001; Rout and Rout, 2002). It describes stress in terms of the individual's response to a threatening or disturbing stimulus (Bemansour, 1998; Rout and Rout, 2002). In this model the focus is on physiological, psychological and behavioural responses which may appear as consequences of stress (Pelletier and Lutz, 1988; Wilson and Hall, 2002). The physiological and psychological symptoms are not unique to stress and can therefore be attributed to other medical conditions. Applied to the teaching profession the educator in this model is described as a passive recipient who is pressurised by resultant stress (Wilson and Hall, 2002).

(c) Interactional and Transactional Models of Stress : The interactional model of stress is a psychological based approach which views stress as an individual phenomenon which is both interactive and situational (Bemansour, 1998; Motseke, 1998; Nahavandi and Malekzadeh, 1999; Rout and Rout, 2002; Wilson and Hall, 2002). It means that different individuals, when confronted with the same situation respond differently.

The transactional approach views stress as embedded neither in the individual nor in the environment but in the interrelationship between the stressor and the individual's perception of the situation and his or her subjective responses (Lazarus, 1999; Cooper et al., 2001; Mills, 1995).

In this definition the role played by self-appraisal in determining an individual's stress level is recognized (Lazarus, 1999). In a stressful situation the individual appraises the situation (primary appraisal) (Rout and Rout, 2002; Tosi et al., 2000). Stress occurs when the individual perceives the situation as threatening to his or her important goals and feels unable to meet these demands (Rout and Rout, 2002). Secondary appraisal are made when the situation is judged as stressful (Rout and Rout, 2002; Tosi et al., 2000). Therefore, the experience of stress arises from educator's perceptions of demands the inability to meet those demands emanating from a lack of effective coping skills and the ultimate threat to the educators physical or mental well-being (Abel and Sewell, 1999). In this model educators are actors and not passive recipients of the external pressures (Wilson and Hall, 2002)

The transactional model corresponds to the Kyriacou and Sutcliff's (1978) view that the experience of stress is the result of an educators perception that demands are being made on him or her that he or she has difficulty or is unable to meet these demands and that failing to do so threatens his or her mental and/or physical well-being (Bemansour, 1998). This model acknowledges, on the one hand, that teaching and some schools in particular exert certain pressures on the educators and that educators on the other hand may react in different ways to bring a variety of adaptive resources to cope with the stressors (Wilson and Hall, 2002).

Models of Occupational Stress

Models of occupational stress (also termed job stress or work stress) have generally accepted the transactional model of stress proposed by Lazarus (1966), atleast from a theoretical perspective, suggesting that stress results from the transaction or the interaction between the individual and the environment. Empirical work has predominantly used this interactional approach to assess occupational stress and its outcomes (Cooper et al., 2001). The interactional approach to occupational stress focuses primarily on the statistical interaction between the stressor and the response, limiting the ability to infer causal pathways in these relationships. Based on a number of different occupational stress theories and practices, Beehr and Franz (1986) identified four approaches to study occupational stress: medical, clinical / counselling psychology, engineering psychology, and organisational psychology. For each of these approaches, Beehr and Franz indicated what a typical stressor and a typical outcome (or strain) would be. Their medical approach identified the typical stressor as physical and the typical outcome as physical strain (physiological or biochemical). The clinical/counselling psychology approach identified the typical stressor as being psychological and the outcome being psychological strain (for example, anxiety). Thirdly, the engineering psychology approach suggested that the typical stressor was physical (the physical work environment) and the outcome is related to job performance. Finally, the organisational psychology approach suggests that the stressor would be psychological and the outcome would be psychological strain.

(a) Person-Environment (P-E) Fit Model : The person-environment fit (P-E- fit) model has its origin in the work of Kurt Lewin and his view point of interactional psychology, which argues that behaviour is a function of the interaction between the person and the situation, where one aspect of this interaction is the degree to which the person fits the situation (Jex, 1998). The P-E fit model can be discussed as a subjective model, referring to the fit between the subjective person and the subjective environment i.e. the individual's *perceptions* of the P-E fit (Harrison, 1978). Harrison emphasized that there are two kinds of fit between an individual and their environment: the extent to which the skills and abilities of the individual match the demands required of them and the extent to which the environment matches the individual's needs. From this perspective, a model of occupational stress can be proposed to include perceived job demands (the subjective environment) and the individual's perceived abilities to manage those demands (the subjective person), producing strains which are psychological, physical and or behavioural in nature (Harrison, 1978).

(b) Job Demands-Control Model : Several models of stress relating specifically to occupational stress have been developed in an attempt to better understand the relationship between work characteristics and employee well-being. These models include the Job Demands-Control Model (Karasek, 1979; Karasek and Theorell, 1990), the Effort-Rewards Imbalance Model (Siegrist, 1996; Siegrist et al., 1986), the Job-Demands-Resources Model (Bakker et al., 2003; Demerouti et al., 2001), and the Burnout Model (Maslach and Jackson, 1981; Maslach et al., 2001).

The Job Demands-Control Model of occupational stress (Karasek, 1979; Karasek and Thorell, 1990) is based upon the proposition that the interaction between job demand and job control will explain strain outcomes. Karasek defined job demand as the independent variable that measures stressors, such as workload demands. He originally conceptualized job control under the phrase job decision latitude and defined this as the control that the working individual has over tasks and their conduct during their working day. Karasek suggested that when job demands are high and job control is low, strain will occur, leading to both mental and physical health problems. The concept of job control has long been acknowledged as an important factor in the occupational stress process (Cooper et al., 2001).

(c) Effort-Rewards Imbalance Model : In comparison, the Effort-Rewards Imbalance model of occupational stress places emphasis on both the effort and the reward structure of work (Marmot, Siegrist, Theorell and Feeney, 1999) and hypothesizes that work-related benefits depend on a reciprocal relationship between the efforts and the rewards obtained from work. Effort has been defined as the job demands or the obligations that are placed upon the employee, and rewards are considered to be distributed by the employing organisation and include variables such as salary, job security, and career growth opportunities (Siegrist, 1996). This model of occupational stress hypothesizes that an employee's work which is characterised by high effort and low reward represents a deficit between the employee's costs and gains. It is this deficit, or imbalance, that is the cause of stress in the employee which leads to disease and ill-health (for example, cardiovascular disease). Unlike the Job Demands-Control Model of occupational stress, the Effort-Rewards Imbalance Model examines both situational and personal characteristics of the work environment, however, the Effort-Rewards Imbalance Model is limited in that it includes a narrow approach to health outcomes (originally used to predict the onset of cardiovascular problems) in comparison to the Job Demands-Control Model health outcomes (which was developed to predict both individual strain and learning).

(d) Job-Demands-Resources Model : Job-Demands Resources Model of occupational stress (Bakker, et al., 2003; Demerouti et al., 2001) is related to the Burnout Model (Maslach and Jackson, 1981; Maslach et al., 2001). According to Maslach and Jackson, chronic stress is emotionally draining and ultimately leads to a state of 'burnout'. Burnout has been conceptualised as a psychological syndrome developed in response to chronic interpersonal stressors on the job and is characterised by three key dimensions (Maslach et al., 2001). Firstly, burnout is characterised by overwhelming exhaustion, secondly by feelings of cynicism and detachment from the job, and finally by a sense of ineffectiveness and lack of accomplishment. Maslach et al., hypothesize that the exhaustion component represents the stress dimensions of burnout, that the cynicism component represents the interpersonal context of burnout, and that the ineffectiveness and lack of accomplishment components represent the self-evaluation dimension of burnout.

Linked to the Model of Burnout is the Job-Demands-Resources Model of occupational stress. This model proposes that the development of burnout follows two processes (Demerouti et al., 2001). Firstly, extreme job demands lead to constant overtaxing of the individual and in the end, to emotional exhaustion. Secondly, lack of resources available to the employee complicates the meeting of job demands which then leads to withdrawal behaviours and ultimately to disengagement from work. The Job-Demands-Resources model assumes that although employees in different organisations may be confronted with different working environments, the characteristics of these working environments can always be classified into two categories—job demands and job resources (Bakker et al., 2003). According to this model, job demands are defined as physical, psychological, social or organisational aspects of one's job that require sustained effort (cognitive and emotional) and are associated with psychological and physical costs to the individual. Job resources are defined as the same aspects of one's job (physical, psychological, social or organisational) but those aspects are functional in achieving work goals, reducing job demands, and/or stimulating personal development and growth. Similar to the models of occupational stress presented above, the Job-Demands-Resources model works on the assumption that stress in the workplace is a result of the interaction between the person and their environment.

Sources of Occupational Stress

Hock and Roger (1996) indicated that the degree of stress which teachers experience is positively related to the degree which he/she perceives as a lack of control over potentially threatening situations, such as inability to meet the demands of students and a lack of adequate coping mechanisms. Schools are considered as a formal organization (Hoy and Miskel, 1987), and teachers are susceptible to organizational stress of role conflict and role ambiguity. Many researchers have identified sources of stress among post-secondary faculty members. Their findings have indicated that time pressures (Astin, 1993; Barnes, Agago and Coombs, 1998; Smith et al., 1995; Thompson and Dey, 1998) and high self expectations (Gmelch et al., 1986; Smith et al., 1995) are the main sources of stress for teachers.

The stressors may be both outside and inside work and can, therefore, have an effect on the whole family. Cooper and Marshall (1978) identified major causes of stress in the workplace. In a study of the literature, Cooper and Marshall identified over 40 interacting factors which could be identified as sources of work stress. They grouped these into categories and proposed six major causes of stress at work. These six major categories are: (*i*) Factors intrinsic to the job; (*ii*) Role in the organization; iii) Relationships at work; (*iv*) Career development; (*v*) Organizational structure and climate; and (*vi*) Organizational interface with outside.

A Model of Occupational Stress, (Source : Cooper et al., 1988a)

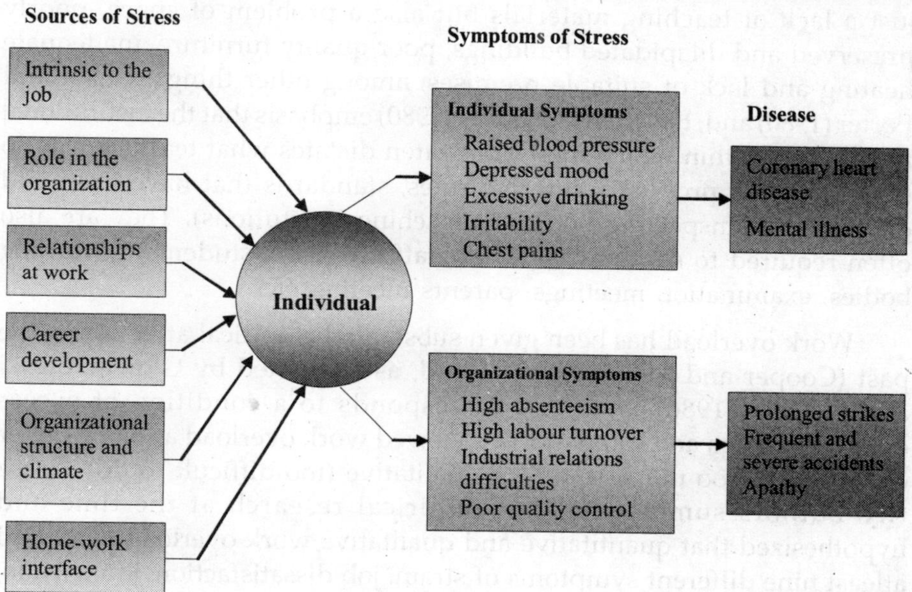

(i) Factors Intrinsic to the Job : The first category identifies causes of stress in the workplace that relate to factors intrinsic to the job. Stressors intrinsic to the job itself dominated early research in the area, with the majority of studies examining working conditions and work overload (Cooper and Marshall, 1978). Since this early research, longer lists of factors intrinsic to the job which may cause stress have been identified. As noted in Cartwright and Cooper (1997) poor working conditions, long hours, shift work, travel, risk and danger, new technology, work overload and work under load may all be factors relating to the experience of occupational stress.

Aspects of working conditions that have received attention in the past include class sizes, unsuitable buildings, noise levels and inadequate resources (Connors, 1983; Kyriacou and Sutcliffe, 1978a). Working conditions of a particular job can create stress due to the environment. Evidence presented by Cooper and Marshall (1978), Cartwright and Cooper (1997) show a link between poor mental health and unpleasant work conditions (including aspects of the physical environment, such as lighting, speed of work required and office design). Much research into teacher stress has revealed a general lack of resources as one of the most important factors (Laughlin, 1984) more specifically, inadequate school buildings and equipment (Smith and Cline, 1980). The International Labour Organization-ILO Report (1981) and the Breuse Report (1984) have revealed that the lack of resources in teaching does not necessarily imply just a lack of teaching materials but also a problem of space, poorly preserved and dilapidated buildings, poor quality furniture, inadequate heating and lack of suitable premises, among other things. Goble and Porter (1980) and, Bayer and Chauvet (1980) emphasis that the institutional framework within which they work often dictates what teachers can do (e.g. timetable problems, internal rules, standards that have been laid down by the inspecting bodies or teaching institutions). They are also often required to set time aside for staff meetings, students, governing bodies, examination meetings, parents meeting etc.

Work overload has been given substantial empirical attention in the past (Cooper and Marshall, 1978) and, as suggested by Glowinkowski and Cooper (1986), overload corresponds to a condition of excess demand. French and Caplan (1973) viewed work overload as being either quantitative (too much to do) or qualitative (too difficult to do). These two authors summarised the empirical research at the time and hypothesized that quantitative and qualitative work overload produced atleast nine different symptoms of strain: job dissatisfaction, job tension, lowered self-esteem, threat, embarrassment, high cholesterol, increases in heart rate, skin resistance, and increased smoking behaviour. Work overload is also heavily linked to time pressures not only in terms of the amount of work teachers have to fit in during the day, but also the amount that they have to take home at night, intruding into their personal life (Smith and Cline, 1980; Fimian and Santoro, 1983).

(ii) Role in the Organization : The second category of antecedents of stress in the workplace is that of role in the organisation. Roles encompass the demands and behaviours associated with the job an individual perform (Cooper et al., 2001). Role-related strain was first identified by Kahn, Wolfe, Quinn and Snoek (1964), whose research in this area has provided the foundation for most of the empirical work on role strain. Kahn et al. posited two primary ways of role dysfunction: role ambiguity and role conflict. Role ambiguity exists when the individual has inadequate information in order to carry out the task or does not fully understand the requirements. The outcomes of this can be job dissatisfaction, lack of self-confidence, feelings of futility, lack of self-esteem, depression, low motivation and the behavioural outcomes of increased intention to leave the job. Other manifestations may be physiological (increased blood pressure and pulse rate) (Kahn et al., 1964; French and Caplan, 1970; Margolis et al., 1974). There are a number of situations that may lead to role ambiguity and these are contemporary issues in teaching (i.e. job relocation, changes in the method of working, new organizational structure and changes in actual requirements of the job). Role ambiguity is a pervasive part of the teachers experience due to the endemic uncertainty regarding the teacher's role in the school (Schwab and Iwanicki, 1982).

Role conflict exists when the individual is 'torn' by conflicting job demands or when the individual is required to do things that they do not want to do and that are not part of their job. The results of this conflict have been found to result in lower job satisfaction and higher job tension. The issue of role conflict may be seen to be very relevant to teachers as it may include both intra-role conflicts due to teachers having to assume several roles within the school setting. The multiplicity of roles that the teacher may have to fulfill can include that of a diagnostician, guidance, counsellor, remediator, parent record keeper, evaluator and finally teacher. Increasingly the role of social worker is becoming part of the teacher's role (Phillips and Lee, 1980; Austin, 1981; Sparks and Hammond, 1981). Sometimes role conflict may require teachers to reject their own principles and better judgments (Dunham, 1980). For example, due to staff shortages they may be forced to teach a subject outside of their own expertise area and for which they have no desire or skill (Burke and Dunham, 1982; Schwab and Iwanicki 1982; Kalker, 1984). They may also have to spend a considerable amount of time controlling pupils and dealing with discipline problems at the cost of time spent on actual teaching (Kalker, 1984).

The work of Kahn and colleagues has added two additional roles in the organization as being related to occupational stress: role overload and responsibility (Cooper and Marshall, 1978; Cartwright and Cooper, 1997; Cooper et al., 2001). Role overload (similar to work overload) comprises the number of different roles an individual needs to fulfill and leads to excessive time demands and uncertainty as to the ability to perform these different roles adequately (Cartwright and Cooper, 1997). Problems connected with role overload may include: constant interaction with pupils which allows little time for relaxation, lunch etc. (Weiskopf, 1980); constant interaction with others (Schwab, 1983); too many roles altogether (Austin, 1981); and the problem of being physically and emotionally drained (Sparks, 1979). Responsibility is another important potential stressor associated with organizational roles. Responsibility can be differentiated into responsibility for people and responsibility for things (for instance, equipment, budgets, and buildings). As noted by Cartwright and Cooper, too much responsibility exceeding the individual's belief that they are able to manage is a clear source of stress; however, a lack of responsibility may also be a source of stress if the individual's perception is work under load. Responsibility for people has been identified as being particularly stressful, with studies in the 1960's showing an increased incidence of poor physical health when responsibility for people was high (Cooper and Marshall, 1978; Cartwright and Cooper, 1997).

Another potential stressor is role preparedness i.e. being inadequately prepared for the role of a teacher because of inadequate training (Fimian and Santoro, 1983). Minkler and Biller (1979) explain that the stresses and tensions manifested as discontinuity are encountered when moving from familiar to unfamiliar roles. These unfamiliar roles may constitute totally new role or familiar old roles which are played differently in a new situation. With the amount of rapid changes in teaching, it is possible that the teachers training may well be out of date by the time he or she actually starts to teach.

(iii) Relationships at Work : The third category of potential causes of stress in the workplace is relationships at work. A review of the research literature with regard to teacher stress reveals that the teachers are experiencing stress from their relationships with fellow teaching colleagues (Wanberg, 1984; Brenner et al., 1985), head-teachers (Clark, 1980; Needle et al., 1980; Tellenbeck et al., 1983), administrators/ education authorities (Hawkes and Dedrick, 1983; Kalker, 1984; Wanberg, 1984; Russell et al., 1987), parents (Kalker, 1984; Mykletun, 1984; Wanberg, 1984), the community (Cox, 1977; Needle et al., 1980) and pupils (Tellenbeck et al., 1983; Brenner et al., 1985).

Relationship with others in the workplace (bosses, peers, subordinates) in terms of quality of these interpersonal relationships and social support are suggested to be potential sources of job-related strain (Cartwright and Cooper, 1997; Brenner et al., 1985). The work of Kahn et al. (1964) and, French and Caplan (1970) concluded that a breakdown in relationships with the people one works which can lead to psychological strain in the form of lowered job satisfaction and to feelings of threat to one's well-being.

Kyriacou (1987) explains that although absenteeism may enable some teachers to cope the role overload, it may have a resulting negative impact, as it can worsen relationships when the classes of an absent teacher have to be covered by others on the staff. One of the major stressors the teachers facing was the pupil's attitudes and behaviour. Student misbehaviour is reported to be a major teacher stressor (Abel and Sewell, 1999; Borg et al., 1991; Chan and Hui, 1998; Dorman, 2003; Kelly and Berthelsen, 1995; Makinen and Kinnunen, 1986; Manassero et al., 2006; Newmann et al., 1989). Kyriacou and Sutcliffe (1978) found four factors of teacher stress that includes pupil misbehaviour, poor working conditions, time pressure and poor school ethos.

Research has shown that particular individuals in a working environment may cause undue stress to others, because they do not recognize the interpersonal feelings and sensibilities in social interaction (Sutherland and Cooper, 1991). Levinson (1978) has devised the label 'abrasive personalities' to describe this character type. These people are usually achievement oriented, intelligent, hard driving, though less efficient with regard to emotional situations. It is suggested that if a leader is of this personality type, then stress may result for the subordinates. For example, if the head teacher of a primary school has the above characteristics, is a perfectionist and is self-centered, then this might create feelings of inadequacy and conflict between staff.

Another relevant feature is that of leadership style, as this is a potential source of stress for employees in whatever type of occupation. The effects of exposure to an authoritarian style of leader have been well documented by Lewin et al. (1939). If a head teacher, for example, does not engage in participation, encourage feedback on his or her decisions or performance and does not give recognition for good work, the head teacher-teacher relationship could be at risk.

(iv) Career Development : The fourth category identifies antecedents of occupational stress, and is termed career development. Cooper and Marshall (1978) identified two clusters of potential stressors in the area of career development: lack of job security (a fear of job loss, obsolescence or forced retirement) and status in-congruency (reaching career ceiling, under or over-promotion). For many employees career progression is valued, with promotion generally leading to an increase in income, job status and new challenges. Often when an employee reaches middle age he finds his career progress has slowed or stopped with job opportunities becoming fewer, knowledge becoming obsolete and energy waning (Cartwright and Cooper, 1997). The insecurity of teacher's jobs is well documented (Needle et al., 1980). Status incongruence is a feature that is also relevant to the section concerning relationships at work and refers to the situation where the actual status bestowed on an individual does not match that individual's status expectations and beliefs. This is of particular relevance to teachers at the moment, as they complain that they are suffering from a poor public image in terms of prestige, salary and respect for their professional status (Laughlin, 1984; Wanberg, 1984). Cooper et al. (2001) suggested that strain is often caused by a lack of advancement in the organisation, however, it may also be present when employees feel promoted beyond their capabilities. These authors hypothesize that under and over-promotion can have serious detrimental effects on the well-being of the employee and on levels of job satisfaction. Wisniewski and Gargiulo (1997) observed that professional training is required to meet the demands of the profession. Inadequate training programmes may directly or indirectly influence the development of stress because they often fail to provide educators with specific skills to meet the demands of teaching.

(v) Organizational Structure and Climate : The fifth major category of potential causes of occupational stress is organizational structure and climate. Simply being in an organisation can threaten an individual's freedom, autonomy and identity. An increasing number of researchers are investigating this area and problems include: lack of participation in decision-making processes; lack of a sense of belonging; lack of effective consultation; poor communication; restrictions on behaviour; and office politics (Cooper and Marshall, 1978). In summing the literature of the 1970's, Cooper and Marshall stated that employee participation in the organisation is related to lowered turnover and increased productivity, however, when participation is absent, lowered levels of job satisfaction and higher levels of poor mental and physical health (Cooper et al., 2001).

Hall (1979), Hall and Rutherford (1976) identified that organizational structure and working conditions influencing the teaching profession. As such they include : insufficient planning and long working hours to meet either instructional objectives or students needs; demands of accountability and excessive paperwork interferes with classroom responsibilities; inadequate instructional support material and resources; lack of professional opportunities and opportunities for professional growth; inadequate programme facilities for students with special needs; loss of teacher control to design and implement curricular practices and innovations; and lack of participation and influence in decision-making. Another potential source of stress was noted by Rout and Rout (2002) in organizational structure and climate of the any organization. They found that the process and implementation of appraisal systems (performance appraisal) can be a source of stress to individuals, especially when the outcome may influence the person's salary or promotion.

Reddy (2007) studied the occupational stress of special education teachers and found that lack of opportunities for promotion, insufficient planning time for planning instructional activities, inadequate instructional supportive materials and resources, inadequate salary and job demands are the potential sources of stress among special education teachers.

Gersten, Keating, Yovanoff and Harniss (2001) study indicated that stress in job design (administration support, inadequate resources, limited decision-making power). The job design for special education teachers is very encumber-some and ambiguous. Also, Andrews, Evans and, Miller (2002) state that the main factor of retention for special education teachers is support i.e. financial, administration, etc. Many educators responses to researchers about attrition focuses on disillusionment and the lack of value placed on the work that is expected.

(vi) Organizational Interface with Outside : The final source of occupational stress outlined by Cooper and Marshall (1978) was labelled as organizational interface with outside. These are the potential stressors that exist in the life of the teacher, outside the work arena and affecting behaviour at work, which require consideration when assessing the sources and impact of teacher stress. These stressors include stressful life events, pressure resulting from conflict between organizational and family demands, financial difficulties and conflicts between organizational and personal beliefs. The area that has received the most research interest is that of the work-family interface (sometimes referred to as work-family conflict). In case of teachers, the main stresses from the home/work interface are those resulting from dual-career couples and relationships between work and family. One aspect of home life that may help exacerbate pressure is that of being part of a dual-career couple. Lewis and Cooper (1989) outline conflict, overload, role cycling dilemmas, relationship dilemmas and dilemmas of equality as stressors of being a member of a dual-career family. On the other hand, the interaction between home and work can create stress. Family based strains can result from role pressure or overload (e.g. due to homemaking), interpersonal conflicts (between couples and between parents and children) and role captivity (where they are bound by one role, but would prefer another).

Emphasized by Cooper et al. (2001) changes in the structure of families, the increase of women in the workforce, and changes in technology (for example, portable computers and the internet) which enable the employee to perform work-related tasks in a variety of locations have blurred the boundary between life on and life off the job. This conflict between roles has been consistently linked with psychological strain (Frone, Russell and Cooper, 1992).

Concept, Meaning and Definitions of Job Satisfaction

Job satisfaction is an integral component of organizational climate and an important element in management-employee relationships. Job satisfaction is a positive emotional state that occurs when a person's job seems to fulfill important job values provided these values are compatible with one's needs. Job satisfaction in simple words is an individual's emotional reaction to the job itself. Job satisfaction may be general or specific. Sometimes job satisfaction is referred to as overall feeling of satisfaction i.e. satisfaction with the situation as a whole. At some other point of times, job satisfaction refers to persons feelings towards specific dimensions of the work environment. In reviewing the literature it becomes apparent that job satisfaction can be defined in a number of ways.

In a study on job satisfaction, Hoppock (1935) proposed the following six major components of job satisfaction : (*i*) the way the individual reacts to unpleasant situation; (*ii*) the facility with which he adjusts himself to other persons; (*iii*) his relative status in the social and economic group with which he identified himself; (*iv*) the nature of the work in relation to his abilities, interests and preparation for the job; (*v*) security; and (*vi*) loyalty. Vroom (1964) listed the following seven dimensions which go into job satisfaction : (*a*) attitude towards the company and company management; (*b*) attitude towards promotional opportunities; (*c*) attitude towards the job content; (*d*) attitude towards supervision; (*e*) attitude towards financial rewards; (*f*) attitude towards working conditions; and (*g*) attitude towards co-workers.

Milkovich and Boudreau (1988) define job satisfaction as 'a pleasurable or positive emotional reaction to a persons job experiences'. According to Ramayah, Jantan and Tadisina (2001), job satisfaction explains what makes people to come to work? and what makes them happy about their job or not to quit their job? Similarly, Ranft and Ranft (1999), defines job satisfaction as 'the constellation of a persons attitudes towards or about the job'. Organ and Bateman (1991) view job satisfaction as a reflection of perceived fairness on the job. In other words, job satisfaction scores correspond to an evaluation of the job and its various aspects against some intuitive idea of what they ought to be.

Hoppock (1935) mentioned in Brokke (2002) views job satisfaction as any combination of psychological, physiological and environmental circumstances that would cause a person to state, 'I am satisfied with my job'. According to Rocca and Kostanski (2001), job satisfaction is the degree to which people like their jobs. It is a general attitude toward the job, the difference between the amount of rewards employees receive and the amount they believe they should receive. A person with a high level of job satisfaction holds positive attitudes towards the job, while a person who is dissatisfied with his or her job holds negative attitudes about the job (Robbins et al., 1994).

Busch, Fallan and Pettersen (1998) defined job satisfaction as the positive emotional response to a job situation resulting from attaining what the employee wants and values from the job. This implies that job satisfaction can be captured by either a one-dimensional concept of global job satisfaction or a multidimensional, faceted, construct of job satisfaction capturing different aspects of a job situation that can vary independently and should be measured separately. The facet-specific job satisfaction might include aspects like inner rewards, conflict-balance dimensions, recognition and support and economic compensation.

Different operational definitions of job satisfaction given by Wanous and Lawler (1972) may be quoted : (1) Overall job satisfaction is the sum of job facet satisfaction across all facets of job; (2) Job satisfaction has been conceptualized as a weighted sum of job facet satisfaction; (3) Job satisfaction has been operationalised as the sum of goal attainment or need fulfillment when summed across job facets; (4) Job satisfaction has been operationalised as a discrepancy between 'how much is there on' and 'how much should there be'.

Reddy (2007) refers job satisfaction of special education teachers as the degree of satisfaction the special education teachers enjoyed with reference to the organizational climate; inter and intra personal relationships; motivational climate and security; and financial status that they ensign in special education schools.

Models of Job Satisfaction

Several theories have been propounded concerning the dynamics of job satisfaction and its general impact upon worker behaviours. The important theories that reflect the job-satisfaction models are Herzberg's Two-Factors Theory (1959); Maslow's Hierarchy of Needs Theory (1943); Vroom's Expectancy Theory (1964) and Porter-Lawler Model (1968).

(a) Maslow's Hierarchy of Needs Theory (1943) : Jobs which are able to satisfy most of the Maslow's (1943) needs would be jobs which would result in greater satisfaction on the part of the employee. Maslow's (1943) theory is based on a hierarchy of five needs (Physiological, Safety/Security, Belongingness/Social, Self-esteem and Self-actualization); each need is assumed to motivate behaviour in varying degrees. Maslow argues that lower-level needs in the hierarchy take precedence; behavior is directed toward satisfying these needs sufficiently to make the next higher order need dominant.

1. *Physiological needs*—these are the basic needs of the organism such as food, water, oxygen and sleep. They also include the somewhat less basic needs such as sex or activity.
2. *Safety needs*—Here Maslow is talking about the need of a person for a generally ordered existence in a stable environment which is relatively free of threats to the safety of the persons existence.
3. *Love needs*—these are the needs for affectionate relations with other individuals and the need for one to have a recognized place as a group member—the need to be accepted by one's peers.
4. *Esteem needs*—the need for self-respect, for accomplishment and for achievement. The desire for prestige and status is an important aspect of the drive for achievement. Attaining goals leads to feelings of self-respect, strength and confidence.
5. *Self-actualization needs*—the needs for self-fulfillment. The need to achieve one's full capacity for doing.

Blai (1982) hypothesized that, in the work environment, degrees of self assessed job satisfactions vary with the strength of the psychological needs satisfied. The degree of satisfaction of any person is dependent upon the extent of fulfillment of his needs. If the structure of the work situation is such that it is not possible for an employee to select goals or to obtain goals which are necessary to satisfy his needs, then frustration—instigated behaviour is likely to occur. It is therefore, a system of goals or rewards will be made available to the employee that well satisfy whatever the needs he brings into the work situation.

(b) Herzberg's Two-Factors Theory (1959) : The original study of Herzberg, Mausner and Synderman (1959) was concerned with an investigation into causes of job satisfaction and job dissatisfaction among engineers and accountants. The results of their study did indicate that things which were associated with high satisfaction (satisfiers) were somewhat different from the things which were associated with situations of low satisfaction (dissatisfiers). They found that the discriminations of good periods included such things such as achievement, recognition, advancement, responsibility, advancement etc. All of these things seemed to relate to the actual content of the job. They were therefore called 'content factors'. Descriptions of dissatisfying work periods seemed to be filled with items dealing with company policy, supervision, salary and working conditions. These items were seemed to relate to the context in which a person performed his task and were therefore referred to as 'context factors'.

Herzberg et al. (1959) from their study postulated two general classes of work variables—'satisfiers' and 'dissatisfiers'. Satisfiers are those things which lead to job satisfaction. They are generally job 'content factors' or 'motivators'. Dissatisfiers are those things which result in job dissatisfaction. They are generally job 'context' or 'hygiene' factors. According to Brokke (2002), the central hypotheses derived from Herzberg's research were as follows : (1) the factors involved in producing job satisfaction were separate and distinct from the factors that led to job dissatisfaction; (2) the opposite of job satisfaction would not be job dissatisfaction, but rather no job satisfaction; (3) the factors that is, they contribute very little to job dissatisfaction; and (4) conversely, the dissatisfiers contribute very little to job satisfaction. Herzberg (1966) argues the fact that job satisfaction is made up of two unipolar is not unique, but it remains a difficult concept to grasp.

(c) Vroom's Expectancy Theory (1964) : The Expectancy Theory of Victor Vroom deals with motivation and management. Vroom's theory assumes that behavior results from conscious choices among alternatives whose purpose it is to maximize pleasure and minimize pain. Together with Edward Lawler and Lyman Porter, Vroom suggested that the relationship between people's behavior at work and their goals was not as simple as was first imagined by other scientists. Vroom realized that an employee's performance is based on individual's factors such as personality, skills, knowledge, experience and abilities.

The expectancy theory says that individuals have different sets of goals and can be motivated if they believe that: there is a positive correlation between efforts and performance; favourable performance will result in a desirable reward; the reward will satisfy an important need; and the desire to satisfy the need is strong enough to make the effort worthwhile. Vroom's Expectancy Theory is based upon the following three beliefs:

1. *Valence :* Valence refers to the emotional orientations people hold with respect to outcomes [rewards]. The depth of the want of an employee for extrinsic (money, promotion, time-off, benefits) or intrinsic (satisfaction) rewards. Management must discover what employee's value;
2. *Expectancy :* Employees have different expectations and levels of confidence about what they are capable of doing. Management must discover what resources, training, or supervision employees need;

3. *Instrumentality* : The perception of employees whether they will actually get what they desire even if it has been promised by a manager. Management must ensure that promises of rewards are fulfilled and that employees are aware of that.

Vroom suggests that an employee's beliefs about expectancy, instrumentality, and valence interact psychologically to create a motivational force such that the employee acts in ways that bring pleasure and avoid pain. This force can be 'calculated' via the following formula: *Motivation = Valence × Expectancy* (Instrumentality). This formula can be used to indicate and predict such things as job satisfaction, ones occupational choice, the likelihood of staying in a job, and the effort one might expand at work.

(d) Porter-Lawler Model (1968) : Luthans (1998) states that the 'Herzberg model is really a theory of job satisfaction, but still it does not adequately deal with the relationship between satisfaction and performance'. The Vroom model also avoids the relationship between satisfaction and performance, Porter and Lawler refined and extended Vroom's model that the relationship between satisfaction and performance.

Porter-Lawler Theory of motivation, which was developed by Lyman W. Porter and Edward E. Lawler, supports a belief that actual performance in a job is primarily determined by the effort spent. This belief supports the idea that performance is also affected by the personal ability to do the job and also by individual's perception of what the required task is. So performance is the responsible factor that leads to intrinsic as well as extrinsic rewards. This reward along with the equity of individuals leads to satisfaction. Hence, satisfaction of the individual depends upon the fairness of the reward. Porter-Lawler model tells what happens after the performance, the rewards that follow and how these are perceived will determine satisfaction.

(e) Adam's Equity Theory (1963) : Adams (1965) argues that individuals compare their inputs and outcomes to those of relevant other persons in determining whether they are equitably (fairly) treated. Stated another way, the comparison process is a comparison of ratios:

$$\frac{\textit{Persons outcomes}}{\textit{Person's inputs}} \ \textit{compared to} \ \frac{\textit{Other's outcomes}}{\textit{Other's inputs}} \longrightarrow \textit{Employee Behaviour}$$

This model suggests that individuals consider the ratio of the outcomes or rewards they receive to the inputs they provide and compare their ratio to their perceptions of the ratio for some relevant other person or group. When the two ratios are unequal, an individual is motivated to reduce the perceived inequity.

Factors Influencing Job Satisfaction Among Teachers

Job satisfaction is the result of various attitudes possessed by an employee (Blum and Naylor, 1968). In a narrow sense, their attitudes are related to the job and are concerned with such specific factors as : (*i*) wages; (*ii*) supervision; (*iii*) steadiness of employment; (*iv*) conditions of work; (*v*) opportunities for advancement; (*vi*) recognition of ability; (*vii*) fair evaluation of work; (*viii*) social relations on the job; (*ix*) prompt settlement of grieveness; (*x*) fair treatment by the employer; and (*xi*) other similar factors. Other aspects such as employee's age, health, temperament and level of aspirations should be considered.

Rogers and McIntire (1983) state that the responses an individual makes in a given situation are the result of two basic types of factors i.e. external and internal factors. External factors operates from outside the person and in an organizational setting, the external factors would include among other things, specific job requirements, the person's position in the organizational hierarchy and the behaviour of superiors, subordinates and co-workers. On the other hand, internal factors operate within the person and in an organizational context internal factors would include the person's interest in the job, job satisfaction and feelings toward superiors, subordinated and co-workers. An extensive review of the literature indicated the Herzberg Two-Factor Theory (Herzberg, Mausner and Synderman, 1959) as a prominent model for identifying the satisfiers or intrinsic factors and the dissatisfiers or extrinsic factors.

(a) Intrinsic/Content Factors : Davis (1972), states that the distinction between job content and job context is similar to the distinction between intrinsic and extrinsic factors in the field of psychology. Intrinsic or content factors are those which occur at the time of performance of the work, so there is a direct satisfaction to perform the work. According to Perie, Baker and Whitener (1997) for teachers, intrinsic satisfaction can come from classroom activities. Daily interactions with students inform teacher's feelings about whether or not students have learned something as a result of their teaching. Student characteristics and perceptions of teacher control over the classroom environment also are intrinsic factors affecting teacher satisfaction (Lee, Dedrick and Smith, 1991). Several studies have found that these factors are related to both attrition and satisfaction in teaching, as well as other profession (Boe and Gilford, 1992; Lee et al., 1991). The job that provides a greater degree of freedom and control (autonomy) in work method and work pace also enhances satisfaction with the work (Vroom, 1964; Hughey and Murphy, 1982; Brodinsky, 1984). Satisfaction of subordinates is positively associated with the degree to which they are permitted an opportunity to participate in making decisions (Vroom 1964, Belasco and Alutto, 1972, Sweeney, 1981; Schneider, 1984). Vroom (1960) showed that the amount of participation was most positively related to satisfaction of persons high in need for independence. Recognition for one's task performance/ accomplishment has been found to be a significant contributor to job satisfaction. Locke (1973) found recognition to be one of the single most frequently mentioned events causing satisfaction/dissatisfaction. According to Gannon (1977) perhaps most important influence on a person's job satisfaction is his or her occupational or organizational level (Locke, 1976 and Robinson, 1969). The design or structure of the organization also appears to relate to job satisfaction. The larger the subunit or work group, the lower the satisfaction of those in it (Porter, Lawler and Hackman, 1975). As the size of the subunit increases, individual's relationships with their fellow employees seem to become more impersonal (Ingham, 1970).

One's schedule of work can also influence his or her level of job satisfaction (Wheeler, Gurman and Tarnowieski, 1972). Research on the schedule has indicated that job satisfaction does seem to increase when the new approach is introduced (Nord and Costigan, 1973). The job satisfaction of these workers declines after about a year. A second distinct method of scheduling work, flexi time, appears to create a high level of job satisfaction both in the short run and in the long run (Hedges, 1973). Ellis (1984) mentions that teachers obtain their greatest satisfaction through a sense of achievement in reaching and affecting students, experiencing recognition and feeling responsible. According to Ganzach (2002) people assign greater weight to intrinsic satisfaction than to pay satisfaction; that is, intrinsic satisfaction has a larger influence on global satisfaction than pay satisfaction.

In a study Brunetti (2001) examined teacher satisfaction in a group of high school teachers and found that the teachers were highly satisfied with their jobs. Also, the study identified that working with young people and seeing them learn and grow as principal motivators. Other important motivators included 'professional satisfaction factors such as teaching one's subject, serving society, and having autonomy in the classroom. Of less importance were 'practical satisfaction factors' such as salary and benefits and job security.

(b) Extrinsic / Context Factors : Davis (1972) states that extrinsic factors are those which occur after work or away from work, providing no direct satisfaction at the time the work is performed. The employee cannot enjoy them until he stops working. Examples of extrinsic satisfiers are retirement plans, health insurance and vacations because none of them provides satisfaction during work. Perie, Baker and Whitener (1997) state that a variety of extrinsic factors have been associated with teacher satisfaction, including salary, perceived support from administrators, school safety and availability of school resources, among others (Bobbitt et al., 1994; Choy et al., 1993). A study by Misshawk (1971) confirms that employees look for more than human relations skills in their supervisors, whatever their occupational levels. For high, medium and low-level skill groups, Misshawk found that all regarded technical skills of importance to their job satisfaction in addition to human relational skills. A study by French, Israel and As (1960) examined the effects of participation in decision-making and found that in only three out of fourteen items was there is a significant improvement in job satisfaction. Keller (1975) showed that role ambiguity to be associated with low levels of satisfaction with the work itself, whereas role conflict was associated with lower levels of satisfaction with supervisory behaviour, pay and promotion. As Keller points out the findings in this area have clear practical implications. Where a supervisor fails to agree with a subordinate as to which role should be performed, the uncertainty can lead to a lowering of job satisfaction. Johnson and Stinson (1975) found that those with a high need for achievement were more affected by role ambiguity and conflict.

Perie, Baker and Whitener (1997) states although organizational factors related to teacher satisfaction are often the focus of research efforts, several teacher and school characteristics are also related to satisfaction. For instance, Choy et al. (1993) research examining the satisfaction of public and private school teachers indicates that teaching in a private school is associated with greater job satisfaction on average. Similarly, elementary school teachers tend to be more likely to be highly satisfied with their working conditions than secondary school teachers.

According to Gruneberg (1979) a number of investigators have examined the relationship between organizational climate and job satisfaction. Friedlander and Margulies (1969) found that satisfaction with task involvement was greatest in climates, high in management thrust whereas satisfaction with interpersonal relationships was highest in organizations where the climate was low in routine. Friedlander and Margulies also found organizational climate affected satisfaction with personal relationships more than the other aspects of satisfaction. Pritchard and Karasick (1973) in their study of the relationship between organizational climate and job satisfaction also found significant correlations between job satisfaction and aspects of organizational climate such as supportiveness, concern or social relationships and so on. As with the study of Friedlander and Margulies they also found individual differences in the relationship between job satisfaction and organizational climate.

Klassen and Anderson (2009) found that teachers in 1962 were most concerned with external sources of job dissatisfaction (e.g. salary, condition of buildings and equipment and poor human relations), whereas the teachers in 2007 expressed the most concern about factors relating to teaching itself (e.g. time demands and pupils behaviour). Ma and MacMillan (1999) found that the teachers who stayed in the profession longer were less satisfied with their professional role. Workplace conditions positively affected teacher satisfaction; administration control was the most important, followed by teaching competence and organizational culture. Ololube (2006) found that the teachers were dissatisfied with the educational policies and administration, pay and fringe benefits, material rewards and advancement. Price and Terry (2008) found that the higher levels of teacher satisfaction were associated with fewer children assigned to a class. Bhandari and Patil (2009) found that few of the women teachers are facing certain problems due to lack of coordination and cooperation in the workplace. Majority of the women teachers are satisfied with their work, job and salary and majority of them said that they have not recognized for the job and work done.

Ghazi (2004) found that the head teachers were 'slightly satisfied' with compensation, working conditions, social status, school system policies and practices; 'satisfied' with advancement, social service, creativity, recognition, supervision human relation, security, independence, colleagues, supervision technical, authority, responsibility, achievement, ability utilization and variety; 'very satisfied' with moral values and activity aspects of their job. Nazar and Ahmad (1998) found that the factors like promotion, responsibility, salary and interpersonal relations were significant determinants of overall job satisfaction of teachers whereas the factors like job security, salary, working conditions and institutional policies and practices were significant determinants of overall job dissatisfaction of teachers. Hurren (2006) found that the principals who share humour in the workplace have teachers with higher job satisfaction than those principals who share very little or no humour in the workplace.

Relationship Between Emotional Intelligence, Occupational Stress and Job Satisfaction

Built into the emotional-cognitive structures of the brain are many evolutionary functions that date back to our species struggle for survival and the mechanisms that evolved to cope with that stress. Brain structures like the amygdala in the emotional or limbic regions of the brain can 'hijack' intellectual processes when intense emotions are experienced in the system. This is why even very smart people can make very foolish choices when under emotional stress.

According to Ashforth and Humphrey (1995, p.98) 'emotions are an integral and inseparable part of everyday organizational life'. Also, Lazarus (1995) has made clear that emotions offer a rich and useful source of information about what is happening to a person. Hochschild (1983) who introduced the concept of emotional labour examined the relationship between emotions and aspects of work and strain. Hochschild's (1983) primary concerns were with the emotional consequences of emotional labour, including estrangement of self, depersonalization, detachment, stress, burnout, or even drug use. In the elaborate model, Marris and Feldman (1996) proposed that emotional labour has four dimensions : frequency of appropriate emotional display, attentiveness required to display rules, variety of emotions to be displayed and emotional dissonance. The more these dimensions are present in the workplace, the more emotional labour employees provide. Moreover, some of these dimensions are positively related (for example, frequency and emotional dissonance; attentiveness and variety; and attentiveness and emotional dissonance), while others are negatively related (frequency and attentiveness as well as variety and emotional dissonance). Emotional exhaustion was proposed as the outcome of the four dimensions of emotional labour, while job dissatisfaction was hypothesized to be the outcome of only emotional dissonance. Brotheridge and Grandey (2002) distinguished between two types of emotional labour: job-focussed emotional labour, which represents the level of emotional requirements of a job, and employee-focussed emotional labour, which is the process or experience of managing emotions and expressions to meet work demands, including surface acting (measured as emotional dissonance) and deep acting (measured as emotion regulation). Classifying emotional labour into self-focussed and other-focussed emotion management, Pugliesi (1999) found that both forms of emotional labour had negative effects on employees, in terms of increasing distress and perceptions of job stress, as well as decreasing job satisfaction, with self-focussed emotion management having the most pervasive and detrimental impacts.

Within an organizational stress framework, many scholars think that occupational stress, emotional intelligence and job satisfaction are distinct constructs, but highly interrelated. For example, the ability of employees to properly manage their emotions and manage other employee's emotions will strongly increase their abilities to cope with physiological and psychological stresses in implementing job. As a result, it may lead to higher job satisfaction in organizations (Guleryuz et al., 2008; Sy et al., 2006; Thiebaut et al., 2005). The employee who cannot control stresses may have job dissatisfaction, lower commitment and productivity at the workplace (Seaward, 2005; Newell, 2002; Sy et al., 2006; World Health Organization, 2005). The ability of employees to manage their physiological and psychological stresses may have a significant impact on job satisfaction (Fairbrother and Warn, 2003; Snelgrove, 1998; Swanson et al., 1998). Further, Salaski and Cartwright (2002) suggested that higher levels of emotional intelligence might increase an individual's resilience to stress in the workplace. Findings from the surveys (Gillespie et al., 2001; Salaski and Cartwright, 2002; Nikolau and Tsaosis, 2002) showed that the properly controlled physiological and psychological stresses had increased employee capabilities to manage (understand, use and regulate) their emotions and other employee emotions in implementing job. These findings are consistent with the emotional intelligence theories of Bar-On, 1997; Goleman, 1998, 2003; Salovey and Mayer, 1990, 1997, which posits that the level of emotional intelligence will increase individual's competencies and this can increase their ability to decrease stress situations and increase positive individual attitudes and behaviours.

In a chapter investigating the role of emotions specific to the occupational stress process, Spector and Goh (2001) outlined their emotion-centered occupational stress model and suggested how a focus on emotions can enhance employee well-being. These authors note that the continual experience of negative emotions in the workplace is likely to induce job dissatisfaction, a decline in organisational commitment, and increased withdrawal.

Fisher (2000) hypothesised that emotions should be directly attributable to the job because emotions have a target and are often triggered by actual events in the workplace (being angry at someone, feeling frustrated because of an obstacle in reaching a goal, being proud of an accomplishment). Internal features of a job such as the relationship the employee has with supervisors and colleagues is likely to be related to emotion and therefore influence an employee's perception of job satisfaction, more so than external features such as pay and promotion. In analysing data from 121 employees, Fisher (2000) reports that the experience of emotions is related to job satisfaction, with the experience of positive emotions being related to increased job satisfaction, and negative emotions being related to decreased job satisfaction, whereby employees who report experiencing positive emotions in the workplace also report greater feelings of satisfaction with their job than employees who report experiencing negative emotions in the workplace.

Also, there are several studies that determined the link between teacher's occupational stress and job satisfaction. Research study by Reddy (2007) reveals that there was a significant negative relationship between occupational stress and job satisfaction of special education teachers. Also, De Nobile and McCormick (2005) identified that all four occupational stress domains (student, information, personal, school domains and general occupational stress) predicted job satisfaction of primary school teachers. According to Stamps and Piedmonte (1986) job satisfaction has been found to be significantly related with job stress and identified four job stressors that were predictive of job dissatisfaction (Cooper et al., 1989). In other study, Vinokur-Kaplan (1991) stated that organization factors such as workload and working conditions were negatively related with job satisfaction. Fletcher and Payne (1980) identified that a lack of satisfaction can be a source of stress, while high satisfaction can alleviate the effects of stress. This study reveals that, both of job stress and job satisfaction were found to be interrelated. The study of Landsbergis (1988) and Terry et al. (1993) showed that high levels of work stress are associated with low levels of job satisfaction. Moreover, Cummins (1990) have emphasized that job stressors are predictive of job dissatisfaction and greater propensity to leave the organization.

The ability of teachers to properly manage their emotions and other's emotions will increase their ability to cope with the stressors and which in-turn decreases their job dissatisfaction. Recent studies (Hsieh et al., 2004; Leka et al., 2003; Wetzel et al., 2006; Adler et al., 2006; Hourani et al., 2006; Zhong et al., 2006 mentioned in Ismail et al., 2010) showed that the ability of employees to manage their physiological and psychological stresses may have a significant impact on job performance. Also, the ability of employees to properly control and manage their physiological and psychological stresses in performing job may lead to higher job performance in organizations.

Roles and Responsibilities of the Special Education Teachers

As inclusion is gaining ground throughout the world, teachers and others involved in education are working to develop positive educational experiences to all children with disabilities. For an inclusive setup, any educational system should change to better accommodate the diversity of needs that pupils have and include them in all aspects of school life, identify any barriers within and around the school that hinder learning and participation and reduce or remove these barriers. In this context, both the special education teacher and the general education teachers have to play multiple roles in the organization of the class, teaching and training, guidance and counselling, intra and interpersonal relations apart from research activities.

As a teacher, he / she have to play various roles. The National Policy on Education (1986) emphasis the teacher accountability to the pupils, their parents, the community and to their own profession. In specific terms, it emphasis, the specific activities of the teachers :

1. Teaching and guidance of pupils
2. Research, experimentation and innovation
3. Extension and social services
4. Management of various services and activities that institutes undertake to implement their programmes
5. Diagnoses children needs and potentialities
6. Encouraging curiosity in students
7. Teaching by example as well as by percept

Due to increased demands and changes, the special education teachers in both special education and in regular schools have to play the following roles and responsibilities.

(a) Planning and Organizational Roles : First and foremost, any special education teachers should organize and co-ordinate the educational programme of the students with disabilities, should know the causes and characteristics (both physiological and psychological aspects of children with disabilities), and should be aware of the diagnostic and assessment procedures to identify the disability (Reddy, 2007). In addition, the special educators should gather data for planning and designing instructional programmes according to the students needs and serve as case managers for developing, implementing and evaluating individualized educational programmes-IEP. Also, it is the sole responsibility of any special educator to maintain student's records like IEP, documentation, progress report, behaviour plan etc., to do follow up activities. Also, they should involve themselves in preparing budget for designing, implementing and evaluating IEP. Before planning and designing IEP and instructional programmes, it is special educator who should involve in identification and assessment of the special needs children, as early identification of a child with special needs is essential to intervene early in their education. In the process of early identification and intervention, the special education teachers make use of direct observation, conduct formal and informal tests and identify the abilities and disabilities of each child by using various technological resources. They should also be involved in planning and designing effective learning environments and experiences supported by technology like—designing developmentally appropriate learning opportunities that apply technology enhanced instructional strategies to support the diverse needs students. In addition, they should plan for the management of technology resources in the context of the learning activities. They should play a major role in decision making process as they are directly involved with the children. Apart from these responsibilities, they should co-operate with the research personnel in research and extension activities.

(b) Teaching and Training Roles : Teaching and training is one of the major roles to be played by the special educator. They should teach regular academic subjects by adopting the curriculum to meet the students individual needs through IEP apart from giving training in life skills like plus curricular skills—shopping, cooking, self-care etc., Educating all the special education children by today's standards and for tomorrows living, most certainly includes the use of technology. Its relationship in providing essential supports for students with disabilities in areas of self-care, education, employment, recreation/leisure and community living are readily accepted. Additionally, access to technology can provide meaningful learning experiences to develop problem solving and higher order thinking skills and to function in the world beyond the classroom.

The appropriate and successful integration of technology into learning environments has the potential to benefit all students with disabilities. Specifically, technology assists students to : (*a*) maximize independence in academic and employment tasks; (*b*) participate in classroom discussion; (*c*) gain access to peers, mentors and role models; (*d*) self-advocate; (*e*) gain access to the full range of educational experiences; (*f*) participate in experiences not otherwise possible; (*g*) success in work-based learning experiences; (*h*) secure high levels of independent learning; (*i*) prepare for transitions to college and careers; (*j*) work side-by-side with peers; (*k*) master academic tasks that they cannot accomplish otherwise; (*l*) enter high-tech career fields; and (*m*) participate in community and recreational activities (Burstahler, 2003). Also, Wiener (1987) has rightly pointed out that "the potential for computers in special education is without limits. Computer technology can provide a voice for students with oral communication problems; serve as writing medium for students who have difficulty manipulating a pencil; open the world of written communication problems; open the world of written communication for the blind; enable the deaf to communicate in a hearing classroom; and allow the physically disabled the opportunity to control their learning environment". These recent trends in special education that includes the use of technology provides essential supports to students with disabilities to access, participate in and demonstrate progress in standards-based curriculum. Thus the special education teacher should be responsible enough to use technological services meant for the students with disabilities. They should demonstrate introductory knowledge, skills and understanding of technology operations and concepts as well as should maintain and troubleshoot, if need arises.

Further, the teacher should have a sound mastery over the peculiar skills in preparing the teaching aids and teaching-learning materials and use of relevant equipments like braille embossers, thermoform braille duplicators, graphics machine, amplification devices, mobility materials, screen readers, screen magnifiers, job access with speech (JAWS) etc. Apart from these, the special educator should use various strategies like cognitive, meta-cognitive and cognitive behaviour modification techniques to deal children with disabilities (Santakumari, 2003; Shyamala, 2004; and Jayaprabha, 2003).

In the teaching-learning process, the mantra of reinforcement is a well known fact. It is the duty of a teacher to motivate aptly to receive appropriate behaviour and learning from any child. Motivation is the central factor in effective management of the process of learning. It is the special educator who should think of the ways and means for achieving motivation in the teaching-learning process. In order to reinforce the special child, the teacher should make use of child-centered approach, link the new learning with the past, make use of effective methods, aids and devices in teaching and create appropriate learning situation and environment to motivate a child in any set up. In addition, he/she should make use of the competition based on co-operation learning to inculcate the feeling of self-improvement in the child. This will develop team spirit, community feeling, a sense of unity and other socially desirable habits.

(c) Guidance and Counselling Roles : Guidance and counselling service may be in personal, social, psychological, educational or vocational area given to the students with disabilities, parents of children with disabilities, peer group or to the other person related to the children who are in need of the services. Guidance and counselling includes a variety of group oriented activities designed to enhance students attitudes and values

and refers to an individualized, small-group or class process that assists disabled students with specific personal/social issues and difficulties and educational or career issues. Counselling services may be developmental, preventive or crisis-oriented. Special educator should play a role of guide and a counsellor to motivate the students in learning activities, modify the undesirable behaviour, motivate the desirable behaviour, to create awareness on various aspects of the disability like legal issue i.e. policies, regulations, concessions, reservations, job opportunities etc., and change stereotypic attitudes towards disability; discuss problems arising during transition period and how to tackle these problems and suggesting management tactics during crisis. Effective guidance to peer group by teachers will promote peer acceptance. This in-turn will facilitate the children with disabilities to develop self-confidence, self-esteem and self-realisation.

(d) Intra and Inter Personal Roles : As the special education programme is a joint venture, most of the responsibilities of special educators are to be shared with the other staff members and parents. A close rapport with the psychologists, ophthalmologists, otologists, orthopaedists, paediatricians, therapists, social worker, vocational rehabilitator etc., is essential to get comprehensive view about the nature and type of impairment and the cause of action to be taken for improvement. Also, this type of rapport helps them to overcome the impairment or for further rehabilitation service. Sharing ideas and making decisions by involving other professionals demands higher order of inter-personal skills in special education teachers, where they should apply their personal skills and knowledge to manage their own behaviour and encourage others appropriate behaviour in a wide range of situation. They should describe many aspects of relationships and use skills to interact positively and communicate the results with the colleagues, parents and para-professionals in diverse settings at school and in community for the well-being of the children. Further, they should identify the variety of characteristics, skills, competencies, qualities and talents of students, their parents, peers, administrators and para-professionals and should demonstrate social responsibility both at school and community levels.

Apart from these responsibilities, they should identify their personal interests, strengths, competencies and accomplishments in the field to equip themselves with the necessary skills and qualifications. Thus in the modern era, a teacher has innumerable responsibilities as our society becomes very complex. Teacher has to play the several roles to develop special children. The most important qualities of teacher are sincerity, honesty and involvement in teaching. The knowledge of teaching, training and instruction can be effectively used by incorporating important basic skills like learning strategies and speaking skill, complex problem solving skills through idea generation, implementation, planning and social skills through instruction, service orientation and social perceptiveness in managing special children.

Need for Identification of Emotional Intelligence, Occupational Stress and Job Satisfaction of Special Education Teachers

Goleman through his best-selling books like 'Emotional intelligence—why it can matter more than Intelligence Quotient (IQ)' and 'Working with emotional intelligence', has stresses the following factors while showing the importance of emotional intelligence : (*i*) emotional intelligence is as powerful, and at times more powerful than IQ; (*ii*) unlike IQ, emotional intelligence, may be the best predictor of success in life; (*iii*) unlike what is claimed of IQ, we can teach and improve in children and in any individual, some crucial emotional competencies, paving way for increasing their emotional intelligence and thus making their life more healthy, enjoyable and successful in the days to come; (*iv*) the concept of emotional intelligence is to be applauded not because it is totally new but because it captures the essence of what our children or all of us need to know for being productive and happy; (*v*) IQ and even standard achievement test (SAT) scores do not predict any person's success in life. Even success in academics can be predicted more by emotional and social measures than by academic ability; (*vi*) in working situations too, emotional intelligence helps more than one's intellectual potential in terms of one's IQ or even professional skills and competencies; (*vii*) a person's emotional intelligence helps him in all spheres of life through its various constituents or components namely knowledge of his emotions (self-awareness), managing the emotions, motivating oneself and recognizing emotions in others (empathy and handling relationships). Further, EI has been related significantly and positively to increased adapted behaviour such as : higher quality social relationships (Gil-Olarte et al., 2006; Lopes et al, 2004; Lopes et al, 2003), longer retention in the educational system (Parker et al., 2006), pro-social behaviour (Lopes et al., 2005), more satisfaction in life (Extremera and Fernandez-Berrocal, 2005; Palmer et al., 2002; Palomera and Brackett, 2006), the use of better adapted coping strategies (Fernandez-Berrocal and Extremera, 2006; Gohm and Clore, 2002), better mental health (Fernandez-Berrocal et al., 2006) and a greater capacity for interrupting negative emotional states and prolonging positive ones (Salovey et al., 2002).

Success in teaching requires considerable capacities in emotional competence. In general, teaching professionals need social-emotional competencies to be able to build resilience to adversity in the field, to self-monitor performance, and to regulate emotions through both reactive and proactive coping. Teachers in particular need sound organizational skills. They need to be self-aware of abilities and skills required for the range of roles, responsibilities, and demands of their work. They need to be able to seek support from educational leaders and managers when they self-perceive weaknesses in these abilities and skills. Also, they need social-emotional competencies to be able to effectively manage and develop student's emotional development.

Any special education programme, whether it is for physically challenged, intellectually impaired, sensorally deprived, emotionally disturbed and talented should focus on the innate abilities of the child rather than expecting the child to do extraordinary things. In other words, what is available in the child is more important rather than the things which are not available within the child. The human personality should be developed in-terms of the minimum knowledge, skills and capabilities required to perform the functions for healthy living. In this context, a special education teacher is one who should know the innate abilities and compensate the disabilities of the child by promoting the inner strengths of the individual. For this, a special education teacher's role is not just information provider but a facilitator to the child in every walk of life. Special education teacher should have better patience, perseverance and cognicising the needs of not only the child, but also his/her parents. In other words, he/she should have mind to do something to others than the routine things what we call it as emotionally intelligent. Further, the special school teachers are often witness to their student's emotional outbursts, in addition to the known deficits, which are extremely demanding and consuming of their cognitive and affective resources. The special school teachers adopt to a good extent a child-centered approach and spend a lot of time in interacting with individual students to be able to understand their needs and capabilities and to provide them constant help and supervision. This consumed a great deal of their time and energy adding to their isolation and work overload (Weiskopf, 1980; Shaw, Bensky and Dixon, 1981).

The need of flexibility, autonomy and novelty makes their job definitions inherently ambiguous making room for more role conflicts (Epstein, 1990). The students in special schools need constantly teachers help and supervision which leaves little time for them to interact with colleagues and induced in them a sense of social isolation (Shaw, Bensky and Dixon, 1981). The challenge of performing the tasks in special school is such that teachers need high degree of emotional strength, flexibility of procedures and routines, freedom to act according to the student needs and collegial support and none of these are found forthcoming. Also, in case of special schools the problems with students arise because of the inability of students to understand the rules and instructions.

Yate (1977) in his research found that different jobs require different levels of EQ and listed various jobs on the basis of level of EI they require for success and satisfaction. It is clear that special education teacher requires the highest level of EQ to deal with special needs children. The job of special school teachers is much more demanding of experimentation with novel activities. Rewards will go a long way to motivate the teachers for their creative activities, but none of the school system has any extrinsic rewards for teachers doing the job well, in the special schools even the intrinsic reward of the student progress is denied to teachers as children do not make a consistently upward progress. Children progress slowly and erratically. Markham (1999) found that by sharing the feelings with others and taking others support or direct action will make the teachers to feel better. In this perspective, emotional competence helps the special education teachers to identify the feelings and fears of students, recognize their feelings and can see their unmet emotional needs. Teachers thereby accept their limits, work towards their potentials to reach students with the socio-emotional learning activities during growth and development and can also provide the necessary support to enhance learning activities and educational experience. In this context, teachers have an important role in helping the disabled learners in expanding both IQ and EQ potentials. Moreover, the roles of special education teachers in emotional development of students are important since socio-emotional learning helps the children with disabilities to succeed both academically and socially. An emotionally intelligent person will not only be aware of himself or his role in a particular context but also what he/she should be, to tune the environment to make the fellow being to be more functional. As an emotionally intelligent person, the major roles she/he has to play are providing good organizational/classroom climate, adequately equipping himself/herself to meet the diverse needs of children within and outside the classroom, developing adequate intra and inter relationships and providing suitable instructional assignments and arrangements.

The literature provides evidence of teacher stress (Cooper and Travers, 1996), often linked with diversification of roles and increased responsibilities. Teachers need skills to deal with student behaviour problems and bullying (Nelson and Roberts, 2000). Increasing organisational and systemic increasing expectations from parents and the general community seems to propel these extra demands. The demands placed on teachers in the current climate would seem to be increasing and the demands are changing. Yet workplace support for teachers, through management practices and other strategies to help teachers to cope with these demands is often lacking (Cooper and Travers, 1996). A full range of interpersonal skills and competencies seem to be essential to manage a broad range of professional roles and responsibilities and self-management skills seem to be essential to cope with these demands. Teachers, therefore, need to better understand the development of these intrapersonal (self-management) and interpersonal skills.

Littrell et al. (1994) found that emotional support (e.g., showing appreciation, taking an interest in teachers work, maintaining open communication) is perceived as most important to special educators. They also found that emotional and instructional support (providing needed materials, space, and resources) correlate positively with both job satisfaction and school commitment. Corcoran et al. (1988) suggests that the lack of resources increases the teachers work load. And a heavy work load makes it very difficult to use the available resources.

Billingsley (2003) in analyzing the literature studies on special education teacher retention and attrition observed that the majority of attrition studies focussed on the effects of district and school working conditions, work assignment factors, and teachers affective reactions to their work. Work environment factors associated with staying include: (1) higher salaries; (2) positive school climate; (3) adequate support systems, particularly principal and central office support; (4) opportunities for professional development; (5) reasonable role demand; and (6) manageable case loads. Problematic district and school factors especially low salaries, poor climate, lack of administrative support and role overload and dissonance lead to negative affective reactions, e.g., high levels of stress, low levels of job satisfaction, and low levels of commitment. These negative reactions can often lead to withdrawal and eventually attrition.

Singhal (2004) observed that teachers in special schools have higher workload than regular schools. Also, the research studies by Reddy (2007) revealed that the organizational structure, professional training, inter and professional interaction and instructional assignments and arrangements are the major sources of stress factors contributing to the occupational stress of the special education teachers.

The special education teachers undergo stress and strain because of various stressors arising out of diversified roles and responsibilities. These stress factors make the person cynical towards work, colleagues, children and the school as a whole and have low self-efficacy, less organizational commitment and results in job dissatisfaction which further deteriorates the performance. Dissatisfied teachers may deliver poor service to the children with disabilities and affects the well-being of the teachers themselves. Research studies that explore the special education teachers emotional intelligence, occupational stress and job satisfaction facilitate to identify the emotional intelligence skills they possess, sources of occupational stress and the factors influencing job satisfaction among special education teachers working in the schools for the visually impaired, hearing impaired and the mentally retarded. This facilitates the school management to give training in emotional intelligence skills that they are lacking and reduces the sources of occupational stress by creating good organizational structure and climate, enhancing intra and interpersonal relationships, equip the teachers with necessary skills needed for the profession and control the environmental factors that are causing stress in teachers. All these contribute to the motivation, leading to the job satisfaction of the special education teachers. The present study is a modest attempt to identify the emotional intelligence, occupational stress and job satisfaction of special teachers.

The review of literature specifically related to the present problem under investigation is given in the succeeding chapter.

CHAPTER

2 Review of Related Literature

The review of related literature is an important aspect as any other components of the research process. The major purpose of reviewing the literature is to determine what has already been done in the research area selected and the research gaps. Being familiar with the previous research also facilitates interpretation of the results of the study. The review of literature gives information which can either support or challenge the conclusions of the investigations concerned to the present research and therefore provide clues for later research.

The review of literature highlights and evaluates the empirical data to understand the relation between emotional intelligence, occupational stress and job satisfaction of teachers, student teachers and special education teachers. It helps to gain an in-depth knowledge of the topic and confirm the need for the present study in Indian context. The reports and the results of the earlier studies have been reviewed in detail in order to get clear picture of the present study. The studies collected and reviewed are presented under the following headings:

Studies Conducted in India

Studies on Emotional Intelligence of Teachers

Studies on Emotional Intelligence of Student Teachers

Studies on Occupational Stress in Teachers

Studies on Occupational Stress in Special Education Teachers and Parents

Studies on Job Satisfaction of Teachers

Relationship Studies on Emotional Intelligence, Occupational Stress and Job Satisfaction

Studies Conducted Abroad

Studies on Emotional Intelligence of Teachers and Student Teachers

Studies on Antecedents / Stressors of Occupational Stress

Studies on Consequences of Occupational Stress among Teachers

Studies on Occupational Stress in Teachers

Studies on Occupational Stress in Special Education Teachers

Studies on Job Satisfaction of Teachers

Relationship Studies on Emotional Intelligence, Occupational Stress and Job Satisfaction

Studies Conducted in India

Studies on Emotional Intelligence of Teachers

Emotional intelligence is increasingly recognized as a major success factor in business. The components of emotional intelligence have always led to success in business. Now the term itself is gaining popularity and more attention is being given to its components and its benefits in leadership. In the field of teaching, the teachers teaching the diverse learners requires a new approach where they have to manage the classroom climate, teach qualitatively, adapt to the social changes and has to exhibit good decision-making skills. Thus, it is essential to identify the emotional intelligence and the allied areas. The research studies conducted in this regard in Indian context are discussed hereunder.

Amirtha and Kadhiravan (2006) explored the relationship between emotional intelligence and personality of 207 school teachers working in different schools of Chennai city. The results revealed that gender, age and qualification influence the emotional intelligence of teachers. Teachers also differ in some of their personality dimensions with respect to different descriptive variables. It was also found that extroversion, introversion and feeling dimensions of personality have a negative impact on emotional intelligence of teachers, whereas thinking and judging dimensions have a positive impact on their emotional intelligence. Bansibihari and Pathan (2004) examined the level of emotional intelligence of secondary school teachers in relation to gender and age. Five hundred secondary school teachers from Dhule district of Maharasthra state were administered Emotional Intelligence Test. The results revealed that majority of teachers fall under low category of emotional intelligence. There is no significant difference between the emotional intelligence of males and females, and age was independent of emotional intelligence.

Date (2006) investigated emotional maturity of male and female secondary school teachers of Dhule district. The sample consists of 141 male and 136 female teachers. Emotional Maturity scale was administered to the sample of the study. Findings indicate significant variation between two groups. Jayanthi and Agarwal (2006) attempted to study the socio-economic climate of the classroom in respect of teaching experience, total income, age, teaching subject and sex of 100 secondary school teachers. The results showed that the teachers creating different socio-emotional classroom climates do not differ significantly with respect to their teaching experience; teachers teaching science subjects are positively and significantly correlated with socio-emotional classroom climate as well as teachers creating positive classroom climate differ significantly from their negative counterparts with respect to teaching subject.

David and Roy (2010) conducted a study to examine the effect of emotional intelligence on teacher competencies at secondary school level of education. The study was conducted on 80 secondary school teachers of Secunderabad city. The analysis revealed that there was a moderate relationship between emotional intelligence on teacher competencies at secondary school level. The differential study of teacher competencies among high and low emotional intelligence teacher was also found to be positive.

Khan and Kumar (2008) studied the emotional intelligence and achievement motivation of 40 women teachers in secondary schools. Results showed that 33 per cent of teachers demonstrated high level of emotional intelligence and 70 per cent had high level of achievement motivation. Also, there was positive moderate correlation between emotional intelligence and achievement motivation.

Latha et al. (2005) conducted a study on emotional intelligence and its effect among school teachers. From the results and interpretations, it can be concluded that emotional intelligence does not influence the teacher effectiveness in general. But emotional intelligence affects certain aspects of teaching process i.e. teachers sense of humour and mastery in the subject.

Neelakandan (2007) studied the emotional competence of primary school teachers. Three hundred primary school teachers from Cuddalore district were administered Emotional Competence Scale. The results revealed that the primary school teachers have average level of emotional competence. The results revealed that the teachers having higher qualifications are found to have better emotional competence than teachers having essential qualifications only. Also, there was no significant difference between any two categories of sub-samples of teachers belonging to different group's in-relation to their experience, in respect to their emotional competence. Similarly, there was no significant difference between the teachers of government schools and private schools in respect to their level of emotional competence.

Sibia et al. (2004) attempted to distinguish the idea of emotional intelligence based on the perspectives of parents, teachers and children in the contemporary Indian society. A total of 1047 participants from eight cities in different parts of the country were included in the study. Results indicated that Indian view of emotional intelligence is embedded in its highly valued social concerns, virtues, cultural traditions and practices. The indigenous view of emotional intelligence takes into cognizance such factors as social sensitivity, pro-social values, action tendencies and affective states. Swani (2008) opined that positive emotions produce optimal functioning not just within the present but over the long term. Negative emotions, on the other hand, produce and intensify a variety of health threat and diseases. She suggested cultivating positive emotions within a self and in those around us as a means of achieving improved psychological and physical health over time.

Usha Rao (2008) in her article emphasised the importance of emotional maturity among teachers for enhancing the professional role of teachers. Emotional maturity was exemplified in various response patterns like attention getting : clowning, affected speech, bizarre appearance; rationalization : giving foolish reasons or undesirable behaviour; projection : placing blame on another for one's own shortcomings; day-dreaming : refusing the reality; others ego: satisfying reactions include undue criticism of others, display of jealous and generally inconsistent behaviour. Those teachers who do not show such response patterns definitely are emotionally matured and those will run after their own professional development. She suggested that the working conditions of the teachers should be improved for attaining emotional maturity.

Studies on Emotional Intelligence of Student Teachers

There has been substantial interest in the role of emotional intelligence among prospective teachers during the past ten years. The prospective teachers should be able to impart character among the pupils. They are expected to arouse enthusiasm and be a source of inspiration for the pupils. Being prospective teachers, like in-service teachers should possess emotional intelligence skills. The research studies conducted in assessing emotional intelligence among the student teachers and the influence of their personal variables like age, gender, community, educational qualification, locality etc., on emotional intelligence is discussed hereunder. Reviewing such studies will throw light on the emotional intelligence possessed by the prospective teachers, relationship between the emotional intelligence and the teacher's personality factors, influence of demographic variables on emotional intelligence and so on.

Gupta and Kaur (2006) studied the emotional intelligence of 200 B.Ed. students of Guru Nanak Dev University, Amristar. Results revealed that there were nine per cent male and 22 per cent female B.Ed. students with high emotional intelligence while, six per cent male and 12 per cent female B.Ed. students had low emotional intelligence. Male and female B.Ed. students differed significantly on self-management dimension of emotional intelligence while arts and science stream B.Ed. students differed on social skills dimension of emotional intelligence. Also, B.Ed. students of non-working mothers scored more on internality while, B.Ed. students of working mothers scored more on empathy. Gupta and Ram (2006) also studied the role of gender difference and emotional intelligence in the transactional styles of 201 prospective teachers studying in various colleges of education in Jalandhar city. The results indicated that supportive style is the dominant style and rescuing style is back up style in both male and female students. Also, the results showed that emotional intelligence had the main effect on aggressive style while gender had main effects on rescuing style, normative style, problem-solving style, innovative style, resilient and sulking styles.

Indu (2009) studied the emotional intelligence of 502 secondary grade teacher trainees from Coimbatore city. The findings revealed that majority of the teacher trainees possessed average emotional intelligence and there was no significant difference in the emotional intelligence of the sub-samples i.e. gender, type of family and type of institution. Neetha (2008) investigated the interaction effect of language proficiency, emotional intelligence and reasoning ability on teaching competency of 600 B.Ed. students. The results revealed that there was positive significant relationship between emotional intelligence, its dimensions—self regulation, motivation, social awareness, social skills and teaching competency. Also, the results revealed that there was no significant relationship between language proficiency and emotional intelligence.

Panda (2009) studied the emotional intelligence and personality traits of 130 pupil teachers belonging to different localities, gender and personalities with an objective to find out the significant relationship in emotional intelligence of normal and neurotic pupil teachers. Emotional

Intelligence Test and Neurotic Personality Inventory were administered. Results revealed that there was a significant positive correlation between emotional intelligence and normal behaviour of pupil teachers; significant negative correlation between emotional intelligence and neurotic behaviour of pupil teachers; there was significant difference between normal and neurotic behaviour of pupil teachers in emotional intelligence; and no significant difference between male and female teachers in emotional intelligence.

Remould (2006) assessed the effectiveness of the Enneagram educational programme on the five competencies of emotional intelligence namely emotional self awareness, emotional expression, emotional awareness of others, creativity and interpersonal connections among 40 student teachers. Enneagram was a tool for conversion, for tuning ourselves around. Enneagram educational programme was given to the experimental group for the duration of three months. Administering of Emotional Intelligence Scale to both the experimental and control group revealed that there was significant difference in the mean scores of emotional self-awareness, emotional expression, emotional awareness of others, creativity and interpersonal connections (the components of emotional intelligence) of the experimental and the control group in the pre and post intervention.

Sahaya Mary and Samuel (2010) attempted to find out the influence of emotional intelligence on attitude towards teaching of 191 student teachers at two government colleges of education in Chennai. The study was on the basis of their gender, subject, educational qualification, community, previous teaching experience and the influence to be a teacher of student-teachers. The findings of the study revealed that there was a significant difference between qualification, community influence to be a teacher and attitude towards teaching of student-teachers. There was no significant difference between gender, subject, community, influence of others, previous teaching experience and the emotional intelligence of the student teachers. There was a significant relationship between emotional intelligence and attitude towards teaching profession of student teachers.

Sharma (2008) correlated emotional intelligence, creativity and achievement motivation with art competencies in 805 B.Ed. students. Results demonstrated the significant correlation between art competencies and emotional intelligence. Suresh and Rao (2009) conducted a study on social intelligence of 307 student teachers pursuing B.Ed. course in the Colleges of Education in Guntur district. The social intelligence dimensions like patience, cooperativeness, confidence level, sensitivity, recognition of social environment, tactfulness, sense of humour and memory have been measured. The results revealed that the student teachers possessed high level of social intelligence irrespective of their gender, locality, teaching methodology and educational qualification.

Suresh and Joshith (2008) conducted a study on emotional intelligence as a correlate of stress among 602 student teachers of various training colleges of Kerala. The investigator finds a significant negative relationship between emotional intelligence and stress for the total sample and sub-samples and concludes that individuals having high emotional intelligence may have low stress and this will directly contribute to the positive development of the individual and the society. Umadevi (2009) examined the relationship between emotional intelligence, achievement motivation and academic achievement of 200 primary school student teachers studying in various B.Ed. colleges of Davanagere city. The results revealed that there was a positive relationship between emotional intelligence, achievement motivation and academic motivation. Male and female, arts and science student teachers do not differ significantly in emotional intelligence and achievement motivation.

Studies on Occupational Stress in Teachers

Because of the changing roles and responsibilities of the teachers in the new millennium, the teachers experience stress due to various stressors available in the working environment. The researchers have concentrated on the occupational stress in teachers during the past two decades in Indian context. Reviewing such literature will throw light on the models of stress and occupational stress, sources of stress, consequences of stress, tools used to measure occupational stress in teachers, influence of teachers demographic variables on occupational stress etc.,. Few such studies are reviewed hereunder.

Amirtagowri and Thiagarajan (2005) analysed the occupational problems of working women in Thoothukudi. The sample of the study was 665 women in teaching service from schools, colleges, private training cadres, clerical service, medical service centres, anganwadi centre, and police service. The data were analysed on the basis of their age, marital status, educational level, nature of job, sector of employment, co-workers, boss and years of experience. The results revealed that women police and anganwadi workers had significant problems. Women working under the male boss had more problems than their counterparts.

Arora and Hussain (2008) studied the work alienation among 500 primary school B.T.C and special B.T.C. teachers. The results revealed that special B.T.C teachers were more alienated from their work as compared to the B.T.C teachers. The work alienation components have not significantly differed in B.T.C. and special B.T.C. teachers of both rural and urban areas. Further, male B.T.C. teachers were highly alienated from their work than female B.T.C teachers.

Brahmaiah and Rao (2009) studied the stress of 310 student teachers studying in the Colleges of Education in Andhra Pradesh State. The analysis of data revealed that the student teachers are holding an average level of stress irrespective of their gender, locality, teaching methodology and educational qualifications. Also, the student teachers belonging to female category, graduate qualification, science methodology are holding more stress than male student teachers, post graduates and student teachers in arts methodology respectively.

Chaturvedi and Purushothaman (2009) investigated the role of certain demographic variables in determining stress-coping behaviour of female teachers. The sample consisted of 150 female teachers selected by stratified sampling method from various schools of Bhopal. Stress-coping behaviour was measured with the help of a subscale of 'The Occupational Stress Indicator' (Wendy Lord, 1993) consisting of 28 items encompassing six dimensions of coping strategies i.e. logics, involvement, social support, task strategies, time management and, home and work relations. The scores of the subjects were compared in terms of marital status, age, and level of teaching with the help of t-test and F value was used for comparing experience. The results revealed that marital status, age, and experience were found to be significant determinants of stress-coping, whereas the scores did not differ significantly on the basis of level of teaching. Further, the married teachers in the age range of 40-60 years, with higher experience had coped better with the job stress than their counterparts.

Chopra and Gartia (2009) studied the accountability and occupational stress of 120 secondary school teachers belonging to private and government secondary schools in Kurushetra. The results revealed that occupational stress had a negative impact on accountability of secondary school teachers. Teachers who had high occupational stress are less accountable towards their job and teachers with low occupational stress are more accountable towards their job. Also, the results found that the female teachers were more accountable towards their job than their male counterparts.

Gupta (2009) conducted a study with the following objectives: (1) To study the values and attitude of public and government school principals towards modernization; (2) To compare the different dimensions of values and modernization between public and government school principals; (3) To study the organizational climate of public and government schools; (4) To compare the different dimensions of organizational climate between public and government schools; (5) To study relationship between values, modernization and organizational climate of public schools and government schools. Value Test and Modernization Test were conducted to 51 school principals. Tool on Organizational Climate was administered to 354 school teachers. The finding of the study reveals that: (1) public and government school principals are quite positive towards values in general and its different dimensions also; (2) attitude of both the school principals is also positive towards modernization and its various dimensions except religiosity; (3) there was a significant difference in the climate of public and government schools. Public schools possess 'Controlled' type of climate whereas government schools possess 'Familiar' type of climate. (4) correlation studies between values and organizational climate of public schools and government schools revealed that there was no significant relation between them; (5) no correlation was also found between modernization and organizational climate of public schools and government schools; (6) no correlation was there between values and modernization of public schools but significant relationship was found in government schools.

Jamal et al. (2007) studied the influence of variables—teacher stress, job satisfaction, teacher morale and socio-emotional school climate on the level of organizational commitment of 615 secondary school teachers. Step-wise multiple regression analysis of the data revealed that teacher stress was negatively correlated with organizational commitment while job satisfaction, teacher morale and socio-emotional school climate are positively correlated with organizational commitment; and teacher stress was the most important predictor of organizational commitment followed by teacher morale.

Joolideh and Yeshodhara (2008) compared the organizational commitment of high school teachers in India and Iran, and studied the influence of teacher's gender and types of school on organizational commitment of teachers. Data were obtained from 215 high school teachers in Bangalore and from 215 high school teachers in Sanandaj (Iran), using Organizational Commitment Questionnaire. Results revealed that female teachers had better organizational commitment than male teachers. Also, in normative commitment, significant difference was observed between government and private high school teachers. Indian and Iranian female high school teachers have better organizational commitment than Indian and Iranian male teachers. When both countries are compared separately and together, Iranian private high school teachers have better organizational commitment than Indian government high school teachers.

Joshi and Singhvi's (2000) study revealed that Machiavellianism was not found to be correlated with stress among teachers. Kaur (2008) studied the relationship between occupational stress and teacher effectiveness among government secondary school teachers in Punjab State. The Teacher Effectiveness Scale was administered to identify the effective and ineffective teachers. The occupational stress of the teachers was studied using Occupational Stress Scale. The results revealed that the less effective teachers are under a higher level of occupational stress than the highly effective teachers, while the female secondary school teachers are significantly under more occupational stress than their male counterparts. The correlation analysis revealed that occupational stress was negatively correlated with the teacher effectiveness.

Kumar (2007) examined the stress factors among public and private teachers and found that men and women teachers differed in their level of occupational stress and men teachers expressed high level of stress compared to women teachers; job satisfaction, job involvement, achievement motivation and personality characteristics are significantly related with the stress factors; and private school teachers expressed significant stress in all the factors compared to the public school teachers.

Kumaran (2003) conducted a study on organizational health and academic performance. The organizational health of the school was studied by adopting the Ipsative method, where the measures of organizational health of the schools were studied through the responses given by the teachers of the concerned schools. Eight hundred and fifty two higher secondary school teachers from Chennai, Kanchipuram and Thiruvallur were studied. The study shows that the variables academic emphasis and principal influence had direct impact on academic performance of the schools. Mishra (1996) reported that female teacher's experienced greater role related stress, interpersonal stress and workload as compared to their male colleagues.

Manoj Kumar (2006) in his study on the occupational stress of high school teachers found that nine of the twelve job stressed factors—role overload, role ambiguity, role conflict, unreasonable group and political pressure, responsibility for persons, powerlessness, intrinsic impoverishment, low status and strenuous working conditions made the teachers found to be significant factors causing stress among them; men and women teachers differed significantly in their level of occupational stress; teachers working in rural schools had more occupational stress than the teachers in the urban schools; the age, experience and educational qualifications of the teachers were found to be the significant predictors of the occupational stress of teachers.

Misra (1986) conducted a study on secondary school teachers and found that stress had become basic characteristic with teachers and burnout becomes their apparent reaction. The results demonstrated that age difference was significant with respect to stress of teachers, stress was positively related to burnout with respect to emotional exhaustion and depersonalization and there was a negative relationship between meaning in life and stress variable. Pareek and Metha (1997) in comparison of role stress experienced by officers, bankers and school teachers found that teachers experienced least role stress.

Ravichandran and Rajendran (2007) attempted a study to investigate the various sources of stress experienced by higher secondary teachers. A sample of 200 higher secondary teachers was randomly selected. They were administered Teacher Stress Inventory developed by Rajendran, which measures eight independent factors of sources of stress. The result of one way ANOVA indicated that the personal variables: sex, age, educational levels, years of teaching experience and types of school, play a significant role in the perception of various sources of stress related to the teaching profession.

Shejwal and Mohammadi (2006) examined the relationship between job burnout variables and coping mechanism variables among the 300 high school teachers in Pune. The results showed that the male teachers compared to the female teachers, used more of problem-focussed and emotion-focussed coping mechanisms. The male teachers, compared to the female teachers, had higher job burnout in the areas of emotional exhaustion and depersonalization but not in the area of loss of personal accomplishment. Among the male teachers, there were no significant correlations between coping mechanism variables and any of the job burnout variables. Among female teachers, there were no significant correlations between the coping mechanisms and the job burnout variables except for depersonalization, which showed a significant positive correlation with both the coping mechanisms.

Shukla and Trivedi (2008) investigated the status of burnout among 320 secondary school teachers in Lucknow city and assessed its extent in Indian teachers. The findings demonstrated that burnout was presented in secondary school teachers in varying degrees. Moderate level of burnout was found in the emotional exhaustion and personal accomplishment dimensions and a low level of burnout in the depersonalization dimension. Teachers, when grouped on the basis of gender and medium of instruction showed no significant difference in their burnout tendencies. However, teachers belonging to the arts subject stream and the science subject stream, when compared, showed a significant difference in their level of burnout in the depersonalization dimension. Science stream teachers are higher in their burnout levels than arts stream teachers in this dimension.

Sud and Malik (1999) found that the perception of social support was found to reduce stress among teachers. Sultana (1995) noted significant differences between both professional male and female teachers on the dimensions of inter-role distance, role stagnation, role erosion, role overload and role ambiguity. Vaijayanthi and Sunny (2010) investigated the stress of 650 student teachers studying in Coimbatore B.Ed. colleges. Data were collected using the standardized multi dimensional stress inventory. The collected data was analyzed using mean, SD, t-test and F-test. The results revealed that 86 per cent of the B.Ed. students experience moderate level of stress. The results of F-values revealed that there was no significant difference among the B.Ed. students stress level due to variations in their type of colleges and their optional subjects.

Studies on Occupational Stress in Special Education Teachers and Parents

In Indian context, the literatures on the occupational stress in special education teachers are sporadic in nature. Only few studies are available and are reviewed hereunder. The studies reviewed highlight the sources of stress in special education teachers, level of stress and strain experienced by the caregivers, mothers of children with disabilities, problems faced by the special education teachers in special and inclusive set up.

Balabaskar (2010) investigated the occupational stress of teachers working in schools meant for children with mental handicap, hearing handicap, visual handicap and physical handicap. The study constituted of a total sample of 300 teachers divided in four groups. Each of the four group comprised of 75 special educators. The tool used in the study was Occupational Stress Index. The statistical techniques used for analyzing the data were mean, SD and ANOVA. Educators working for children with mental retardation experienced more occupational stress when compared to other groups of special educators. Role ambiguity, role conflict and intrinsic improvement were reported by special educators working with the mentally retarded as important factors for occupational stress. Special educators teaching mentally retarded children and physically handicapped reported 'responsibility for persons' as a central factor. 'Poor peer relations' was seen as an imperative factor leading to occupational stress by special educators working with the visually impaired. Similarly, special educators working with the hearing impaired reported 'role overload' and 'un profitability' as significant factors.

Basu et al. (2004) through qualitative interview explored the cognitive and affective responses of the 80 mothers of mentally challenged children to the disability and the child itself. Content analysis and ratings revealed that the mothers were apparently aware of the scientific status of the disability in terms of its clinical status and prognosis; the affective reactions towards the child were ambivalent, characterized by both love and rejection. Overall, the mother's inner strength from formal and informal social support dealt effectively with the stressful situation.

John (2007) conducted a study to find out the level of occupational stress of 150 teachers working in the schools for visually impaired children in the Malabar region of Kerala. Also, the study aimed to find out the influence of personal variables like gender, age, community, educational qualification, training in special education, salary per month, years of experience, type of school, nature of job, locale of the school and teachers visual condition on their occupational stress. The analysis of data revealed that nearly 70 per cent of the teachers had experienced high and moderate levels of occupational stress. The teachers occupational stress does not differed significantly with respect to their gender, age, educational qualification and locale of the school; whereas the teachers community, training in special education, salary and type of management have significant influence on the teachers occupational stress.

Khalid and Kausar (2008) explored the quality of life among caregivers of people affected by stroke. The samples covered are 25 caregivers of people affected by stroke. Hospital Anxiety and Depression Scale and WHO Quality of Life Scale were administered to assess depression and quality of life respectively. It was found that almost half of the caregivers were depressed while some of them were at risk of developing depression and that depression affected their quality of life.

Mathew (2005) conducted an experimental study to examine the sources, effects and the coping strategies of occupational stress among special educators of two districts of Kerala. Sample of the study consisted of 35 special education teachers having more than two years of experience. Occupational Stress Indicator developed by Cooper et al. (1988) was used to evaluate the five key factors—sources of stress, individual characteristics, locus of control, coping strategies and effects of stress. The results of the study revealed that sources of stress spread from school structure and climate, home-work interface, relationship with other people, intrinsic job factors. The common effect of stress on special educators was found to be health related problems (both physical and mental) and job dissatisfaction. Job security, work overload, and high teacher-student ratio also lead to job stress among special school teachers.

Pandey (2009) carried out a study to attain the following objectives: (*i*) to review the existing special educational programme; (*ii*) to study the perception of various persons related to special need education; (*iii*) to identify the barriers in the implementation of inclusive education policies; (*iv*) to develop relevant tools to study the barriers in the implementations of inclusive educational programme; and (*v*) to suggest measures to promote inclusion. The sample of the study consisted of 40 Head/Principals and regular teachers of all (public-20, government-20) school that had children with special needs in Delhi. One principal and three regular teachers from every school were interviewed. The major findings of the study revealed the following:

(*i*) The majority of the principals of public and government schools did not understand or, were not aware of inclusive education. They could not differentiate between inclusion and integration. Hence the concept of inclusion as whole was not clear to the principals. However, principals of public schools were better aware than the principals of government schools;

(*ii*) Majority of principals had partial awareness about the types of children with special educational needs (CWSEN). However, comparatively principals of public schools had somewhat better awareness than principals of government schools;

(*iii*) The majority of principals from public and govt. schools faced problems while introducing inclusive education for CWSEN in their schools;

(*iv*) The majority of principals of both types of regular schools did not take initiatives to facilitate the education of CWSEN. The results showed that public schools were better than government schools in facilitating inclusion of CWSEN;

(*v*) The principals of government schools had better awareness level than the principals of public school regarding various facilities available to CWSEN from the state. Overall, majority of the principals were not aware about the various schemes, concession facilities available to CWSEN from the states;

(*vi*) Most of the principals of both types of schools did not accept that it was feasible to educate CWSEN in their regular schools;

(*vii*) A large majority of the principals of both public and govt. schools were not aware of the procedure for availing the facilities provided to CWSEN by the states;

(*viii*) A large majority of the principals of both types of public and government school were unaware of the resources. They could not make use of the resources for providing supportive services needed by CWSEN for their education in inclusive set up;

(*ix*) More than half of the principals of both public and government schools accepted that they do not have knowledge and awareness about legal provisions for education of CWSEN;

(*x*) More than half of the principals of the regular schools (both type) confirmed that there was no drop out in their schools;

(*xi*) More than half (73.5%) of the regular teachers of public and government schools had no concept and definition of visual-impairment and blindness;

(*xii*) More than half (55%) of the regular teachers both types of school confirmed that they had problems in teaching of visually impaired children while teaching;

(*xiii*) The result shows that participation of visually impaired children and support of sighted children was not better. They got partial support from sighted peers and also partially participated in activities;

(*xiv*) Almost all regular teachers of both types of schools were affirmative about the need for specialist support;

(*xv*) Eighty per cent of regular teachers of both types of schools were positive towards inclusive education;

(*xvi*) The majority (80%) of both types of schools did not have essential physical infrastructure facilities like ramps, disabled friendly toilet, sitting and lighting arrangement etc.;

(*xvii*) The result shows that almost all schools (91.9%) did not have teaching learning materials like braille papers, braille books, tactile maps, embossed diagram, large print books etc. for use of visually impaired children;

(*xviii*) Eighty seven per cent government schools and 72.2 per cent public schools did not have educational aids and appliances like braille duplicators and writers, writing devices etc. Most of schools did not have basic equipments, aids and appliances for children with special educational needs. They have only computers with text to speech software.

Ushasree and Jamuna (1990) conducted a study to examine role conflict and job stress among special and general school teachers. The sample comprised 40 special school teachers of Tirumala Tirupati Devasthanam's (TTD) school for the deaf and dumb and a random sample of 60 teachers from TTD's high school. Role Conflict Inventory and Teachers Burnout Scale were used to assess the role conflict and job stress. The analysis of data did not reveal any gender differences among teachers from special schools on role conflict and job stress. However, women teachers in general schools were found to experience greater role conflict and had poor attitudes towards their students and were less satisfied with their careers as compared to male counterparts in general schools. Teachers from special schools, both men and women were found to experience significantly greater role conflict and job stress compared to their counterparts in general schools.

Rajeswari et al. (2008) in an empirical research found the stress level and attitude of 100 women teachers handling normal and special children (visually impaired, hearing impaired and mentally retarded). The major findings of the study was that the stress of women teachers as a whole is of moderate level, but those teachers handling mentally retarded children was found to be relatively high compared to other teachers. The teachers handling hearing impaired children are found to have relatively low level of stress and high attitude towards their profession. Teachers of age group of below 40 years and below 15 years of experience are found to have more stress and low attitude towards their profession. Moderately high level of stress and low level of attitude was found in the teachers working under private management schools.

Reddy and Poornima (2009) examined the occupational stress of teachers working in the special schools for visually impaired children. The study was conducted in the four districts of the two States (Chittoor and Hyderabad in Andhra Pradesh and Madurai and Chennai in Tamilnadu) in South India. The sample consisted of 87 teachers working in the schools for visually impaired children. A five point Rating Scale to assess the occupational stress of teachers and a Checklist to identify the infrastructure facilities in the schools for visually impaired children were used. The results revealed that 70 per cent of the teachers were experiencing high and moderate levels of occupational stress, whereas 30 per cent are with low level of stress. Further, lack of opportunities for promotion, development of materials to meet the individual needs of each child, insufficient time for planning instructional activities, inadequate instructional support material, inadequate salary, job demands and over expectations of the job, long school hours, giving more thrust on development of curricular innovations, too many responsibilities, giving more and more assessment and diagnostic responsibilities, students indiscipline, inadequate ongoing professional training without necessary organizational resources, feeling of physical and mental discomfort, preparation of teaching learning materials to implement instruction in meeting the diverse special needs population, inadequate funding for school programmes, job related work after hours, poorly motivated students and lack of time for individual attention are the potential sources of stress for the teachers working in the schools for visually impaired children. The study also revealed that the teachers working in the schools with good and moderate infrastructure facilities were experiencing low levels of stress compared to the teachers working in the schools with poor infrastructure facilities. These results indicate the need to strengthen the organizational structure of the schools for visually impaired with respect to enrichment of professional training components with adequate supportive systems, provision for strengthening interpersonal and professional interactions among the teachers and the need to provide supportive environments for proper instructional assignments and arrangements within the school.

Reddy and Poornima (2008) also attempted to develop a checklist to identify the problems of special education teachers working in schools for mentally retarded. Survey method was employed in the study. The sample consisted of 293 teachers from 40 special schools meant for mentally retarded children located in four districts of Andhra Pradesh (Hyderabad and Chittoor) and Tamil Nadu (Chennai and Madurai) States. The study revealed that the problems such as: lack of clarity in the concept of disabilities, non-availability of academic records, inadequate infrastructure facilities, lack of collaboration with other professionals, inadequate salary and job security, problems in involving parents, competency in organizing special sports and cultural activities to mentally retarded children are the problems faced under the dimension 'Planning and Organization'. Likewise, inadequate knowledge about the fundamental aspects of human body, lack of skill in modifying the curriculum to the needs of children with disabilities, lack of knowledge in the use of novel methods such as peer-tutoring, co-operative learning, problems in auditory and speech training in classroom setup and lack of proficiency in multi-sensory approach are the problems faced by the teachers under the dimension 'Teaching and Training'. Similarly, under the dimension 'Guidance and Counselling', the teachers face problems such as lack of conceptual clarity about the disabilities and developmental delays, lack of expertise in group counselling to develop positive attitude towards children with different disabilities.

Vijesh and Sukumaran (2007) studied the stress experienced by fifty mothers of children with cerebral palsy attending special schools in Kerala State. Stress level was assessed using the Questionnaire on Resources and Stress and the data were analyzed with respect to certain child related and mother related variables. The study revealed that the stress experienced by mothers of these children was at a moderate level and the pessimism expressed regarding the child's ability towards achieving self sufficiency was found to be most stress producing factor. Among the child related and mother related variables, only multiple disabilities along with cerebral palsy was a significant variable in deciding the difference in the severity of stress among the mothers.

Singhal (2004) conducted a study on stress and burnout of teachers in government regular and special schools in New Delhi. The sample comprises of 120 teachers from regular schools and 188 teachers from special schools teaching upper primary and middle levels. The results revealed that teachers in special schools have higher workload than regular schools. Also, the scope of student contact has been higher among teachers in special schools, as they work closely and deal with fewer students more intensively. Even the social isolation and role conflicts have been experienced more by the special school than the regular school teachers. The more the variety of activities assigned to teachers, sometimes of unexpected type, the more was perhaps the role conflict generated, they all know what they should do, but the overlapping and conflicting assignments and the urgency of immediate needs of children create role conflicts and affect their work. They also, found that lack of competence was equally stressful. Overall, the teachers in special schools perceive their work-setting more demanding and less conducive to task accomplishment than the regular schools.

Sreedevi and Sarada Devi (2008) studied the stress and coping methods of 60 parents of children with learning disabilities using ex-post facto research design. Results revealed that majority of parents experienced greater financial burdens, reduced social and recreational participation and mental worries about child's future. Also, they experienced moderate level of physical care burdens, strained relationships with family members and teachers, reduced family support and self-esteem. Further, majority of the parents adopted medium-level approach followed by high-level approach and avoidance coping strategies to cope with stress. Positive reappraisal, logical analysis, emotional discharge and resigned acceptance were frequently used strategies.

Studies on Job Satisfaction of Teachers

Literatures related to job satisfaction of teachers are innumerable in Indian context. Research studies for the past three decades focussed on job satisfaction and motivational factors, stress and burnout, job characteristics, nature of work, work environment, job behaviour, management, principal, supervision, co-workers, students, security, rewards, recognition and praise, advancement, qualification. marital status, salary, occupational level, sex, age, experience, family background, personality, adjustment, anxiety, authoritarianism and neurotic behaviour. Also, the studies focussed on the relationship of job satisfaction with stress, occupational stress, teaching competency etc., few such studies are reviewed hereunder.

Amaladoss Xavier (2009) studied the relationship between job satisfaction and teaching competency of the chemistry teachers in Kanyakumari. The sample covered in the study was 96 chemistry teachers working in higher secondary schools. The main objectives of the study was to find out the level of job satisfaction of postgraduate chemistry teachers; to find out the level of teaching competency of postgraduate chemistry teachers and to study the significant relationship between teaching competency of postgraduate chemistry teachers and job satisfaction. The study revealed that the teaching competency of postgraduate chemistry teachers was average. There was significant relationship between high-level competence of postgraduate chemistry teachers and their job satisfaction.

Balabaskar (2009) conducted a study on job satisfaction of 300 special educators teaching children with mental retardation, hearing impairment, visual impairment and physically handicapped working in six districts of A.P. State. The Job Satisfaction Scale (JSC) developed by Pramod Kumar and Muthash (1986) was used to measure job satisfaction in teachers. The results revealed that overall special educators have higher level of job satisfaction and in particular job satisfaction was found to be high among special educators teaching children with mental retardation. Whereas, job satisfaction of special educators teaching physically handicapped children was low. The factor 'satisfaction with authority including school management' contributed for higher job satisfaction among teachers teaching mentally retarded children.

Beegam and Dhamangadan (2000) examined gender differences in job satisfaction in a sample of 415 college teachers (age 23-55 years) with an equal number of males and females. Female teachers were more satisfied with their jobs than male teachers. Bhandari and Patil (2009) investigated the job satisfaction of 295 women teachers working in primary and upper primary schools of Gulbarga city. The results showed that few of the women teachers are facing certain problems due to lack of coordination and cooperation in the workplace. Majority of the women teachers were satisfied with their work, job and salary and majority of them said that they have not recognized for the job and work done.

Chamundeswari and Vasanthi (2009) conducted a study to identify the job satisfaction and occupational commitment among 588 teachers of state, matriculation and central board schools. The results revealed that there was a significant difference in job satisfaction and occupational commitment between teachers in different categories of schools. Further, job satisfaction and occupational commitment were positively correlated with each other. Matriculation school teachers have better job satisfaction and occupational commitment compared to the state and central board teachers. Gakhar et al. (2005) explored the relationship of the self-concept, anxiety and attitude of teachers towards teaching with the job satisfaction of teachers. The main aim of the study was to find the relationship of self-concept, anxiety and attitude towards teaching with job satisfaction of scheduled caste and non-scheduled caste teachers. The results revealed that the difference in job satisfaction due to sex-differences and also difference in the job-satisfaction of scheduled and non-scheduled caste teachers.

Ghazi (2004) investigated the job satisfaction of 207 elementary head teachers of Toba Tek Singh districts in Punjab. The main purpose of the study was to document intrinsic, extrinsic and facet-specific levels of job satisfaction of head teachers and the influence of selected demographic characteristics on general job satisfaction of head teachers. The results revealed that the head teachers were 'slightly satisfied' with compensation, working conditions, social status, school system policies and practices; 'satisfied' with advancement, social service, creativity, recognition, supervision human relation, security, independence, colleagues, supervision technical, authority, responsibility, achievement, ability utilization and variety; 'very satisfied' with moral values and activity aspects of their job. Also, the head teachers with demographic characteristics younger and older, females, bachelor degree holders, minimum and maximum experienced, from urban and smaller schools obtained higher means than the head teachers with middle age, males, master degree holders, medium experienced, from rural and larger schools. Demographically, significant differences were found among four demographic variables (age, gender, experience and school location) with intrinsic and general job satisfaction, whereas the other two variables—degree status and school size have not predicted the job satisfaction of the head teachers.

Gupta (1997) explored the relationship between job satisfaction and personal values among 32 college teachers. There was a significant correlation between teacher's job satisfaction and their personal values. Teachers with high academic and social values express higher job satisfaction. Economic and democratic values were significantly but negatively correlated with job satisfaction. Religious, aesthetic, domestic and physical values were not significantly related with teacher's job satisfaction.

Kumar and Rao (2007) conducted a study to find out the job satisfaction of 160 school teachers working in the Guntur district. The analysis of data revealed that the school teachers have higher job satisfaction irrespective of gender, area (rural/urban), type of school they are working (i.e. govt., or private), varied teaching experience (low/high), position they are holding (secondary grade/school assistant) and medium of instruction (English/Telugu). Also, the results revealed that teachers in urban schools, holding secondary grade position and women teachers possess high job satisfaction than the teachers in rural schools, holding school assistant position and men teachers respectively.

Kumaraswamy and Sarma (2005) studied the influence of personal and demographic variables on job involvement of 180 secondary school teachers in Anantapur district. The results revealed that the variables like age, caste, experience, marital status and participation in the in-service programmes have significantly influenced the job involvement of secondary school teachers; whereas, the variables like gender, education, locality of working, income, subject of teaching have not significant influence on the job involvement. Manjunathaiah (2003) studied the personality adjustment (home, health, social, emotional) and job satisfaction of 240 teachers (visually impaired teachers and sighted teachers) working in the schools for visually impaired children. Results revealed that sighted teachers had significantly better job satisfaction than the visually impaired teachers. Also, the variables like gender, school type and length of service influenced the job satisfaction of both sighted and visually impaired teachers.

Musthafa and Jaseena (2008) conducted a study to find out the level of job satisfaction of pre-school teachers in Kerala. The study also investigated the effect of certain variables on job satisfaction. The data was collected from 400 pre-school teachers using Job Satisfaction Scale. The study revealed that the pre-school teachers are not satisfied with their job. The variables like locale, type of management, teaching experience and educational qualification have significantly influenced job satisfaction.

Natarajan (2001) conducted a study with the objective of investigating the types of organizational climate existing in higher secondary schools and its overall influence on the job satisfaction of postgraduate teachers working in such schools. Organizational Climate Descriptive Questionnaire and Job Satisfaction Scale were administered to the 256 higher secondary teachers in Tirupatur. The analysis of data revealed that there was a significant relationship between the school organizational climate and the job satisfaction of teachers.

Nazar and Ahmad (1998) studied the sources of satisfaction and dissatisfaction among teachers and attempted to confirm Herzberg's two factor theory. Satisfaction and dissatisfaction were independent of each other. Hygiene factors contributed to both satisfaction and dissatisfaction. Motivators and hygiene factors were not mutually exclusive and could not be classified distinctively. Promotion, responsibility, salary and interpersonal relations were significant determinants of overall job satisfaction on a unipolar satisfaction scale. Job factors on the unipolar dissatisfaction scale contributing to overall job satisfaction were job security, salary, working conditions and institutional policies and practices.

Neelakandan and Rajendran (2007) studied the level of job satisfaction of 320 employees. The results revealed that employees differed in job satisfaction on the basis of marital status and years of experience. Raj (2001) examined the relationship between teaching effectiveness and job satisfaction and motivation to work among 100 secondary school teachers from both rural and urban areas. Results indicated that motivation to work had a significant effect on teaching effectiveness. The effect of job satisfaction as well as the interaction effect of motivation to work and job satisfaction was found to be non-significant. Teachers high on motivation to work were significantly better than poorly motivated teachers on teaching effectiveness.

Ramathulasamma and Rao (2003) explored the job satisfaction of 172 teacher educators working in 47 Colleges of Education in Andhra Pradesh. The main aim of the study was to find out to what extent the job satisfaction of teacher educators influenced by the organizational climate of teacher education colleges and the personality characteristics of teachers and to what extent are they related to one another. The results revealed that the teacher educators possessed average levels of job satisfaction. Also, strong significant association was found between the job satisfaction and organizational climate. The relationship between job satisfaction and personality characteristics was not significant. A similar study was conducted by Rao and Sridhar (2003) to identify the job satisfaction of 80 secondary school teachers. The results revealed that secondary school teachers have good job satisfaction irrespective of the age, sex, experience, qualification, location and type of school management. Also, the results revealed that the teachers less than 30 years of age are with very good job satisfaction than the other age groups.

Saveri (2009) explored the relationship between job satisfaction and life satisfaction among 300 government and aided higher secondary B.T. Assistant teachers from urban and rural schools in Trichy and Lalgudi. The results revealed that the majority of B.T. Assistants showed moderate level of job satisfaction and life satisfaction. Significant association was found between job satisfaction and total number of teaching experience of teachers, type of management i.e. aided and government school and there was positive relationship between job satisfaction and life satisfaction among B.T. Assistant teachers. Further, there was no significant difference in job satisfaction of men and women B.T. Assistant teachers.

Sharma and Patnaik (2009) studied the organizational health of 39 government and private elementary schools and job satisfaction of 184 elementary school teachers in Bhopal city. The results demonstrated that the total organizational health of the private schools was better than the government schools. The teachers of private schools are highly satisfied in their job than the government school teachers. Further, the organizational health of schools and job satisfaction of teachers are positive and significantly correlated.

Singh (2007) studied the job satisfaction of 250 teacher educators from 20 colleges of education affiliated to Punjab university, Guru Nanak Dev University and Punjabi University in relation to their attitude towards teaching. Results revealed that job satisfaction of teacher educators was positively but not significantly related to attitude towards teaching. Also, the job satisfaction of male teacher educators was positively but not significantly related to attitude towards teaching. Further, the relation between job satisfaction and attitude towards teaching of female teacher educators was positive but not significant.

Shafeeq (2000) conducted a study on job satisfaction of teachers teaching visually impaired in relation to their adjustment. The objectives of the study was to know the correlation between job satisfaction and adjustment of teachers teaching in the schools meant for visually impaired, and to know whether there exists any significant difference between the mean scores of teachers who are low and highly adjusted on their job satisfaction. The sample in this study comprised of 37 teachers who were randomly selected from two schools. The data were analyzed and based on the findings it revealed that low adjusted teachers have got higher mean scores on job satisfaction in comparison to their counterparts. Adjustment of the teachers teaching visually disabled children at secondary stage had no relationship with the satisfaction of their job.

Srivastava and Krishna (1994) compared the work motivation and job involvement of 100 male and 100 female teachers teaching various subjects of arts, science and commerce. The results indicated that male teachers maintain markedly higher level of work motivation and job involvement. Also, the results showed that work motivation generated by most of the teacher needs positively correlated with the job involvement. Usmani et al. (2006) attempted to investigate the levels of job satisfaction among secondary school teachers in relation to their personality type and the type of school. The sample of the study comprised of 450 teachers selected randomly from 30 secondary schools. The result showed that government and government aided school teachers are highly satisfied; whereas unaided or private school teachers are least satisfied.

Vijayalakshmi (2005) studied the relationship between teacher effectiveness and job satisfaction. The effect of locality, management and subject of teaching on teacher effectiveness and job satisfaction was also studied. Teacher Effectiveness and Job Satisfaction Scales were administered to a sample of 120 women teachers working in high schools of Chittoor district. The finding showed low and positive correlation between teacher effectiveness and job satisfaction. Among locality, management of the school and subject of teaching, only management of the school had significant impact on both teacher effectiveness and job satisfaction.

Relationship Studies on Emotional Intelligence, Occupational Stress and Job Satisfaction

A few studies have been noticed on emotional intelligence, occupational stress and job satisfaction of people working in different professions and such studies are presented hereunder.

Bindhu (2006) conducted a study to find out the job satisfaction and stress coping skills of 500 primary school teachers (165 male and 335 female) of Kerala state. The Job Satisfaction Scale and Stress Coping Skills Inventory were administered. Differential and correlational analysis was used in the analysis of data. The study revealed that job satisfaction differentiates male and female primary school teachers and there was a positive correlation between job satisfaction and stress coping skills. On the basis of results, the authors suggested for creating a supportive organizational climate, managing of task design, clear institutional goals for providing guidance and counselling services to improve job satisfaction and stress coping skills among primary school teachers.

Chandraiah (1993) investigated occupational stress, job satisfaction, job involvement and locus of control among 440 public and private college teachers. Results indicated that public and private college teachers does not differed with respect to their occupational stress but were significant among college teachers with respect to their experience. Also, occupational stress decreased with increase in age of the teachers.

Mehrotra (2002) compared the leadership styles of principals in relation to job satisfaction of 1120 teachers and organizational climate in government and private senior secondary schools of Delhi. The results revealed that the leadership style of principals, job satisfaction of teachers and organizational climate differed from school to school. The leadership in private schools had not been found very influential as far as the job satisfaction of the teachers was concerned. It had also been observed that there was no significant difference between the organizational climate of the government and private schools. Teachers of government schools are found to be more satisfied than the teachers of private schools. The factors like less pressure of work, low supervision and high job security may be held responsible for this. The findings of the present study suggested that the educational administrators should ensure that more autonomy should be provided to the teachers in government and private schools to enhance their level of job satisfaction which may subsequently create conducive environment in the schools. The principals of the present decade have been working under the administrative and managerial pressures. The educational implication of the study was that the teachers and the principals should be provided in service training in human relations to achieve a good school climate and a higher job satisfaction among teachers. Although new visions of the school principal as leader are emerging, the new goals required of them in the changing educational environment needs to be addressed.

Singh and Koteswari (2006) explored the relationship between emotional intelligence and the types of coping resources of stress among 50 project managers belonging to different information technology companies in Hyderabad. Effect on emotional intelligence and coping resources of stress used across age was also explored. The findings of the study revealed that highly emotional intelligent people use more of coping resources of stress and emotional intelligence increases with increase in age.

Sinha and Jain (2004) examined the relationship between emotional intelligence and job satisfaction, personal effectiveness, organizational commitment, reputational effectiveness, general health, trust, turnover intention, organizational effectiveness and organizational productivity. The data was obtained from 250 middle-level male executives of two wheeler automobile manufacturing organizations. The results revealed that personal effectiveness and reputational effectiveness was predicted by assertiveness and positive self concept; Organizational productivity was positively predicted by controlled problem solving dimension of EI; Positive attitude about life predicted sense of accomplishment and contribution and botheration free existence positively; Reality awareness dimension of emotional intelligence predicted sense of attachment and normative commitment dimensions of organizational commitment are conceptualized as true kinds of commitment; Job satisfaction and turnover intention was found to be negative predictor of conditional continuance commitment and resource acquisition related organizational effectiveness. Also, vertical trust was positively predicted by controlled problem solving, reality awareness and impulse control.

Sumangala and Ushadevi (2009) studied the effectiveness of role conflict, job satisfaction and attitude towards teaching in predicting success in teaching among 300 secondary school women teachers working in 53 government and private-aided secondary schools of Kerala. The survey revealed that all the three variables are related to success in teaching. Role conflict and attitude towards teaching profession are capable of predicting success in teaching; whereas, job satisfaction have not predicted success in teaching and role conflict contributed more to the variation in success in teaching than the attitude towards teaching profession.

Suryanarayana et al. (2009) studied the relationship between the dimensions of teacher stress and teacher job satisfaction. Also they found the significance of difference between demographic and professional variables like sex, locality, qualification, age, marital status, experience and type of institution in respect of teacher stress and job satisfaction of 178 secondary school teachers. The analysis of data revealed that there was significant relationship between stress and job satisfaction among the secondary school teachers, significant relationship between the dimensions of teacher stress, significant relationship between the dimensions of teacher job satisfaction. Further, with respect to teacher stress, there was significant difference between the variables—sex, locality, qualification, age and type of institution, whereas the teachers with respect to experience and marital status have not differed significantly. With respect to teacher's job satisfaction, there was significant difference between the variables—locality, experience, age, marital status and type of institution, whereas the teachers with respect to sex and qualification have not differed significantly.

Studies Conducted Abroad

The theoretical and empirical literature on emotional intelligence, occupational stress and job satisfaction in western world is abundant. Similarly, the relationship between emotional intelligence, occupational stress and job satisfaction are conducted in good number with special reference to teachers, such studies are reviewed hereunder.

Studies on Emotional Intelligence of Teachers and Student Teachers

Chan (2008) assessed the emotional intelligence (intrapersonal and interpersonal) and general teacher self-efficacy to represent personal resources facilitating active and passive coping in a sample of 273 Chinese prospective and in-service teachers in Hong Kong. Intrapersonal and interpersonal emotional intelligence were found to predict significantly the active coping strategy, but teacher self-efficacy have not contributed independently to the prediction of active coping even though there was some evidence that teacher self-efficacy might interact with intrapersonal emotional intelligence in the prediction of active coping, especially for male teachers.

Dominguez-Cruz (2003) conducted a study to understand the school principal's leadership orientations and their emotional intelligence. The results indicated motivation as one of the dimensions in emotional intelligence that had no relationship with leadership orientations. The study indicated that principals viewed themselves in different ways when leading. It also indicated the absence of social skills and self-awareness among the principals.

Haskett (2003) compared the emotional intelligence and teaching success in higher education. This study compared the emotional intelligence of 286 faculty members with their teaching effectiveness. Based on the results of the study, a significant link was found between specific emotional intelligence competencies and behaviours of effective teaching. Based on these findings, the researcher concluded that it was not only the actions/behaviours taken by faculty that are important, but the underlying attitude behind the actions that had the greatest influence on effective teaching.

Hay/McBer (2000) conducted a study of the heads of forty-two schools in the United Kingdom. The results suggested that leadership style drove up student's academic achievement by directly affecting school climate. When the school head was flexible in leadership style and demonstrated a variety of EI abilities, teacher's attitudes were more positive and student's grades higher; when the leader relied on fewer EI competencies, teachers tended to be demoralized and students underperformed academically. Effective school leaders have not only created a working climate conducive to achievement but were more attuned to teacher's perceptions of such aspects of climate and organizational health as clarity of vision and level of teamwork.

Kaplan (2003) evaluated the effects of a psycho-educational training programme on the development of emotional intelligence in preschool and elementary educators and caregivers. The intervention was designed to develop their ability to perceive, understand and manage emotions and to successfully implement a social-emotional learning programme with children. Findings suggested that, the emotional intelligence appeared to be weak in pre-programme and it improved significantly after post-training. The study suggested practical implications for preparing teachers to implement social-emotional learning programmes, as well as for retooling tests for assessing emotional intelligence in culturally and educationally diverse populations.

Lee (2003) conducted a study to identify the conflict-management styles and emotional intelligence of 290 faculty and staff member's at a selected college in Taiwan. Analyses of the data indicated that the majority of faculty and staff members used the integrating style most often and the obliging style least often. With regard to the five dimensions of emotional intelligence—self awareness, managing emotions, self-motivation, empathy, and handling relationships, the faculty and staff member's scores were highest in self-motivation and lowest in managing emotion. The results of the ANOVAs showed that EI level, gender and position affected faculty and staff members' conflict-management styles. In addition, gender, academic rank and position influenced emotional intelligence. Significant interaction effects were found between emotional intelligence level and academic rank as well as between emotional intelligence level and age in faculty and staff member's conflict-management styles. The results of Pearson Product Moment correlations revealed that both integrating and compromising styles have significant and positive relationships with emotional intelligence. The findings also showed that self-motivation, managing emotions, and self-awareness of emotional intelligence were significant predictors in predicting both the integrating and compromising conflict-management styles.

Reed (2005) explored teachers (n=1598) perceptions of principal (n=700) emotional intelligence, principal leadership behaviour, and principal openness working in 67 public elementary schools throughout Ohio. The results revealed that the three competencies in the self-awareness domain exhibit relatively high means, suggesting that principals were perceived as often exhibiting emotional self-awareness, accurate self-assessment and self-confidence; competencies in the self-management domain indicated that principals were perceived as demonstrating high levels of optimism followed closely by a strong orientation toward achievement, two highly correlated competencies of self-management; self-management competency that scored marginally lower than the others was principal initiative. The highest mean in the relationship management domain was teamwork and collaboration. Further, conflict management, the ability to handle difficult individuals, groups of people, or tense situations with diplomacy and tact, yielded the lowest mean overall of the 18 emotional intelligence competencies.

Salami (2007) investigated the relationship of emotional intelligence and self-efficacy to work attitudes of secondary school teachers in south western Nigeria. The sample consists of 475 secondary school teachers (230 males and 245 females) randomly selected from south western Nigeria. Measures of demographic data form, career commitment, organizational commitment, emotional intelligence, self-efficacy and, work-family conflict were administered to the teachers. Data collected was analysed using hierarchical multiple regression analysis. Results of the study indicated that emotional intelligence and self-efficacy had significant relationships with work attitudes. However, age, sex and work experience had none. The study recommended that emotional intelligence and self-efficacy of the teachers should be enhanced to improve their work attitudes.

Williams (2008) identified emotional and social competencies that distinguished outstanding urban principals based on data from behavioural event interviews using a double coding method. The design utilized a criterion group of 20 principals from a large mid-western school district (12 outstanding and 8 typical performers) drawn from a population size of 120 urban school principals. A multiple source nomination process, which included peer nominations, supervisor nominations and teacher ratings over two years, was used to identify the criterion sample. Results revealed that outstanding principals demonstrated competencies related to emotional and social intelligence. In addition, the study found that outstanding principals interact with a broader range of key constituents (e.g. parental, district and community leaders). The major implication of the study was the potential benefits of a competency based approach to help urban school districts, create systems to better recruit, select and prepare principal candidates and provide more effective professional development for current principals.

Studies on Antecedents/Stressors of Occupational Stress

Stressors that have been identified among samples of teachers include- role overload (being overwhelmed by the amount or complexity of work), role ambiguity (uncertainty about job description), conflicting job roles, lack of influence over the work environment, inadequate work environment, demands made by external agencies, poor relations with colleagues, poor relations with students, lack of support from the principal, school climate and culture (Borg and Falzon, 1991; Dinham, 1993; Kyriacou, 1989; Mathei and Gilmore, 1996; McCormick, 1997; 1997a; O'Connor and Clarke, 1990; Otto, 1986; Solman and Feld, 1989; Whitehead and Ryba, 1995).

Thomas, Clarke and Lavery (2003) found time and workload pressure, parental expectations and negative community attitudes rated higher as stressors than school administration. In their extensive review of teacher stress, Chen and Miller (1997) identified two types of stressors: organizational, and individual. Similarly, Forlin (2001) indicated that a detailed review of research in this area has revealed three categories of stressors for teachers: administrative, classroom-based and personal. Administrative stressors include workload, time pressure, and lack of support from the administration, excessive paper work, extracurricular demands and interpersonal conflicts (Chen and Miller, 1997; Forlin, 2001). The last three administrative stressors identified above as well as work overload were found to be the most stressful (Forlin, 2001). Classroom-based stressors that have been reported most frequently were the ones that required direct contact with students. These are disruptive behaviour, lack of student discipline, student's abilities, lack of materials or appropriate curriculum, with disruptive behaviour and a lack of student discipline being identified as potential stressors more frequently than the others. However, researchers also point out that isolated incidents of misbehaviour are considered to be minor or insignificant causes of stress. It is the persistence of these minor misbehaviours or cumulative effect of constant or repeated minor misbehaviours that causes stress (Dunham, 1992; Travers and Cooper, 1996). Finally personal stressors include age, years of experience, and lack of appropriate professional training (Forlin, 2001).

Other studies on teacher stress also indicated that the most commonly identified stressor for teachers are time pressures, work overload, staff relationships, classroom discipline, lack of resources, poor management, role conflict, as well as size and spatial arrangements of classrooms (Antoniou et al. 2006; Brown and Nagel, 2004; Kyriacou, 2001; Trendall, 1989; Wiley, 2000). In fact, when Trendall (1989) asked 237 primary, secondary and special school teachers to rank/order five stressors from a list of 20, found that there was agreement among all of the participants that the most prevalent stressors were: 1) lack of time; 2) large classes; 3) teaching workload; and 4) pupil misbehaviour. Kitle and Leynen (2003) reported higher physical exertion, job demands, somatic complaints and lower job control, social support and personal accomplishment as the major causes of teachers stress. Kyriacou and Sutcliffe (1978) found four factors of teacher stress—pupil misbehaviour, poor working conditions, time pressure and poor school ethos.

In a study of Australian teachers, McCormick (1997b) reported that job satisfaction was strongly associated with stress from external forces (such as system expectations and government policies) than stress arising from personal issues (such as perceived suitability to teaching). On the other hand, teachers reporting higher job satisfaction were more likely to identify stress arising from personal issues as sources of stress.

Some of the most common teacher reported sources of stress include lack of time (Kyriacou, 1987), poor relationships with colleagues and principals (Troman, 2000), large class size (Trendall, 1989 cited in Nagel and Brown, 2003), inadequate resources (Chaplain, 1995), poor student behaviour (Friedman, 1995), adapting to change (Kyriacou, 2001) and role conflict (Pearlin, 1989). Student misbehaviour is a major teacher stressor (Abel and Sewell, 1999; Borg et al., 1991; Chan and Hui, 1998; Dorman, 2003; Kelly and Berthelsen, 1995; Makinen and Kinnunen, 1986; Manassero et al., 2006; Newmann et al., 1989).

Siegall and Cummings (1995) theorised that the relation between role conflict and role stress was moderated by the strain existing within a persons social network; this strain was produced by two factors, the perceived power of the role sender and the importance of the senders expectations to the focal person; the relation between role stress and role distress (felt emotional discomfort) was moderated by several personality characteristics; the relation between role distress and coping (actual behaviour aimed at reducing distress) was moderated by both individual-level and situational-level factors; and the relation between coping and strain can be reciprocal. Also, there is a strong positive correlation between isolation and stress (Dussault et al., 1999; George, et al., 1995; Lawrenson and McKinnon, 1982; McManus and Kauffman, 1991). Negative interpersonal relations and the absence of support from colleagues or superiors can be significant stressors for employees (O'Driscoll and Beehr, 1994).

Studies of correlates of teacher well-being consistently stress the benefits of a positive school culture. The primary dimensions of these cultures include: (*a*) colleague supportiveness (Brouwers et al., 2001; Burke and Greenglass, 1995; Burke et al., 1996; Chan and Hui, 1998; Dussault et al., 1999; Gersten et al., 2001; Griffith et al., 1999; Newmann et al., 1989; Talmor et al., 2005; 2005a); (*b*) principal (Burke and Greenglass, 1995; Brouwers et al., 2001; Davis and Wilson, 2000; Gersten et al., 2001) and other administrative support (Betoret, 2006; Burke and Greenglass, 1995; Newmann, et al., 1989); (*c*) participatory decision-making (Ingersoll, 1996); (*d*) autonomy (Burke and Greenglass, 1995; Ingersoll, 1996); and (*e*) shared values and goals (Burke and Greenglass, 1995; Chubb, 1988; Dorman, 2003). Support is particularly important for new teachers. Smith and Ingersoll (2004) found that new teachers with mentors (particularly related to collegial support) in their first year were less likely to leave or transfer. On average, 29 per cent of new teachers changed schools (15%) or left teaching (14%). Without mentoring, the probability of leaving rose to 40 per cent (Smith and Ingersoll, 2004).

Studies on Consequences of Occupational Stress Among Teachers

Occupational stress can result in psychological, physical and behavioural consequences for individuals. These outcomes, in their various forms, can prove quite costly to individuals and organizations to which they belong. For schools, these costs are not just monetary. Student learning can be disrupted or otherwise affected. For these reasons, the reduction of occupational stress should be of great importance to schools and other organizations. Psychological consequences include job dissatisfaction, reduced job commitment, anxiety, frustration, anger and of most concern, burnout (Aluja et al., 2005; Angerer, 2003; Borg et al., 1991; Hanson and Sullivan, 2003; Luthans, 2002; Manthei and Gilmore, 1996; Maslach, 1982; Sarros and Sarros, 1992; Troman, 2000).

Physical consequences of occupational stress involve changes to normal bodily functioning (Ashcraft, 1992). Research conducted in numerous settings, including schools, have established links between the following and occupational stress (and burnout); hypertension, elevated blood pressure, dryness in the throat, nervous tics, stomach complaints, ulcers, neck or back pain, headache, migraine, tiredness, chest pain, heart disease and stroke (Angerer, 2003; Ashcraft, 1992; Brown and Ralph, 1992; Burke and Greenglass, 1994; Caputo, 1991; Dunham, 1993; Kyriacou and Sutcliffe, 1977).

Behavioural consequences of occupational stress are the actions by individuals. These may arise directly from stress or as a result of psychological or physical reactions. The five major behavioural consequences identified in the literature are withdrawal, reduced performance, deteriorating collegial relations, substance abuse and accidents (Aluja et al., 2005; Angerer, 2003; Dunham, 1993; Hanson and Sullivan, 2003; Kalliath and Beck, 2001; Kyriacou and Sutcliffe, 1979; Muchinsky, 2000; Saros and Sarros, 1992; Solman and Feld, 1989; Spector, 2000; Troman, 2000).

McEwen and Thompson (1997) investigated stress and morale amongst 459 teachers following the introduction of a new national curriculum. The results revealed that male teachers rated too much to do, pupil behaviour, pupil's attainments, lack of standards and poor pay as being the most stressful aspects of their jobs. Similarly, female teachers rated too much to do as the most stressful, followed by pupil behaviour, pupil's attainments and a lack of standards. Also, the research indicated that teachers in both primary and post-primary teaching positions indicated they experienced problems with their school principals which they cited as one of their most highly rated stressors. They also indicated their pay to be unsatisfactory and as a contributory factor in their level of stress.

Pithers (1995) states that high levels of stress among teachers have been identified as having important implication for work performance, health and psychological status of the teachers. Furthermore, teachers work experiences can have detrimental effects not only on them, but also on their students and the learning environment which causes their feelings about themselves, their students and their profession to become more negative over time (Wiley, 2000). In his examination of the role of hardiness in the stress-burnout relationship among teachers, Chan (2003) indicates that stress and the resulting burnout can impair the quality of teaching, lead to job dissatisfaction, work alienation, and even to leaving the profession. Similarly, Tatar and Horenczyk (2003) state that chronic work stress leads to emotional exhaustion, depersonalization which is described as an unfeeling response toward students, and decline in feelings of competence and achievement in one's work. Wiley (2000) indicates that effects of stress may be physical such as ulcers and cardiovascular diseases, psychological leading to depression or anxiety, or behavioural such as decline in work performance which effects the students most directly. He also points out that stress can affect the teacher's personality causing him/her to become cold, insensitive, and possibly excessively authoritative and rigid, which will lead to ineffective teaching.

Stress and burnout may also impact how teachers perceive or appraise behaviours of their students. In their examination of the correlates of teacher appraisals of student behaviours, Kokkinos et al. (2005) tested the hypothesis that burned-out teachers will perceive the same behaviour problem as more serious than their non-burned-out colleagues. They found no significant main effect of burnout on severity ratings of misbehaviour; however, burnout did have a significant effect on severity ratings for anti-social and defiant behaviours. They also indicated that although the effect was not significant there was a tendency of burnout to increase teacher's severity ratings of students externalizing behaviour (i.e. anti-social, oppositional, inattention/carelessness).

Researchers like Dunham (1992) and Travers and Cooper (1996) discuss the impact of stress on teachers in terms of stress reactions. According to Dunham (1976) (as cited in Punch and Tuettemann, 1990), there are two main teacher responses to stress: frustration and anxiety which could manifest themselves through a variety of physiological and psychological symptoms. Frustration is usually associated with physiological symptoms such as headaches, sleep disturbances, and stomach upsets, while anxiety was associated with loss of confidence, feelings of inadequacy, confusion in thinking and panic (Travers and Cooper, 1996). Dunham (1992) indicates that under high levels of anxiety teachers ability to make decisions was impaired, and concentration was reduced. High anxiety of teachers may also effect student performance negatively and influence how teachers handle responsibilities in the educational setting. Specifically, 'high anxiety teachers use significantly less task-oriented behaviour with students and they have a tendency to provide fewer positive reinforcements for their students' (Wiley, 2000, p. 84).

The relationship between stress and anxiety is also highlighted by Spielberger (1979), who indicated that the stress process starts with an external stimulus or situation that could be harmful or threatening. If the stimulus was perceived as threatening, an anxiety reaction (state anxiety) will be elicited. Similarly, Baumann et al. (2001) indicated that the subjective experience of acute stress (a state that occurs when there was high physiological arousal, and a need to make multiple decisions rapidly in an uncertain situation with important consequences) involves anxiety, and that it was the anxiety induced by these stressors but not the stressors themselves that had a negative impact on performance. Meijer's (2001) examination of the relationship between stress, trait anxiety and state anxiety with cognitive performance also indicated that state anxiety induced by high levels of stress leads to lower quality of performance. The anxiety reaction had two psychological components—worry and emotionality. It was the worry component of anxiety that impacts cognitive processes such as decision making. Infact, Baumann et al. (2001) asserted that anxiety was negatively related to performance due to narrowing of focus and negative self-reactions (worry). Depression and burnout are more likely in schools with high levels of student disruptiveness (Beer and Beer, 1992; Dorman, 2003; Hasting and Bham, 2003; Schonfeld, 1992). At the same time, distressed teachers are less able to handle misbehaviour or provide nurturance.

Teacher's intolerance of challenging behaviour (Kokkinos et al., 2005) impairs their ability to handle it. Yoon (2008) found elementary teachers who reported stress in handling student misbehaviour had much more negative relationships with students. Burnout also has a relationship to teacher's uncertainty about dealing with problem behaviour. Jackson et al. (1986) studied burnout among New Hampshire teachers and found all three burnout dimensions predicted whether teachers had left teaching a year later. Collegial social support predicted personal accomplishment. Role conflict predicted emotional exhaustion, which predicted turnover.

Factors associated with teacher attrition involve school organization. They include administrative support (Betancourt-Smith et al., 1994; Certo and Fox, 2002; Ingersoll, 2001), student discipline problems (Certo and Fox, 2002; Langdon, 1996), colleagues social and emotional support (Guarino et al., 2006; Kim and Loadman, 1994; Rosenholtz, 1985; Shann, 1998), and professional development, participation in decision-making, and support for student discipline (Yee, 1990).

Ceyanes (2004) analyzed teacher trust in the principal and teacher burnout as identified by teachers in selected Texas public schools using a cross-tabulation. The Pearson product-moment correlation produced a strong, positive correlation between teacher trust in the principal and teacher burnout. In addition, teachers who indicated low trust in the principal are about 28 per cent more likely to experience high teacher burnout. In fact, out of the 315 teachers, not one teacher who reported high teacher trust in the principal scored high on teacher burnout. Further, the researcher explored how selected demographic variables influenced the teacher trust-burnout relationship. The number of years that the teacher has worked with the principal had a strong influence on the teacher trust-burnout relationship, and the teacher's age and experience have a moderate effect. In addition, teacher gender appears to have a slight effect on the teacher trust-burnout relationship, and principal gender, principal age, and principal race appear to not affect the teacher trust-burnout relationship at all. The multivariate regression analysis suggested that teacher trust in the principal and the demographic variables account for nearly 40 per cent of the variance for teacher burnout. The results of this study suggested that principals must focus on developing trusting relationships with their teachers to reduce teacher burnout.

Chan and Hui (1995) studied the burnout and coping among 415 Chinese secondary school teachers in Hong Kong. The tripartite components (emotional exhaustion, depersonalization and personal accomplishment) of burnout and eight coping strategies (confrontive coping, distancing, self-control, seeking social support, accepting responsibility, escape-avoidance, plan-full problem-solving and positive reappraisal) were assessed. The results reported that reduced sense of accomplishment as a distinct component of burnout while emotional exhaustion and depersonalization were relatively undifferentiated among these teachers. The findings that avoidant coping strategies were consistently related to all three aspects of burnout suggested that teachers employing escape-avoidance to cope with stressors might be more prone to burnout. The study suggested that cognitive restructuring, positive reappraising, seeking support, problem-solving skill may help teacher guard against becoming depersonalized and may also increase the sense of personal achievement.

Studies on Occupational Stress in Teachers

Ahghar (2008) studied the influence of the organizational climate of a school on the occupational stress of secondary school teachers. Using a multi-stage random sampling method, a sample volume of 220 people was determined using the Cochran formula. Two main instruments were used to measure the study variables—a 27-item questionnaire on organizational climate and a 53-item occupational stress questionnaire by Vingerhoets. The frequency, percentage, and mean values were calculated and a step-wise regression analysis was performed to evaluate the statistical significance of the findings. The study results revealed that: (*a*) 40.02 per cent of secondary school teachers experience occupational stress at a moderate or higher level; (*b*) the rate of occupational stress among teachers can be predicted using the scores on the school organizational climate, this predictability is highest for the open climate and gradually decreases through the engaged and disengaged to the closed climate; (*c*) among the teachers working in the disengaged and closed climate, the rate of occupational stress significantly exceeds that recorded among the teachers working in the open climate.

Al-Fudail and Mellar (2008) explored the stress experienced by teachers using ICT in the classroom by using a 'teacher-technology environment interaction model'. The methodology used involved a comparison of three datasets obtained from: direct observation and video-logging of the teachers in the classroom; recordings of their galvanic skin response (GSR) taken while teaching; and interviews. Data were obtained from nine teachers. The main results of this study were: (*a*) the demonstration that teachers do suffer stress associated with the use of technology in the classroom (i.e. techno-stress); (*b*) the identification of causes, symptoms and coping strategies associated with techno-stress in the classroom. The study, points to an alternative way of thinking about the problems of implementing e-learning by conceptualizing some of these implementation problems in terms of techno-stress (and in particular of teacher-technology environment fit model).

Antoniou et al. (2006) identified the specific sources of occupational stress and the professional burnout experienced by teachers working in Greek primary and secondary schools. A special emphasis was given to gender and age differences. A cross-sectional design was used. Two self-report measures was administered to a sample of 493 primary and secondary school teachers, a self-report rating scale of specific occupational stressors and the Maslach Burnout Inventory (education version). The results revealed that the most highly rated sources of stress referred to problems in interaction with students, lack of interest, low attainment and handling students with 'difficult' behaviour. Female teachers experienced significantly higher levels of occupational stress, specifically with regard to interaction with students and colleagues, workload, student's progress and emotional exhaustion. Younger teachers experienced higher levels of burnout, specifically in terms of emotional exhaustion and disengagement from the profession, while older teachers experienced higher levels of stress in terms of the support they feel they receive from the government.

Axup and Gersch (2008) conducted a small-scale study on teacher attitudes regarding the impact of student behaviour on their professional lives. They formulated a brief questionnaire to explore teacher perceptions of the student responses that appeared to cause them stress. Anecdotal evidence within a local authority educational psychology service suggested that increasing teacher concern about student disruptive behaviour was causing significant professional anxiety. The key favoured coping strategies report included behaviour management techniques, praise and trying to understand the difficult behaviour, while personally talking to peers, switching off after the lesson, taking exercise and talking to family and friends. For future help, the preferred teacher options included the employment of more specialist behaviour support staff.

Betoret (2006) examined the relationships among teacher occupational stressors, self-efficacy, coping resources, and burnout in a sample of 247 Spanish secondary school teachers. The study examined the effect of teaching stressors on teacher burnout and the role of self-efficacy and school coping resources as mediator or moderator variables in the stressor-burnout relationship. Teachers reported that when their pedagogical practice in the school setting was being interfered with or hindered by a set of factors from the multiple contexts involved in students learning, problems of burnout occurred. In addition, results revealed that teachers with a high level of self-efficacy and more coping resources reported suffering less stress and burnout than teachers with a low level of self-efficacy and fewer coping resources, and vice versa.

Brundage (2007) surveyed the EFL Foreign Teachers stress in Korea. This study aimed to find the causes of teachers stress and the coping mechanisms. The study covered 53 foreign EFL (English as a Foreign Language) public and private school and university teachers (2004 and 2006) in Jeonju City, South Korea. Results showed that foreign EFL teachers reported moderate levels of stress and attribute stresses in roughly equal measures to student misbehaviour and school director/ administrative sources. Survey results also suggested primary coping mechanisms include drinking alcohol, sports, conversation with friends, hobbies including watching TV and movies and listening to music. A strong correlation (r=.622; t= 4.53) was found between foreign EFL teachers perceptions of stress in Korea and perceptions of stress at their teaching job. No significant correlation were found between foreign EFL teachers perception of stress and gender, length of time teaching in Korea or plans to renew teaching contracts. Teachers interviewed in 2006 were an average of five years younger than those interviewed in 2004 and reported slight but not significantly higher levels of stress.

Chan et al. (2010) comprehensively investigated the occupational health problems among teachers of primary and secondary schools in Hong Kong. A random sample of 6000 teachers was generated from the database of Hong Kong Professional Teachers Union (HKPTU) members. A self-administrated questionnaire was used to collect the data. A total of 1,710 usable questionnaires were returned. The results indicated that comparing with one year and five years ago, 91.6 per cent and 97.3 per cent of the responding teachers reported an increase of perceived stress level, respectively. Heavy workload, time pressure, education reforms, external school review, pursuing further education, and managing student's behaviour and learning were the most frequently reported sources of work stress. The four most frequently reported stress management activities were sleeping, talking to neighbours and friends, self-relaxing, and watching television, whereas the least frequently reported activity was doing more exercises or sports. The findings of this research served to be useful reference for the government and related organizations such as the Education and Manpower Bureau and Professional Teachers Union while formulating the policies and strategies to help the teachers to relieve and cope with their work-related health problems.

Cinamon et al. (2007) studied to know how work and family generic and occupation-specific stressors and support variables related to family interfering with work and work interfering with family among 230 Israeli high school teachers. Also, the authors examined the work- family conflict effects on burnout and vigour. Results indicated that conflict was related to generic variables and more so to distinctive teaching characteristics (e.g. investment in student behaviour and parent-teacher relations). Both work-family conflict and family-work conflict predicted burnout, whereas only family-work conflict predicted vigour.

Dworkin et al. (1990) conducted a study on stress and illness behaviour among 291 urban public school teachers. This study tested a series of hypotheses concerning the relationships among job stress associated with teaching, stress-induced illness behaviour and social support by principals and co-workers. The analysis of data revealed that the illness increases as job stress increases, except that teachers assigned to schools where the principal was seen as supportive are significantly less likely to report stress-induced illness behaviour than teachers in schools where the principal was seen as unsupportive. Supportive co-workers have no effect upon stress-induced illness behaviour, nor was there a statistical interaction effect between principals and co-workers.

Evers et al. (2004) explored the students and teachers perception of teacher burnout in relation to the occurrence of disruptive student classroom behaviour and the teacher's competence to cope with this kind of behaviour. The results showed that the students perceptions do not differ according to their age; there was a significant difference between the perceptions of male and female students in respect of emotional exhaustion and depersonalization, but not in respect of personal accomplishment; according to the students perceptions, a considerable percentage of variance in each of the three burnout dimensions was explained by teachers competence to cope with student disruptive behaviour and perceived disruptive student behaviour; and with respect to the teachers self-reports, it appeared that teachers and students reports differed significantly with respect to depersonalization, personal accomplishment and the competence to cope with disruptive student behaviour. The hierarchical regression analyses of the teacher's data showed that the competence to cope with disruptive student behaviour significantly contributed to depersonalization and personal accomplishment, whereas the teacher's age was significantly related with personal accomplishment.

Fordasz and Leder (2006) investigated work patterns and stressors of experienced and novice mathematics teachers. The data collection focussed on the activities the teachers undertook in and out of working hours, and their reactions to them. The range of tasks was found to be extensive, and stretched well beyond formal school hours. There were similarities and differences in the activities and work patterns of the experienced and novice teachers, and in what they found stressful. Administrative tasks were more likely to be the cause of stress for the experienced teachers; teaching-related activities for the novice teachers.

Geving (2007) conducted a study with an objective to identify the student behaviours associated with teacher stress and determined the types of teacher behaviours that may elicit these stressful student behaviours. Student teachers (n = 186) and their supervising teachers (n = 77) completed a stressful student behaviour questionnaire, a teacher behaviour questionnaire, and a teacher stress survey. Results showed that student lack of effort in class was most strongly associated with teacher stress. In addition, teacher behaviours were correlated with student's behaviours of coming to class unprepared. However, few significant correlations were obtained when student behaviour and teacher behaviour data were provided by different sources.

Grayson and Alvarez (2008) investigated components of school climate (i.e. parent/community relations, administration, student behavioural values) and assessed their influence on the core burnout dimensions of emotional exhaustion, depersonalization, and feelings of low personal accomplishment. The study weighed the relative contributions of demographic factors (i.e. gender, age and years of teaching experience), teacher satisfaction, and teacher-rated school climate that predict resultant levels of teacher stress and burnout from 17 rural schools in south-eastern Ohio. Results revealed that different aspects of school climate related to each of the three primary burnout dimensions. Further, the inverse relationship between school climate and burnout was mediated by teacher satisfaction levels for both emotional exhaustion and depersonalization dimensions.

Kyriacou and Chien (2004) studied the stress of primary school teachers in Taiwan. A questionnaire was used to explore teacher stress amongst 203 teachers in primary schools. Results revealed that 26 per cent of the teachers reported that being a teacher was either very or extremely stressful. The main source of stress identified was the changing education policies of the government. The most effective coping action reported was having a healthy home life. Teachers reported that the most effective action that schools or the government could take to reduce teacher stress was to decrease teachers workload.

Leung et al. (2009) examined occupational stress and mental health among secondary school teachers in Hong Kong, and identified the differences between those actively engaged in stress management behaviours and those who were not. Survey design was adopted using validated instruments including Occupational Stress Inventory (OSI-R), Depression Anxiety Stress Scale (DASS-21), and Health-Promoting Lifestyle Profile (HPLP II). The sample covered was 89 secondary school teachers who attended a professional development course offered by the University of Hong Kong. The results revealed that the majority of participants (75.3%) reported fair to very low satisfaction with the teaching career, and 82 per cent of them felt unaccountably tired or exhausted. Results of OSI-Revised showed that 38.6 per cent had experienced strong maladaptive stress due to vocational strain but coping resource was limited with most deficits on rational and cognitive coping. Analysis of DASS-21 indicated that 30.3 per cent had severe to extremely severe anxiety and 12.3 per cent had severe to extremely severe depression. HPLP II revealed that participants paid little attention to their own health and the management of stress. Those who exhibited more stress management behaviours showed significantly less physical symptoms, higher satisfaction with teaching and, lower occupational stress. The investigators reported that the secondary grade teachers have high occupational stress but insufficient stress coping resources. They recommended cognitive-behavioural programmes to enhance teachers stress management resources.

Ling-feng (2005) explored the relationships between mental health status and stress of kindergarten teachers and provided basis for improving their mental health. Self-administered questionnaire were adopted to test the kindergarten teachers status of mental health and stress in Huzhou. Results revealed that 39.2 per cent and 4.7 per cent of the teachers felt they were under the medium and heavy stress and the highest stress was caused by the infants and their parents. The prevalence of mental problems was 10.38 per cent. Mental health of the kindergarten teachers under 39 years old were poorer than that of 40-49 years old and the teachers with the first grade title of the technical post had the poorest mental health. Some of the kindergarten teachers have mental disorders. Stress plays an important role in the mental health of the kindergarten teachers.

McCarthy (2009) examined levels of elementary teacher's burnout symptoms: (1) between schools, with individual/teacher perceptions of demands and resources aggregated to the group level; and (2) at the individual teacher level within schools, where perceptions of classroom demands and resources, as well as teacher's personal coping resources and experience, were taken into account. Also, assessed the specific classroom demands and resources hypothesized to contribute to elementary teachers burnout symptoms using the Classroom Appraisal of Resources and Demands and used the Preventive Resources Inventory to measure teachers psychological coping resources. Burnout symptoms were measured using the Maslach Burnout Inventory. Data were collected from 451 teachers in 13 elementary schools in the south-eastern United States. Results indicated that although there was little variance in reported burnout symptoms between schools, each of the individual teacher-level variables was associated in the predicted direction with burnout symptoms. These findings supported transactional models of stress in that individual difference among teachers within schools in perceptions of demands and resources predicted burnout symptoms and differences in school context were not.

Mokdad (2005) conducted a study on 'occupational stress among Algerian teachers'. The main aim of the study was to find out the sources of stress, symptoms of ill-health and study the stress coping strategy among 126 Algerian primary school teachers. The results revealed that the major sources of teachers stress were society, parents, teaching, the teaching environment, pupils, supervision, the curriculum, colleagues and administration. Also the teachers suffered from many health problems. More than seven out of ten teachers (74%) reported headaches. Other health problems (sensual problems, arthritis, respiratory problems, ulcers, hypertension, heart problems, and diabetes) were also reported by many teachers but not by the majority. As to strategies for coping with stress, 62 per cent of teachers said they watch TV programmes, 59 per cent talk with their friends, and 54 per cent pray to cope with occupational stress. As to demographic variables (age, sex, work experience and training) the differences were significant only for age and gender. The researcher suggested for the educational ergonomics. The major areas of educational ergonomics are: teaching (teaching methods, teaching aids, increasing learners motivation); academic curricula (design, development, enrichment, evaluation); assessment of academic performance (developing evaluation tools, assessing evaluation tools, academic achievement tests, exams); development of individuals (students, teachers, administrators); the design of context design (study place, the design of classrooms and amphitheatres, computer stations, the physical environment); and the legislative framework (laws and regulations). The investigator believed that if educational ergonomics were widely taught and applied in practice, much occupational stress among teachers would be eliminated.

Prakee et al. (2007) conducted a study on 'challenging parents, teacher occupational stress and health in Dutch primary schools'. The main aim of the study was to identify the risk teachers (i.e. the most vulnerable to the presence of behaviourally challenging parents). The study examined teacher's perceptions of their own ability to handle challenging parent behaviour and to establish positive relationships as a possible influence on the quality of teacher-parent relationships. The participants in the study were 212 elementary school teachers in the Netherlands. The results revealed that unsatisfied parents, overprotective parents, neglectful parents and excessively worried parents have the largest impact on teacher stress. Teachers experiencing stress from challenging parent behaviour, suffer mostly from negative feelings toward parents, frustration on working with parents, loss of satisfaction with teaching and to lesser extent health problems.

Qiang et al. (2008) studied the main sources of school teachers work stress and their coping styles in Guangzhou so as to provide some evidence for improving teachers' working conditions as well as maintaining their mental health. 600 teachers in Guangzhou are randomly selected and were administered School Teacher Work Stress Scale and Coping Style Questionnaire developed by Xiao Jihua and Xu Xiufeng. The results revealed that gender, grade of teaching, school type and marital status were closely related with teachers work stress and they have different coping styles towards the stress. School teachers in Guangzhou have work stress in general and the stress sources are diversified. In addition, they have different coping styles towards the stress.

Rieg et al. (2007) explored the teacher's stressors in elementary classroom and ways to alleviate stress. The results showed that the twenty-five to fifty per cent of beginning teachers resign during their first three years of teaching and among all the causes, stress from teaching was one of the salient causes.

Salo (2002) aimed to study the teacher stress processes and the connections between stress processes, potential stressors, ways of coping, coping resources, and background variables (short-term effects), the connections between teachers subjective stress, coping, and health over eight-year period of time (long-term effects). Teachers from comprehensive and upper secondary schools in five municipalities (n=70) were studied in two phases by means of questionnaires. Information on the teacher's way of living, work and coping was obtained through interviews. The level of teacher stress increased towards the end of the autumn term in both years. During autumn in the second phase, coping resources explained job exhaustion best, while stressors and ways of coping explained anxiety. Also, large inter individual differences in stress during the autumn term were noticed in both years. Teachers work had become more stressful and their well-being declined during the past eight years. The results suggested that teacher stress was not necessarily a short-lived problem, and individual intervention methods of preventing or reducing stress should be employed.

Stress Report, (1999) reported the causes of stress and its effects among teachers. The study received a total of 25 responses from its members in Europe covering 16 countries from central, eastern, northern, southern and, western Europe. From the respondents, it was apparent that the majority of causes are related to how work is organised, and following that are societal and personal pressures related to the teaching profession. With regard to professional development, there was a lack of training and continuing education available to keep up with the changes in teaching methods, curriculum, and aid materials. Furthermore, education policy reform and political restructuring tend to bring a heavy burden upon teachers, not only relating to the implementation of changes but also in terms of job security. Frequent budget cuts were cited as a major factor in this area. Teachers are not remunerated according to the same salary scale as a majority of other professions, and this weighs heavily upon them financially and sends a message that their work is not highly valued.

Although the students were not noted as the main source of stress, it is rather that the organisational structure had not determined how to empower teachers to best deal with specific student issues. They are not always equipped with the proper means to handle the increase in violence and aggression; the lack of attention, interest and motivation; disciplinary problems; drugs; and an expanding class size per teacher. These challenges are only worsened by increasingly poor parent-teacher relations and decreased parent participation. The teacher experiences greater pressure from parents and society as a whole to play a larger role in the upbringing of a child—not only concerning ethical issues but also providing assistance and counselling for issues such as suicide, bulimia, abortion, and divorce. The responsibility for students overall welfare and well-being was a strain resulting in stress for teachers. It was also noted that women are often more susceptible to work-related stress due to a number of other outside pressures, such as having the same type of emotional and psychological responsibilities at home and at work, for her family and her students.

The school was also viewed as a stressful working environment both physically and psychologically. Lack of financial resources for sufficient materials, class rooms and equipment; environmental noise; poor ventilation; and problems with hygiene and safety are just some of the bad working conditions. These are coupled with a lack of time and unrealistic workload, excessive paperwork and administrative duties, lack of personnel and allocation, and a strong administrative hierarchy with a lack of support. A combination of these factors places the environment in a position of low morale and lack of solidarity, and often the teacher experiences enormous isolation, being alone against their class. This causes a great deal of stress because these feelings clash with the teacher's personal ambitions and goals for fulfilling their job and providing a quality education, and the educator was left at a loss.

The stress manifests behavioural, physical or psychological distress in teachers. One of the greatest risks of stress was the decrease in the quality of education and the reduction in teacher effectiveness. The combination of all of these elements means that the overall quality of education provided by the institutions also suffers. The consequences of stress for the entire organisation can be widespread. An organisation affected by stress displayed the following symptoms: High levels of sickness and absenteeism, frequent and severe accidents, high labour turnover, dysfunctional personal relationships, apathy among the workforce, poor quality and low levels of performance.

In order to reduce the causes of stress in teachers, the following recommendations/claims were made by the teachers union and existing studies:

1. Better working conditions;
2. Ensuring favourable fiscal policy towards teachers in terms of increased salaries and benefits, terms and conditions of employment;
3. Recruitment and maintenance of adequately qualified staff;
4. Respect from the parents and a commitment to working together with the parent associations;
5. A financial commitment from the state to respond to the demands of the 21st century in education, allowing for equipment improvements and modern communication tools;

6. Involvement of the teachers and their organisation in the educational system at all levels;
7. Integrated health education programmes in the curriculum;
8. A firm support system for young people at risk and their families;
9. Developing solidarity at the heart of the trade unions, including more international cooperation and professional exchange, in order to reduce the educators feeling of isolation;
10. Better continuing education possibilities and programmes;
11. Comprehensive initial and in-service training programmes including handling criticism and conflict, communication theories, setting achievable goals and limits, stress management, career development;
12. Recognizing teaching profession as valuable and sensitising the society to be more understanding and helpful;
13. Improved planning and programming including personnel, time and resource allocation;
14. Supporting leadership, leadership training and facilitating adaptation to the educational working environment through strengthened support networks;
15. Implement preventative and supportive measures of occupational health care—obligatory medical exams at the beginning of the academic year and periodic stress evaluations;
16. Concretising the objectives of education and training;
17. Integrating quality of teachers working life into education quality assessment and evaluation of professional aptitude;
18. More manageable class sizes, an effective code of discipline, a decrease in classroom hours per teacher;
19. Protecting teacher's rights; economic and social interests.

Tsai et al. (2006) examined the sources and manifestations of stress of Hong Kong female kindergarten teachers. Results suggested that time management and work-related stressors are more common sources of stress whereas feelings of fatigue and emotional related symptoms are more common manifestations of stress.

Wu et al. (2006) evaluated the effectiveness of the interventions on occupational stress among teachers in middle schools. The study group consists of 459 teachers (247 men and 212 women) from four middle schools in China. The control group consists of 502 teachers (271 men and 231 women). The three dimensions of occupational adjustment (including occupational stress, psychological strain, and coping resources) were measured with the Occupational Stress Inventory-Revised Edition (OSI-R) and the work ability was assessed with the Work Ability Index (WAI) among teachers. The integrated interventions (involving organizational and individual level intervention) were taken to the teachers in the study group. The scores of some scales of occupational role questionnaire and personal strain questionnaire decreased significantly and the scores of some scales of personal resources questionnaire and WAI increased significantly after intervening. The study suggested that interventions were efficient in reducing the teacher's occupational stressors, increased their coping resources and improved their work ability.

Zhihong et al. (2008) explored the relationships among teacher's occupational stressors, teaching efficacy and burnout among a sample of 728 Chinese secondary school teachers. The results showed that teachers with a higher level of stress reported less burnout than those with a lower level of stress, and vice versa. In addition, general teaching efficacy partially mediated the impact of occupational stressors on emotional exhaustion and cynicism; personal teaching efficacy fully mediated the relationship between occupational stressors and reduced accomplishment, and partially mediated the influence of occupational stressors on cynicism.

Studies on Occupational Stress in Special Education Teachers

Antoniou et al. (2009) investigated the specific work-related stressors affecting special educational needs teachers in Greece and the coping strategies applied by them. 158 special education teachers participated in the study. Pilot interviews were conducted in order to generate a scale for measuring specific sources of stress in Greek special education teachers. The resulting scale(s), together with the Coping sub-scale of the Occupational Stress Indicator were administered to the sample, and a number of socio-demographic factors were also obtained by the use of a detailed biographical questionnaire. The results identified five key stressors, loading mainly onto the domains of working conditions, workload, and organisational problems, which appear to have an impact on teachers of special educational needs students in Greece. Furthermore, a number of key coping strategies were identified by the teachers, as a means of dealing with work-related stress.

Billingsley and Cross (1991) investigated why some special education teachers choose to stay in teaching, but leave their special education assignments. In addition, they identified deterrents and potential incentives that had lead former special educators to reconsider teaching positions in special education. Questionnaires from 286 respondents were analyzed. The primary reasons cited for leaving special education suggested that the teachers transfer from special to general education because of administrative factors and the stress involved in working with special education students. Billingsley and Cross (1992) conducted a study to identify the variables that influence teachers commitment and job satisfaction among both general and special educators. A secondary purpose was to determine the extent to which these commitment and satisfaction variables influence teacher's intent to stay in teaching. A questionnaire using primarily existing measures was sent to a random sample of 558 special educators and 589 general educators in Virginia. Completed questionnaires were received from 83 per cent of both samples. Cross validated regression results suggested that work related variables, such as leadership support, role conflict, role ambiguity, and stress, are better predictors of commitment and job satisfaction than are demographic variables. Generally, the findings were similar for general and special educators.

Billingsley (2002) based on his research experience and findings on special education teacher's attrition discussed eight recommendations to improve special educators work environment and increase retention. Hiring certified teachers; paying high salaries and bonuses as incentives; developing responsive induction programmes to support beginning special educators; creating positive work environments and systems of support; increasing the level and quality of administrative support; fostering professional development to encourage teacher effectiveness; structuring teachers roles to focus on student learning; and providing programmes to help teachers deal with work stress.

Boutskou (2007) explored as how special education teachers perceive their job and their role. The author explored as how teachers give meaning to their experiences and how these experiences influence their practice. The different discourses and ambiguities over inclusion, integration and special education indicated the complexity of this area and of teacher's roles. The uncertainty over their role, the tensions with other professionals and the changing policy context and policy shifts create significant inconsistencies.

Chambers (2008) reported that the feelings of isolation, too little time with students, lack of administrative support and increasing demands are challenges that are faced by the special education teachers and contributing to teacher shortages. If educators are to provide the high quality programmes necessary for their children and youth with disabilities, while ensuring that they make good progress toward attaining their goals and meeting increasingly rigorous academic standards, the recruitment and retention of qualified, committed and talented teachers was essential. School administrators must use strategies that give their district an advantage by learning what compels a teacher to work and remain in a district.

Christina et al. (2004) investigated the relationship of occupational stress, psychological strain, and coping resources to the turnover intentions of full-time rehabilitation counsellors of the American Rehabilitation Counseling Association. The Occupational Stress Inventory—Revised and an individual data form were used to determine the turnover intentions of rehabilitation counsellors, based on an interactive model of stress, strain, and coping as well as various demographic variables. The results indicated that it was the occupational stress inherent in the job functions of rehabilitation counsellors, and not individual coping resources or demographic variables that accounts for the turnover intentions of counsellors in the field of rehabilitation.

Eichinger (2000) conducted a study to find out the job stress and satisfaction among special education teachers and found that the undifferentiated orientation was associated with lower levels of satisfaction and higher level of stress. Similarly, Engelbrecht et al. (2001) identified the stressors in teachers in an inclusive educational approach and coping skills employed to ameliorate the negative effect of these stressors from ten mainstream primary school teachers with a learner with Down's syndrome in their classrooms. Teacher's knowledge, attitudes, stressors and coping skills were qualitatively analysed with the help of semi-structured interviews and a questionnaire. Preliminary findings indicated that the stressors experienced and coping skills vary. The variation appears to be related not only to their perceived professional and personal ability to handle the needs of the learners but also to external factors such as collaboration with support groups and parents. Also, they highlighted that the behaviour of learners was rated as one of the factors that were found to cause more stress to teachers.

Forlin's (1997) research based on 571 teachers revealed that teachers attributed the most stressful aspects of their work in inclusive environments as being due to professional competence, administrative issues and issues relating to the classroom. There is consistent evidence that employees with more support from others experience lower strain and burnout (Lee and Ashforth, 1996), and where an employee was faced with potentially stressful demands, conflicts and problems in the workplace, having support from others may reduce the impact of the pressures on the individuals well-being (Jarvis, 2002; O'Driscoll and Cooper, 2002).

Crane and Iwanicki (1986) examined the relationship of role conflict and role ambiguity to teacher burnout among Connecticut urban special education teachers (n = 443) after controlling selected personal and professional background variables. The relationship of these background variables to teacher burnout was also examined. Role conflict and ambiguity explained a significant amount of variance in feelings of emotional exhaustion and depersonalization. When perceived burnout among teachers was moderate, the level varied significantly with respect to age, experience, sex, and whether one taught in a resource room or a self-contained classroom.

Embich (2001) conducted a study with a purpose to extend previous research on teacher burnout by delineating factors which contribute to secondary learning disabilities teachers feelings of emotional exhaustion, depersonalization, and reduced sense of personal accomplishment. Data were collected via a survey that employed the use of the Maslach Burnout Inventory (Maslach and Jackson, 1986) and the Role Conflict and Role Ambiguity Questionnaire (Rizzo et al., 1970). Overall, findings revealed that secondary learning disabilities teachers (n = 300) were experiencing high levels of emotional exhaustion, specifically those who team teach with a general educator. Following regression analysis, findings concluded that each of the seven variables chosen for the study contributed significantly to burnout, however, the relationship between those variables and the three determinants of burnout changed across teaching positions.

Fimian and Blanton (1986) reported on role, stress, and burnout problems experienced by 379 special education teacher trainees and 36 first-year teachers. Correlational analyses were used to determine the degree to which these were related to personal, academic, and organizational variables. Regression analyses were employed to establish how and to what degree these variables, in combination, acted as significant predictors of trainee and inexperienced teacher stress and burnout. Finally, analysis of variance was used to identify significant differences between and among three levels of traineeship and one of teaching, with respect to role, stress, and burnout problems in special education classrooms. Results indicated that the majority of such problems were significantly interrelated, that not all of the background variables predicted significant stress and burnout levels, and that different levels of role, stress, and burnout problems were observed in respondents at various stages of professional development.

Frank and McKenzie (1993) examined the phenomenon of burnout among special educators and the manner in which stress developed over time. The special educators were followed over the five-year period following the receipt of their undergraduate degrees in special education. Participants responded to a questionnaire and the Maslach Burnout Inventory, which was administered three times in Years 1-2 and three times in years 4-5. Results indicated that teachers (n = 41) who remained in special education experienced slow but steady increases in emotional exhaustion over the course of the five years. Some differences concerning trends in emotional exhaustion were observed among subgroups of teachers.

Griffin et al. (2008) reviewed a pertinent literature regarding novice teachers, with a focus on the changing roles of special educators, relationships between novice teachers and their colleagues, and accessibility of the general education curriculum to students with disabilities. The investigations have documented numerous factors in special education settings that contributed to the stresses of the first year of teaching for them, including: role ambiguity, students posing complex behavioural and academic challenges, large caseloads, insufficient curricular and technical resources, inadequate administrative support, inadequate time for planning, few opportunities for collaboration and professional development, and excessive procedural demands. Findings from this study suggested that supportive relationships with general education teachers are important to the professional lives of novice special educators. Helping the beginning teachers develop the skills to work in, and advance, a collaborative school culture may be one way that teacher educators and school administrators can begin to foster these relationships.

Harris et al. (2009) measured the stress levels of 97 school-based speech language pathologists using the Speech-Language Pathologist Stress Inventory. Results indicated that participant's emotional-fatigue manifestations, instructional limitations, bio-behavioural manifestations, lack of professional supports, and total stress were significantly below that of the original national sample. However, of the 48 survey items, participant's responses indicated more stress in three specific areas, namely, case load size, salary, and the use of prescription drugs. No significant differences in stress were identified with the type of school district (rural and urban), number of years of experience, or number of students served. Efforts to reduce stress levels of SLP's should be aimed at increasing supports, reducing caseloads, and increasing salaries.

Hart et al. (1995) conducted a longitudinal study to assess the effectiveness of the school discipline policy on teacher stress and the relationship between student misbehaviour and teacher stress. Data were obtained from 4,072 primary, secondary and special school teachers. The results showed that the school discipline programme was effective in reducing teacher stress and there was no mean change in student's misbehaviour. Structural equation analysis showed that there was little relationship between school's discipline policy and the perceived level of student's misbehaviour. It was also found that student suspension rates were not related to student's misbehaviour, but could be predicted on the basis of a schools discipline policy and self-esteem of teachers. Also, it showed that there is little point in trying to reduce teacher stress by reducing student misbehaviour; rather, it was more appropriate to develop a supportive organizational climate that enables to cope with the student misbehaviour that confronts them.

Kaufhold et al. (2006) conducted a study to examine the supplies, materials and resources for the special education teacher existed in the Texas public schools. Also, the study examined the attitudes of the 228 teachers in relation to their perceptions of federal financial support. Individuals interviewed personally indicated that the lack of sufficient supplies, coupled with the necessity of using out-of-pocket money in order to accomplish their teaching tasks caused a high degree of frustration which, in some teachers, led to burnout. The researchers suggested the administrators to channel allotted funds to these teachers and to ensure that they have the necessary resources and administrative support in order to perform their duties.

Lees and Barnard (1999) studied the climates of individual classrooms, concluding that teachers who are more aware of how students feel in the classroom are better able to design a learning environment that suits students and better able to guide them toward success. Teachers who have a leader who has created a positive school climate will be better equipped to do the same in their own classrooms. Indeed, several dimensions of school climate identified in the earlier study correspond to dimensions of classroom climate. For instance, clarity of vision in a schools purpose parallels clarity of purpose in class lessons; challenging yet realistic performance standards for teachers translate into like standards for students.

Lin et al. (2009) investigated the staff job strain profile and its determinants which included the worker characteristics and the psycho-social working environments in Taiwan. A cross-sectional study survey was carried out among 1243 workers by means of a self-answered questionnaire. The outcome variable (high-strain job) was evaluated. The explanatory variables were: worker characteristics and the psycho-social working environment evaluated according to Karasek's Job Demand-Control-Support model. The results revealed that many staff characteristics were correlated with job strain, such as staff working hours, age, gender, job title, educational level, religion, in-job training, working years in disability institutions and Effort-Reward Imbalance factors. Organization factors, such as geographical, institutional ownership and accreditation performance and size were also correlated with staff job strain. In multiple a logistic regression model of the job strain, the authors found that the factors of financial reward, extrinsic effort and perceived job stress of the staff were significantly correlated to the high job strain of the staff. The authors suggested that an important focus of future research should extend the findings to consider the factors to affect the high job strain to improve the well-being for staff working for people with intellectual disability.

Maolin and Xiaoxin (2008) studied the job stress and coping strategies of 182 special school teachers. The Questionnaire and Interview were employed. The results showed that special school teachers are experiencing moderate stress and the major sources of stress were the problems caused by students. Secondly, the most popular coping strategy used by teachers was problem solving, followed by seeking support. Thirdly, there was significant difference of special school teachers in gender, teaching experience and professional background in terms of job stress and coping strategies.

Male and May (1997) investigated stress, burnout and workload in teachers of children with special educational needs. A postal questionnaire was used to collect data from 221 teachers from 56 ordinary schools and eight schools for children with moderate learning difficulties (MLD), eight for children with severe learning difficulties (SLD) and eight for children with emotional and behavioural difficulties (EBD). The schools were situated in inner city, urban and rural areas in the south-east of England. Results indicated that, all three special school settings showed the evidence of a high level of emotional exhaustion. In addition, all groups were subject to long hours of work, and work overload was high for ordinary school teachers followed by SEN teachers and teachers working in MLD and SLD settings. Reference to sources of intense stress indicated some differences according to setting but generally implicated workload and challenging behaviour. In-particular, the results indicated that for schools with special education needs, most teachers cited excessive work (45%), paperwork (41%) and challenging behaviour (21%) as the most stressful, while inspection was the least stressful (1%).

For those schools for children with emotional and behavioural disorders, Male and May (1997) report challenging behaviour to be the most stressful for teachers (66%), followed by relationships with colleagues (43%) and workload (33%). Less than one per cent rated resources as stressful in their environments. In their research in schools categorized as having pupils with moderate learning difficulties, Male and May (1997) reported that workload (42%), paperwork (39%) and curriculum (29%) were the most stressful for teachers, while the least stressful was considered to be managing support staff (2.5%).

In schools with severe learning difficulties, Male and May (1997) indicated that teachers maintained that workload was the most stressful (63%), followed by challenging behaviour (33%) and curriculum (27%), while the least stressful was rated to be inspection (3%). Although reference to sources of stress indicated some differences according to the setting in which the research was conducted, workload was a frequently cited source of stress. Also, Male (1996) and Lewis et al. (1997) reported that challenging behaviour was amongst the most frequently cited sources of stress for teachers involved in inclusive education environments.

Miller et al. (1999) surveyed 1,576 Florida special education teachers and examined predictors of their leaving the field or transferring in two years. Perceptions of high stress insufficient certification and poor school climate were two of the most important predictors of leaving or transferring.

Nance and Calabrese (2009) described the reasons as why the current or former tenured special education teachers in a Local Education Agency remain or leave their special education teaching positions through the theoretical perspectives of organizational learning and organizational culture. Also, described the influence of increased legal requirements on current or former tenured special education teacher attrition or retention by reporting their reasons for staying or leaving. A qualitative multiple case studies of two units of analysis was conducted through a constructionist epistemology. Data were collected from 40 current and former tenured special education teachers through focus groups, semi-structured interviews, the left hand and right-hand column case method, and review of appropriate documents. The data collected were analyzed using text analysis software, content analysis, and pattern matching. The findings demonstrated that current tenured special education teachers want to be listened to and have their needs considered; current tenured special education teachers feel overwhelmed by the workload related to state assessments; current and former tenured special education teachers believe that legally-required changes affected them in practice; and current and former tenured special education teachers perceive that time requirements for administrative tasks reduce time for student services. The practical implications includes organizational learning and organizational culture that encourage listening to the experience of tenured special education teachers and including them in decisions that affect them in an effort to retain them.

Nelson et al. (2001) examined the sources of occupational stress for teachers of students with emotional and behavioural disorders. The occupational stress ratings from 415 teachers of students with emotional and behavioural disorders (EBD) was represented by regression, using teacher demographic characteristics, working conditions, and ability to work with children with EBD as factors in the analysis. Working condition variables (principal-teacher relationship, capacity to contribute to decisions, and working relationships), as well as years of professional experience and ability to work with externalizing children, had a significant effect on occupational stress. Additionally, within-inventory analyses pointed to ability to contribute to decisions as more influential than positive relationships with principals or colleagues.

Oliva (2003) observed that the attrition of special education teachers is a point of research focussed on in the light of our information age and the possibilities for increased understanding in special education teacher preparation programmes. The isolation factor was focussed on and the uses of e-mail as a communication device are studied. The study attempted to understand what effect the e-mail communication had on the retention of special education teachers in their preparation programmes and the field of special education. Natale (1993) argues that teacher's sense of isolation and lack of support from experienced colleagues and administrators contributed to their decisions to leave the profession. The use of electronic mail as a mentoring tool allowed the teachers to get support, feedback and break down the barriers of isolation that teachers often get their first year on the job (Eisenman and Thornton, 1999).

Paulse (2005) investigated the sources of stress of teachers involved in inclusive education. The study also explored the significant difference in stress experienced by teachers based on their biographical details. Teacher Stress Questionnaire was administered to 115 teachers teaching at the various schools located in the Cape Town area of the Western Cape. The results revealed that student behaviour was regarded as the most stressful; whereas, the administration was regarded as the least source of stress factor. Further, the seven independent variables (age, gender, experience, level taught, position, years of involvement in inclusive education and access to professional development and training received) significantly explained the variance in stress experienced by teachers involved in inclusive education.

Platsidou and Agaliotis (2008) conducted a study to find out the burnout, job satisfaction and instructional assignment related sources among 127 Greek special education teachers at the primary school level. The sample was given Maslach Burnout Inventory, the Employee Satisfaction Inventory, and the Inventory of Job-related Stress Factors. Results indicated that Greek special education teachers reported average to low levels of burnout. They reported moderately high levels of satisfaction with their job, the principal, and the school organisation as a whole; they also reported average satisfaction with work conditions and low satisfaction with prospects of promotion and pay. Four factors were identified on the job-related stress factors: teaching in a multi-category classroom, programme organisation and implementation, assessment of students, and collaborations with other special education experts and parents. The special education teachers perceived none of these issues as particularly overwhelming. Moreover, few significant effects of age, gender, and family status were identified.

Singh and Billingsley (1996) examined the effects of work-related variables on two groups of special educator's intent to stay in teaching. The study was carried out using Lisrel Annalyses. The final sample included 658 special educators (159 teachers of students with emotional disorder and 499 special educators from other special education areas). Results indicated that for both groups of teachers, the most important determinant of intent to stay in teaching was workplace conditions. For both groups, job satisfaction had the strongest direct positive effect on intent to stay and role-related problems had negative effects on intent to stay. Principal support influenced intent to stay indirectly through role-related problems and job satisfaction. Further, stress had an adverse indirect effect on intent to stay through job satisfaction and professional commitment.

Research by Trendall (1989) cited in Nagel and Brown, 2003 based on a comparison of special school teachers and mainstream teachers found special school teachers to be less stressed by their school situation. In contrast with Trendall's (1989), cited in Nagel and Brown, 2003 finding that teachers in special schools were less stressed than mainstream teachers, Williams and Gersch's (2004) research comparing 41 mainstream and special schools, indicates no overall difference in the total level of stress experienced by mainstream and special school teachers.

Williams and Poel (2006) designed the self administered tool for awareness and relaxation (STAR) to manage stress in special educators. The STAR is a colour-coded model for stress management that shows the interconnected relationship between the brain, body, and emotions. The STAR is comprised of four levels that progress sequentially. *Level—I* consist of seven elements pertaining to the category of inner realms: basic needs; physical body; will power; emotions; communication; intuition and inspiration. These involve the internal experiences and inherent physical, mental, and emotional aspects of life. Inner realms are significant to everyday functioning, since they interact with the external environment. By bringing awareness to the inner realms, the teacher can identify the source and impact of stressors. *Level—II* introduces six relationships, which encompass a broad range of interpersonal relationships. *Level—III* includes the four external environments, which cover the full spectrum of physical locations where individuals live, work, play, or interact with others. *Level—IV* provides the four dimensions of existence and six symbolic guides, designed to facilitate the process of relieving stress and experiencing relaxation. This tool helped teachers to gain a sense of control by facilitating increased awareness of the impact of job-related stress. Further, the tool assisted teachers in managing stress by providing positive affirmations that had increased teacher's sense of self-esteem and job satisfaction.

Job Satisfaction of Teachers

Job dissatisfaction and reduced job satisfaction have been associated with several outcomes for employees and in-turn organizations. For schools, these often lead to the added cost of disrupted learning for students. Among the most costly of these to organizations are absenteeism and turnover (which together can be classed as withdrawal), lowered commitment, lowered productivity (often a result of the preceding outcomes) and diminished health of staff members (Australian Teaching Council, 1995; Bruce and Cacciope, 1989; Muchinsky, 2000a; Rosenblatt and Shirom, 2004; Singh and Billingsley, 2001; Spector, 2000; Starnaman and Miller, 1992).

Abd-El-Fattah (2010) investigated the longitudinal effects of a pay-increase schema, known as the teacher's cadre, on teacher's job satisfaction. A total of 155 primary school teachers responded to a questionnaire tapping their overall job satisfaction over four occasions. The results of the study showed that pay increase did not have a significant effect on teacher's job satisfaction. After pay increase, teachers with high academic attainments were significantly less satisfied with their teaching profession than teachers with low academic attainments. After pay increase, male teachers were significantly more satisfied with their teaching profession than female teachers. Length of service did not have a significant effect on teachers' job satisfaction.

Al Khateeb and Hadidi (2009) reported the results of an investigation of satisfaction of 135 resource room teachers and 190 mothers of children served in resource room programmes in Jordan. Information from teachers was gathered using questionnaires, semi-structured interviews, and classroom visits. Information from parents was gathered using a brief questionnaire. Teachers reported a moderate level of satisfaction with working conditions in resource rooms. They were most satisfied with their job as resource room teachers and relationships with colleagues. They were most dissatisfied with salary and fringe benefits and family involvement in educational programmes. Mothers were highly satisfied with resource room teachers. They were most satisfied with the improvement in the academic performance of their children in the resource room and least satisfied with the schools communication with them.

Beverly (2009) conducted a study to determine the best indicators of special education teacher's job satisfaction and barriers that threaten their satisfactory working conditions. An online survey was designed to capture 29 areas to explore qualifications and working environments of teachers. Of the 600 targeted teachers, 332 individuals participated in Likert-like scales to determine their degree of satisfaction or dissatisfaction for working conditions, use of intervention strategies, and areas of commitment. Closed-ended and multiple-choice questions were used. The resulting factors indicated that, although some respondents pointed to job dissatisfaction within the subset of questions, participants who worked for more than six years were less likely to vacate their positions than teachers working for less than six years.

Bishay (1996) studied the levels of teacher motivation and job satisfaction of teachers. A sample of 12 teachers was studied using the Experience Sampling Method (ESM). Teachers were randomly beeped by special pagers five times a day for five days and completed surveys on mood and activity for each beep, resulting in 190 reports of teacher's daily experiences. Conventional survey data corresponded with ESM data. The results revealed that job satisfaction and motivation correlated significantly with responsibility levels, gender, subject, age, years of teaching experience, and activity. For this group of teachers who work in a school with a selective student body, overall motivation and job satisfaction levels were high. Based upon the findings, it appeared that gratification of higher-order needs was more important for job satisfaction.

Brunetti (2001) examined teacher satisfaction in a group of high school teachers from a large school district in Northern California. The study was based on survey responses and on interviews with a select group of satisfied experienced teachers. The study found that the teachers were highly satisfied with their jobs. Also, the study identified that working with young people and seeing them learn and grow as principal motivators. Other important motivators include 'professional satisfaction factors' such as teaching one's subject, serving society, and having autonomy in the classroom. Of less importance were 'practical satisfaction factors' such as salary and benefits and job security.

Chen (2010) examined teacher job satisfaction in Chinese middle schools from the aspects of school, community, and life and the relationships between these factors and teacher moving. A sample of 294 teachers completed a 35-item questionnaire. The results revealed that: (1) Chinese middle school teachers were dissatisfied with their job in general. (2) younger, less-experienced, junior teachers were more satisfied, most groups of teachers were more satisfied with their working conditions, but less satisfied with income; (3) the sub-factors of leadership, professional opportunities, working conditions, and income had significant relationships with teachers future career planning.

Crossman and Harris (2006) examined job satisfaction among secondary school teachers in different types of secondary school. The results indicated a significant difference in the overall job satisfaction scores of teachers by type of school. Teachers in independent and privately-managed schools exhibited the highest satisfaction levels while those in foundation schools exhibited the lowest. No significant difference in satisfaction was found when the data were analysed by age, gender and length of service.

Davis (2009) conducted a study among the population of teachers working in international schools around the world (Africa, Eastern Africa, South-Central Asia, South-East Asia, Eastern and Southern Europe, Northern and Western Europe, the Caribbean, South and Central America, North America, Australia and Micronesia/Polynesia/Melanesia), focussing on change, job satisfaction and the transition process. The purpose of the study was two-fold. First, it aimed to determine if any association exists between an individuals change style and job satisfaction. Secondly, it aimed to provide a more comprehensive understanding of cultural, technical and political factors connected with professional satisfaction and the relocation process. An exploratory case study was conducted, incorporating both qualitative and quantitative data collection and analysis. Quantitative data collection included a psychometric assessment tool on change styles and a survey questionnaire, completed by 204 respondents. The qualitative element consisted of semi-structured interviews with seven volunteers, identified from the quantitative data set. Qualitative responses were separated by themes, which in turn were refined into broader categories, leading to systematic interpretations of change styles among this specific group of international teachers. Quantitative data provided descriptive statistics with which to compare qualitative interpretations. Quantitative and qualitative data were compared and contrasted throughout, leading to greater credibility and applicability of the study.

Hurren (2006) analyzed how teacher job satisfaction was influenced by principal's frequency of humour use in different groups. Results indicated that the idea that principals who shared humour in the workplace have teachers with higher job satisfaction than those principals who share very little or no humour in the workplace.

Klassen and Anderson (2009) explored the level of job satisfaction and the sources of job dissatisfaction for 210 secondary school teachers in southwest England and compared the results with the results from a similar study published in 1962. Questionnaires were given to 210 secondary teachers in southwest England (63% female) to rate their level of job satisfaction and to rate 16 sources of job dissatisfaction that are from the 1962 study. Teachers in 2007 rated their job satisfaction significantly lower and ordered the sources of job dissatisfaction significantly differently than did teachers in 1962. Whereas, teachers in 1962 was most concerned with external sources of job dissatisfaction (e.g. salary, condition of buildings and equipment and poor human relations), teachers in 2007 expressed the most concern about factors relating to teaching itself (e.g. time demands and pupils behaviour). The changes in sources of dissatisfaction hold true for male and female teachers, with no difference in rankings according to years of teaching experience.

Marston et al. (2006) examined career satisfaction among a group of elementary teachers in California and Pennsylvánia who had been teaching for 15 or more years and explored factors that motivated these teachers to continue as classroom practitioners. Quantitative data from the experienced teacher survey and qualitative data from individual interviews were collected from a sample of teachers from each state. Research questions focused on the nature and extent of job satisfaction, teacher relationships with colleagues and administrators, and perceived balance between their personal and professional lives. The findings revealed that California and Pennsylvania teachers indicated that core professional values such as satisfaction in working with young people and satisfaction in fulfilling a professional commitment, were powerful motivators for keeping them in the classroom. Pennsylvania teachers valued practical concerns such as job security, salary, and benefits more than their California counterparts. Social factors, such as relationships with colleagues and administrators, were another source of satisfaction for teachers in both groups. California teachers valued having a good principal more than their Pennsylvania counterparts. In addition, both groups expressed how time-consuming and challenging the profession was for them and their families, and how life experiences, such as parenthood, influenced their work in the classroom.

Ma and MacMillan (1999) studied the influence of workplace conditions on teacher's job satisfaction of 2,202 teachers working in New Brunswick Elementary School. They examined as how teacher professional satisfaction was related to background characteristics and workplace conditions measured through teaching competence, administration control, and organizational culture. Results showed that female teachers were more satisfied with their professional role as a teacher than their male counterparts. Teachers who stayed in the profession longer were less satisfied with their professional role. Workplace conditions positively affected teacher satisfaction; administration control was the most important, followed by teaching competence and organizational culture. Significant interactions between teacher background characteristics and workplace conditions occurred. The gender gap in professional satisfaction grew with increased teaching competence.

Mertler (2001) examined the current state of teacher (n=969) motivation and job satisfaction. Participants were predominantly white, female elementary, middle, and high school teachers. They responded to a web-based survey that examined their overall level of job satisfaction as a teacher, whether they would choose to become a teacher again if starting all over in a new career, the extent to which teachers in general are motivated, and how many teachers they knew or worked with who were unmotivated. Data analysis indicated that 77 per cent of teachers were satisfied with their jobs as teachers. Males were slightly more satisfied as teachers than females. Teachers early in their careers and near the end of their careers indicated the highest levels of job satisfaction. More teachers in their early 20s and 30s indicated a desire to enter the field of teaching again if given the opportunity.

Michaelowa (2002) conducted a study to find out the low teacher motivation and its detrimental effect on student achievement as they are central problems of many education systems in Africa. Using standardized data for student achievement in Burkina Faso, Cameroon, Cote d'Ivoire, Madagascar and Senegal, the author analyzes the empirical links between various policy measures, teacher job satisfaction and primary education outcomes. It appears that there was only very limited evidence for the effectiveness of intensively debated and costly measures such as increasing teachers salaries, reducing class size, and increasing academic qualification requirements. Other, simpler measures such as improved equipment with textbooks are both more effective and less costly. It also appears that teacher job satisfaction and education quality are not necessarily complementary objectives. Especially those measures ensuring control and incentive related working conditions for teachers, significantly increased student achievement while reducing teacher job satisfaction. In addition, teacher's academic qualification beyond the baccalaureate, while beneficial for students learning, tends to lead to a mismatch between teachers expectations and professional realities, and thereby reduces teacher's job satisfaction.

Michelle (2009) examined the components of novice teacher induction which may have a positive impact on novice teacher's intentions to stay in that teaching position and to determine which aspects of induction will increase teacher job satisfaction by examining the commonalities among their perceptions of their induction. Eight variables were identified for the study. The independent variables are new teacher orientation, presence of a mentor, participation in team lesson planning, regular meetings, observations of novice teacher by mentor, observations of veteran teachers by novice teacher, specific activities to be completed each month and personal reflection by the novice teacher. The researcher used intention to leave as a measure of teacher attrition. A sample of 40 novice teachers was randomly selected. The results indicated that seven variables reported by novice teachers increases their job satisfaction. The same seven independent variables were linked to intention to stay.

Ololube (2006) assessed the differences and relationship between the level of teacher's job satisfaction, motivation and their teaching performance in Rivers State of Nigeria. A questionnaire was used to collect data for the study. While the data for the study was analyzed using multiple statistical procedures: mean point value, standard deviation, and variance, t-test of significance and one-way-analysis of variance (ANOVA). The survey results revealed that teacher related sources of job satisfaction seem to have a greater impact on teaching performance, as teachers are also dissatisfied with the educational policies and administration, pay and fringe benefits, material rewards and advancement. From qualitative and quantitative data, Otto (1986) reported that occupational stress was highest among the most dissatisfied teachers and lowest among the satisfied.

Price and Terry (2008) examined the relationship between small class size in early elementary grades and teacher job satisfaction in a single school district using 20 elementary schools involving 135 teachers. Results of the study indicated that higher levels of teacher satisfaction were associated with fewer children assigned to a class. Specifically, statistically significant correlations were found for the relationship between small class sizes and the use of enriched activities in the classroom, ability to reconfigure classrooms for learning, and increased ability to respond to student needs, all factors enhanced through smaller class sizes and related to teacher job satisfaction. The analysis conducted found that job satisfaction could be predicted from effective relationships, time management, and classroom configurations. The correlational analysis also provided evidence of statistically significant correlations with these three variables and class size, providing further support that class size had a strong influence on teacher satisfaction. Effective relationships between teacher, parents, and students can be enhanced with fewer students. Teachers with fewer students can spend more time with parents at parent-teacher conferences and communicate with them on a regular basis. Time management skills can assist teachers in implementing district curriculum requirements, optimize instructional time, and leave the school by not feeling overwhelmed at the end of the day. As the number of children in a classroom decreases, the space available for each child increases, allowing teachers to provide innovative learning centers for special projects. These factors can increase job satisfaction for teachers making them less likely to depart the profession. Viewed from this perspective, investments in small class-sizes may well be cost effective when compared to the annual costs of recruiting and training new teachers and the loss of sustained learning for students.

Sargent and Hannum (2003) explored the factors that keep teachers satisfied who teach to the poor communities. With multivariate analyses of a survey of rural primary school teachers, principals and village leaders in one of China's poorest provinces, the authors investigated the role of individual teacher background, school environment, and community factors as influences on three measures of teacher work satisfaction. The results showed that younger, better-educated teachers are less satisfied, and suggested that teachers may be more satisfied in schools with an organizational climate that supports collaboration and in communities where village leaders support education. More surprisingly, models showed ambiguous effects of economic resources in the community and school, while timely payment of salaries and school expenditures are positively linked to teacher satisfaction, other indicators of economic status of communities and schools such as village income per capita, contributions of the village collective to the school, and teacher salary were negatively linked to teacher satisfaction, or not linked at all. These results underscore the challenge that faces rural, impoverished communities as they seek to retain teachers, and especially well educated teachers. Results also suggested that economic development alone may not ameliorate the problem.

Stempien and Loeb (2002) compared the satisfaction and dissatisfaction of teachers of emotionally/behaviourally impaired students in special education, teachers of students in general education, and teachers responsible for both groups of students. Teachers of students in special education programmes were found to be the most dissatisfied. Specific stresses and frustrations, both from within and from outside the classroom, were found to be associated with the dissatisfaction. The difficulties were particularly common in younger, less experienced special education teachers.

Tasnim (2006) conducted a study to analyse the job satisfaction among the female teachers of government run primary schools in Bangladesh. 57 teachers from seven government run primary schools in urban and rural areas have been selected. Both open-ended and close-ended questionnaire are used. Fredrick Herzberg's theory of motivation, power distance and masculinity-femininity theory of Hofstede, teacher's job satisfaction model by Linda Evans have chosen to analyse data as well as variables. The results revealed that some factors like salary, academic qualification, career prospects, supervision, management, working environment, culture etc. affected job satisfaction of both male and female teachers. Few perceptions of job satisfaction and the factors those affect it are same to the male and female teachers. But there are many perception as well as factors in which the male and female teachers are in two opposite pole. These different opinions are mostly interpreted in masculinity-femininity and power distance model of Hofstede. It is found that both the male and female teachers are dissatisfied but the female section is more dissatisfied than those of the male teachers.

Zembylas and Papanastasiou (2004) examined job satisfaction and motivation among 461 K-12 teachers in Cyprus. An adapted version of the questionnaire developed by the 'Teacher 2000 Project' was translated into Greek and used for the purpose of the study. The findings showed that, unlike other countries in which this questionnaire was used, Cypriot teachers chose this career because of the salary, the hours, and the holidays associated with this profession. It had been found that context seems to be the most powerful predictor of overall satisfaction.

Relationship Studies on Emotional Intelligence, Occupational Stress and Job Satisfaction

Adeyemo and Ogunyemi (2007) studied the interactive and relative effects of emotional intelligence and self-efficacy on occupational stress of University academic staff. Emotional intelligence scale, General perceived self-efficacy scale and Occupational stress scale was administered to a sample of 300 academic staff from all the eight faculties of Olabisi Onabanjo University, Nigeria. Data analysis involved the use of Pearson correlation and multiple regression procedure to investigate predictive capacity of the independent variables on the dependent variable. The results indicated that the two independent variables, when taken together, were effective in predicting occupational stress. Each of the variables contributed significantly to the prediction of occupational stress with self-efficacy making higher contribution to the prediction of occupational stress. The findings suggested that emotional intelligence programming and self-efficacy intervention techniques will benefit teachers immensely in coping with stress.

Betoret (2009) examines the relationship between school resources, teacher self-efficacy, potential multi-level stressors and teacher burnout using structural equation modelling. The causal structure for primary and secondary school teachers was also examined. The sample of 724 primary and secondary Spanish school teachers was taken. The changes occurring in the Spanish teacher role in the last decade were taken into account to select job stressors. The results obtained revealed that external (school support resources) and internal (management classroom self-efficacy and instructional self-efficacy) coping resources have a negative and significant effect on job stressors. In turn, job stressors have a positive and significant effect on teacher's burnout considering it as both a unidimensional and multidimensional construct. Furthermore, the hypothesised structure of burnout dimensions revealed that emotional exhaustion plays a key role in explaining Spanish school teacher's burnout.

Bogler (2001) examined the effects of principals leadership style (transformational or transactional), principals decision-making strategy (autocratic versus participative), and teachers occupation perceptions on teacher satisfaction from the job. A quantitative questionnaire using Likert-type scales was administered to 745 teachers in Israeli schools. Path analysis was used to explain teacher job satisfaction by the exogenous variables. The most salient finding was that teacher's occupation perceptions strongly affected their satisfaction. Principal's transformational leadership affected teacher's satisfaction both directly and indirectly through their occupation perceptions.

Boyle et al. (1995) made a comprehensive survey of teacher stress, job satisfaction and career commitment among 710 full-time primary school teachers in the Mediterranean islands of Malta and Gozo. Results revealed that the pupil misbehaviour, time/resource difficulties, professional recognition needs and poor relationships as major sources of teacher stress along with evidence of an additional teacher stress factor work overload. Consequently, structural modelling of the 'casual relationships' between the various latent variables and self-reported stress was undertaken on the combined samples. Although, both non-recursive models incorporating poor colleague relations as mediating variable were tested for their goodness-of-fit, a simple regression model provided the most parsimonious fit to the empirical data, wherein workload and student misbehaviour accounted for most of the variance in predicting teachers stress.

Brackett et al. (2010) examined the relationship between emotion-regulation ability (ERA), as assessed by the Mayer-Salovey-Caruso Emotional Intelligence Test (MSCEIT), and both job satisfaction and burnout among secondary-school teachers (N = 123). It also examined the mediating effects of affect and principal support on these outcomes. ERA was associated positively with positive affect, principal support, job satisfaction, and one component of burnout, personal accomplishment. Two path models demonstrated that both positive affect and principal support mediated independently the associations between ERA and both personal accomplishment and job satisfaction.

Brand (2007) explored the relationship between burnout, occupational stress and emotional intelligence in the nursing industry. Sources of Work Stress Inventory, Maslach Burnout Inventory, and Emotional Intelligence Test were administered to a sample of 220 nurses working in medical industry. The results showed that significant positive relationships exist between occupational stress and two dimensions of burnout, emotional exhaustion and depersonalization. Significant negative relationships were found for emotional exhaustion and two dimensions of emotional intelligence, emotional management and emotional control and between depersonalization and emotional management and emotional control. Accomplishment showed significant positive relationships with four of the five dimensions of emotional intelligence. Significant relationships were found between depersonalization and emotional exhaustion. Further, the sources of stress found to be the strongest predictors of burnout. Understanding emotions, emotional management and emotional control were all significant contributors to variance in occupational stress.

Camilli (2004) determined whether years of teaching experience is a predictive factor of job satisfaction and burnout in 60 teachers, ranging in teaching experience from 1 year to 44 years. It was hypothesized that teachers who have been in the profession for 1-2 or 3-10 years will be less satisfied and will have lower rates of burnout than teachers who have been in the profession 11-19 and 20 or more years. It was also hypothesized that teachers who have scored high on the burnout scale will have lower scores on the locus of control scale. A two-way analysis of variance (ANOVA) and the Pearson correlation were used to determine significance. The results of the study revealed that years of teaching experience was not a significant predictor of teacher job satisfaction and burnout.

Chaplain (2001) examined the levels of perceived stress and job satisfaction among primary head teachers. Around half reported high levels of occupational stress but some half were satisfied with their work. Sources of stress and job satisfaction were examined under four headings: managing oneself and others; managing finances; managing the curriculum; and managing change. The highest levels of satisfaction came from personal factors and organizational factors. School organization was a source of stress and of satisfaction. The lowest level of satisfaction was with the level of social support. Two subgroups reporting 'very high' levels of stress differed markedly in levels of job satisfaction—one 'very satisfied', the other 'not satisfied'. These differences were related to gender and perceived sources of job satisfaction and stress.

Clunies-Ross et al. (2008) investigated the relationship between primary school teachers self-reported and actual use of classroom management strategies, and examined how the use of proactive and reactive strategies was related to teacher stress and student behaviour. The total sample consisted of 97 teachers from primary schools within Melbourne. Teachers completed four questionnaires which gathered information on demographics, disruptive student behaviour, teacher management strategies, and teacher self-reported stress. In addition, 20 of the 97 teachers were observed in their classrooms while teaching, with teacher behaviour management strategies and student on-task behaviour recorded. The findings indicated that teacher self-reports accurately reflect actual practice, that relatively minor forms of student misbehaviours are a common concern for teachers, and that teachers are spending a considerable amount of time on behaviour management issues. The findings also revealed that the use of predominantly reactive management strategies has a significant relationship with elevated teacher stress and decreased student on-task behaviour.

Colangelo (2004) tested the hypothesis that teachers who participate in aerobic exercise and have increased parent involvement in their classrooms will have lower stress and consequently are significantly less likely to experience burnout and job dissatisfaction. The results found that teachers who participated in moderate physical activity reported less stress. The data also suggested that teachers who have positive relationships with parents expressed less burnout but there was no significant relationship with stress.

De Nobile and McCormick (2005) studied the job satisfaction and occupational stress of teachers working in Catholic primary schools. The sample of 356 teachers from 52 primary schools of six Catholic school systems in New South Wales, Australia was involved in the study. Nine (responsibility for work, relationships with the students, work itself, relationship with the principal, colleagues, job variety, supervision, working conditions, feedback, general job satisfaction) and four occupational variables (student domain, information domain, personal domain, school domain, general occupational stress) were identified from factor analyses. It was found that the staff members (teaching and non-teaching alike) were highly satisfied with their work overall and that this same group were experiencing mild to moderate levels of occupational stress overall. The study identified several moderate to strong correlations between facets of job satisfaction and domains of occupational stress, especially in the school and information domains. Only one occupational stress domain correlated moderately with general job satisfaction, while four job satisfaction facets correlated moderately with general stress. The multiple regression analyses suggested that all four occupational stress domains were predictors of job satisfaction. The results indicated that, if the organizational communication variables were not in the regression models, occupational stress, especially school domain and student domain stress, could predict substantial variance in job satisfaction.

Gokalp (2008) addressed the strategies that the teachers choose in dealing with pupil behaviour problems, and the influence of the strategies in their level of stress. Also, explored the role of teacher's years of experience and amount of behaviour management training they received in making the choices. Further, the impact of different types of behaviour problems on teacher's strategy selection was examined. 84 elementary school teachers with varying years of teaching experience completed two questionnaires, and responded to three vignettes (short descriptive essay) that described student behaviour problems that occurred during instruction. The independent variables were teacher stress (measured by the Teacher Stress Inventory), participant's years of teaching experience, and the amount of behaviour management training they received. The dependent variables were teacher's probability rating for using each of the seven strategies for each of the three vignettes and the types of information they used in deciding what strategy to select. The results indicated that as stress level increased, likelihood of using effective strategies decreased, and likelihood of using ineffective strategies increased. Results also showed that having more experience and more behaviour management training had not necessarily lead to more effective strategy selection. Finally it was found that the type of behaviour problem described in the vignettes had impact on the type of strategies selected by the teachers to deal with the misbehaviour.

Hopkins et al. (2007) examined the relationship between emotional intelligence and effective school board governance, as assessed using the Board Self Assessment Questionnaire which consisted of descriptive behavioural statements that measure individual and collective progress in six practice domains (i.e., making decisions, functioning as a group, exercising authority, connecting to the community, working towards board improvement and acting strategically). Each statement in the questionnaire was coded for the presence or absence of 18 emotional intelligence (EI) competencies defined in the Emotional Competence Inventory (ECI). The current and former school board members in two urban areas rank-ordered the most critical EI competencies for effective board governance and offered explanations for their most highly-rated competencies. Results revealed that a set of six core competencies are universal across the six board practice domains: transparency, achievement, initiative, organizational awareness, conflict management, and teamwork and collaboration. Each board practice domain was also characterized by one or two key EI competencies. The findings suggested that EI competencies are critical factors for effective school boards.

Hollifield (2005) examined the relationship between 136 teachers (from elementary, middle and high schools) job satisfaction and school climate/organizational culture through non-experimental, descriptive research design. Results indicated that teachers who had positive perceptions of school effectiveness significantly differenced in their job satisfaction or work-related stress indicating that teachers at each building level were experiencing moderately high levels of job satisfaction and low levels of work-related stress. Building level to which the teacher was assigned was a statistically significant predictor of safe and orderly environment, clear school mission, high expectations, opportunity to learn/time on task, and home school relations. Further, middle and high school teachers were not as satisfied as teachers at the elementary level.

Iordanoglou (2007) examined the relationship between emotional intelligence, leadership, job commitment and satisfaction among 332 primary education teachers in Greece. Results showed that emotional intelligence especially the intrapersonal and interpersonal dimensions had a positive effect on leadership effectiveness and was also strongly related to teacher's commitment and satisfaction. The findings suggested that besides cognitive abilities, the selection criteria in education should also include emotional competencies to ensure adequate performance of educators.

Ismail et al. (2010) conducted a study to measure the effect of occupational stress (i.e. physiological stress and psychological stress) and emotional intelligence on job satisfaction in private institutions of higher learning in Sarawak, Malaysia. A survey method was used to gather 80 usable questionnaires from academic employees who have worked in the organizations. The results of exploratory factor analysis confirmed that the measurement scales used in this study satisfactorily met the standards of validity and reliability analyses. The outcomes of testing research hypothesis using a hierarchical regression analysis showed two major findings: first, interaction between emotional intelligence and physiological stress significantly correlated with job satisfaction. Second, interaction between emotional intelligence and psychological stress insignificantly correlated with job satisfaction. This result demonstrated that the capability of academic employees to manage their emotions and other employee emotions has increased their abilities to control psychological stress in implementing job. As a result, it could lead to higher job satisfaction. Conversely, the incapability of academic employees to manage their emotions and other employee emotions had decreased their abilities to control psychological stress in implementing job. Consequently, it could lead to lower job satisfaction. Further, this study confirmed that emotional intelligence does act as a partial moderating variable in the occupational stress models of the organizational sector sample.

Kafetsios and Loumakou (2007) compared the effects of trait emotional intelligence (EI) and emotion regulation on positive and negative affect at work and job satisfaction among 475 teachers in Greece. Among the trait EI branches, only general mood had consistent predictive value for positive and negative affect at work. The interpersonal branch of EI was a predictor of job satisfaction and positive affect for the older age group, whereas emotion regulation was a predictor of affect and job satisfaction for the younger age group. There was minimal evidence for emotion regulation being a mediator between EI and affect at work in either age group suggesting that trait EI and emotion regulation may refer to distinct processes.

Kafetsios and Zampetakis (2008) tested the links between emotional intelligence (EI), affect at work and job satisfaction among 523 educators in Greece. The results demonstrated that EI was an important predictor of work affectivity and job satisfaction. Results also indicated that positive and negative affect at work substantially mediated the relationship between EI and job satisfaction with positive affect exerting a stronger influence. Among the four EI dimensions, use of emotion and emotion regulation were significant predictors of affect at work; whereas, perceiving others emotions was uniquely associated with job satisfaction.

Klassen et al. (2009) examined the efficacy beliefs, stress and job satisfaction of teachers teaching in the Yukon Territory in northern Canada. In *Study—1* the investigators used questionnaires to examine job beliefs of 221 teachers from the Yukon and western Canada. Teacher's self and collective efficacy and workload stress were lower for teachers, but levels of overall stress and satisfaction were similar across settings. In *Study—2* they conducted interviews to examine how geographical, community, and cultural factors were related to teacher's job beliefs. Results showed that job stress and job satisfaction were influenced by physical and human geography, level of connection with the community and by the communities cultural transitions. The findings highlighted the influence of cultural and community factors on teachers working lives.

Lisa (2005) studied the emotional intelligence and occupational stress among 320 employees (Accountant—3; Administration—46; Analyst—8; Consultant—25; Engineer—30; Information Technology—19; Manager-103; Teacher—62 and Others—24). The results of study indicated that four dimensions of emotional intelligence were particularly important in the occupational stress process: emotional recognition and expression, understanding emotions, emotional management and emotional control. Further the intervention of emotional intelligence training programmes demonstrated the effectiveness in terms of improving levels of emotional intelligence, decreasing feelings of stress and strain and improving the outcomes of stress.

Mohammadyfar et al. (2009) studied the determination of the effect size of emotional intelligence and occupational stress on mental and physical health. For this purpose 250 primary and high school teachers were selected with stratified random sampling selection from schools of

Tehran, Iran. Three questionnaires Emotional Intelligence Scale (EIS - Singh, 2004), Teacher's Occupational Stress Questionnaire (TOSQ-Mohammadyfar and Khan, 2008), and Mental Health Inventory (MHI - Srivastava and Jagdish, 1983), and one checklist (Physical Health Checklist) were administered among the school teachers. The results showed that emotional intelligence and job burnout were explained 43.9 per cent of mental health and 13.5 per cent of variance of physical health. Also, emotional intelligence and occupational stress were explained 13.5 per cent of variance of physical health in Indian teachers sample. Results showed that occupational stress was positive significant predictor (ß=0.253, P<0.001) in prediction of physical health. It means higher perceived stress will produce worse physical health.

Nikolaou and Tsaousis (2002) explored the relationship between emotional intelligence and occupational stress sources and outcomes on a sample of professionals in mental health institutions. A total of 212 participants were administered the Emotional Intelligence Questionnaire (EIQ) as well as the ASSET, a new 'Organisational Screening Tool', which measures workplace stress. The results showed a negative correlation between emotional intelligence and stress at work, indicating that high scorers in overall EI suffered less stress related to occupational environment. A positive correlation was also found between emotional intelligence and organisational commitment, which according to the ASSET model is considered as a consequence of stress, suggesting a 'new' role for EI as a determinant of employee loyalty to organisations.

Petrides and Furnham (2006) investigated the relationships between trait emotional intelligence and four job-related variables (perceived job control, job stress, job satisfaction, and organizational commitment). Gender-specific data (N=167, 87 females) were analyzed via multi-group structural equation modelling. Perceived job control had a negative effect on stress and a positive effect on satisfaction. Stress had a negative effect on satisfaction, which, in turn, had the strongest positive effect on commitment. There were many gender differences in the model, mainly concerning age, which was negatively related to control and commitment in the female sample only. Trait EI had specific, rather than widespread, effects in the model.

Platsidou (2009) investigated the relationship between burnout, job satisfaction and perceived emotional intelligence (EI) of 127 Greek special education teachers working at primary school level. The present study aimed to investigate their perceived burnout, job satisfaction and EI, in relation to individual differences such as age, gender, teaching experience, marital status, and to examine which of the above variables could be used as significant predictors of burnout dimensions. Results showed that the Greek teachers reported lower levels of burnout compared to their American and European counterparts; also, they reported fairly high scores in the specific EI factors and the overall EI. Regression analysis revealed that emotional exhaustion can be predicted by satisfaction with the job itself and with the principal subscales; depersonalization was predicted by satisfaction with the job and with prospective promotions; personal accomplishment was predicted by satisfaction with the job itself as well as by an EI factor, optimism/mood regulation, and a demographic variable, age. The findings suggested that teacher's burnout and low job satisfaction is likely to be preventable, if they are helped to enhance their EI with intervention programmes that would be available in both in-service and pre-service teacher education.

Platsidou (2010) investigated the perceived emotional intelligence (EI) in relation to burnout syndrome and job satisfaction in primary special education teachers from Greece. EI was measured by the Emotional Intelligence Scale (EIS) developed by Schutte et al. (1998). Factor analysis revealed that four factors can be identified in the EIS. Results showed that Greek teachers reported fairly high scores in the specific factors and the overall EI. Perceived EI was significantly related to burnout syndrome and job satisfaction, indicating that teachers of high-perceived EI are likely to experience less burnout and greater job satisfaction. Regression analysis revealed that emotional exhaustion can be predicted by satisfaction with the job itself and with the principal subscales; depersonalization was predicted by satisfaction with the job and with prospective promotions; personal accomplishment was predicted by satisfaction with the job itself as well as by an EI factor, optimism/ mood regulation and a demographic variable, age.

Ross Azura and Normah (2008) studied the factors influencing teaching performance among the rural elementary schools teachers (n=102). The elements studied are the relationship between stress, self-efficacy and teaching performance, comparison of stress and self-efficacy with genders and prediction of factors influencing teaching performance. The results revealed that self- efficacy had significant positive correlations with stress particularly time management stress and work-related stress. Teacher's performance had weak negative correlations with emotional manifestation. Level of stress among male differs significantly in terms of discipline and motivation compared to female. Emotional manifestation of stress and fatigue manifestation significantly influenced teaching performance.

Salami (2008) investigated the impact of job satisfaction and organizational commitment (OC) on organizational citizenship behaviour

(OCB) and also examined the moderating role of group cohesiveness on the relationship of job satisfaction and OC with OCB. The sample consisted of 420 secondary school teachers randomly selected from five states in Southwest Nigeria. Measures of job satisfaction, OC, OCB and work group cohesiveness were administered to the samples. Data obtained were analyzed using hierarchical multiple regression analysis. Results of the study indicated significant relationships of job satisfaction and OC with OCB. Group cohesiveness moderated the relationships of job satisfaction and OC with OCB. Based on the findings, it was recommended that human resource managers and school administrators should provide motivation, improved salaries and attractive working environments for the teachers. Also, counselling and personnel psychologists should design intervention strategies for improving group cohesiveness among the teachers.

Santavirta et al. (2007) investigated how different formulations of high demands and low decision latitude were related to teacher's burnout and estimated the possible interaction between these factors. The sample consisted of 1,028 school teachers. Multivariate covariant analyses (MANCOVA) were used to evaluate the relationship between a high-strain job defined by three different cut-off points and burnout. Logistical regression analysis was used to estimate the separate and joint effects of demand and decision authority on emotional exhaustion. Interaction between high demands and low decision authority was analysed using relative excess risk due to interaction. Attributable proportion (AP) was calculated in order to estimate the proportion of emotionally exhausted teachers among those exposed to both risk factors that was attributable to their synergistic interaction. The group of teachers who perceived their job as a low-strain job was used as the reference group in the analysis. The results indicated that the effect of job strain on burnout was proved to be consistent and robust across alternative formulations. The main effect of high demands exceeded that of low decision authority in relation to emotional exhaustion. Furthermore, the two factors acted synergistically to increase the risk of burnout.

Schwarzer and Hallum (2008) examined the relationships between self-efficacy, job stress, and burnout, focussing on mediation (self-efficacy job stress burnout). Moreover, the study examined whether such a mediation, if found, would be dependent on the levels of other variables (moderated mediation). *Study—I,* with two samples of teachers (n = 1,203), examined this assumed mechanism cross sectionally and found such an effect, in particular for younger teachers and those with low general self-efficacy. *Study—II,* with 458 teachers, replicated the results longitudinally over a period of one year by employing structural equation models. In a cross-lagged panel design, low self-efficacy preceded burnout.

Singh and Billingsley (1998) conducted a national survey database to examine the effects of professional support on teacher's commitment to the teaching profession. Principal leadership/support influenced teacher's professional commitment directly and also indirectly through peer support. The largest direct effect on teacher's professional commitment was from peer support. The findings indicated the importance of principal's leadership in enhancing teacher's commitment and the effect principals can have on teacher's collegial relationships.

Toni (2005) explored the factors that lead to special education teacher attrition and retention involving 212 special educators in the Commonwealth of Virginia. Structural equation modelling was used to test a hypothesized model of the relationship between teacher/administrative support, role dissonance, psychological strain, satisfaction with job, commitment to the profession, age, and psychological resilience to determine which variables directly and indirectly affect the turnover intentions of special education teachers. Structural equation modelling identified a path model wherein nine variables had a statistically significant influence on special education teacher turnover intentions. The confirmed path model suggests that one's perception of the effects of adversity due to physical or sexual abuse and adversity due to family loss play some role related to resilience. As the perception of psychological resilience increases, commitment to the profession increases and the intent to leave the field of special education decreases.

Wong et al. (2010) empirically investigated the potential effect of school leaders (i.e., senior teachers) EI, as measured by the 16-item scale developed by Wong and Law (2002), on teachers job satisfaction in Hong Kong. In *Study—1*, 107 teachers were asked to list the attributes of successful senior teachers/mentors in their schools. In *Study—2*, 3866 school teachers and middle-level leaders were surveyed on their EI and job satisfaction level. Middle-level leaders average EI was significantly related to the average of ordinary frontline teacher's job satisfaction. Results showed that school teachers believe that middle-level leaders EI is important for their success and a large sample of teachers surveyed also indicated that EI was positively related to job satisfaction. The main implication of this study was that the teaching profession requires both teachers and school leaders to have high levels of EI. Practically, this implies that in selecting, training and developing teachers and school leaders, EI should be one of the important concerns and that it may be worthwhile for educational researchers to spend more efforts in designing training programmes to improve the EI of teachers and school leaders.

An Overview of the Literature Reviewed

The above cited review, clearly indicates that studies are attempted on emotional intelligence of teachers, student teachers; occupational stress among teachers, special education teachers both in India and Abroad. It is also noted that good number of studies are found on antecedents of occupational stress and consequences of occupational stress among teachers, particularly in the western world. Similarly, a good number of empirical researches are found on job satisfaction of teachers, apart from relationship studies on emotional intelligence, occupational stress and job satisfaction both in India and western world. A close look at the review also, clearly indicates that the researches conducted in Indian continent is more sporadic in nature compared to rest of the world, in the sense that, the western studies are more in depth in nature than the Indian ones. In India, studies on relationship between emotional intelligence and occupational stress, emotional intelligence and job satisfaction and, occupational stress and job satisfaction are very limited and require the researcher's attention. It is also noted that whatever the limited studies available on this aspect, they are more on regular school teachers and the special school teachers spectrum is wide open to the researchers, considering the complexity of the nature of job they are engaged. Further, researches probing into the factors contributing to the emotional intelligence, occupational stress and job satisfaction are of vital importance for planning, development and implementation of not only the special education programmes but also for promoting inclusive classrooms, schools and societies at large.

The statement of the problem of the present investigation is presented in the subsequent chapter-III.

CHAPTER

3 Statement of the Problem

Introduction

Once the problem has been identified, stating the problem is an important task that has to be carried out. Defining the problem helps to specify the problem under study in a clear cut manner. This process helps the investigator to separate her study carefully from other previous studies. It will also lead to find a method to arrive at the right type of conclusion. Operational definition of the terms helps to view the general problem in terms of more specific, measurable and observable variables. Hypotheses are a powerful tool in the process of research to achieve tentative solution for the problem. Hypotheses of the study with specific objectives enable to identify the variables involved in the study and suggest methodological procedures to be employed. The scope and need of the study shows the worth and urgency of the study. This chapter deals with the title of the problem, operational definitions of the terms used in the study, objectives of the study, assumptions of the study, hypotheses of the study, scope, need and delimitations of the study.

Title of the Problem

'Emotional Intelligence, Occupational Stress and Job Satisfaction of Special Education Teachers'.

Operational Definitions of the Terms Used in the Study

The operational definitions of the terms used in the study are:

Emotional Intelligence

The Oxford Dictionary (2003) termed the word emotion as 'a strong mental or instinctive feeling'; 'emotional intensity or sensibility' and the word emotional is termed as 'readily displaying emotion'. The word intelligence refers to 'the quickness of understanding'. Similarly, Oxford English Dictionary (2005) defines emotion as 'any agitation or disturbance of mind'. Goleman (1995) refer emotion as a 'feeling and its distinctive thoughts, psychological and biological states and range of propensities to act'. Goleman (1995) defined emotional intelligence as 'the ability to know and manage one's own emotions, recognize them in others and handle relationships'.

In this study, emotional intelligence of the special education teachers refers to the ability of the teacher to be responsive of the self and the social environment thereby managing the self and acquiring relevant social skills to better discharge the duties as a special educator.

Occupational Stress

The Oxford Advanced Learners Dictionary (2003) defines occupation as 'connected with a person's job or profession' and stress as 'pressure or worry caused by the problems in life'. Similarly, the Cambridge Learner's Dictionary (2000) defined occupation as 'relating to one's job' and stress as 'feeling of worry caused by difficult situation such as problem at work'. Kyriacou (1997, p.156) defined teacher stress as the experience by a teacher of unpleasant emotions such as tension, frustration, anxiety, anger and depression resulting from aspects of his or her work as a teacher.

In this study, occupational stress of the special education teacher refers to the negative emotional state experienced by a teacher out of challenged organizational structure and climate, inadequate personal and professional efficiency, strained intra and interpersonal interactions and environmental factors existing within the school climate.

Job Satisfaction

The Oxford Dictionary (2003) termed job as 'a piece of work'. The Oxford Advanced Learner's Dictionary (2003) refers satisfaction as 'the good feeling one derives from what he does or when things happen as we think it to be ?'. Collins Dictionary (2005) explains job satisfaction as 'the extent to which the desires and hopes of a worker are fulfilled as a result of his work'. Blum and Naylor (1968) defined that job satisfaction is the result of various attitudes the employee holds towards his/her job related factors and towards life in general.

In this study, job satisfaction of special education teachers refer to the extent of pleasure experienced by a teacher from their job with reference to the school organizational aspects, intra and interpersonal relationships, motivational climate existing and the security and financial grade of their profession.

Special Education Teachers

The term 'special' is applied to a trait or to a person possessing the trait, if there is a considerable extent of deviation from the normal possession of that trait. The various types of disabilities that qualify individuals for special education programmes include specific learning disabilities, speech or language impairments, mental retardation, emotional disturbance, multiple disabilities, hearing impairments, orthopaedic impairments, visual impairments, autism, combined deafness and blindness, traumatic brain injury, and other health impairments. These children require education and related services with special care. The teachers who are involved in such educational programme are called as special education teacher.

In this study, the term special education teachers refers to those working in the schools for visually impaired, mentally retarded and hearing impaired.

Objectives of the Study

The following objectives have been framed for the present study :

1. To develop a tool to assess the level of emotional intelligence (EI) of teachers working in the special education schools;
2. To develop a tool to assess the level of occupational stress (OS) of teachers working in the special education schools;
3. To identify the level of job satisfaction (JS) of teachers working in the special education schools;
4. To find out the significant difference, if any, in the emotional intelligence, occupational stress and job satisfaction of special education teachers due to variations in their age, community, educational qualification, nature of special schools the teachers working in, training received in special education, level of classes handled, nature of job, years of experience and salary they receive;
5. To develop a tool to assess the level of infrastructure facilities (ISF) available in the special education schools, rated by the special education teachers;

6. To find out the significant difference if any, in the emotional intelligence, occupational stress and job satisfaction of special education teachers due to variations in the level of infrastructure facilities available, as rated by them in the special schools they are working;
7. To find out the relationship between the:
   (*a*) emotional intelligence and occupational stress of special education teachers;
   (*b*) occupational stress and job satisfaction of special education teachers; and
   (*c*) emotional intelligence and job satisfaction of special education teachers.
8. To study how far and to what extent the independent variables (age, community, educational qualification, nature of special schools the teachers working in, training received in special education, level of classes handled, nature of job, years of experience and salary they receive) influence the dependent variables (emotional intelligence, occupational stress and job satisfaction);
9. To study how far and to what extent the independent variable (emotional intelligence dimensions) contribute to the dependent variables (occupational stress and job satisfaction); independent variable (occupational stress dimensions) to the dependent variable (job satisfaction).

Assumptions of the Study

1. It is possible to develop tools to assess the level of emotional intelligence, occupational stress and job satisfaction of special education teachers.
2. The emotional intelligence, occupational stress and job satisfaction of special education teachers may vary.
3. The infrastructure facilities available in special schools as rated by the special education teachers may vary.
4. It is possible to predict the contribution of independent variables (age, community, educational qualification, nature of special schools the teachers working in, training received in special education, level of classes handled, nature of job, years of experience and salary they receive) to the dependent variables— emotional intelligence, occupational stress and job satisfaction) of the special education teachers.

5. It is possible to predict the contribution of emotional intelligence dimensions to the occupational stress and job satisfaction; occupational stress dimensions to the job satisfaction of special education teachers.

Hypotheses of the Study

1. There is significant difference in the emotional intelligence of special education teachers due to variations in their age, community, educational qualification, nature of special schools the teachers working in, training received in special education, level of classes handled, nature of job, years of experience and salary they receive.
2. There is significant difference in the occupational stress of special education teachers due to variations in their age, community, educational qualification, nature of special schools the teachers working in, training received in special education, level of classes handled, nature of job, years of experience and salary they receive.
3. There is significant difference in the job satisfaction of special education teachers due to variations in their age, community, educational qualification, nature of special schools the teachers working in, training received in special education, level of classes handled, nature of job, years of experience and salary they receive.
4. There is significant difference in emotional intelligence, occupational stress and job satisfaction of special education teachers working in the schools with poor, moderate and good infrastructure facilities available, as rated by them in special schools they are working.
5. There is significant relationship between the:
   (*c*) emotional intelligence and occupational stress of special education teachers;
   (*b*) occupational stress and job satisfaction of special education teachers; and
   (*c*) emotional intelligence and job satisfaction of special education teachers.

Scope of the Study

Researches in the field of special education are scanty in India. Most of the researches in the field of special education are centered on special child. The problems associated with the teacher who is the pivotal point in the special education field are neglected. The multiple roles played by the special education teacher demand intra and interpersonal skills and exert lot of stress and strain in them. The present study aims to identify the emotional intelligence, occupational stress and job satisfaction of special education teachers working in the schools for visually impaired, hearing impaired and mentally retarded children. For this purpose, the investigator developed the rating scales to assess the emotional intelligence and occupational stress of special education teachers. The job satisfaction scale developed by Reddy (2007) has been adopted and modified the same to identify the factors influencing job satisfaction of the special education teachers.

As resource inadequacy is a major problem faced by the special education teachers in transacting the curriculum, the study attempts to explore into the infrastructure facilities available in the special education schools using the infrastructure facilities rating scale developed by the investigator. Also, the study intends to find out the significant differences, if any, in the emotional intelligence, occupational stress and job satisfaction of the special education teachers due to variations in their age, community, educational qualification, nature of special schools the teachers working in, training in special education, level of classes handled, nature of job, years of experience, salary they receive and the infrastructure facilities available in the special education schools.

Further, the study deliberated the relationship between emotional intelligence and occupational stress, emotional intelligence and job satisfaction and occupational stress and job satisfaction of the special education teachers. Also, the study focussed on how far and to what extent the personal variables viz. age, community, educational qualification, nature of special schools the teachers working in, training in special education, level of classes handled, nature of job, years of experience and salary they receive are contributing to the dependent variables i.e. emotional intelligence, occupational stress and job satisfaction of special education teachers. In addition, it also focusses its attention on the contribution of emotional intelligence dimensions to the occupational stress and job satisfaction; occupational stress dimensions to the job satisfaction of special education teachers working in different types of special schools.

Need and Importance of the Study

The task of the teacher working in special school is a complex task as students needs are more diversified in nature demanding their intense attention, specific competencies and skills to handle specific situations (say for example early identification and assessment at right time), development of teaching-learning materials to accommodate each child and planning and development of individualized educational programmes apart from continuous monitoring and evaluation of the educational assignments. Also, the special education teachers have to think and work to meet the needs of the special children in inclusive setup. As the task of switching over to the pattern of inclusive setup on the part of the teachers all over the country is really a tedious and challenging one. All the specific needs and challenges encountered by children in special schools require the teachers to have a flexible control system, freedom to experiment and follow the child rather than the planned programme for needed strategies. The special school teachers are often witness to their student's emotional outbursts, in addition to the known deficits, which are extremely demanding and consuming of their cognitive and affective resources. The special school teachers adopt to a good extent a child-centered approach and spend a lot of time in interacting with individual students to be able to understand their needs and capabilities and to provide them the constant help and supervision. This consumes a great deal of their time and energy adding to their isolation and work overload.

Billingsley (1993) and Brownell and Smith (1993) stated that in comparison with general educators, special educators have been found to have higher attrition rates. Singer (1993) also reported the differential pattern of attrition was seen among special educators teaching different population of learners with special needs. Attrition rates were found to be higher among special educators teaching within hearing and visually impaired (secondary and elementary), mental retardation/developmental disabilities, (secondary), speech and language impaired (secondary) categories. Attrition rates were found to be higher in those who provide support and related services for students with special needs (elementary and secondary). Boomer and King (1981), Lawrenson and Mckinnnon (1982) and Zabel and Zabel (1982) revealed that teachers who work with students having behaviour/emotional disabilities are at the highest risk of leaving the classroom. The literature in Indian and western world provides evidence of special education teachers stress (Antoniou et al., 2009; Billingsley, 2002; Boutskou, 2007; Harris et al., 2009; Male and May, 1997; Al Khateeb and Hadidi 2009; Nance and Calabrese, 2009; Reddy, 2007; Singhal, 2004; Balaabaskar, 2010; Belcastro and Gold 1983; Bensky, et al., 1980; Buckhalt et al., 1990; Caton et al., 1988, Cook and Leffingwell, 1982; Currie and Rotatori, 1987; Dedrick and Raschke, 1980; Farber, 1991; Fimian, 1985, 1986, 1986a; Fimian and Blanton, 1986; Fimian and Santoro, 1983; Johnson et al., 1982; Pullis, 1992 and; Zabel, et al., 1984) often linked with diversification of roles, increased responsibilities, inadequate salary and poor fringe, lack of supplies and materials, difficulty in meeting student's needs and instructional objectives, excessive interactions and growth, lack of recognition and stressful interpersonal interactions. Cross and Billingsley (1994) states that the principals support will help to alleviate stress, increase leadership roles, and produce job satisfaction that can influence commitment and teachers intent to stay in teaching. In other words it leads to better job commitment and satisfaction.

A good number of research studies (Bishay, 1996; Brunetti, 2001; Crossman and Harris, 2006; Davis, 2009; Klassen and Anderson, 2009; Marston et al., 2006; Ma and MacMillan, 1999; Mertler, 2001; Michaelowa, 2002; Ololube, 2006; Price and Terry, 2008; Salami, 2008; Hollifield, 2005; Sargent and Hannum, 2003; Zembylas and Papanastasious, 2004; Amalados Xavier, 2009; Chamundeswari and Vasanthi, 2009; Gakhar et al., 2005; Ghazi, 2004; Kumar and Rao, 2007; Ramathulasamma and Rao, 2003; Rao and Sridhar, 2003; Saveri, 2009; Sharma and Patnaik, 2009 and Vijayalakshmi, 2005) have been noted on job satisfaction of teachers working at various levels. In case of special education teachers, the studies of Billingsley and Cross, 1992; Singh and Billingsley, 1996; Yezzi and Lester, 2000; Shafeeq, 2000; Reddy, 2007 and Balabaskar, 2009 are noted. Billingsley (2002) in analyzing the literature studies on special education teachers retention and attrition found that problematic district and school factors especially low salaries, poor climate, lack of administrative support, role overload and dissonance lead to negative affective reactions e.g. high levels of stress with low levels of job satisfaction and low level of commitment.

Research studies in Indian context (Reddy, 2000) reveal that the role performance of special education teachers is low with regard to the guidance and counselling role, organization of teaching and training roles and also low salary, temporary nature of the job is the common feature observed in the special education jobs. Further, studies (Reddy, 2004) also reveal that the special education teachers possess moderate and low level of awareness in most of the aspects of dealing children with disabilities. Their attitude was also negative in most of the aspects of disabilities. Their competencies too go hand in hand with their awareness and attitude. It means, special education teachers possess low level of attitude and competency on several aspects of disabilities in children. The research study also revealed that around 20 to 25 per cent of special schools and 70 to 80 per cent normal school were lacking infrastructure facilities for the education of children with disabilities. It is also revealed that better the infrastructure facilities, the less will be the percentage of drop out rate both in normal and special schools and, less the infrastructure facilities more will be the dropout rates (Reddy, 2004).

Reddy (2007) also found that more than 70 per cent of the special education teachers are experiencing high and moderate levels of occupational stress; 60 per cent of the teachers are showing high and moderate levels of professional burnout and, 70 per cent of them possess low and moderate levels of job satisfaction. Further, the infrastructure facilities available in the special education schools are also poor. Reddy found that the factors like development of materials to meet the individual needs of each child, insufficient planning time for planning instructional activities, inadequate instructional support material and resources, inadequate salary, job demands and over expectation of the job and lack of opportunities for promotion are the potential sources of stressors related to the organizational structure of the special education schools. From the same research study, it is also noted that good adjustment and relationships with job personnel contributes to the higher rates of job satisfaction of teachers. Similarly, Balabaskar (2009) observed that the factor 'satisfaction with authority including school management' contributed for higher job satisfaction among teachers teaching mentally retarded children. Reddy and Poornima (2009), studied that the stress factors viz., lack of opportunities for promotion, thrusting on development of curricular innovations and materials, giving more and more assessment and diagnostic responsibilities and preparation of teaching learning materials and implementation of instruction cause high level of occupational stress in teachers working in the schools for visually impaired. Singhal, (2004) found that teachers in special schools have higher workload than the teachers in regular schools.

Though the special education teachers cannot control issues related to salary, teaching assignment, paper-work, student behaviour, and support from administrators, they can learn and choose to develop skilled behaviours to deal with these stressors. The challenge of performing the tasks in special school is such that teachers need high degree of emotional strength, flexibility of procedures and routines, freedom to act according to the student needs and collegial support. Payne (2005) observed that special education teachers lack the leadership qualities that heighten the ability for them to deal with the demands of the job. Payne also noted that special education teachers must develop leadership skills that will assist in becoming effective advocates in the field of education. In simple terms, special education teachers need to be: (*a*) self aware of abilities and skills required for the range of the roles, responsibilities and demands of their work; (*b*) manage emotional reactions to specific situations and people; (*c*) accurately pick up on emotions in other people and react to others emotions and understanding others needs; and (*d*) socially skilled enough to use awareness of one's own emotions and the emotions of others to manage interactions successfully.

A close look at the research studies conducted in India and abroad on Emotional intelligence reveals that there are studies related to the emotional intelligence of *teachers* (Amirtha and Kadiravan, 2006; Bansibihari and Pathan, 2004; Date, 2006; Khan and Kumar, 2008; Latha et al., 2005; Neelakandan, 2007; Sibia et al., 2004; Swani, 2008; Usha Rao, 2008; Chan, 2008, Carbonneau et al, 2008; Kaplan, 2003; Salami, 2007 and David and Roy, 2010), *student teachers* (Gupta and Kaur, 2006; Gupta and Ram, 2006; Indu, 2009; Neetha, 2008, Panda, 2009; Sharma, 2008; Umadevi, 2009 and Sahaya Mary and Samuel, 2010) are noticed.

Further, a growing body of interdisciplinary research clearly has connected the relationship of emotional intelligence to achievement, productivity, leadership, personal health and occupational stress (Goleman, 1995, 1998; Epstein, 1998; Sternberg, 1996; Gardner, 1983; Weisinger, 1998; Low, 2000; Nelson and Low, 1999, 2003, 2005). The relationship of emotional intelligence to occupational stress of *teachers* (Gardner, 2005; Mohammadyfar et al., 2009), *nurses* (Brand, 2007), *university teachers* (Adeyemo and Ogunyemi, 2007; Ismail et al., 2010) and *professionals in mental health institutions* (Nikolaou and Tsaousis 2002) have been carried out in recent years. Further, the researches by Platsidou (2010) on *special education teachers*, Kafetsios and Zampetakis (2008); Wong et al. (2010); Brackett et al. (2010); Iordanoglou (2007) on *teachers*, Sinha and Jain (2004) on *male executives* have related emotional intelligence to the job satisfaction. Also, a good number of research studies (Chandraiah, 1993; Bindhu, 2006; Sumangala and Ushadevi, 2009; Suryanarayana et al., 2009; Chaplain, 2001 and De Nobile and McCormick, 2005; Boyle et al., 1995; Klassen et al., 2009) have been observed linking occupational stress and job satisfaction of teachers. It is observed that there is only few specific research studies focussed on the special education teacher's emotional intelligence, occupational stress and job satisfaction, giving vast scope for the researchers in this area.

It is clear from the literature reviewed in chapter—II, the special education teachers in both India and west are experiencing occupational stress and they are in need of emotional stability to face the challenges that are ahead in their way. A critical view at the research studies also indicates that the research on the combination of the three variables i.e. emotional intelligence, occupational stress and job satisfaction of special education teachers are limited and sporadic in nature. Further, the available studies are of foreign origin. The Indian scene is wide open for the researchers. A comprehensive study on emotional intelligence, occupational stress and job satisfaction of special education teachers will give clear cut picture about the emotional intelligence, occupational stress and job satisfaction and the relationship among these three. Infact, researches in this area provide better insights to create effective organizational environment, healthy intra and inter-personal relations, professional interactions, strengthening of the professional training components, the ways and means to equip teachers with instructional assignments and arrangements to meet the needs of the global society. Similarly, the studies on emotional intelligence, occupational stress and job satisfaction of teachers facilitate to know what factors contribute to job satisfaction/dissatisfaction among the special education teachers. Also, such studies will give better insight into the influence of teacher's personal variables on their emotional intelligence, occupational stress and job satisfaction which can provide for better policy planning, policy development and implementation in education, selection and training of special education teachers.

Delimitations of the Study

1. The emotional intelligence, occupational stress and job satisfaction of the special education teachers have been assessed only based on the self-ratings of the teachers.
2. The study is confined to Chennai city of Tamil Nadu State.
3. The study is limited only to the special education teachers working in the schools for hearing impaired, mentally retarded and visually impaired children.
4. Rating scale is the only tool used to assess the emotional intelligence, occupational stress and job satisfaction of the special education teachers
5. The dimension 'home-work interface', which is one of the sources of the occupational stress, is not included in the tool, as the investigator concentrated only on the work environment of the special education teacher.
6. The Infrastructure Facilities Rating Scale is rated by the special education teachers only.

The methodology used in the study is given in the next chapter.

CHAPTER

Methodology

Introduction

This chapter describes design of the study, various procedures adopted in the construction and development of the data gathering instruments to measure different variables which are included in the study and methods adopted in the selection of the sample, locale of the sample, data collection and the different statistical techniques employed in the analysis of the data.

Design of the Study

There are commonly three methods of research to solve the problems in education viz. historical, descriptive and experimental. According to Best (1963), historical research describes 'what was', descriptive research describes 'what is' and the experimental research describe 'what would be'. Descriptive study is concerned with conditions or relationships that exist, opinions that are held, processes that are going on, effects that are evident, or trends that are developing and survey is used for this type of research. The method adopted by the investigator in the present study was survey method. Survey studies are mainly of the 'what exists' type, they are designed to determine the nature of an existing state of affairs. The survey is very useful in doing what it is designed to do, i.e. it gathers descriptive data which people can provide from their own experiences.

Construction of the Tools used in the Study

In the survey method, data can be collected commonly in two ways viz. data can be obtained personally through face to face contact or through some kind of paper pencil test. In the present study, data were collected using the Rating Scales developed by the investigator.

The rating scale is the most commonly used device. Moulay (1964) stated 'the rating scale is best conceived as an instrument, which permits the quantification of numerical values to the ratings, cumulated points, multiple choice method etc., were carefully examined. Considering the nature and purpose of the study, the investigator developed Likert type Rating Scale to assess the emotional intelligence and occupational stress of the special education teachers and adopted Job Satisfaction Scale (Reddy, 2007) to evaluate the job satisfaction of the special education teachers working in special schools.

Development of the Research Tools

The prime objective of the investigation is to identify the emotional intelligence, occupational stress and the job satisfaction of the special education teachers. To achieve the above stated objectives, the researcher developed and adopted the following tools:

(*i*) Rating Scale to assess the Emotional Intelligence of the Special Education Teachers (developed by the investigator);

(*ii*) Rating Scale to assess the Occupational Stress of the Special Education Teachers (developed by the investigator);

(*iii*) Rating Scale to assess the Job Satisfaction of the Special Education Teachers (adopted and modified from Reddy, 2007);

(*iv*) Rating Scale to assess the Infrastructure Facilities available in the Special Education Schools (developed by the investigator);

The brief discussions of the research tools developed are as follows:

Rating Scale to assess the Emotional Intelligence of Special Education Teachers

To develop the rating scale to assess the emotional intelligence of the special education teachers, the investigator has constructed the statements to measure the emotional competencies possessed by the special education teachers. The investigator went through various tools developed to assess the emotional intelligence and reviewed the literature to construct the statements.

Salovey and Mayer (1990) used the 30 item self report Trait Meta Mood Scale (TMMS) to measure the attitudes about emotions and mood regulation. The scale is divided into three sub-scales viz. attention to feelings, clarity in discrimination of feelings and mood repair. Mayer et al. (1999) used 402 items Multifactor Emotional Intelligence Scale (MEIS) to measure the performance based emotional intelligence. It is designed to comprehensively assess the four branches (perceiving, using, understanding and managing emotions) of the emotional intelligence model developed by Mayer and Salovey (1997). Similarly, a subsequent revised 294 item Mayer, Salovey and Caruso Emotional Intelligence Test (MSCEIT, Mayer et al., 1999) was developed and it is based on a series of emotion-based problem solving items. In 2000, Boyatziz et al., used 110 item Emotional Competence Inventory (ECI) which is a 360 degree measure designed to assess the self-awareness, self-regulation, motivation, empathy and social skills of a person. Bar-On (1997) developed a self report Emotional Quotient Inventory (EQi) which includes 133 items to assess five specific dimensions viz. intra personal skills, interpersonal skills, adaptability, stress management and general mood of a person.

Another measure of emotional intelligence developed by Palmer and Stough (2001) is Swinburne University Emotional Intelligence Test (SUEIT). It is a self-report inventory with 64 items assessing the way people typically think, feel and act with emotions at work. The inventory consists of five sub scales i.e. emotional recognition and expression, understanding emotions, emotions direct cognition, emotional management and the last subscale is emotional control.

Cameron (2004) used Work Profile Questionnaire-Emotional Intelligence version (WPQ-ei) to measure the personal qualities and competencies that employees need to develop to manage emotion at work which includes seven components : innovation, self awareness, intuition, emotions, motivation, empathy and social skills. Likewise, Petrides and Furnham (2004) used Trait Emotional Intelligence Questionnaire (TEIQUE) to measure the four factors of emotional intelligence viz. well being, self-control, emotionality and sociability and encompasses 15 sub-scales.

In Indian context, Sharma and Bharadwaj (1995) developed the Emotional Competencies Scale that encompasses 30 items to measure five competencies (adequate depth of feeling, adequate expression and control of emotions, ability to function with emotions, ability to cope with problem emotions, encouragement of positive emotions) to assess the students emotional competencies. Similarly, Hyde (2002) developed

Emotional Intelligence Scale with 34 items that measure 10 factors of emotional intelligence: self awareness, empathy, self motivation, emotional stability, managing relations, integrity, self-development, value orientation, commitment and altruistic behaviour.

The available tools and the literature on emotional intelligence have not specifically concentrated on the emotional intelligence of special education teachers but they provide better insights into the concept under investigation. Considering the available tools and the literature on emotional intelligence, the investigator developed Emotional Intelligence Rating Scale with four dimensions viz. self awareness, self management, social awareness and social skills. These four dimensions encompass certain emotional competencies from the Goleman (2001) model of Emotional Intelligence. At the initial stage, the draft pool of 96 statements on emotional intelligence of special education teachers was prepared based on the emotional competencies and arranged under the four dimensions. Care was taken to present the statements in a clear and concise form for better understanding. This rough draft pool of items was given to the psychologists, educational experts, professionals, teachers and special educators and discussed critically about the emotional abilities of the special education teachers. Based on the discussion, the statements were further refined to avoid ambiguity and repetition. At the final stage, 58 statements, both positive and negative items were framed and arranged under the following four dimensions of emotional intelligence.

(*i*) *Self awareness :* self awareness refers to the ability to understand one's own emotions as well as understanding the impact of one's emotions on specific situations and people and recognize the impact of a particular emotions. This dimension assesses the emotional competencies like emotional awareness, accurate self-assessment and self confidence of the special education teachers;

(*ii*) *Self management :* self management refers to the ability to use awareness of one's emotions to stay flexible and positively direct behaviour and managing emotional reactions to specific situations and people. The items in this dimension measure self-control, trustworthiness, conscientiousness, adaptability, achievement drive and initiative;

(*iii*) *Social awareness :* this refers to the ability to accurately pick up on emotions in other people and react to other emotions and understanding other needs. The emotional competencies like empathy, service orientation and the institutional awareness are included in this dimension;

(*iv*) *Social skills* : social skill is the ability to use awareness of one's own emotions and the emotions of others to manage interactions successfully. This includes clear communication and effectiveness in handling conflict. Developing others, effective communication, conflict management, leadership, change catalyst, building bonds, teamwork and collaboration are the emotional competencies included in this dimension.

Thus the final form of the Emotional Intelligence Rating Scale (EIRS) includes part I and part II. The demographica/personal characteristics of the special education teachers like gender, age group, educational qualification, nature of special school the teachers working in, community, training received in special education, nature of job, salary per month, years of experience and level of classes handled have been included in part I of the rating scale. Wherein part II, 58 statements and the specific directions for the respondents to fill the rating scale have been given. To avoid the tendency to give a stereotyped response, items of positive and negative responses were evenly arranged. The distribution of statements in the final form is given under:

Distribution of Statements in the Emotional Intelligence Scale

Emotional Intelligence Dimensions	Serial Number of the Statements		Total number of state-ments
	Positive Items	Negativae Items	
Self awareness	1, 2, 4, 5, 6, 7, 8, 10, 11, 12	3, 9	12
Self management	15, 16, 17, 19, 21, 22, 23, 25, 27, 28	13, 14, 18, 20, 24, 26	16
Social awareness	29, 30, 32, 33, 34, 35, 36, 37, 38, 39	31, 40	12
Social skills	41, 42, 43, 44, 45, 48, 49, 50, 51, 53, 55, 58	46, 47, 52, 54, 56, 57	18

To measure the emotional competencies of the special education teachers, against each statement five gradations are given namely Strongly Disagree (SD), Disagree (D), Undecided (UD), Agree (A), Strongly Agree (SA) having the scores 1, 2, 3, 4 and 5 respectively for positive items and reverse scoring for negative items.

Rating Scale to assess the Occupational Stress of Special Education Teachers

To develop the rating scale to assess the occupational stress of the special education teachers, the investigator has constructed the statements to measure the sources of stress in special education teachers. The investigator went through various tools developed to assess the occupational stress and reviewed the literature to construct the statements.

Osipow (1998) used a revised edition of the Occupational Stress Inventory- Revised (OSI-R^{TM}) which is divided into three questionnaire viz. Occupational Role Questionnaire (QRQ) (having subscales like role overload, role insufficiency, role ambiguity, role boundary, responsibility and physical environment), the Personal Strain Questionnaire (PSQ) (having four subscales viz. vocational stress, psychological strain, interpersonal strain and physical strain) and the Personal Resources Questionnaire (PRQ) (having four subscales like recreation, self-care, social support and rational/cognitive coping). These questionnaires provide concise measure of three important dimensions of occupational adjustment, occupational stress, psychological strain and coping resources. For each of these dimensions, scales measure specific attributes of the environment or individual that represents important characteristics of occupational adjustment.

Job Stress Survey (JSS) developed by Spielberger and Vagg (1999) assesses generic sources of work related stress experienced by men and women in a wide variety of business, industrial and educational settings. The tool measures 30 factors viz. assignment of disagreeable duties, working overtime, lack of opportunity for advancement, assignment of new or unfamiliar duties, fellow workers not doing their jobs, inadequate support by supervisor, dealing with crisis situations, lack of recognition for good work, performing tasks not in job description, inadequate or poor quality equipment, assignment of increased responsibility, periods of inactivity, difficulty getting along with supervisor, experiencing negative attitudes towards the organization, insufficient personnel to handle an assignment, making critical on-the-spot decisions, personal insult from customer/consumer/colleague, lack of participation in policy-making decisions, inadequate salary, competition for advancement, poor or inadequate supervision, noisy work area, frequent interruptions, frequent changes from boring to demanding duties, excessive paperwork, meeting deadlines, insufficient personal time, covering work for another employee, poorly motivated coworkers and, conflicts with other departments.

Similarly, the Occupational Stress Indicator (OSI) developed by Cooper, Sloan and Williams (1988) assesses the causes and effects of stress in both groups and individuals and also identifies what coping strategies are currently being used. This includes six questionnaires each measuring different dimension of stress. The OSI consists of 25 subscales with a total of 167 items. The scales look at sources of pressure (61 items, six subscales: intrinsic to the job, organizational role, relationship with others, career and achievement, organizational structure and climate, home/work interface), type A behaviour (14 items, three subscales: attitude to living, style of behaviour, ambition), locus of control (12 items, three subscales: organizational forces, management process, individual influence), coping styles (28 items, six subscales: social support, task strategies, logic, home/work relations, time management, involvement), job satisfaction (22 items, five subscales: achievement, value and growth, job itself, organizational design and structure, organizational processes, personal relationships) and health (30 items, two subscales: mental ill-health, physical ill-health). These six questionnaire focus on four closely defined areas like sources of stress, individual characteristics, coping strategies and the effects on the individual and the organization. Dunham (1992) developed a questionnaire to identify the reported pressures, coping strategies of support teacher—special educational needs, early years of hearing impaired teacher, emotional and behaviour support teacher, visually impaired support teacher, visually impaired resources coordinator and center manager-family centre.

Winefield (2002) used 17 survey measures to assess the occupational stress among university teachers in Australia. The 17 survey measure includes General Health Questionnaire (Goldberg and Williams, 1988), job satisfaction scale (Warr et al., 1979), organizational commitment scale (Porter et al., 1974), work pressure scale (Beehr et al., 1976), work-home conflict scale (Frone and Yardley, 1996), job insecurity measure (Ashford et al., 1989), job involvement scale, (Lodahl and Kejner, 1965), job autonomy sub scale (Moos Work Environment Scale—Moos and Insel, 1974), procedural fairness scale was measured using the items developed from focus group discussions (Gillespie et al., 2001), trustworthiness scale (Mayer and Davis, 1999 and; Butler, 1991), likewise, negative affectivity, hardiness, coping, satisfaction with resources was assessed by the appropriate scales.

Pethe et al. (2001) developed Organizational Climate Scale (OCS) with 24 items assessing the employee results, clarity of roles and sharing of information and altruistic behaviour. Srivastava and Singh (1981) developed Occupational Stress Index with 46 items that assess the extent of stress, employees experiences in context of their job life that assess twelve sources of stress viz. role over-load, role ambiguity, role conflict, group and political pressures, responsibility for persons, under participation, powerlessness, poor peer relations, intrinsic impoverishment, low status, strenuous working conditions and unprofitability. Similarly, Srivastava and Krishna (1981) developed a 13 item Functional Job Stress Scale to assess the extent of job stress which is caused from demanding but desirable job situation.

Reddy (2007) developed occupational stress scale to assess the extent of occupational stress among special education teachers with 46 items measuring four factors of occupational stress viz. organizational structure, professional training, interpersonal and professional interaction and instructional assignments and arrangements. Likewise, Mathew (2005) used Stress Indicator to identify the sources, effects and the coping strategies of occupational stress among special education teachers in India.

From the review of the research tools, it is understood that in western context, a good number of tools are available to assess the occupational stress in teachers in particular and other employees in general. In India too, there are tools developed by Reddy (2007) and Mathew (2005) to assess the occupational stress in special education teachers. However, the investigator felt that the certain factors like the problems arising out of personal and professional efficiency of the special education teachers and the environmental factors like problems with student discipline, working environment, reinforcement etc., had to be included with the other stress factors. Thus, the available tools and the literature reviewed helped the investigator to develop Occupational Stress Rating Scale to assess the sources of stress among special education teachers. At the initial stage, the draft pool of 72 statements on the sources of occupational stress among special education teachers was prepared and was arranged under the four dimensions viz. organizational structure and climate, personal and professional efficiency, intra and interpersonal interactions and environmental factors. Care was taken to present the statements in a clear and concise form for better understanding. These rough draft pools of items was given to the educational psychologists, professionals, teachers and special educators and discussed critically about the sources of stress in special education teachers. Based on the discussion, the statements were further refined to avoid ambiguity and repetition. At the final stage, the Rating Scale encompasses 52 items under the following dimensions of the occupational stress:

(i) *Organizational structure and climate :* organizational structure and climate is one of the major potential sources of stress factors. This dimension includes items which identifies the sources of stress experienced by special education teachers arising out of the organizational factors like role overload, role ambiguity, role conflict, little or no participation in decision making, stringent rules and regulations, resource constraints and, problematic instructional assignments and arrangements.

(ii) *Personal and professional efficiency* : The second major source of stress in special education teachers is the personal and professional efficiency. The statements in this dimension spots the causes of stress in teachers due to inadequate personal and professional training, poor self-efficacy and management and technological advancement in special education field.

(iii) *Intra and interpersonal interactions* : The quality of intra and interpersonal relationship at work plays a dominant role in determining the special education teachers job behaviour and stress. The factors such as negative feelings in teachers, strained relationship with colleagues, students, parents, administration and para-professionals which create stress in special education teachers are included in this dimension.

(iv) *Environmental factors* : This dimension includes a set of factors in work setting causing stress in special education teachers that are related to the violence and danger caused by the pupils and co-workers, reward structure and recognition, negative publicity and physical working conditions.

Thus in the final form of the Occupational Stress Rating Scale (OSRS), 52 statements assessing the sources of stress along with the specific directions for the respondents to fill the rating scale were incorporated. All the statements are framed in negative format. The distribution of statements under each dimension in the final form is given hereunder.

Distribution of the Statements in the Occupational Stress Scale

Occupational Stress Dimensions	Serial Number of the Statements	Total number of Statements
Organizational structure and climate	1, 2, 3, 4, 5, 6, 7, 8, 9, 10, 11, 12, 13, 14, 15, 16	16
Personal and professional efficiency	17, 18, 19, 20, 21, 22, 23, 24, 25, 26, 27, 28	12
Intra and interpersonal interactions	29, 30, 31, 32, 33, 34, 35, 36, 37, 38, 39, 40	12
Environmental factors	41, 42, 43, 44, 45, 46, 47, 48, 49, 50, 51, 52	12

To measure the occupational stress in special education teachers, against each statement five gradations are given namely Strongly Disagree (SD), Disagree (D), Undecided (UD), Agree (A), Strongly Agree (SA) having the scores 1,2,3,4 and 5 respectively.

Rating Scale to assess the Job Satisfaction of Special Education Teachers

The term job satisfaction refers to the perceived feelings of an employee towards his job. It is a psychological feeling and has both rational and emotional elements. The job satisfaction, being global aspect is affected by a large array of variables such as salary, promotion, experience, primary and secondary needs, opportunities for advancement, congenial working conditions, rewards, job security, competent and fair supervision, degree of participation in goal setting and perception of the employees. Job satisfaction is presumed to wield considerable influence on job performance. In particular, in the field of special education, teachers satisfaction go a long way in improving the quality of instruction, educational and research output, developing social competence in special children and student teacher relationships. A close look at the literature reveals that there are various tools available to measure the job satisfaction of the teachers both in western and in Indian contexts.

Weiss et al. (1967) used Minnesota Satisfaction Questionnaire (MSQ) to measure an employee's satisfaction with their particular job. There are three forms of MSQ: two long forms (1977 version and 1967 version) and a short form. Long form MSQ consists of 100 items measuring 20 facets of job satisfaction: ability utilization, achievement, activity, advancement, authority, company policies, compensation, co-workers, creativity, independence, security, social service, social status, moral values, recognition, responsibility, supervision-human relations, supervision-technical, variety and working conditions. The short form MSQ consists of 20 items from the long-form MSQ that best represent each of the 20 scales.

Job Descriptive Index (JDI) developed by Smith et al. (1969) measures five major factors associated with job satisfaction: the nature of the work itself, compensations and benefits, attitudes towards supervisors, relations with co-workers, and opportunities for promotion. Likewise, Spector (1994) used Job Satisfaction Survey (JSS) to evaluate nine dimensions (pay, promotion, supervision, fringe benefits, contingent rewards, operating procedures, coworkers, nature of work and communication) of job satisfaction related to overall satisfaction. Warr et al. (1979) used Job Satisfaction Scale to assess satisfaction towards both internal and external work features including level of responsibility, chance of promotion and amount of variety in job (internal features) and pay, security and management (external features). Saxena (1994) used Job Satisfaction Scale to identify four different aspects of job satisfaction in teaching : (1) work; (2) salary, security and promotion; (3) institutional plans and procedures; and 4) authority including school management.

Dhar and Dhar (2001) used Job Involvement Scale to measure two factors viz. identification with the job and job centricity. Singh and Sharma (1999) developed Job Satisfaction Scale with 30 statements for assessing job intrinsic and job extrinsic factors like excursions, place of posting, working conditions, co-operation, democratic functioning, intelligence, social circle, salary, allowance, quality of life and national economy. Similarly, the Teachers Job Satisfaction Scale developed by Mudgil et al. (1991) with 75 statements assesses the job satisfaction of college and university teachers. In order to find the job satisfaction of the primary and secondary school teachers, Dixit (1993) includes job factors like (1) intrinsic aspect of the job; (2) salary, promotional avenues and service conditions; (3) physical facilities; (4) institutional plans and policies; (5) satisfaction with authorities; (6) satisfaction with social status and family welfare; (7) rapport with students; and (8) relationship with co-workers. Reddy (2007) developed rating scale with 54 items under four dimensions viz. organizational climate, inter and intrapersonal relationships, motivational climate and security and financial status to identify the job satisfaction of the special education teacher.

After going through the tools that are previously developed by the researchers, the investigator felt that the tool developed by Reddy (2007) to identify the job satisfaction of the special education teachers more appropriate, as the researcher has covered the teachers working in different special schools. However, the investigator felt that there is a need to change some of the items. Likewise, the investigator adopted the tool, modified and deleted certain statements. The so prepared 50 statements were given to the educational experts, special educators and psychologists. Based on their suggestions, some 4 statements have been deleted and some modifications have been made. Thus a final form of 46 statements was framed and arranged under the following four dimensions of the job satisfaction:

(i) *Organizational aspects* : The items in this dimension identify whether the special education teacher is satisfied with the organizational aspects like workload, environment, resources, training, rules and regulations, policy and leisure;

(ii) *Intra and interpersonal relationships :* This dimension includes the items that measure special education teachers satisfaction with the personal and social relationship within the school. This includes teacher's satisfaction in relationship with the school management, co-teacher, students, professionals and satisfaction with the self;

(iii) *Motivational climate :* The statements in this dimension deal with the intrinsic and extrinsic motivation of the special education teachers and their satisfaction with the extrinsic rewards and recognition.

(iv) *Job security and financial status :* This dimension evaluates the teachers satisfaction in relation to their salary, job security and job status.

Thus the Job Satisfaction Rating Scale (JSRS) includes 46 statements and the specific directions for the teachers to fill the rating scale. To avoid the tendency to give a stereotyped response, items of positive and negative responses were evenly arranged. The distribution of statements in the final form is given below:

Distribution of the Statements in the Job Satisfaction Scale

Job Satisfaction Dimensions	Serial Number of the Statements		Total number of statements
	Positive Items	Negativae Items	
Organizational aspects	1, 3, 4, 7, 8, 12	2, 5, 6, 9, 10, 11	12
Intra and interpersonal relationships	13, 14, 15, 16, 19, 21, 22	17, 18, 20	10
Motivational climate	23, 24, 25, 26, 27, 28, 29, 31, 32, 33, 34, 35, 36	30	14
Job security and financial status	37, 40, 41, 44	38, 39, 42, 43, 45, 46	10

To measure the job satisfaction of the special education teachers, against each statement five gradations are given namely Strongly Disagree (SD), Disagree (D), Undecided (UD), Agree (A), Strongly Agree (SA) having the scores 1, 2, 3, 4 and 5 respectively for positive items and reverse scoring for negative items.

Rating Scale to Assess the Infrastructure Facilities Available in Special Education Schools

In any educational institutions, the infrastructural facilities are essential in order to carry out the professional responsibilities in an effective and efficient manner. In special education too, these infrastructural facilities play a major role as the teaching learning materials, aids and appliances, adequate space etc., will facilitate the special education teacher to transact the curriculum in a more methodical way. Corcoran et al. (1988) suggests that the lack of resources increases the special education teachers work load. And a heavy work load makes it very difficult to use the available resources.

Reddy and Poornima (2008) identified that special education teachers teaching mentally retarded children, face problem in teaching and training due to the lack of adequate facilities to provide stimulative environment and the non-availability of structures and systematic learning materials for a child in learning. Similarly, the study carried out by Reddy (2007) revealed that only less than 50 per cent of the schools are equipped with magnifying devices, large print materials, overhead-projectors, audio-video materials, computer assisted instruction and speech synthesizers. Likewise, Reddy (2005) found that 90 per cent of the special education teachers dealing visually impaired children face problem due to lack of ventilation and adequate flexible seating arrangements to each child and 85 per cent of them face problem due to inadequate materials to diagnose visual efficiency in children.

For the purpose of the study, the investigator went through the Problem Checklist developed by Reddy (2005) to identify the problems faced by the special education teachers dealing children with visual impairment, hearing impairment, mentally retarded and the orthopaedic handicapped. The Problem Checklist developed assessed the teachers problem related to organization, teaching and training and guidance and counselling. Also, the questionnaire developed by Reddy (2007) to identify the infrastructure facilities available in the special schools was reviewed. After going through the tools and the literature related, the investigator prepared draft pool of 42 items related to the infrastructural facilities available in the special education schools which was given to the educational experts and the special education teachers for their review. Based on their suggestions, certain items have been deleted and finally 30 items were retained to identify the availability of the infrastructural facilities in special education schools meant for the visually impaired, hearing impaired and the mentally retarded.

To measure the infrastructure facilities available in the special education schools, against each statement three gradations are given namely Poor, Moderate and Good having the scores 1,2 and 3 respectively.

Pilot Study

A pilot study has been carried out by the investigator to find out the suitability of the test items for the investigation. Pilot study aimed to find out the reliability and the validity of the Rating Scales. The developed Rating Scales viz. Emotional Intelligence Scale, Occupational Stress Scale, Job Satisfaction Scale and Infrastructure Facilities Scale were administered to 20 special education teachers (10 % of the total sample) randomly selected from three schools meant for visually impaired, hearing impaired and mentally retarded from the study area. The teachers were oriented to rate the statements of the Rating Scales to indicate their responses using the gradations. The completed Rating Scales were collected and statistically analyzed to establish reliability and the validity of the tools.

Reliability of the Research Tools

Henry, E. Garrett (1966) says, "A test score is called reliable when we have reasons for believing the score to be stable and trustworthy". The correlation of the test with itself-computed in several ways is called the reliability co-efficient of the test.

Garrett (1966) describes four methods of establishing the reliability of a test. They are : (*a*) Test-retest method; (*b*) Alternate or parallel forms; (*c*) Split-half method; and (*d*) Rational equivalence method. Of these four procedures, the split-half method is regarded by many as the best of the methods for measuring test reliability (Garrett and Woodsworth, 1981). This method is used by many investigators because the data for calculating reliability are obtained from one occasion so that variations brought about by differences between the two testing situations are eliminated. In Split-Half Method, the tool was divided into two equivalent halves and the correlation was found for these half-tests by using the following Karl Pearson's Correlation Co-efficient formula.

$$r_{1/2} = \frac{N\Sigma xy - \Sigma x \times \Sigma y}{\sqrt{(N\Sigma x^2 - (\Sigma x)^2\ (N\Sigma y^2 - (\Sigma y)^2)}}$$

Where

$r_{1/2}$ = Correlation co-efficient

x = Score obtained one half of the test

y = Score obtained in another half of the test

Σx = Sum of obtained x values

Σy = Sum of obtained y values

Σx^2 = Sum of squared x values

Σy^2 = Sum of squared y values

$(\Sigma x)^2$ = Squared value of the sum of obtained x values

$(\Sigma y)^2$ = Squared value of the sum of obtained y values

N = Total number of sample

From the reliability of the half test, the self-correlation of the whole test is then estimated using Spearman Brown Prophecy formula.

$$r_{11} = \frac{2r_{1/2}}{1+r_{1/2}}$$

r_{11} = Reliability co-efficient of the whole test.

$r_{1/2}$ = Reliability co-efficient of the half test found experimentally.

The obtained reliability values for the tools used in the study through Split-Half Method are presented hereunder:

Name of the Scale	Reliability value through Split-Half Method	
	Half test reliability ($r_{1/2}$)	Whole test reliability (r_{11})
Emotional Intelligence Rating Scale	0.78	0.88
Occupational Stress Rating Scale	0.95	0.97
Job Satisfaction Rating Scale	0.84	0.92
Infrastructure Facilities Rating Scale	0.76	0.86

Validity of the Research Tools

Validity is the quality of the research tool or procedure that measures what it purports to measure. According to Best (1989), validity is the quality of a data gathering instrument or procedure that enables it to measure what it is supposed to measure. The index of reliability is sometimes taken as a measure of validity (Garrett and Woodworth, 1981). Several kinds of validity are ascertained, they are:

Content Validity

The content validity shows the adequacy of the content of a test. The items in the rating scales are based on the review of related literature and the tools already available. Also the items thus framed are consulted with related field experts. Their suggestions have been taken into account to enhance the contents and quality of items. Therefore, the research tools used in the study possess content validity.

Face Validity

This is the term used to characterize test materials that appear to measure what the test desires to measure. In other words, it refers to the way the test appears to those it is meant, to experts and educationalists. That is, the test items should be related to the variable being measured. Based on the expert's consultation and opinion, it can be said that the tools used in the study possess face validity.

Intrinsic Validity

Intrinsic validity shows how well the obtained scores measure the test's true score component. The square root of the reliability is the intrinsic validity of the tools. The obtained intrinsic validity of the Emotional Intelligence Rating Scale (0.93), Occupational Stress Rating Scale (0.98), Job Satisfaction Rating Scale (0.96) and Infrastructure Facilities Rating Scale (0.92) were high and hence the tools used in the study possessed intrinsic validity.

Locale and Sample of the Study

The area of the study encompasses Chennai City of the Tamilnadu State. As per the directory of the Office of the State Commissioner for the Disabled, Tamil Nadu and the District Disabled Rehabilitation Office, Chennai, there are totally 46 special education schools meant for the visually impaired (15), hearing impaired (15) and the mentally retarded (16) duly recognized by the Government. For the purpose of the study, the investigator randomly selected 12 special education schools (4 schools for visually impaired, 4 schools for hearing impaired and 4 schools for mentally retarded i.e. 26 per cent of the total schools available) by using Simple Random Sampling Technique. There are totally 226 teachers working in these schools. All the special education teachers were considered for the study. But due to absence and non-response of some teachers, 202 special education teachers formed the sample of the present study. The background characteristics of the sample are given in chapter-V of Table-1.

Data Collection

The investigator got the permission from the State Commissioner for the Disabled, Chennai, Tamil Nadu, the District Disabled Rehabilitation Officer, Chennai, and the Principals of the respected special education schools to collect data from the special education teachers. Good rapport was established with the special education teachers before administering the tools. They were explained about the purpose of the study. It was emphasized that the data will be kept confidential and they were instructed not to leave any item without rating. The developed Rating Scales were administered to the special education teachers to know their emotional intelligence, occupational stress and job satisfaction. At the beginning, the teachers were asked to provide their personal information in Part-A of the Emotional Intelligence Rating Scale. Later, they were oriented as how to rate their gradations against the statements under each dimensions of the Emotional Intelligence Rating Scale. Similarly, the Occupational Stress Rating Scale, Job Satisfaction Rating Scale and the Infrastructure Facilities Rating Scale were administered to the special education teachers. Teachers were directed to go through the instructions before rating the statements of the tools. No time limit to respond to the rating scale was fixed. The investigator collected the filled up rating scale personally.

Statistical Techniques used in the Study

The collected data were analyzed by using appropriate statistical techniques such as number and percentage, mean, SD, t-test, F-test, correlations and step-wise multiple regression analysis with the help of computer. To find out the number and percentage of special education teachers coming under low, moderate and high level of emotional intelligence, mean and standard deviation of the emotional intelligence scores have been computed. By using mean ± 1 SD, the number and percentage of teachers coming under low, moderate and high emotional intelligence were identified by category wise special schools as well as special schools together. Likewise, the same procedure is followed for identifying the number and percentage of special education teachers with low, moderate and high occupational stress and job satisfaction. In the second stage, to identify the level of emotional intelligence in special education teachers, mean and SD of the emotional intelligence scores have been computed. Mean ± 1 SD is used to categorize the statements into low, moderate and high level of emotional abilities. The similar procedure was used for identifying the sources of occupational stress and the factors influencing job satisfaction.

To find out the effect of age group, community, educational qualification, nature of special school the teachers working in, training in special education, level of classes handled, nature of job, salary per month and years of experience on special education teachers emotional intelligence, mean and standard deviation, t-test and F-test had been worked out. Whenever two groups are involved in a variable, t-test had been used. F-test was used when more than two groups are involved in a variable. Similarly, the same procedure was adopted to find the effect of the personal variables on occupational stress and job satisfaction of the special education teachers.

To find out the infrastructure facilities (ISF) available in the special education schools, the number and percentage of special education teachers working in the schools with poor, moderate and high infrastructure facilities (ISF), as rated by them were calculated. Further, mean ± 1 SD were calculated to categorize the teachers coming under poor, moderate and good level of ISF based on the mean and SD scores. The mean and SD of EI, OS and JS scores of the respective categories of teachers have been worked out to find out any significance difference if any, in the emotional intelligence, occupational stress and job satisfaction of special education teachers due to variations in the availability of the ISF's.

Correlations were computed to find out the relationship between emotional intelligence and occupational stress, occupational stress and job satisfaction, emotional intelligence and job satisfaction of special education teachers working in each type of special education schools and special education schools together. To find out the contribution of the independent variables (age group, community, educational qualification, nature of special school the teachers working in, training in special education, level of classes handled, nature of job, salary per month and years of experience) on the dependent variables (emotional intelligence, occupational stress and job satisfaction), step-wise multiple regression analysis was carried out. This analysis aimed to predict to what extent and to how far the independent variables contribute to the dependent variables (emotional intelligence, occupational stress and job satisfaction) of special education teachers. Also, using step wise multiple regression analysis, the contribution of independent variable—emotional intelligence dimensions (EI) to the dependent variables—occupational stress (OS) and job satisfaction (JS); and independent variable—occupational stress dimensions (OS) to the dependent variable—job satisfaction (JS) were found.

The obtained results are presented and discussed in detail in the subsequent chapter.

CHAPTER 5

Results and Discussion

Introduction

This chapter deals with the analysis and interpretation of data collected from the sample of the study. The results and discussion are presented in two parts. The first part deals with the descriptive analysis. In this part, the description of the sample with background characteristics, mean scores and level of emotional intelligence, occupational stress and job satisfaction of special education teachers were analyzed.

The second part deals with the differential analysis, where the effect of personal variables such as age, community, educational qualification, nature of the special schools the teachers working in, training received in special education, level of classes handled, nature of job, years of experience and salary on the emotional intelligence, occupational stress and job satisfaction of the special education teachers was analyzed. The low, moderate and high infrastructure facilities available in special schools as perceived by the teachers in terms of their number and percentage were calculated. Also, the special education teacher's emotional intelligence, occupational stress and job satisfaction based on the infrastructure facilities have been analyzed.

Further, the relationship between emotional intelligence, occupational stress and job satisfaction of special education teachers and the contribution of the independent variables of special education teachers (such as age, community, educational qualification, nature of special schools the teachers working in, training received in special education, level of classes handled, nature of job, years of experience and salary) to the dependent variables (such as emotional intelligence, occupational stress and job satisfaction) of the teachers have been calculated. Further, the contribution of the independent variable (EI) to the dependent variables (OS and JS) and, independent variable (OS) to the dependent variable (JS) have been calculated.

PART—I : DESCRIPTIVE ANALYSIS

Descriptive Analysis of the Emotional Intelligence (EI), Occupational Stress (OS) and Job Satisfaction (JS) of Special Education Teachers

In this part the description of the background sample of the study is presented in Table—5.1. The independent variables of the special education teachers like age, community, educational qualification, nature of special schools the teachers working in, training received in special education, level of classes handled, nature of job, years of experience and salary have been discussed in detail. In addition, the number and percentage of special education teachers falling under low, moderate and high emotional intelligence, occupational stress and job satisfaction have been calculated as it is one of the major objectives of the study. For this, Mean and SDs of the emotional intelligence, occupational stress and job satisfaction scores have been calculated for each teacher working in the schools for hearing impaired (HI), mentally retarded (MR), visually impaired (VI) and special schools as a whole (SAW). By using mean ± 1 SD, the emotional intelligence, occupational stress and job satisfaction scores of special education teachers have been divided into three levels i.e. low, moderate and high. Accordingly, the teachers coming under emotional intelligence scores 3.88 and above are categorized as high, 3.25 to 3.87 are moderate and 3.24 and below are low. Similarly, the teachers with occupational stress scores 3.22 and above are categorized as high, 2.18 to 3.21 are moderate and scores 2.17 and below are categorized as low. Likewise, the teachers with mean job satisfaction scores 3.91and above are categorized as high, 3.07 to 3.90 are moderate and scores 3.08 and below are categorized as low. The number and percentage of teachers falling under each category have been worked out and are presented in Table—5.2.

Likewise, to identify the emotional competencies possessed by the special education teachers, sources of occupational stress and job satisfaction of teachers, mean and standard deviation for each aspect of emotional intelligence, occupational stress and job satisfaction have been computed for the total sample of the study. By using mean ± 1SD, the statements have been divided in each scale into three categories i.e. low, moderate and high. This analysis facilitates to identify the emotional abilities, sources of occupational stress and job satisfaction of the special education teachers. The obtained results were presented in the form of tables and are discussed in Table—5.3 to 5.5.

Background Characteristics of the Sample

The area of the study is the Chennai city of Tamil Nadu State. In Chennai City, there are totally 46 special education schools for children with HI, MR and VI. For the purpose of the study, the investigator randomly selected 12 special education schools, where 226 teachers are working. Out of 226 teachers, 202 teachers responded out of which 66 were working in the schools for visually impaired (VI), 64 are working in the schools for mentally retarded (MR) and 72 are in the schools for hearing impaired (HI). All these teachers working in the three categories of schools are selected as a sample of the study. The background characteristics of the sample are presented in Table—5.1.

Out of 202 special school teachers, 42 belong to 30 and below years of age group, 90 are in the age group of 31-45 years and 70 of them belong to 46 and above years of age group. With regard to community, 44 teachers belong to OC category, 122 belong to BC category and 36 teachers to MBC/SC & ST category. Under educational qualification, 95 special school teachers possess teacher training, 66 teachers have graduation with B.Ed. and 41 teachers possess graduation with B.Ed. and M.Ed. qualifications. Out of 202 special school teachers, 146 teachers are with diploma in special education and 56 are trained graduates with B.Ed. in special education. When the level of classes handled is considered, 81 teachers handle primary classes, 77 handle secondary classes and 44 teachers handle higher secondary classes. With regard to the years of experience, 85 special educators are with 1 to 10 years of experience, 61 are with 11 to 20 years of experience and 56 are with 21 and above years of experience.

Out of 202 special educators, 156 are in permanent position and 46 are in temporary position. With respect to the monthly salary, 74 special education teachers draw monthly salary below ₹ 10,000, 89 of them receive ₹ 10,001 to 20,000 per month and 39 teachers receive ₹ 20,001 and above per month.

Table 5.1 : Background Characteristics of the Sample

Name of the Variable	Number of Teachers
(*a*) Age	
30 and below yrs	42
31-45 yrs	90
46 and above yrs	70
(*b*) Community	
OC	44
BC	122
MBC / SC & ST	36
(*c*) Educational Qualification	
Teacher Training	95
Graduation with B.Ed.	66
Graduation with B.Ed. and M.Ed.	41
(*d*) Nature of Special School the Teachers Working in	
School for Visually Impaired	66
Schools for Mentally Retarded	64
Schools for Hearing Impaired	72
(*e*) Training Received in Special Education	
Diploma in Special Education	146
B.Ed. in Special Education	56
(*f*) Level of Classes Handled	
Primary	81
Secondary	77
Higher. Secondary	44
(*g*) Years of Experience	
10 yrs and below	85
11-20 yrs	61
21 yrs and above	56
(*h*) Nature of Job	
Permanent	156
Temporary	46
(*i*) Salary per Month	
₹ 10,000 and below	74
₹ 10,001-20,000	89
₹ 20,001 and above	39

Special Education Teachers with Low, Moderate and High Levels of EI, OS and JS

Table—5.2 illustrates the number and percentage of teachers falling under low, moderate and high levels of emotional intelligence (EI), occupational stress (OS) and job satisfaction (JS).

Table 5.2 : Number and Percentage of Teachers Working in Different Types of Special Education Schools (HI, MR and VI) with Low, Moderate and High Levels of EI, OS and JS

Nature of Special Education Schools	Number and Percentage of Teachers with Low, Moderate and High		
	EI	OS	JS
HI (n=72)			
Low	11 (15.28)	5 (6.94)	11 (15.28)
Moderate	54 (75.00)	57 (79.17)	60 (83.33)
High	7 (9.72)	10 (13.89)	1 (1.39)
MR (n=64)			
Low	13 (20.32)	8 (12.50)	9 (14.06)
Moderate	41 (64.06)	46 (71.88)	42 (65.63)
High	10 (15.63)	10 (15.63)	13 (20.31)
VI (n=66)			
Low	10 (15.15)	10 (15.15)	9 (13.64)
Moderate	46 (69.70)	51 (77.27)	46 (69.70)
High	10 (15.15)	5 (7.58)	11 (16.67)
Special Schools as a Whole (n=202)			
Low	29 (14.36)	25 (12.38)	32 (15.84)
Moderate	144 (71.29)	143 (70.79)	148 (73.27)
High	29 (14.36)	34 (16.83)	22 (10.89)

Note: Number mentioned in the brackets denotes percentage

From Table—5.2 it is clear that out of 202 teachers working in special schools, 144 (71.29%) teachers possess moderate level of emotional intelligence, followed by 29 (14.36%) teachers with high level of EI and the remaining 29 (14.36%) teachers exhibit low level of emotional intelligence. The school-wise analysis of emotional intelligence reveals that more percentage (75%) of teachers working in the schools for HI possess moderate level of emotional intelligence followed by the teachers working in the schools for VI (69.70%) and MR (64.06%), whereas, 15.63 per cent of teachers working in the schools for MR possess high level of emotional intelligence followed by the teachers working in the schools for children with VI (15.15%) and HI (9.72%). The remaining 20.32 per cent of teachers working in the schools for MR possess low level of emotional intelligence followed by the teachers working in the schools for children with HI (15.28%) and VI (15.15%). The present findings are in agreement with the results of Neelakandan (2007), Khan and Kumar (2008), Indu (2009) and, Bansibihari and Pathan (2004) where the majority of primary, secondary school teachers, teacher trainees and secondary school teachers possessed moderate and low level of emotional intelligence respectively.

In occupational stress too, majority (143) of special education teachers experience moderate level of stress followed by 34 (16.83%) teachers with high level of OS and the remaining 25 teachers are with low level of stress. Further, 79.17 per cent of teachers working in the schools for HI experience moderate level of stress, followed by the teachers working in the schools for children with VI (77.27%) and MR (71.88%). The high level of occupational stress is experienced by the teachers working in the schools for MR (15.63) followed by teachers working in the schools for HI (13.89%) and VI (7.58%), whereas, 15.15 per cent of teachers working in the schools for children with VI experience low level of occupational stress followed by the teachers working in the schools for MR children (12.50%) and HI (6.94%). These findings confirm the results of Reddy (2007) and Reddy and Poornima (2009), where the majority of special education teachers working in the schools for HI and VI exhibit moderate level of occupational stress. Also, the results of Rajeswari et al. (2008) are akin to the present findings, where the majority of teachers experience moderate level of stress.

With regard to job satisfaction, more percentage (83.33 %) of teachers working in the schools for the HI are with moderate level of job satisfaction followed by the teachers working in the schools for children with VI (69.70%) and MR (65.63%). At the same time, 15.28 per cent of teachers working in the special schools for HI are with low level of job satisfaction followed by the teachers working in the schools for children with MR (14.06%) and HI (13.64%). On the other hand, 20.31 per cent of teachers working in the schools for MR are with high level of job satisfaction followed by 16.67 per cent of teachers working in the schools for VI and 1.39 per cent of teachers in the schools for HI. When special schools as a whole, are taken into account, 148 teachers enjoy moderate level of job satisfaction followed by 32 teachers with low and 22 teachers with high levels of job satisfaction. The results of Reddy (2007) corroborate with the present findings where the majority of special education teachers working in the schools of VI, HI and MR enjoy only moderate level of job satisfaction.

It is also noted that within the three categories of special schools, majority (90%) of teachers working for the HI children possess only moderate and low level of emotional intelligence demonstrating moderate and high levels of stress (93% of teachers) with moderate and low levels of job satisfaction (98% of teachers). It implies that teachers working in the schools for HI experience more stress with low job satisfaction and emotional intelligence.

From the above, it is inferred that, more than 85 per cent of the teachers working in the special education schools possess moderate and low level of emotional intelligence, whereas 86 percentage of special education teachers experience moderate and high level of occupational stress. Likewise, more than 88 percentages of teachers are with moderate and low level of job satisfaction irrespective of the special schools they are working in. This trend indicates that there is a need to look into the emotional competencies possessed by the special education teachers that helps them to manage various sources of occupational stress that leads to job satisfaction in special education profession.

Level of Emotional Intelligence of Special Education Teachers Working in Different Types of Special Schools

Gold and Roth (1993) identified teacher self awareness as a key component for managing stress. Gold and Roth (1993) defined self awareness as 'a process of getting in touch with their feelings and behaviours'. Increased self-awareness involves a more accurate understanding of how students affect the teachers own emotional processes and behaviours and how teachers affect students, as well. Special educator's self-awareness of primary emotions triggers and improves their chances of making rational decisions based on conscious choice, rather than unconscious emotional conditioning. Further, they should be aware of their own abilities and skills to carryout the multiple roles and responsibilities. Self-awareness of special educators helps them to stay with confidence in establishing the objectives, plan and conduct the activities for a balanced programme of instruction.

From Table—5.3 *(See on page 163 to 168)* it is clear that the teachers working in the schools for HI, MR and VI possess moderate level of self awareness in identifying and separating their emotions (S.No.1), acknowledging their own strengths and weaknesses (S.No.5) and, feeling confident in delivering the goods upto the expectations in their job (S.No.12). Likewise, in emotional abilities such as: self-evaluating to overcome difficult situations (S.No.6) and in feeling good about themselves (S.No.9), the teachers working in the schools for HI and MR possess moderate level of self awareness, whereas the teachers working in the schools for VI possess low level of self-awareness. Also, the teachers working in the schools for HI and MR possess moderate level of self awareness in knowing the feelings and their impact on actions (S.No.4) and, in feeling good about themselves while looking at their both good and bad points (S.No.10). The teachers working for the VI children possess high level of self-awareness in these aspects. In the other self-awareness aspects such as: continuing to act on their beliefs even under criticism (S.No.7) and in defending while receiving negative feedback (S.No.2), the teachers working for HI and MR possess low level of self-awareness whereas, the teachers working for the children with VI possess moderate level of self-awareness in these aspects. The teachers working for the children with HI and VI possess high level of self-awareness by knowing their priorities clearly (S.No.8), while the other category of teachers working for the children with MR possess moderate level of self-awareness in these aspect. Similarly, in aspect of being happy while looking at the things (S.No.11), the teachers working in the schools for HI and MR possess high level while the teachers working for the children with HI possess moderate level of self-awareness. Further, in knowing their own feelings (S.No.3), only the teachers working for HI children possess high level of self-awareness while the teachers working for MR exhibit low level of self-awareness and the teachers working for VI have moderate level of self-awareness.

The demands placed on the special education teacher in current climate are increasing and at the same time, it is changing to a greater extent. In order to meet these challenges they should effectively manage their own emotions. The teachers, who can manage their own as well as students emotions while teaching, can create a more open and effective teaching and learning environment with fewer distractions. Similarly, those who can control their emotional reactions and effectively influence how others feel can deal better with difficult conversations with parents and administrators. In addition, managing their own time, monitoring and assessing their own performance in order to take corrective action, initiating novel ideas and taking up new assignments, changing the ideas based on the goals, understanding the implications of new ideas for both current and future problem-solving and decision-making skills will help the special educators to organize, plan and prioritize their work demands in a comprehensive manner.

In the dimension 'self-management', the teachers working for the children with HI, MR and VI evince moderate level of EI in aspects such as controlling their anger (S.No. 13), being patient (S.No.14), having presence of mind (S.No. 15), ability in changing ideas and goals based on new information (S.No. 16), taking calculated risks to reach the goals (S.No. 22), initiating action to create possibilities for the future (S.No. 23), optimistic behaviour (S.No. 25) and in achieving small goals (S.No. 26). In other aspects such as; maintaining the standards of honesty and integrity (S.No. 21) and, in organizing the work environment (S.No. 28), the teachers working for the children with HI and MR exhibit moderate level of self-management skills while, the teachers in schools for visually impaired children possess high level of self-managing skills. Likewise, the teachers working in MR and VI schools possess moderate level of self-management skills of behaving quietly in stressful situations (S.No.17) and in acting on their own values in risky and challenging situations (S.No.27), whereas the teachers from the schools of HI possess low level of self management skills on the same aspect. Similarly, by feeling easy on occasions where new ideas and information are to be accepted (S.No. 18), the teachers working in the schools for HI and MR possess moderate level, whereas the teachers working in the school for VI exhibit low level of this self-management skill. Further, the teachers working in the schools for HI, MR and VI possess high level of self management skills by doing their duties with responsibility and commitment (S.No. 20). Contrary to this, in admitting the mistakes publicly (S.No. 19), the teachers working in the schools for HI and MR children possess low level, whereas, the teachers working for the VI children demonstrate moderate level of self-management skills. Further, the teachers working in the schools for MR and VI exhibit low level of initiative skills in taking up new assignments (S.No. 24), whereas the teachers working for HI children possess moderate level of initiative skills.

Special educators should be aware of the people's reactions and their emotions. Also, they should pay full attention to understand the reason for others actions and emotions. Social awarenes helps the special educators to identify the educational needs of the students and developing formal educational or training programmes or classes, teaching or instructing parents of the students with disabilities, selecting and using training/instructional methods and procedures appropriate for the situation while learning or teaching new things. Special educators should observe and receive information from all relevant sources to be socially aware of the issues related to the profession.

Table 5.3 : Mean Emotional Intelligence Scores and Level of Emotional Intelligence of Teachers Working in the Special Education Schools for HI, MR and VI

S.No.	Dimensions of Emotional Intelligence	HI (n = 72)		MR (n = 64)		VI (n = 66)		School Together (n = 202)	
		MEI	LEI	MEI	LEI	MEI	LEI	MEI	LEI
1	2	3	4	5	6	7	8	9	10
	I. Self Awareness								
1.	I am able to identify and separate my emotions	3.44	M	3.48	M	3.65	M	3.52	M
2.	I am defensive when I am receiving negative feedback	2.89	L	3.20	L	3.32	M	3.13	L
3.	I am unaware of my own feelings	3.92	H	3.14	L	3.48	M	3.53	M
4.	I know how feelings impact my own actions	3.76	M	3.72	M	4.03	H	3.84	M
5.	I acknowledge my own strengths and weaknesses	3.38	M	3.80	M	3.85	M	3.66	M
6.	My ability of self-evaluation has helped me to overcome many difficult situations	3.61	M	3.22	L	3.64	M	3.50	M
7.	I can continue to do what I believe in, even under severe criticism	3.14	L	3.03	L	3.55	M	3.24	M
8.	I know my priorities very clearly	3.96	H	3.77	M	4.00	H	3.91	H
9.	In many times, I don't feel good about myself	3.65	M	3.03	L	3.80	M	3.50	M

...(Contd.)

1	2	3	4	5	6	7	8	9	10
10.	Looking at both my good points and bad points, I feel good about myself	3.72	M	3.50	M	4.15	H	3.79	M
11.	I am happy with the way I look at the things	4.04	H	3.97	H	3.80	M	3.94	H
12.	I feel confident that I can deliver the goods the expectations in my job	3.57	M	3.45	M	3.79	M	3.60	M
	II. Self-management								
13.	It is a problem for me to control my anger	3.36	M	3.63	M	3.42	M	3.47	M
14.	In many times, I am impatient	3.53	M	3.63	M	3.65	M	3.60	M
15.	I have presence of mind in any situation	3.54	M	3.59	M	3.58	M	3.57	M
16.	I can change my ideas and goals based on new information to fit into the situation	3.86	M	3.52	M	3.58	M	3.66	M
17.	I can behave calmly even in stressful situations	3.13	L	3.56	M	3.32	M	3.33	M
18.	I feel restless on occasions when new ideas and information are to be accepted	3.24	M	3.33	M	2.89	L	3.15	L
19.	I admit my mistake publicly when it demands	3.04	L	2.97	L	3.39	M	3.13	L
20.	I am not able to do the duties entursted to me with responsibility and commitment	3.94	H	3.92	H	3.94	H	3.94	H
21.	I am able to maintain the standards of honestry and integrity	3.58	M	3.81	M	3.91	M	3.76	M
22.	I take calculated risks to reach the goals	3.58	M	3.52	M	3.67	M	3.59	M

...(Contd.)

1	2	3	4	5	6	7	8	9	10
23.	I initiate actions to create possibilities for the future	3.44	M	3.28	M	3.56	M	3.43	M
24.	I hesitate to take up new assignments	3.35	M	3.08	L	3.11	L	3.18	L
25.	My optimism motivates me to overcome any hurdless and go forward	3.31	M	3.30	M	3.77	M	3.46	M
26.	I find it difficult to reach even small things	3.50	M	3.72	M	3.77	M	3.66	M
27.	I always act on my own values even when there is a significant risk	3.17	L	3.41	M	3.41	M	3.32	M
28.	I am organized in my work	3.86	M	3.78	M	4.17	H	3.94	H
	III. Social Awareness								
29.	I am sensitive to the feelings of others	3.50	M	3.63	M	3.39	M	3.50	M
30.	It is hard for me to see people suffer	3.71	M	3.58	M	4.02	H	3.77	M
31.	I won't interfere in other feelings and help them to overcome	3.10	L	3.27	M	3.42	M	3.26	M
32.	I am able to confront with the un-ethical actions of others	3.13	L	3.00	L	3.44	M	3.19	L
33.	I listen attentively to the school needs	3.92	H	3.81	M	4.17	H	3.97	H
34.	I am capable of using equipments to cater to the needs of the students with special needs	3.93	H	3.80	M	4.38	H	4.03	H
35.	I make myself available to the students and parents even out of office hours when they are in need	3.83	M	3.69	M	4.23	H	3.92	H

...(Contd.)

1	2	3	4	5	6	7	8	9	10
36.	In many times, I feel it difficult in making the curriculum to relate the diverse background of special needs students	3.21	L	3.25	M	2.89	L	3.12	L
37.	In many situations, I understand the organizational values and un-spelt out rules	3.18	L	3.48	M	3.44	M	3.36	M
38.	I always work by understanding the organizational financial constraints and act accordingly	3.65	M	3.38	M	3.77	M	3.60	M
39.	I always recognize the forces in the school and work to meet the requirements of the job	3.58	M	3.36	M	3.56	M	3.50	M
40.	I am not fully aware of the Infrastructure facilities available in the School	3.44	M	3.48	M	3.30	M	3.41	M
	IV. Social Skills								
41.	I can encourage colleagues to work even when things are not favourable	3.63	M	3.61	M	3.32	M	3.52	M
42.	I don't insist the students to learn what they lack	2.61	L	2.56	L	2.47	L	2.55	L
43.	I appreciate others for their success	4.22	H	3.95	H	4.38	H	4.19	H
44.	I try to provide on going mentoring or coaching to my colleagues	3.72	M	3.55	M	3.41	M	3.56	M
45.	It is easy for me to make friends	3.96	H	4.06	H	4.17	H	4.06	H

...(Contd.)

1	2	3	4	5	6	7	8	9	10
46.	I don't get along with others easily in work situations	3.25	M	3.11	L	3.73	M	3.36	M
47.	I feel it difficult to seek help from others when needed	3.26	M	2.94	L	3.64	M	3.28	M
48.	I interact well with the students and parents and provide guidance and counselling	4.11	H	4.03	H	4.06	H	4.07	H
49.	I maintain good relations and co-operate with the school personnel	4.31	H	4.03	H	4.06	H	4.14	H
50.	I can lead others by setting an example	3.94	H	3.83	M	3.83	M	3.87	M
51.	I have clear ideas to realize the vision of the school, I am working	3.83	M	3.55	M	3.83	M	3.74	M
52.	I try to be away from the conflict situations	2.50	L	2.66	L	2.38	L	2.51	L
53.	I always like to be the active partner in solving the conflicts in my school	3.40	M	3.67	M	3.27	M	3.45	M
54.	I engage myself in quarrel when things have not favoured me	3.43	M	3.20	L	3.62	M	3.42	M
55.	I will always try new methods and techniques to make all the students learn effectively	3.72	M	3.86	M	3.82	M	3.80	M
56.	I will not convince by appealing to the students and parents interest	3.36	M	3.02	L	3.55	M	3.31	M

1	2	3	4	5	6	7	8	9	10
57.	I believe that working with group leads to failure	3.75	M	3.47	M	3.89	M	3.71	M
58.	I establish and maintain close relationship with other professionals at work	3.65	M	4.06	H	3.70	M	3.80	M

Note: Level of Emotional Intelligence

1. Low : Values 3.22 and below
2. Moderate : Values from 3.21 to 3.89
3. High : Values 3.90 and above

With regard to the dimension of 'social awareness', the teachers working in the schools for HI, MR and VI exhibit moderate level of social awareness skills in being sensitive to the feelings of others (S.No.29), working by understanding the organizational financial constraints and acting (S.No.38), recognizing the forces in the school and working to meet the requirements of the job (S.No.39) and being aware of the infrastructure facilities available in the schools (S.No.40). In the other social awareness skills like—empathetic feeling (S.No.30) and service orientation (S.No.35), the teachers working in the schools for VI possess high level of competency in these skills whereas, the teachers working in the schools for HI and MR exhibit moderate level of competency in these aspects. Also, in listening attentively to the school needs (S.No.33) and ability in using equipments to cater to the needs of the students with special needs (S.No.34), the teachers in schools for HI and VI exhibit high level of social awareness skills, whereas the teachers working in the schools for MR exhibit moderate level. Likewise, in aspects such as—teachers ability of interfering in others feeling and helping others to overcome the problem (S.No.31) and the ability of understanding the organizational values and un-spelt out rules (S.No.37), the teachers working in the schools for MR and VI have exhibited moderate level whereas, the teachers working in HI schools have exhibited low level in the above aspects. In confronting with the un-ethical actions of others (S.No.32), the teachers working in the schools for HI and MR have demonstrated low level while the teachers in VI schools has evinced moderate level of social awareness. For teachers working in the schools for HI and VI, it is very difficult to design the curriculum to meet the diverse needs of students (S.No.36), as they exhibit low level of mean scores (HI: 3.21; and VI : 2.89) and at the same time teachers working for MR children evince moderate level of mean scores (MR: 3.25).

The social skills are essential to the special educators as it helps them to develop constructive and cooperative working relationships with others and maintain them over time, meet parents to discuss their children's progress and to determine priorities for their children and their resource needs, work in groups with parents, administrators, testing specialists, social workers, and professionals to develop individualized educational plans which should be designed to promote students educational, physical, and social development, analyze information and evaluate results to choose the best solution and solve problems, communicate effectively to meet the needs of the stakeholders and provide personal assistance, medical attention, emotional support, or other personal care to the stakeholders (such as co-workers, parents, students).

With regard to the dimensions 'social skills', the teachers working for the children with VI, MR and HI exhibit moderate level of social skills in six aspects i.e. encouraging colleagues (S.No.41), providing on going mentoring / coaching to colleagues (S.No.44), having clear ideas to realize the vision of the school (S.No.51), being active partner in solving the conflicts (S.No.53), trying new methods and techniques in teaching-learning process (S.No.55) and believing in team work (S.No.57). In the aspects such as - insisting students to learn what they lack (S.No. 42) and trying to be away from the conflict situations (S.No.52), the teachers working in all the three categories (HI, MR and VI) of schools exhibit low level of social skills. Contrary to this, the teachers working in all the three categories of schools have demonstrated high level of social skills in four aspects such as appreciating others for their success (S.No.43), making friends easily (S.No.45), interacting well with the students, parents and providing guidance and counselling (S.No.48) and maintaining good relations and co-operating with the school personnel (S.No.49). In aspects such as - getting along with others easily in work situations (S.No.46), seeking help from others (S.No.47), engaging in quarrel (S.No.54) and convincing to the students and parents interest (S.No.56), the teachers working for the children with HI and VI exhibit moderate level of social skills, whereas the teachers working in the schools for MR children exhibit low level of social skills. The teachers working in the schools for mentally retarded children possess high level of social skills and the teachers working in the schools for HI and VI possess low level of social skill in establishing and maintaining close relationship with other professionals at work (S.No.58). The mean emotional intelligence score of the aspect teaching others by setting an example (S.No.50) is high i.e. 3.94 for the teachers working in the schools for HI, while the teachers working for MR and VI children exhibit moderate level in these aspect.

From the above, it is concluded that out of 28 personal competencies listed under self awareness and self management dimensions, the teachers working in the special schools possess moderate level of EI in 20 aspects *(self awareness—S.No. 1, 3, 4, 5, 6, 7, 9, 10 and 12; self management—S.No. 13, 14, 15, 16, 17, 21, 22, 23, 25, 26 and 27)*, whereas they evince only low level of EI in 4 aspects *(self awareness—S.No. 2; self management—S. No.18, 19 and 24)* and high level of EI in the rest of the 4 aspects *(self awareness - S.No. 8 and 11; self management—S. No. 20 and 28)*. Likewise, in social competencies, out of 30 aspects, the special education teachers have demonstrated moderate level of EI in 19 aspects *(social awareness—S.No. 29, 30, 31, 38, 37, 39 and 40, social skills—41, 44, 46, 47, 50, 51, 53, 55, 57, 54, 58 and 56)* and low level of EI in 4 aspects *(social awareness—S.No. 32 and 36, social skills—S.No. 42 and 52)*. Contrary to this, on 7 aspects *(social awareness—S.No. 33, 34 and 35*, social skills—*S.No. 43, 45, 48 and 49*), their EI is at high level.

Sources and the Level of Occupational Stress of Special Education Teachers Working in Different Types of Special Schools

One of the major objectives of the study is to find out the level of occupational stress of special education teachers working in the schools for HI, MR and VI. Also, this study attempts to identify the potential sources of stress in special education teachers. The potential sources of stress may be due to different sources like organizational structure and climate, personal and professional efficiency, intra and interpersonal relationships and environmental factors. To identify the level of occupational stress of teachers working in different types of special schools, mean and SD for each stressor of the occupational stress dimensions have been calculated for the whole sample of teachers and the teachers working—school-wise. By using mean ± 1SD, the low, moderate and high stressors have been identified. The same is presented in Table 5.4. *(See on page 174 to 178)*

It is a known fact that the nature of organization structure and climate plays a vital role in promoting job involvement in the employees. This is also true with regard to the teachers working in the special schools. The stressors like role ambiguity, role conflict, little or no participation in decision making, stringent rules and regulations, resource constraints, problematic instructional assignments and arrangements and, behaviour constraints in organizational structure and climate evoke occupational stress in special educators.

From table 5.4, it is clear that the long working hours and expectations to do more work (S.No.1), lack of equipments and teaching-learning materials (S.No.6), inadequate supportive staff (S.No.7), problematic individualized educational plan for pupils with multiple disabilities (S.No.8), inadequate trained human resources (S.No.9), lack of time to pay individual attention (S.No.11), stringent rules and regulations in the school (S.No.15) are the major stressors for the teachers working in the schools for VI, as their mean occupational stress scores fall under high level category; whereas for the teachers working in the schools for HI and MR, they are the moderate stressors as their mean OS scores fall under moderate level category. For teachers working in the schools for MR and VI, the stressors such as—carrying multiple responsibilities (S.No.2) and taking responsibilities of others (S.No.16) are creating high level of stress, whereas for the teachers working in the schools for HI,

S.No. 2 and 16 cause moderate level of stress. Likewise, role conflict in their profession (S.No.4) and the large class size with diverse needs students (S.No.10) create high level of stress among teachers working in the schools for HI and VI. The same stressors have created only moderate level of stress among teachers working in the schools for MR. The stressor 'working on assignments that are unnecessary to their profession' (S.No.5) has generated moderate level of stress in all the teachers working in the schools for HI, MR and VI children, as the mean occupational stress scores fall under moderate level category. The teachers working in the schools for hearing impaired feel that lack of information in carrying out the professional responsibilities (S.No.3) has evoked high level of stress among them, while the teachers working for VI and MR have felt that it has evoked only moderate level of stress in them. Similarly, the stressor 'lack of opportunities for promotion' (S.No.13) has produced moderate level of stress in teachers working in the schools for HI and VI, whereas it has evoked high level of stress in teachers working in the schools for MR. Inadequate salary (S.No.14) is not a major source of stress for teachers working in the schools for VI, as their mean occupational stress score fall under low level category. But, it has generated moderate level of stress among teachers working in the schools for HI and MR. High level of stress is experienced by the teachers working in the schools for VI, as they are not involved in the decision making process in their profession (S.No.12). Contrary to this, the teachers working in the schools for MR have experienced low level of stress due to this stressor and the teachers working for the HI have experienced moderate level of stress.

The various aspects related to the personal and professional efficiency are also the sources of stress in special education teachers. The aspects such as—inadequate personal and professional training, poor self-efficacy and management and, technological advancement in special education field generate stress in special educators. In this dimension, the stressors such as—the teachers being over qualified to perform the job (S.No.21), facing problems in decision making process (S.No.26) and difficulty in completing the task within a stipulated period of time (S.No.27) have evoked moderate level of stress in the teachers working in all the three categories (HI, MR and VI) of schools. Similarly, moderate level of stress has been generated in teachers working in the schools for VI by the stressors such as—difficulty in managing students (S.No.24) and difficulty in solving the problems (S.No.25), whereas the same stressors have produced only low level of stress in teachers working in the schools for HI and MR. Also, the teachers working in the schools for VI have experienced high level of stress due to lack of opportunities for professional enhancement in the form of participation in professional meetings/seminars/conferences (S.No.18), inadequate knowledge in using aids and appliances (S.No.19) and difficulty in implementing new procedures and policies (S.No.28), while the teachers working in the schools for HI and MR experience only moderate level of stress due to these stressors. High level of stress is evoked in the teachers working in the schools for MR and VI due to thrust on the development of curricular innovations and materials (S.No.20) and the same stressor has triggered only moderate level of stress in teachers working in the schools for HI.

The other stressors such as—inadequate training in special education (S.No.17) and, problem in identification and assessment procedures (S.No.23) have generated high level of stress among teachers working in the schools for VI. On the other hand, the same aspect has created only low level of stress in teachers working for HI children. The stressor 'lack of commitment and interest to perform the job' (S.No.22) is not the major source of stress for teachers working in the schools for HI, MR and VI as their mean occupational stress score fall under low categories.

Different aspects of intra and inter personal interactions like negative feelings of special education teachers, strained relationship with colleagues, students, parents, administration and para-professionals construct stress in special education teachers. From table 5.4, it is clear that the teachers working in the schools for MR and HI have experienced moderate level of stress due to: being angry with the students for their continuous failure (S.No.34) and difficulty to satisfy the requirements of the management (S.No.36), while the same aspects have triggered only low level of stress in teachers working for the hearing impaired children as their mean occupational stress scores fall under the low level category. High level of stress has been experienced by the teachers working in the schools for VI as they had stressful interactions with parents and did not get adequate support from the parents (S.No.32) and also received poor quality of feedback and supervision that address their concerns (S.No.39).

Conversely, the same stressors have produced low level of stress in teachers working for the children with mental retardation. At the same time, it has generated moderate level of stress in teachers working in the schools for HI. The stressor difficulty in discussing the failure of students with their parents (S.No.40) has created moderate level of stress in teachers working in all the three categories of schools. Lack of team work and professional collaboration to meet the divergent needs of children (S.No.33) is the major source of stress among teachers working in the schools for VI, whereas it has created moderate level of stress in teachers working in the schools for HI and MR. Similarly, teachers working in the schools for HI and MR felt that understanding the behaviour of the

Table 5.4 : Mean Occupational Stress Scores and Levei of Occupational Stress of Teachers Workineg in the Special Education Schools for HI, MR and VI

S.No.	Dimensions of Occupational Stress	HI (n = 72)		MR (n = 64)		VI (n = 66)		School Together (n = 202)	
		MOS	LOS	MOS	LOS	MOS	LOS	MOS	LOS
1	2	3	4	5	6	7	8	9	10
	I. Organizational Structure and Climate								
1.	Long working hours and expectations to do more work	3.00	M	2.73	M	3.77	H	3.17	H
2.	Carrying multiple responsibilities in a short span of time	2.85	M	3.34	H	3.73	H	3.29	H
3.	Lack of information in carrying out the professional responsibilities	3.08	H	2.67	M	2.97	M	2.92	M
4.	Receive conflicting requests from two or more people that differ with the realities of daily professional life	3.24	H	2.73	M	3.23	H	3.07	H
5.	Working on assignments that are not necessary to the profession	2.46	M	2.55	M	2.85	M	2.61	M
6.	Lack of equipments and teaching-learning materials	2.60	M	2.45	M	3.56	H	2.87	M
7.	Inadequate supportive staff in the school	2.63	M	2.81	M	3.48	H	2.97	M
8.	Problematic IEP for pupil with multiple disabilities	3.00	M	2.81	M	3.68	H	3.16	H

...(Contd.)

1	2	3	4	5	6	7	8	9	10
9.	Inadequate trained human resources to carry out the work assigned	2.43	M	2.86	M	3.55	H	2.93	M
10.	Large class size with diverse needs students	3.24	H	2.70	M	3.68	H	3.21	H
11.	Lack of time to pay individual attention to each special need student	3.01	M	2.77	M	3.89	H	3.22	H
12.	Lack of involvement in the decision making process of the activities related to the profession	2.54	M	2.23	L	3.21	H	2.66	M
13.	Lack of opportunities for promotion in the school	2.92	M	3.16	H	2.92	M	3.00	M
14.	Inadequate salary for the work done in the school	2.58	M	2.72	M	2.20	L	2.50	M
15.	Stringent rules and regulations in the school that hinders to act independently	2.43	M	2.92	M	3.47	H	2.93	M
16.	Taking responsibility for the activities of others	2.79	M	3.38	H	3.36	H	3.16	H
	II. Personal and Professional Efficiency								
17.	Inadequate special education training to meet the demands of the profession	2.72	M	2.34	L	3.61	H	2.89	M
18.	Lack of opportunities for professional enhancement in the form of participation in professional meetings / seminars / conferences	2.75	M	2.69	M	3.76	H	3.06	H

...*(Contd.)*

1	2	3	4	5	6	7	8	9	10
19.	Inadequate knowledge in using new aids and appliances	2.78	M	2.84	M	3.53	H	3.04	H
20.	Thrusting on development of curricular innovations and materials	2.71	M	3.17	H	3.56	H	3.13	H
21.	Over qualified to perform the job	2.53	M	2.72	M	2.45	M	2.56	M
22.	Lack of commitment and interest to perform the job	2.32	L	2.25	L	1.95	L	2.18	L
23.	Problem in identification and assessment procedures	2.82	M	2.36	L	3.42	H	2.87	M
24.	Difficulty in managing students in the classroom	2.35	L	2.34	L	3.03	M	2.57	M
25.	Difficulty in solving the problems that arise out of my work	2.33	L	2.31	L	2.67	M	2.44	M
26.	Face problems in decision making process	2.60	M	2.80	M	2.97	M	2.78	M
27.	Unable to complete the task within a stipulated period of time	2.49	M	2.56	M	2.70	M	2.58	M
28.	Difficult to implement new procedures and policies in the place of those already in practice	2.53	M	2.69	M	3.36	H	2.85	M
	III. Intra and Interpersonal Interactions								
29.	Difficult to adjust with the fellow teachers in the school	2.22	L	2.33	L	1.94	L	2.16	L

...(Contd.)

1	2	3	4	5	6	7	8	9	10
30.	Lack of healthy interactions between / among the teachers	2.13	L	2.28	L	2.17	L	2.19	L
31.	Inadequate knowledge to provide guidance and counselling to the students and parents	2.13	L	2.19	L	2.15	L	2.15	L
32.	Stressful interactions with parents and lack of parental support	2.57	M	2.33	L	3.23	H	2.71	M
33.	Lack of teamwork and professional collaboration to meet the diverse needs of children	2.49	M	2.39	M	3.11	H	2.66	M
34.	Angry with the students for their continuous failure	2.26	L	2.41	M	2.89	M	2.51	M
35.	Difficulty arising out in understanding the students behaviour	2.04	L	2.22	L	2.58	M	2.27	L
36.	Difficult to satisfy the requirements of the management	2.25	L	2.58	M	3.00	M	2.60	M
37.	Misunderstood the organizational values and goals	2.14	L	2.34	L	2.17	L	2.21	L
38.	Lack of pro-active communication with the school management	2.28	L	2.39	M	2.03	L	2.23	L
39.	Poor quality of feedback and supervision that address teacher concerns	2.50	M	2.36	L	3.09	H	2.65	M
40.	Difficult to discuss the failure of students with their parents	2.39	M	2.45	M	2.83	M	2.55	M

...(Contd.)

1	2	3	4	5	6	7	8	9	10
	IV. Environmental Factors								
41.	Bullying and frightening by the students inside and outside the school	2.11	L	2.56	M	2.47	M	2.37	M
42.	Complaints by the students	2.31	L	2.77	M	2.55	M	2.53	M
43.	Complaints by other staff members	2.44	M	2.92	M	2.73	M	2.69	M
44.	Problems with students indiscipline	2.43	M	2.78	M	3.53	H	2.90	M
45.	Seldom opportunity to utilize the abilities and experience independently	2.51	M	3.34	H	3.39	H	3.06	H
46.	Lack of respect for the special education professionals by the pupils, parents and the society	2.38	M	2.75	M	2.58	M	2.56	M
47.	Seldom rewarded for the hard labour and efficient performance	2.93	M	3.03	H	3.58	H	3.17	H
48.	Problem with the theft and damage of the property by the students	2.42	M	2.61	M	2.58	M	2.53	M
49.	Problem faced with drug abuse by the students	2.13	L	2.80	M	2.21	L	2.37	M
50.	Problem arising out of fraud and financial mismanagement within the school	1.90	L	2.45	M	2.14	L	2.15	L
51.	Polluted working environment	1.93	L	2.33	L	2.18	L	2.14	L
52.	Difficult to solve students disputes	1.92	L	2.36	L	2.68	M	2.31	L

Note : Level of Occupational Stress
1. Low : Values 2.36 and below
2. Moderate : Values from 2.37 to 3.03
3. High : Values 3.04 and above

students is not a difficult task (S.No.35), as the mean occupational stress scores falls under low category. But at the same time, the teachers working in the schools for VI felt that the same stressor has created moderate level of stress in them. Lack of pro-active communication with the school management (S.No.38) was not a major source of stress for teachers working in the schools for HI and VI, as the mean occupational stress scores fall under low level category, but the mean occupational stress scores of the same aspect is 2.39 showing moderate level of stress among teachers working in the schools for MR.

Further, the stressors such as difficult in adjusting with the colleagues (S.No.29), lack of healthy interactions between the teachers (S.No.30), inadequate knowledge to provide guidance and counselling to the students and parents (S.No.31) and misunderstanding the organizational values and goals (S.No.37) have caused only low level of stress in teachers working in all the three categories of schools as their mean occupational stress scores fall under low level only.

The environmental factors such as violence and danger caused by the pupils and co-workers in their work environment, reward structure and recognition by the management, negative publicity by the society and, physical working conditions trigger stress among special educators. The teachers working in the schools for HI, MR and VI felt that complaints by the staff members (S.No.43), lack of respect for the special education professional by the pupils, parents and the society (S.No.46) and, the problem with the theft and damage of the property by the students (S.No.48) have produced only moderate level of stress among them, whereas the same teachers felt that 'polluted working environment' (S.No.51) has triggered only low level of stress in them. But the stressors such as—seldom opportunity to utilize the abilities and experience independently (S.No.45) and seldom reward for the hard labour (S.No.47) have generated high level of stress among teachers working in the schools for MR and VI, whereas the same stressors have evoked only moderate level of stress among teachers working in the schools for HI. Likewise, the teachers working in the schools for the VI face problems due to students indiscipline (S.No.44) and experience high level of stress, while the teachers in other two categories (HI and MR) experience only moderate level of stress due to students indiscipline. Similarly, moderate level of stress is experienced by the teachers working in the schools for MR and VI due to the complaints made by the students (S.No.42) and, bullying and frightening by the students inside and outside the school (S.No.41), whereas the teachers working for HI children face only negligible amount of stress due to these aspects, as the mean occupational stress scores fall under low category. Similarly, the teachers working in the schools for HI and VI have not faced the problem of students drug abuse (S.No.49) and fraud and financial mismanagement within the school (S.No.50), whereas the teachers from the schools for mentally retarded experience moderate level of stress. Problems in solving students disputes (S.No.52) is not a major source of stress to the teachers working in the schools for the VI and MR, but the same aspect generates moderate level of stress in teachers working for the visually impaired children.

Analyzing the special teachers together in the dimension 'organizational structure and climate', out of sixteen stressors the teachers experience high level of stress due to seven stressors *(S.No. 1, 2, 4, 8, 10, 11 and 16)*. The remaining 9 stressors *(S.No. 3, 5, 6, 7, 9, 12, 13, 14 and 15)* have generated only moderate level of stress in them. Further, the eight aspects in personal and professional efficiency dimension *(S.No. 17, 21, 23, 24, 25, 26, 27 and 28)* have evoked moderate level of stress, while *S.No. 22* has generated only low level of stress in special education teachers. In contrast, the three stressors *(S.No. 18, 19, and 20)* have emerged as potential stressors that triggered high level of stress in them. Correspondingly, the stressors mentioned in *S.No. 32, 33, 34, 36, 39 and 40* have generated moderate level of stress, whereas the stressors in *S.No. 29, 30, 31, 35, 37 and 38* have evoked only low level of stress in teachers under intra and interpersonal dimensions. In the dimension of environmental factors, the two aspects *(S.No. 45 and 47)* have evoked high level of stress, while in seven aspects *(S.No. 41, 42, 43, 44, 46, 48 and 49)* the teachers experience moderate level of stress. In remaining three aspects *(S.No. 50, 51 and 52)*, the teachers experience low level of stress.

Level of Job Satisfaction of Special Education Teachers Working in Different Types of Special Schools

The quality of special education depends on the quality and competence of the special educators. In order to retain competitive special education teachers, one has to look into the organizational aspects, intra and interpersonal relationships, motivational climate and, job security and financial status. Organizational aspects refer to how best the school provides the comfortable working environment by giving supportive services and resources. Intra and interpersonal relationships refer to how meaningfully the teachers develop personal relationships with the co-workers, parents and students, which in turn, act as a yardstick for their job satisfaction. Motivational climate for the teachers in the form of rewards, opportunity for promotions, appreciation etc., for the work done play a vital role for job satisfaction of teachers. Further, job security and financial status which gives satisfaction to the teachers in terms of salary, job security and status is also one of the deciding factors of job satisfaction. Table- 5 illustrates the mean job satisfaction score and level of job satisfaction of special education teachers working in the special schools for HI, MR, VI and special schools as a whole.

From Table—5.5, *(See on page 182 to 186)* it is clear that the teachers working in the schools for MR are least satisfied with the organizational aspects such as conflicts in the school that makes them annoyed and embarrassed (S.No.2), lack of proper facilities to prepare materials (S.No.5), inadequate classroom facilities (S.No.6), excess workload (S.No.9), trouble in maintaining discipline in the classroom (S.No.11) and non-participation in the policy formulation (S.No.10). At the same time, the teachers working in the schools for HI and VI are satisfied moderately in the above said organizational aspects. The teachers working in all the three categories of schools are satisfied moderately with the sufficient time they received for rest and recreation (S.No.8). Though the teachers working in the schools for HI and VI are highly satisfied with the working environment (S.No.1), the teachers working for the MR children are least satisfied with their working environment as the mean job satisfaction scores (3.16) fall under low level category. The in-service training received by the teachers (S.No.3) working in the schools for HI and MR make them highly satisfied in their job as it had helped them to perform their job, whereas, it has given only moderate level of job satisfaction to the teachers working in the schools for VI. The teachers working in the schools for HI felt that they had freedom to express their ideas (S.No.4) and because of that they are highly satisfied, with their job than the teachers working in the schools for MR and VI who are moderately satisfied in this aspect. The leave rules in the schools (S.No.7) for MR are flexible as the teachers working in that schools are highly satisfied while the teachers working in the schools for HI and VI are moderately satisfied with the leave rules in their schools. The mean job satisfaction scores of the aspect 'opportunities for promotion in the school' (S.No.12) fall under low level category for the teachers working in the schools for MR and VI. This shows that the teachers are least satisfied with the promotional opportunities in their school, whereas the teachers working in the schools for HI are moderately satisfied in this aspect.

Under the dimension 'intra and interpersonal relationships', it is clearly observed that the teachers working in all the three categories of schools are moderately satisfied in making adjustments in their job as a special education teacher (S.No.13), co-operation and support from the colleagues (S.No.17) and believing people in the job to discuss the

Table 5.5 : Mean Job Satisfaction Scores and Level of Job Satisfaction of Teachers Working in the Special Education Schools for HI, MR and VI

S.No.	Dimensions of Job Satisfaction	HI (n = 72)		MR (n = 64)		VI (n = 66)		School Together (n = 202)	
		MJS	LJS	MJS	LJS	MJS	LJS	MJS	LJS
1	2	3	4	5	6	7	8	9	10
	I. Organizational Aspects								
1.	I am comfortable with a favourable environment provided to perform my work as a special educator	4.15	H	3.16	L	4.03	H	3.80	M
2.	Conflicts arising in my school make me annoyed and embarrassed.	3.26	M	3.06	L	3.36	M	3.23	M
3.	In service training I received in and out of my school helps me to perform my job	3.88	H	3.89	H	3.45	M	3.74	M
4.	I have the freedom to express my ideas for betterment of the school and students	3.85	H	3.39	M	3.74	M	3.67	M
5.	I face problems in preparation of materials due to lack of proper facilities	3.54	M	2.92	L	3.42	M	3.31	M
6.	Inadequate classroom facilities	3.47	M	2.98	L	3.47	M	3.32	M
7.	I am happy with the leave rules of my school	3.54	M	3.86	H	3.64	M	3.67	M
8.	I get sufficient time for rest and recreation	3.32	M	3.41	M	3.44	M	3.39	M
9.	Excess workload leads me to dissatisfaction with my job	3.82	M	3.03	L	3.64	M	3.51	M

...(Contd.)

1	2	3	4	5	6	7	8	9	10
10.	In the policy formulation except the principal/ head teachers, other teachers are not involved	3.47	M	2.98	L	3.21	M	3.23	M
11.	Maintaining discipline and order in the class troubles me	3.89	M	2.91	L	3.55	M	3.47	M
12.	I feel that I have more opportunities for promotion in the school in which I am working	3.43	M	3.11	L	3.11	L	3.22	M
	II. Intra and Interpersonal Relationships								
13.	I make adjustments to my job, as a special education teacher	3.72	M	3.64	M	3.82	M	3.73	M
14.	I always make group relationship with the job personnel's that is needed for my job	3.85	H	3.72	M	3.94	H	3.84	H
15.	The meaningful interpersonal relationships maintained with the students make me satisfied	4.07	H	3.72	M	3.89	H	3.90	H
16.	The Principal helps to improve my personal skills and also maintain good relationships	3.85	H	3.38	M	2.92	L	3.40	M
17.	Lack of cooperation and support from the colleagues makes me embarrassed	3.42	M	3.44	M	3.73	M	3.52	M
18.	Most of the people at my workplace mis-understand me	3.85	H	3.58	M	4.06	H	3.83	M
19.	Students often approach me to discuss their difficulties	3.94	H	3.61	M	3.36	M	3.65	M

...(Contd.)

1	2	3	4	5	6	7	8	9	10
20.	I sometimes feel that there is none in my profession with whom I can confide	3.44	M	3.23	M	3.23	M	3.31	M
21.	The emotional support provided by the colleagues and subordinates working in my field helps me to perform my job better	3.86	H	3.55	M	3.88	H	3.77	M
22.	Students give more respect and expect more attention towards them	4.06	H	3.72	M	3.50	M	3.77	M
	III. Motivational Climate								
23.	I am often rewarded for my individual work	3.51	M	3.27	M	2.59	L	3.13	L
24.	My attitude towards my job and towards life in general is satisfactory	3.96	H	3.58	M	4.05	H	3.87	H
25.	I am often motivated which activates and directs me to perform my job perfectly	3.88	H	3.33	M	3.50	M	3.58	M
26.	The rewards provided for my job motivates me to perform my tasks well	3.72	M	3.06	L	2.45	L	3.10	L
27.	I receive adequate feedback from my Principal to improve myself in the working situation	3.74	M	3.27	M	2.92	L	3.32	M
28.	The adequate opportunities for advancement and growth also motivate me to perform my job	3.68	M	3.14	L	2.71	L	3.19	M
29.	I generally feel tired after returning from my school	2.53	L	2.50	L	2.83	L	2.62	L

...(Contd.)

1	2	3	4	5	6	7	8	9	10
30.	I feel that I have less job involvement	3.81	M	3.38	M	3.62	M	3.61	M
31.	My seniors appreciate my academic knowledge and abilities	3.67	M	3.28	M	2.92	L	3.30	M
32.	I often receive perks for the job well done	3.25	M	3.02	L	2.33	L	2.88	L
33.	I perform the work expected from me devotedly	4.01	H	3.59	M	3.70	M	3.78	M
34.	I derive personal satisfaction with the service I render	4.04	H	3.84	H	3.83	H	3.91	H
35.	I derive great degree of interest from my job	4.06	H	3.84	H	3.85	H	3.92	H
36.	I feel I have selected the right job for myself	4.17	H	4.00	H	3.91	H	4.03	H
	IV. Job Security and Financial Status								
37.	I receive an adequate salary for the work done	3.72	M	2.88	L	3.91	H	3.51	M
38.	Grants for the development of the school are usually inadequate	3.17	L	2.44	L	3.15	L	2.93	L
39.	For the sake of higher salary, I am prepared to change my profession	3.92	H	3.39	M	3.45	M	3.60	M
40.	I am allowed to expose my talents and skills in my job, which leads to personal satisfaction	3.86	H	3.63	M	3.85	H	3.78	M

...(Contd.)

1	2	3	4	5	6	7	8	9	10
41.	I derive self-respect from my profession	3.88	H	3.98	H	3.64	M	3.83	M
42.	I usually think that I earn less as a special educator when compared to the earnings in other profession	3.57	M	2.78	L	3.61	M	3.33	M
43.	I feel in-secured in my job	3.79	M	3.25	M	3.79	M	3.62	M
44.	I occasionally feel like giving up this job and taking up some other job	4.06	H	2.98	L	3.79	M	3.63	M
45.	The temporary nature of my job in the school frequently gives insecure feelings	3.97	H	3.05	L	3.11	L	3.40	M
46.	Salary in special education field are inadequate compared to general education	3.10	L	2.34	L	2.55	L	2.68	L

Note : Level of Job Satisfaction
Low : Values 3.17 and below; *Moderate :* Values from 3.18 to 3.82; *High :* Values 3.83 and above

confidential issue (S.No.20). Further, the teachers working in the schools for HI and VI are highly satisfied with the group relationships with the job personnel's (S.No.14), relationships with the students (S.No.15), better understanding by the people (S.No.18) and the emotional support provided by the colleagues and subordinates (S.No.21); whereas, the teachers working for the mentally retarded children are moderately satisfied in these aspects. High level of job-satisfaction is experienced by the teachers working in the schools for HI, as the students approach them to discuss their difficulties (S.No.19) and students give respect and expect more attention towards them (S.No.22); whereas, moderate level of job satisfaction has been felt by the teachers working for the children with MR and VI. The principals helping tendency in improving the personal skills and their relationship with the teachers (S.No.16) working in the special schools for HI made them highly satisfied. Conversely, teachers working for the VI children are least satisfied with the principal's relationship, while the teachers working for the MR children are moderately satisfied.

In any organization good motivational climate facilitates job satisfaction in the employees. This is also true with respect to the special schools. The study revealed that the teachers working in all the three categories of schools are highly satisfied with their job as they derive personal satisfaction with the service they are rendering (S.No.34), and evince great degree of interest (S.No.35) in the job, they have selected (S.No.36) and, are moderately satisfied with their job involvement (S.No.30). Low level of job satisfaction is observed in teachers working in the schools for VI because of the lack of reward for the individual work from the school (S.No.23), inadequate feedback from their principal for their improvement (S.No.27) and lack of appreciation for the academic knowledge and abilities from the seniors (S.No.31); while the teachers working for the HI and MR children demonstrate moderate level of job satisfaction on these aspects. The teachers working in the schools for MR and VI are dissatisfied with their job as they are not motivated by providing rewards (S.No.26), the teachers are not given adequate opportunities for the advancement and growth (S.No.28) and are not given any perks for their achievement (S.No.32) consequently their mean job satisfaction scores fall under low level category. In case of teachers working for HI children, these aspects have created moderate level of job satisfaction.

Likewise, in S.No. 25, the teachers working in the schools for MR and VI are moderately satisfied as the school management often motivates them which activates and directs them to perform their job, but the teachers in the schools for HI are highly satisfied with this aspect. Further, it is observed that the teachers working for the HI children perform their work with devotion (S.No.33) that makes them highly satisfied, whereas the same aspect has created moderate level of job satisfaction in teachers working in the schools for MR and VI. Also, it is interesting to note the low mean job satisfaction scores of teachers working in all the three categories of schools where they feel tired after returning from their schools (S.No.29), indicating their low level of job satisfaction. The optimistic attitude possessed by the teachers working in the schools for HI and VI towards their job (S.No.24) made them highly satisfied with their job. In case of the teachers working for the MR children, the same aspect has given only moderate level of job satisfaction.

In the dimension 'job security and financial status', the teachers working in the schools for HI and VI have enjoyed the freedom of exposing their talents and skills in their job (S.No.40), as the mean job satisfaction scores fall under high level category and the teachers working in the schools for MR children have enjoyed only moderate level of freedom on this aspect. Similarly, teachers working in the schools for HI and MR have derived high level of self-respect from their profession (S.No.41), while the teachers from the schools for VI felt that they receive only moderate level of self-respect from their profession. The teachers working in the schools for the MR children are least satisfied with the salary they are receiving (S.No.37), as the mean job satisfaction scores fall under low level category. Conversely, the teachers working for the children with VI are satisfied with their salary as their mean job satisfaction scores fall under high level category. On the other hand, the teachers working for HI children are moderately satisfied in this aspect as their mean job satisfaction scores fall under moderate level category. Interestingly, it is noted that the teachers working in all the three categories of special schools have low level of job satisfaction because of the inadequate grants for the development of the school (S.No.38) and inadequate salary received in special education field while comparing with the salary of the general educators (S.No.46). Furthermore, the teachers from all the three categories of special schools felt that they enjoy moderate level of job security (S.No.43) from their profession because of the temporary nature of their job. Job satisfaction of teachers working in the schools for HI is high as they intended to continue in their same profession and have not felt like changing their profession for the sake of high salary (S.No.39). Contrary to this, only moderate level of satisfaction is experienced on this aspect by the teachers working in the schools for MR and VI. The temporary nature of the job (S.No.45) has caused low level of job satisfaction among teachers working in the schools for MR and VI. Conversely, the same aspect has created high level of job satisfaction in teachers working in the schools for HI. High level of job satisfaction is enjoyed by the teachers working in the schools for HI as they occasionally feel like giving up their job and taking up some other job (S.No.44).

The teachers working in the schools for MR children felt low level of job satisfaction on the same aspect, whereas the teachers from VI schools felt moderate level of job satisfaction. Further, the teachers from the schools of MR felt that they earn less as special educators compared to the earnings in other profession (S.No.42) and as a result they are least satisfied with this aspect, whereas the teachers from other two categories of schools (HI and VI) are moderately satisfied in the above said aspect (i.e. S.No.42).

When special education teachers working in special schools as whole are taken into account, the teachers are moderately satisfied in all the organizational aspects *(S.No. 1, 2, 3, 4, 5, 6, 7, 8, 9, 10, 11 and 12)*. Similarly, in the second dimension i.e. intra and interpersonal relationships, out of 10 aspects the teachers are moderately satisfied in 8 aspects *(S.No. 13, 16, 17, 18, 19, 20, 21 and 22)*, while highly satisfied in the remaining two aspects *(S.No. 14 and 15)*. In the dimension 'motivational climate' the teachers are least satisfied in four aspects *(S.No. 23, 26, 29 and 32)*, moderately satisfied in six aspects *(S.No. 25, 27. 28, 30, 31 and 33)* and, highly satisfied in four aspects *(S.No. 24, 34, 35 and 36)*. In 'job security and financial status' dimension, out of 10 aspects, the teachers are least satisfied with two aspects *(S.No. 38 and 46)* and in the remaining eight aspects *(S.No. 37, 39, 40, 41, 42, 43, 44 and 45)*, their satisfaction is at moderate level.

PART—II : DIFFERENTIAL ANALYSIS

Effect of Age, Community, Educational Qualification, Nature of Special School the Teachers Working in, Training Received in Special Education, Level of Classes Handled, Nature of Job, Years of Experience and Salary on EI, OS and JS of Special Education Teachers

In order to study the significant difference between two and more than two group of samples, differential studies are made. One of the major objectives of the study is to find out the significant differences, if any in the special education teachers emotional intelligence, occupational stress and job satisfaction due to variations in their independent variables.

To know the significant differences, if any, in the emotional intelligence of special education teachers due to variations in their age, community, educational qualification, nature of special school the teachers working in, training received in special education, level of classes handled, nature of job, years of experience and salary, mean and SD have been calculated for each group in the variable. Based on the mean and SD's, t / F- values have been worked out to know the significant differences in the emotional intelligence of the special education teachers. The same procedure is adopted for occupational stress and job satisfaction of special school teachers. The obtained results are presented in Tables—5.6 to 5.14.

Effect of 'Age' of Special Education Teachers on their Emotional Intelligence, Occupational Stress and Job Satisfaction

The mean, SD of the emotional intelligence, occupational stress and job satisfaction scores of teachers with three different age groups working in three different types of special schools and the calculated F-values are presented in Table—5.6. Table 5.6 clearly reveals that the teachers working in the schools for MR significantly differ in their emotional intelligence as the calculated F-values is significant (6.06) at 0.01 level. This shows that the variations in age of teachers working in the schools for MR have brought significant differences in their emotional intelligence. *Thus the stated hypothesis, 'there is a significant difference in the emotional intelligence of the special education teachers due to variations in their age' is accepted with respect to the teachers working in the schools for MR.* The mean values also reveal that the teachers belonging to the age group of 46 years and above possess more emotional intelligence (208.90) followed by the teachers belonging to the age group of 31-45 years (205.19) and the age group of below 30 years (189.65). The present findings support the results of the study by Singh and Koteswari (2006) on managers and, Amirtha and Kadhiravan (2006) on regular school teachers where the variations in their age have brought significant differences in their emotional intelligence. On the other hand, the age group has not significantly influenced the emotional intelligence of teachers working in the schools for HI (0.65), VI (0.25) and special schools as a whole (1.49). This shows that the variations in the age group of teachers working in the schools for HI, VI and special schools as a whole have not brought any significant difference in their emotional intelligence. *Hence, the above stated hypothesis is rejected in case of the teachers working in the schools for HI and VI.* Similar findings were observed in the study conducted by Pathan (2004) and Salami (2007) where the secondary school teacher's age did not have significant bearing on their emotional intelligence.

Table 5.6 : Mean and SD Scores of EI, OS and JS of Teachers working in Special Education Schools for HI, MR and VI with respect to their Age and the Calculated F-values

Teachers Age Group	Emotional Intelligence			Occupational Stress			Job Satisfaction		
	Mean	SD	Cal. F-values	Mean	SD	Cal.F-values	Mean	SD	Cal. F-values
HI									
30 yrs and below (n=10)	211.90	14.74		137.30	21.42		174.80	15.20	
31-45 yrs (n=36)	203.31	17.50	**0.65@**	127.47	17.23	**0.71@**	170.69	10.96	**0.59@**
46 yrs and above (n=26)	205.69	27.15		132.08	32.91		169.19	16.70	
MR									
30 yrs and below (n=17)	189.65	21.42		147.06	33.24		150.71	26.57	
31-45 yrs (n=27)	205.19	17.13	**6.06****	134.19	28.65	**1.66@**	155.85	22.13	**0.68@**
46 yrs and above (n=20)	208.90	14.95		131.90	17.81		148.20	20.69	
VI									
30 yrs and below (n=15)	211.73	9.74		161.47	11.59		159.13	9.12	
31-45 yrs (n=27)	209.93	14.70	**0.25@**	152.56	23.60	**0.81@**	158.26	17.88	**0.02@**
46 yrs and above (n=24)	211.67	15.17		151.96	30.71		158.25	15.51	
SAW									
30 yrs and below (n=42)	202.83	19.50		149.88	25.86		159.45	21.07	
31-45 yrs (n=90)	205.86	16.64	**1.49@**	137.01	25.13	**3.42***	162.51	18.16	**0.64@**
46 yrs and above (n=70)	209.00	20.35		138.84	29.75		159.44	19.29	

Note : ** Significant at 0.01 level; * Significant at 0.05 level; @ Not significant at 0.05 level

Similarly, occupational stress of special education teachers has not been significantly influenced by the variations in the age groups of teachers working in the schools for HI, MR and VI as their F-values (0.71, 1.66 and 0.81 respectively) are not significant at 0.05 level. It means, the teachers working in each of these schools with different age groups do not significantly vary in their occupational stress levels. *Hence, the stated hypothesis 'there is a significant difference in the occupational stress of special education teachers due to variations in their age group' is rejected in case of teachers working in the schools for HI, MR and VI.* These findings are in line with the findings of the study conducted by Pisanti (2003) and Reddy (2007) where the occupational stress of secondary school teachers and the special education teachers teaching visually impaired and hearing impaired respectively did not vary significantly due to variations in the age group. In contrast to the above findings, the occupational stress of special education teachers working in the special schools as a whole are influenced by their varied age groups as the F-value 3.42 is significant at 0.05 level. It means the teachers working in special schools together with different age groups vary in their occupational stress levels. Also, it is noted that the teachers belonging to the age group 30 years and below have higher occupational stress compared to their counterparts with age group 46 years and above and, 31-46 years. The results of the study conducted by Reddy (2007) with respect to the teachers working in the schools for HI children, Paulse (2005) on teachers involved in inclusive education, Mokdad (2005) on primary school teachers, Suryanarayana (2009) on secondary school teachers, Rajeswari et al. (2008) on regular and special education teachers and Chandraiah (1993) on college teachers are in line with the present findings where the respective teachers age group has significant bearing on their occupational stress level.

The F-values with respect to the job satisfaction of teachers working in the schools for HI (0.59), MR (0.68), VI (0.02) and special schools as a whole (0.64) are less than the table value indicating the non-influence of age group on teacher's job satisfaction. *Hence, the stated hypothesis 'there is a significant difference in the job satisfaction of special education teachers due to variations in their age group' is rejected.* The results of the study by Reddy (2007), Reddy and Poornima (2009) are in line with the above findings where the special education teachers job satisfaction do not differ significantly due to the variations in their age group. Also, the findings of the study by Rao and Sridhar (2003) and, Crossman and Harris (2006) corroborate with the present findings where the age has not made any significant difference in secondary school teachers job satisfaction, though opposed by the results of Ghazi (2005) and, Platsidou and Agaliotis (2008) where the age group had significantly influenced job satisfaction of elementary head teachers and primary school teachers.

From the above, it is concluded that the variations in the age group has not significantly influenced emotional intelligence, occupational stress and job satisfaction of special education teachers and teachers working in special schools as a whole, except the teachers working in the schools for MR with respect to emotional intelligence and teachers working in special schools as a whole with respect to occupational stress only. Further, lower the age group, lower will be the emotional intelligence of teachers working in the schools for MR children and the teachers of 30 years and below age group experience higher levels of occupational stress followed by teachers belonging to 46 years and above and, 31 to 45 years of age group.

Effect of 'Community' of Special Education Teachers on their Emotional Intelligence, Occupational Stress and Job Satisfaction

Table 5.7, exemplify the mean and SD of the emotional intelligence, occupational stress and job satisfaction scores of special education teachers with varied community background and calculated F-values. The stated hypothesis *'there is a significant difference in the emotional intelligence, occupational stress and job satisfaction of special education teachers due to variations in their community'* is accepted with respect to the emotional intelligence of teachers working in the schools for MR children only. It means, the community of the teachers working in the schools for MR has significant bearing on their emotional intelligence. The obtained F-value (4.39) is significant at 0.05 level, indicating the clear variations in the emotional intelligence scores of OC, BC and MBC/SC & ST community teachers. The mean values, further show that the teachers belonging to BC community possess higher emotional intelligence (Mean value : 207.05) followed by OC teachers (Mean value : 201.27) and MBC/SC & ST teachers (Mean value :190.67).

On the other hand, the emotional intelligence, occupational stress and job satisfaction of teachers working in other categories of special schools have not been significantly influenced by the nature of community of the teachers rejecting the above stated hypothesis. The above findings are in agreement with the findings of Upadhyaya (2008) and Reddy (2007), Reddy and Poornima (2009) where the occupational stress of student teachers, special education teachers teaching VI, HI and MR children respectively did not vary due to variations in their community. Similarly, the results with respect to JS are in line with the findings of the study by Reddy (2007) where the community of teachers working in the schools for MR and OH children has not significantly

Table 5.7 : Mean and SD Scores of EI, OS and JS of Teachers working in Special Education Schools for HI, MR and VI with respect to their Community and the Calculated F-values

Teachers Community	Emotional Intelligence			Occupational Stress			Job Satisfaction		
	Mean	SD	Cal. F-values	Mean	SD	Cal.F-values	Mean	SD	Cal. F-values
HI									
OC (n=18)	208.94	26.67		127.28	23.51		167.72	19.20	
BC (n= 43)	204.14	19.28	**0.34@**	133.12	27.24	**0.62@**	171.14	12.74	**0.75@**
MBC / SC & ST (n=11)	204.27	19.18		125.55	10.60		174.00	3.38	
MR									
OC (n=11)	201.27	21.78		140.09	28.81		160.64	24.06	
BC (n= 38)	207.05	17.25	**4.39***	131.42	25.8	**2.23@**	153.47	23.82	**2.30@**
MBC / SC & ST (n=15)	190.67	17.67		148.40	128.43		142.33	16.47	
VI									
OC (n=15)	208.27	15.26		149.80	22.37		153.53	18.16	
BC (n= 41)	212.02	13.60	**0.50@**	155.49	26.41	**0.34@**	160.98	13.85	**1.57@**
MBC / SC & ST (n=10)	213.10	12.82		156.60	20.35		155.50	14.94	
SAW									
OC (n=44)	206.80	21.86		138.16	25.93		161.11	20.65	
BC (n= 122)	207.70	17.09	**1.80@**	140.11	28.52	**0.41@**	162.22	18.60	**1.65@**
MBC / SC & ST (n=36)	201.06	19.06		143.69	24.95		155.67	18.73	

Note : *Significant at 0.05 level; @ Not significant at 0.05 level

influenced their job satisfaction though the result was not supported by the findings of the study by Gakhar et al. (2005) where the community of teachers teaching normal children significantly influenced their job satisfaction. It means, variations in the community has not brought any significant difference in emotional intelligence, occupational stress and job satisfaction of teachers working either in any school or special schools as a whole, except emotional intelligence in case of teachers working in the schools for MR children.

From the above, it is summed up that the variable 'community' has not significantly influenced the emotional intelligence, occupational stress and job satisfaction of special education teachers, except the emotional intelligence of teachers working in the schools for MR children. The BC community teachers demonstrated higher EI than their counterparts with OC and MBC/SC & ST communities.

Effect of 'Educational Qualifications' of the Special Education Teachers on their Emotional Intelligence, Occupational Stress and Job Satisfaction

The mean and SD of the emotional intelligence, occupational stress and job satisfaction scores of special education teachers with different educational qualifications and the respective F-values are presented in table 5.8.

In table 5.8, it is clear that the obtained F-values with respect to emotional intelligence scores of teachers working in the schools for MR (4.27) and special schools as a whole (4.35) are significant at 0.05 levels.

This indicates that the teachers working in the schools for MR and special schools as a whole with different educational background are significantly varied in their emotional intelligence. The results of the study corroborate with the findings of the studies by Neelakandan (2007) on primary school teachers, Amirtha and Kadhiravan (2006) and Salami (2007) on secondary school teachers, where the educational qualification has influenced their emotional intelligence. Further, the educational background of teachers working in the schools for HI and VI does not influence their emotional intelligence, as the calculated F-values 2.78 and 2.97 are not significant at 0.05 level. *Hence the formulated hypothesis 'there is a significant difference in the emotional intelligence of special education teachers due to variations in their educational qualifications' is accepted only with respect to the teachers working in the schools for MR and special schools as a whole and rejected for the teachers working in the schools for HI and VI.*

Table 5.8 : Mean and SD Scores of EI, OS and JS of Teachers working in Special Education Schools for HI, MR and VI with respect to their Educational Qualification and the Calculated F-values

Teachers Educational Qualification	Emotional Intelligence			Occupational Stress			Job Satisfaction		
	Mean	SD	Cal. F-values	Mean	SD	Cal.F-values	Mean	SD	Cal. F-values
HI									
Teacher Training (n=30)	208.87	13.87		135.73	19.90		173.80	9.78	
Graduation with B.Ed. (n=28)	198.32	21.18	**2.78@**	131.25	29.51	**2.72@**	168.86	14.86	**1.32@**
Graduation with B.Ed and M.Ed. (n=14)	211.93	29.90		117.79	18.26		167.86	18.08	
MR Teacher Training (n=32)	195.59	18.99		137.31	29.73		151.16	23.54	
Graduation with B.Ed. (n=22)	208.32	17.09	**4.27***	137.86	27.53	**0.10@**	157.23	22.66	**1.25@**
Graduation with B.Ed and M.Ed. (n=10)	210.00	17.89		133.40	21.20		143.80	20.06	
VI									
Teacher Training (n=33)	210.61	11.69		159.03	14.81		158.97	13.56	
Graduation with B.Ed. (n=16)	206.31	14.69	**2.97@**	144.75	23.07	**1.88@**	161.06	12.37	**0.69@**
Graduation with B.Ed and M.Ed. (n=17)	217.47	15.13		154.35	36.95		155.00	20.18	
SAW									
Teacher Training (n=95)	205.00	16.46		144.36	24.59		161.02	19.02	
Graduation with B.Ed. (n=66)	203.59	18.76	**4.35***	136.73	27.54	**1.98@**	163.09	17.89	**1.44@**
Graduation with B.Ed and M.Ed. (n=41)	213.76	21.56		136.76	31.87		156.66	21.12	

Note : * Significant at 0.05 level; * Significant of 0.05 level, @ Not significant at 0.05 level

Moreover, the mean emotional intelligence scores of teachers working in MR schools reveal that the teachers having graduation with B.Ed. and M.Ed. possess high emotional intelligence (4.27) followed by teachers having graduation with B.Ed. (208.32) and teacher training (195.59) qualification. In case of teachers from the special schools as a whole, the teachers having graduation with B.Ed. and M.Ed. possess more emotional intelligence as they possess higher mean values of 213.76 followed by the teachers having teacher training (205.00) and teachers having graduation with B.Ed. (203.59) qualification. This trend of results indicates that higher the educational qualification, the better will be the emotional intelligence.

The F-values with respect to the occupational stress and job satisfaction of teachers working in the schools of HI (2.72 and 1.32 respectively), MR (0.10 and 1.25), VI (1.88 and 0.69) and special schools as a whole (1.98 and 1.44) are not significant at 0.05 level indicating that educational qualification of teachers has not any significant bearing on their occupational stress and job satisfaction. *Hence, the formulated hypothesis, 'there is a significant difference in the special education teachers occupational stress and job satisfaction due to variation in their educational qualification' is rejected with respect to the teachers working in all types of special schools.* Though the present findings are not in line with the findings of Suryanarayana (2009) who found that the educational qualification of secondary school teachers had significant bearing on their occupational stress, the findings of the results by Reddy (2007) confirm the above findings where the educational qualification of special education teachers teaching mentally retarded, orthopaedically handicapped and multiple disabled children has not influenced their occupational stress and job satisfaction.

From the above, it is concluded that the variable 'educational qualification' of teachers has significantly influenced the emotional intelligence of teachers working in the schools for MR and special schools as a whole. On the other hand, it has not significantly influenced the emotional intelligence of teachers working in the schools for HI and VI. Higher the educational qualifications, the higher will be the emotional intelligence of teachers working in the schools for MR and special schools as a whole. Contrary to the above, the variations in the educational qualification of teachers working in all types of special schools has not significantly influenced their occupational stress and job satisfaction.

Effect of 'Nature of Special Schools the Teachers Working in' on Special Education Teachers Emotional Intelligence, Occupational Stress and Job Satisfaction

Table 5.9, presents the mean and SD of the emotional intelligence, occupational stress and job satisfaction scores of teachers with respect to

Table 5.9 : Mean and SD Scores of the EI, OS and JS of Teachers Working in the Special Education Schools for HI, MR and VI and the Calculated F-values

	HI (n=72)		MR (n=64)		VI (n=66)		Cal. F-values
	Mean	SD	Mean	SD	Mean	SD	
Emotional Intelligence	205.36	21.12	202.22	19.12	211.33	13.77	4.16 *
Occupational Stress	130.50	24.45	136.89	27.46	154.36	24.51	15.98 **
Job Satisfaction	170.72	13.78	152.09	22.85	158.45	15.20	19.94**

Note : **Significant at 0.01 level
*Significant at 0.05 level

the nature of special schools the teachers working in and the calculated F-values.

Table 5.9 clearly reveals that the obtained F-value with respect to the emotional intelligence (4.16) is significant at 0.05 level and F-values with respect to the occupational stress (15.98) and job satisfaction (19.94) are significant at 0.01 level. It means, variations in nature of special schools have brought significant difference in the emotional intelligence, occupational stress and job satisfaction of teachers. *Hence, the stated hypothesis 'there is a significant difference in the emotional intelligence, occupational stress and job satisfaction of teachers due to variations in the nature of special schools (HI, MR and VI) they are working' is accepted.* Further, the mean values with respect to the emotional intelligence of teachers working in different types of schools clearly reveal that the teachers working in the schools for children with VI possess high emotional intelligence (Mean value :211.33) followed by the teachers working in the schools for HI (Mean value : 205.36) and schools for MR (Mean value : 202.22).

In occupational stress too, the teachers working in the schools for VI experience more stress (Mean value: 154.36) followed by the teachers working in the schools for MR (Mean value :136.89) and HI (Mean value :130.50). The teachers working in the schools for VI possess high level of EI and experience high level of OS, in other categories of teachers the trend is in reverse order. Indepth studies are needed to ascertain the factors contributing to this trend. Furthermore, the teachers working in the schools for HI enjoy high level of job satisfaction (Mean value :170.72), followed by the teachers working in the schools for VI (Mean value :158.45) and MR (Mean value :152.09).

From the above, it can be concluded that the variable 'nature of special schools the teachers working in' has significant influence on their emotional intelligence, occupational stress and job satisfaction. Further, the teachers working in the schools for children with VI possess high emotional intelligence and experience more occupational stress than their counterparts working in the schools for HI and MR. On the other hand, the teachers working for HI children have higher levels of job satisfaction than the teachers working in the schools for VI and MR.

5.3.5 Effect of 'Training Received in Special Education' on the Special Education Teachers Emotional Intelligence, Occupational Stress and Job Satisfaction

Table 5.10, shows the mean and SD of the emotional intelligence, occupational stress and job satisfaction scores of teachers with respect to their training in special education and the calculated t-values.

Table 5.10 : Mean and SD Scores of EI, OS and JS of Teachers working in Special Education Schools for HI, MR and VI with respect to the Training they Received in Special Education and the Calculated t-values

Training in Special Education	Emotional Intelligence			Occupational Stress			Job Satisfaction		
	Mean	SD	Cal. t-values	Mean	SD	Cal. t-values	Mean	SD	Cal. t-values
HI									
Diploma in Special Education (n=52)	205.90	22.65		133.13	26.18		169.60	14.48	
B.Ed. in Special Education (n=20)	203.95	16.95	**0.35@**	123.65	18.04	**1.49@**	173.65	11.61	**1.12@**
MR									
Diploma in Special Education (n=43)	202.30	16.56		138.74	29.58		152.95	22.90	
B.Ed. in Special Education (n=21)	202.05	23.99	**0.05@**	133.10	22.69	**0.77@**	150.33	23.21	**0.43@**
VI									
Diploma in Special Education (n=51)	211.57	13.61		157.92	23.74		156.00	13.79	
B.Ed. in Special Education (n=15)	210.53	14.78	**0.25@**	142.27	23.94	**2.24***	166.80	17.21	**2.52***
SAW									
Diploma in Special Education (n=146)	206.82	18.39		143.45	28.41		159.95	18.56	
B.Ed. in Special Education (n=56)	205.00	19.40	**0.62@**	132.18	22.36	**2.67****	163.07	20.60	**1.04@**

Note : **Significant at 0.01 level; *Significant at 0.05 level; @Not significant at 0.05 level

In table 5.10, it is clear that the obtained t-values with respect to the emotional intelligence of teachers working in the schools for HI (0.35), MR (0.05), VI (0.25) and special schools as a whole (0.62) are not significant at 0.05 level. It means that the variations in the special education training received by the teachers working at different types of special schools have not significantly influenced their emotional intelligence. *Hence the formulated hypothesis, 'there is a significant difference in the emotional intelligence of teachers due to variations in the training received in special education' is rejected.*

On the other hand, the occupational stress of teachers working in the schools for VI and special schools as a whole vary significantly due to variations in the training they received in special education as the calculated t-values 2.24 and 2.67 are significant at 0.05 and 0.01 levels respectively. Similar type of results was observed from the findings of the study by Reddy (2007) and Paulse (2005) where the training received in special education has significantly influenced the occupational stress of teachers working in the schools for MR children and teachers involved in inclusive education respectively. Thus the variable 'nature of training received in special education' has significantly influenced the occupational stress of teachers working in the schools for VI and special schools as a whole, while the same variable has not significant bearing on the occupational stress of teachers working in the schools for HI and MR as their calculated F-values (1.49 and 0.77) are not significant at 0.05 levels. *Hence the stated hypothesis, 'there is a significant difference in the occupational stress of special education teachers due to variations in the training received in special education' is accepted in case of teachers working in the schools for VI and special school as a whole and rejected with respect to the teachers working in the schools for HI and MR.*

Further, the mean values of the teachers working in the schools for VI and special schools as a whole show that the teachers with Diploma in Special Education have higher occupational stress levels (157.92 and 143.45) than the teachers with B.Ed. in Special Education (142.27 and 132.18). This trend indicates that the teachers who received higher professional training like B.Ed. in Special Education have lower occupational stress than their counterparts who pursued only Diploma in Special Education.

Similarly, the job satisfaction of teachers working in the schools for VI differs significantly due to the influence of training they received in special education. This can be observed by the calculated t-value (2.52), which is significant at 0.05 level. Also, the teachers who acquired B.Ed. in Special Education enjoy higher levels of job satisfaction than those with Diploma in Special Education. This can be seen by the mean values of teachers having B.Ed. Special Education (166.80) and teachers having

Diploma in Special Education (156.00). At the same time, the calculated t-values reveal that the job satisfaction of teachers working in the schools for HI (1.12), MR (0.43) and the special schools as a whole (1.04) are not significant at 0.05 level. This indicates the non-influence of the variable 'training in special education' on their job satisfaction. *Hence the formulated hypothesis, 'there is a significant difference in the job satisfaction of special education teachers due to variations in the training received in special education' is accepted in case of teachers working in the special schools for VI and the same is rejected with respect to the teachers working in the schools for HI, MR and the special schools as a whole.* The present findings are in agreement with the results of the study by Reddy (2007) on special education teachers teaching children with VI, HI, MR, OH and, Rao and Sridhar (2003) on teachers teaching secondary school students where their job satisfaction has not significantly differed due to the training they received.

From the above, it is summed up that, the variable 'training received in special education' by the teachers working in all type of special schools has not significantly influenced their emotional intelligence, whereas, it has significantly influenced the occupational stress of teachers working in the schools for VI and special schools as a whole, but has not influenced the teachers working in the schools for MR and HI. Similarly, the job satisfaction of teachers working in the schools for VI differed significantly because of the training they received in special education, whereas it has not influenced the job satisfaction of teachers working in the schools for HI, MR and special schools as a whole. Further, the teachers working in the schools for VI, who received higher order of professional training like B.Ed. in Special Education has lower occupational stress and enjoys higher job satisfaction than their counterparts who have received only Diploma in Special Education.

Effect of the 'Level of Classes Handled' by the Special Education Teachers on their Emotional Intelligence, Occupational Stress and Job Satisfaction

Table 5.11, depicts the mean and SD of the emotional intelligence, occupational stress and job satisfaction scores of teachers handling various levels of classes in special schools and the calculated F-values.

From table 5.11, the calculated F-values with respect to the emotional intelligence of teachers working in the schools for HI (1.37) and VI (0.73) are not significant at 0.05 level. It means, the level of classes handled by the special education teachers working in the schools for HI and VI has not significantly influenced their emotional intelligence, while it has significant influence on the emotional intelligence of the teachers

Table 5.11 : Mean and SD Scores of EI, OS and JS of Teachers working in Special Education Schools for HI, MR and VI with respect to the Level of Classes they Handle and the Calculated F-values

Level of Class the Teachers Handle	Emotional Intelligence			Occupational Stress			Job Satisfaction		
	Mean	SD	Cal. F-values	Mean	SD	Cal. F-values	Mean	SD	Cal. F-values
HI									
Primary (n=30)	208.13	16.27		135.80	19.14		173.07	11.33	
Secondary (n=26)	199.92	22.38	**1.37@**	132.50	30.45	**3.32***	170.15	13.89	**0.96@**
Hr. Secondary (n=16)	209.00	26.17		117.31	18.10		167.25	17.45	
MR									
Primary (n=28)	194.75	16.52		141.54	30.69		147.50	18.03	
Secondary (n=24)	202.04	18.80	**9.25****	139.75	20.27	**2.87@**	154.46	20.96	**1.11@**
Hr. Secondary (n=12)	220.00	14.07		120.33	27.86		158.08	34.17	
VI									
Primary (n=23)	209.17	11.06		158.26	16.15		157.00	12.30	
Secondary (n=27)	211.22	17.14	**0.73@**	156.48	26.13	**1.54@**	158.89	16.99	**0.18@**
Hr. Secondary (n=16)	214.63	10.70		145.19	30.26		159.81	16.51	
SAW									
Primary (n=81)	203.80	16.30		144.16	24.66		159.67	17.86	
Secondary (n=77)	204.55	19.93	**5.06****	143.17	27.72	**5.77****	161.31	18.41	**0.26@**
Hr. Secondary (n=44)	214.05	18.68		128.27	28.30		162.05	22.73	

Note : **Significant at 0.01 level; *Significant at 0.05 level; @ Not significant at 0.05 level

working in the schools for MR and special schools as a whole as their calculated F-values (9.25 and 5.06 respectively) are significant at 0.01 level. *Thus the formulated hypothesis, 'there is a significant difference in special education teachers emotional intelligence due to variations in the level of classes handled' is accepted in case of teachers working in the schools for MR and special schools as a whole and the same is rejected for teachers working in the schools for HI and VI.* The mean values of the teachers working in the schools for MR and special schools as a whole reveal that the teachers handling higher secondary classes possess more emotional intelligence (220.00 and 214.05) than the teachers handling secondary level (202.04 and 204.55) and primary level (194.75 and 203.80) classes.

The occupational stress of teachers working in the schools for MR and VI has not differed significantly due to variations in the level of classes they handled, as the calculated F-values 2.87 and 1.54 respectively are not significant at 0.05 level. This means, the variable 'level of classes handled' does not brought any significant variations in the occupational stress of teachers working in the schools for MR and VI. On the other hand, it has brought significant difference in the occupational stress of teachers working in the schools for HI and special schools as a whole, as the calculated F-values 3.32 and 5.77 are significant at 0.05 and 0.01 levels respectively. *Hence, the stated hypothesis, 'there is a significant differences in the special education teacher's occupational stress due to variations in the level of classes handled' is accepted with respect to teachers working in the schools for HI and special schools as a whole only.*

Further, the mean values for the same indicates that the teachers handling primary classes experience higher level of occupational stress (135.80 and 144.16) followed by the teachers handling secondary classes (132.50 and 143.17) and teachers handling Higher Secondary Levels (117.31 and 128.27). The findings of the study by Paulse (2005), Pratt (1977) and, Borg and Falzon (1991) are similar to the present findings, as the variable level of classes handled brought significant difference in the stress levels of teachers involved in mainstream and special schools. The calculated F-values with respect to the job satisfaction of special education teachers working in the special schools for HI (0.96), MR (1.11), VI (0.18) and special schools as a whole (0.26) are not significant at 0.05 level, indicating the non-influence of the variable 'level of classes handled' on their job satisfaction. It shows that irrespective of the level of classes handled, the special education teacher's job satisfaction is same. So *the stated hypothesis, 'there is a significant difference in special education teachers job satisfaction due to variations in the level of classes handled' is rejected with respect to the teachers working in special schools.*

From the above findings, it can be summed up that, the variable 'level of classes handled' has significantly influenced the emotional intelligence of teachers working in the schools for MR and special schools as a whole and occupational stress of teachers working in the schools for HI and special schools as a whole. Contrary to this, the emotional intelligence of teachers working in the schools for HI and VI, occupational stress of teachers working in the schools for VI and MR and, the job satisfaction of teachers working in all the categories of special schools has not differed significantly due to variations in the level of classes handled by them. Also, the teachers handling higher secondary classes possess higher level of emotional intelligence and experience lower rates of occupational stress than their counterparts who handle secondary and primary level classes.

Effect of the 'Nature of Job' of the Special Education Teachers on their Emotional Intelligence, Occupational Stress and Job Satisfaction

Table 5.12 demonstrates the mean, SD scores of the emotional intelligence, occupational stress and job satisfaction of permanent and temporary teachers working in different categories of special schools and the calculated t-values.

The calculated t-values reveals that the emotional intelligence of teachers working in the schools for HI (4.59), MR (4.31) and special schools as a whole (5.69) differ significantly at 0.01 level due to variations in their nature of job. This shows that the variable 'nature of job' has significantly influenced the emotional intelligence of teachers working in the schools for HI, MR and special schools as a whole. It means the emotional intelligence of permanent and temporary teachers working in the schools for HI, MR and special schools as a whole vary significantly.

Contrary to this, the same has not influenced the emotional intelligence of teachers working in the schools for VI as the calculated t-value is not significant at 0.05 level rejecting the stated *hypothesis, 'there is a significant difference in special education teachers emotional intelligence due to variations in their nature of job' with respect to the teachers working in the schools for VI only.* Furthermore, the mean value reveals that the permanent teachers working in the schools for HI, MR and special schools as a whole possess higher levels of EI (210.53, 207.48 and 210.08 respectively) than their counterparts i.e. temporary teachers (Mean values are 185.33, 186.44

Table 5.12 : Mean and SD Scores of EI, OS and JS of Teachers working in Special Education Schools for HI, MR and VI with respect to their Nature of Job and the Calculated t-values

Nature of Job	Emotional Intelligence			Occupational Stress			Job Satisfaction		
	Mean	SD	Cal. t-values	Mean	SD	Cal. t-values	Mean	SD	Cal. t-values
HI									
Permanent (n=57)	210.53	16.71	**4.59****	130.37	25.54	**0.09@**	171.37	12.56	**0.77@**
Temporary (n=15)	185.33	25.00		131.00	20.52		168.27	18.00	
MR									
Permanent (n=48)	207.48	15.98	**4.31****	129.92	22.21	**3.90****	152.85	23.52	**0.46@**
Temporary (n=16)	186.44	19.50		157.81	31.61		149.81	21.24	
VI									
Permanent (n=57)	212.04	13.90	**0.77@**	153.84	25.89	**0.32@**	157.84	14.51	**0.60@**
Temporary (n=15)	208.93	13.52		156.13	19.77		160.53	17.73	
SAW									
Permanent (n=156)	210.08	15.62	**5.69****	137.90	26.94	**2.35***	161.25	18.87	**0.60@**
Temporary (n=46)	193.54	22.26		148.52	27.17		159.33	20.21	

Note : **Significant at 0.01 level; *Significant at 0.05 level; @ Not significant at 0.05 level

and 193.54 respectively). The t-values related to the occupational stress of teachers working in the schools for MR (3.90) and the special schools as a whole (2.35), are significant at 0.01 and 0.05 level respectively. It reflects that the permanent and temporary teachers in the schools for MR differ in their occupational stress. The findings of the results by Reddy (2007) and Reddy and Poornima (2009) are in tune with the present findings where the nature of job of teachers teaching HI, OH and MR children has significant bearing on their occupational stress. In contrast to the above, the variable 'nature of job' has not influenced significantly the occupational stress of teachers working in the schools for HI and VI, as the calculated t-values (0.09 and 0.32 respectively) are not significant at 0.05 level. Also, the mean values of the teachers working in the schools for MR and special schools as a whole reveal that the teachers in temporary job experience more occupational stress (157.81 and 148.52) than the teachers in permanent job (129.92 and 137.90). *Thus the formulated hypothesis, 'there is a significant difference in the special education teachers occupational stress due to variations in their nature of job is accepted in case of teachers working in the schools for MR and special schools as a whole and rejected with respect to the teachers working in the schools for HI and VI children.*

With regard to job satisfaction, the calculated t-values are not significant at 0.05 levels for the teachers working in HI (0.77), MR (0.46), VI (0.60) and special schools as a whole (0.60). From the above, it can be inferred that permanent and temporary teachers are similar in their level of job satisfaction irrespective of their nature of job. *The result is accepting the stated hypothesis, 'there is a significant difference in the special education teacher's job satisfaction due to variations in their nature of job'*. The findings of Reddy (2007) are in agreement with the present findings where the variable 'nature of job' has not influenced the job satisfaction of teachers working in the schools for VI, HI, MR, OH (orthopaedically handicapped) and MD (multiple disabled) children.

From the above, it can be concluded that the variable 'nature of job' has significantly influenced the emotional intelligence of teachers working in the schools for HI, MR and special schools as a whole and, the occupational stress of teachers working in the schools for MR and special schools as a whole. Contrary to this, it has not influenced the emotional intelligence of teachers working in the schools for VI, occupational stress of teachers working in the schools for HI and VI and, job satisfaction of teachers working in all the categories of special schools. The teachers serving in permanent position possess more emotional intelligence and low level of occupational stress and vice-versa.

Effect of 'Salary of Special Education Teachers' on their Emotional Intelligence, Occupational Stress and Job Satisfaction

Table 5.13 *(See on next page)* illustrates the mean and SD scores of emotional intelligence, occupational stress and job satisfaction of teachers working in different types of special schools and the calculated F-values based on the salary they receive.

The F-values of the emotional intelligence of teachers working in the schools for HI (7.42), MR (8.01) and Special Schools as a Whole (11.64) are significant at 0.01 level, indicating the variations in the emotional intelligence of teachers with varied salary background. This shows the amount of salary, the teachers receive per month has significantly influenced their emotional intelligence. Further, the mean values reveal that the teachers with higher salary possess higher emotional intelligence than their counterparts with lower salary per month. On the other hand, the variation in the monthly salary of teachers has not brought any significant differences in the emotional intelligence of teachers working in the schools for VI as the calculated F-value (0.93) is less than the table value at 0.05 level. *Hence the formulated hypothesis, 'there is a significant difference in special education teachers emotional intelligence due to variations in their monthly salary' is accepted for teachers working in the schools for HI, MR and special schools as a whole only.*

The F-values of occupational stress scores of teachers working in the schools for MR (4.09) are significant at 0.05 level. This indicates that the occupational stress differs due to variations in the monthly salary of teachers. The results of the study by Reddy (2007) are in line with the present findings where the salary has influenced the occupational stress of teachers working in the schools for HI. The mean value depicts that the teachers receiving low salary are with higher occupational stress than their counterparts receiving higher salary with low occupational stress.

Further, the occupational stress of special education teachers working in the schools for HI, VI and special schools as a whole are not significant, as the respective calculated F-values are not significant (1.54, 0.29 and 2.41) at 0.05 level. It means, the occupational stress of teachers working in the schools for HI, VI and special schools as a whole does not differ significantly due to variations in their salary and *the formulated hypothesis 'there is a significant difference in occupational stress of special education teachers due to variations in their monthly salary' is accepted only with respect to the teachers working in the schools for MR.* The calculated F-values for job satisfaction of teachers working in the schools for HI (14.44), MR (3.56)

Table 5.13 : Mean and SD Scores of EI, OS and JS of Teachers working in Special Education Schools for HI, MR and VI with respect to their Monthly Salary and the Calculated F-values

Teachers Salary per Month in ₹	Emotional Intelligence			Occupational Stress			Job Satisfaction		
	Mean	SD	Cal. F-values	Mean	SD	Cal. F-values	Mean	SD	Cal. F-values
HI									
₹ 10,000 and below (n=20)	197.00	27.49		135.85	24.78		158.85	18.71	
₹ 10,001-20,000 (n=40)	203.98	14.59	**7.42****	130.88	21.68	**1.54@**	174.63	6.50	**14.44****
₹ 20,001 and above (n=12)	223.92	17.62		120.33	31.09		177.50	10.48	
MR									
₹ 10,000 and below (n=36)	196.00	19.24		145.14	30.26		151.17	20.34	
₹ 10,001-20,000 (n=17)	204.12	17.12	**8.01****	125.65	21.74	**4.09***	144.47	22.80	**3.56***
₹ 20,001 and above (n=11)	219.64	7.63		127.27	15.06		166.91	25.79	
VI									
₹ 10,000 and below (n=18)	210.72	15.82		157.06	22.46		160.44	15.30	
₹ 10,001-20,000 (n=32)	212.78	13.94	**0.93@**	154.69	25.73	**0.29@**	159.06	16.92	**0.59@**
₹ 20,001 and above (n=16)	209.13	11.26		150.69	25.29		155.00	11.22	
SAW									
₹ 10,000 and below (n=74)	199.85	21.71		145.53	27.84		155.50	19.04	
₹ 10,001-20,000 (n=89)	207.17	15.30	**11.64****	138.44	26.10	**2.41@**	163.27	18.64	**4.82****
₹ 20,001 and above (n=39)	216.64	14.08		134.74	27.94		165.28	18.68	

Note : ** Significant at 0.01 level ; * Significant at 0.05 level ; @ Not significant at 0.05 level

and special schools as a whole (4.82) are greater than the table value (3.07) and significant at 0.01 and 0.05 level. It means, the variations in the salary of teachers working in the special schools for HI, MR and special schools together has brought significant differences in their job satisfaction. The mean values of the job satisfaction scores of teachers working in the schools for HI, MR and special schools as a whole indicates that higher the salary the teacher receives, higher will be the job satisfaction and vice-versa. *Thus the stated hypothesis, 'there is a significant difference in special education teachers job satisfaction due to variations in their salary' is accepted with respect to the teachers working in the schools for HI, MR and special schools as a whole.* The above results substantiate the findings of the study by Reddy (2007) where the job satisfaction differs significantly due to the variations in the salary of teachers working in the schools for HI. On the other hand, it has not influenced the job satisfaction of teachers working in the schools for VI as the calculated F-value (0.59) is not significant at 0.05 level.

To sum up, the variable 'salary of the teachers' has significantly influenced the emotional intelligence of teachers working in the schools for HI, MR and special schools as a whole; whereas, it has not influenced the emotional intelligence of teachers working in the schools for VI. The teachers receiving higher salary possess high level of emotional intelligence and vice-versa. Likewise, the occupational stress of teachers working in the schools for MR is significantly influenced by their salary; whereas, it has not influenced the occupational stress of teachers working in the schools for HI, VI and special schools as a whole. The teachers receiving more than twenty thousand as a monthly salary have low occupational stress rates than their counterparts. The job satisfaction of teachers working in the schools for HI, MR and special schools as a whole is significantly influenced by their salary; whereas, it has not made any significant difference in the job satisfaction of teachers working in the schools for VI. Moreover, the higher the teacher's salary, the better is the job satisfaction of teachers and vice versa.

Effect of 'Years of Experience' of Special Education Teachers on their Emotional Intelligence, Occupational Stress and Job Satisfaction

In table 5.14, the mean and SD of the emotional intelligence, occupational stress and job satisfaction scores of teachers with varied years of experience in special schools are presented along with their respective F-values.

Table 5.14 : Mean and SD Scores of EI, OS and JS of Teachers working in Special Education Schools for HI, MR and VI with respect to their Years of Teaching Experience and the Calculated F-values

Teaching Experience	Emotional Intelligence			Occupational Stress			Job Satisfaction		
	Mean	SD	Cal. F-values	Mean	SD	Cal. F-values	Mean	SD	Cal. F-values
HI									
1-10 yrs (n=24)	200.92	15.34		131.17	17.90		173.13	10.83	
11-20 yrs (n=21)	207.7	18.58	**0.79@**	124.10	18.68	**1.17@**	170.00	13.36	**0.56@**
21 yrs and above (n=27)	1207.48	26.78		134.89	32.05		169.15	16.41	
MR									
1-10 yrs (n=30)	195.53	20.49		140.60	31.90		154.97	24.29	
11-20 yrs (n=23)	206.39	15.23	**4.11***	135.87	25.22	**0.75@**	150.70	22.23	**0.53@**
21 yrs and above (n=11)	211.73	17.36		128.91	16.92		147.18	20.85	
VI									
1-10 yrs (n=31)	212.55	12.49		158.61	19.56		159.97	13.48	
11-20 yrs (n=17)	210.94	14.94	**0.26@**	153.53	24.40	**1.12@**	155.41	18.25	**0.49@**
21 yrs and above (n=18)	209.61	15.31		147.83	31.34		158.72	15.34	
SAW									
1-10 yrs (n=85)	203.26	17.88		144.51	26.56		161.92	18.85	
11-20 yrs (n=61)	208.11	16.22	**2.03@**	136.74	25.38	**1.76@**	158.66	20.05	**0.56@**
21 yrs and above (n=56)	209.00	21.66		137.88	29.90		161.48	18.74	

Note : *Significant at 0.05 level; @ Not significant at 0.05 level

The mean differences in the emotional intelligence scores of teachers working in the schools for MR significantly vary as the calculated F-values (4.11) are greater than the table value (3.04). It means, the emotional intelligence of teachers working in the schools for MR is influenced by the variations in their years of experience. The teachers with 21 and above years of experience (211.73) possess higher levels of emotional intelligence followed by the teachers with 11-20 years (206.39) and teachers with 10 and below years (195.53) of experience. On the other hand, the emotional intelligence of teachers working in the schools for HI, VI and special schools as a whole has not significantly differed due to variations in their years of teaching experience, as the calculated F-values are not significant at 0.05 level. *Thus the hypothesis, 'there is a significant difference in special education teachers due to variations in their years of teaching experience is accepted in case of teachers working in the schools for MR only.* The table also reveals that the F-values related to the occupational stress and job satisfaction of teachers working in the HI (1.17 and 0.56), MR (0.75 and 0.53), VI (1.12 and 0.49) and special schools as a whole (1.76 and 0.56) are not significant at 0.05 level. This indicates the non-influence of the variable 'years of experience' on teacher's occupational stress and job satisfaction.

So, the hypothesis, 'there is a significant difference in special education teacher's occupational stress and job satisfaction due to variations in their years of teaching experience' is rejected. Though the findings of the study by Nelson et al. (2001) differ from the present findings as the variable years of experience has significantly influenced occupational stress of teachers of students with emotional behaviour disorders, the present findings substantiate the results of the study by Reddy (2007) where the years of experience had not significantly influenced the occupational stress and job satisfaction of teachers working for VI, OH, MR and MD children. Also, the present study results confirm the findings of the study by Harris et al. (2009) on speech language pathologists where the years of experience do not influence occupational stress.

In case of job satisfaction, the results of present finding supports the findings of the study by Kumar and Rao (2007), Rao and Sridhar (2003) and, Crossman and Harris (2006) where the teaching experience has not made any significant bearing on the job satisfaction of school teachers and secondary school teachers. Contrary to the above, the findings of the study by Manjunathaiah (2003) are not in tune with the present findings in case of teachers teaching children with VI.

From the above, it can be inferred that the variable 'years of experience' has significantly influenced the emotional intelligence of teachers working in the schools for MR; while the same has not influenced the emotional intelligence of teachers working in the schools for HI, VI and special schools as a whole. The teachers with more years of experience possess higher emotional intelligence than their counterparts with less years of experience. The occupational stress and job satisfaction of teachers working in all the categories of schools have not differed significantly due to variation in their years of experience.

Infrastructure Facilities Available (ISF) in the Special Education Schools as Perceived by the Teachers

One of the main objectives of the study is to identify the infrastructure facilities available in special education schools and to find out the significant differences, if any, in the emotional intelligence, occupational stress and job satisfaction of special education teachers due to variations in the level of infrastructure facilities (ISF) available in the special schools. For identifying the infrastructure facilities in special schools, the perception of the special education teachers working in the respective schools is sought using the Infrastructure Facilities Scale (ISFS). The number and percentage of 202 special education teachers' ratings about the level (poor, moderate and good) of availability of ISF has been worked out and the same is presented in table 5.15. *(See on page 214 and 215)*

Level of ISF in Special Education Schools as Perceived by the Teachers

The special needs children can achieve on par with the normal children. It is not their disabilities that hamper their achievement but the negative attitudes of professionals, parents, teachers and society in general, inaccessibility to education and, inadequate men and material resources that create barriers to the children with special needs. The children with disabilities require accessibility to the special aids and appliances for their daily functioning and learning. Realizing this, the UGC felt the need for ramps, rails and special toilets to suit the special needs of disabled persons and ensured that all existing structures as well as future construction projects in the university/college campuses are made disabled friendly. Also, through HEPSEN (Higher Education for Persons with Disabilities) scheme, they provided access to procure the devices such as low-vision aids, scanners, mobility devices, etc. in the institutes for enriching the educational experiences of persons with disabilities. These facilities are the part and parcel of the special education schools. The special education schools should procure these aids and appliances at any cost to cater to the needs of each child. In special schools or general

Table 5.15 : Number and Percentage of Special Education Teachers Working in the Special Education Schools with Poor, Moderate and Good Infrastructure Facilities

S. No.	Nature of Infrastructure Facilities	Level of ISF available in Special Education Schools as Perceived by the Special Education Teachers		
		Poor ISF	Moderate ISF	Good ISF
1	2	3	4	5
1.	Braille slate and stylus	135 (66.83)	16 (7.92)	51 (25.25)
2.	Magnifying devices and lenses	125 (61.88)	40 (19.8)	37 (18.32)
3.	Large print and coloured print materials	139 (68.81)	26 (12.87)	37 (18.32)
4.	Embossed teaching learning materials	123 (60.89)	43 (21.29)	36 (17.82)
5.	Audio-video instructional materials	82 (40.59)	92 (45.54)	28 (13.86)
6.	Orientation and mobility materials	82 (40.59)	66 (32.67)	54 (26.73)
7.	Ramps / rails and special toilet facilities	85 (42.08)	84 (41.58)	33 (16.34)
8.	Facilities to use Hearing aids and group hearing aids in the classroom	145 (71.78)	8 (3.96)	49 (24.26)
9.	False roofing that facilities to curtail extra noise	190 (94.06)	12 (5.94)	0
10.	Overhead projector	152 (75.25)	23 (11.39)	27 (13.37)
11.	Computer assisted instruction	51 (25.25)	133 (65.84)	18 (8.91)
12.	Physiotherapy and occupational therapy material	137 (67.82)	24 (11.88)	41 (20.3)
13.	Lightening arrangements in the classroom	28 (13.86)	104 (51.49)	70 (34.65)
14.	Low-cost multimedia	37 (8.32)	142 (70.3)	23 (11.39)
15.	Adopted play materials for the disabled children	123 (60.89)	79 (39.11)	0

...(Contd.)

1	2	3	4	5
16.	Speech therapy materials	62 (30.69)	131 (64.85)	9 (4.46)
17.	Sensory training materials	91 (45.05)	82 (40.59)	29 (14.36)
18.	Equipments and materials to identify children with different disabilities	71 (35.15)	131 (64.85)	0
19.	Speech synthesizers for children with disabilities	153 (75.74)	49 (24.26)	0
20.	Braille Typewriters	114 (56.44)	34 (16.83)	54 (26.73)
21.	Talking calculators and books	166 (82.18)	36 (17.82)	0
22.	Mathematical devices and aids like Abacus, Taylor frame, Graphic aids	128 (63.37)	46 (22.77)	28 (13.86)
23.	Closed Circuit Television (CCTV)	121 (59.9)	31 (15.35)	50 (24.75)
24.	Furniture for seating both the staff and the students	12 (5.94)	83 (41.09)	107 (52.97)
25.	Uninterrupted power supply	12 (5.94)	89 (44.06)	101 (50)
26.	Space and proper ventilation in the classroom and the Staff Rooms	34 (16.83)	22 (10.89)	146 (72.28)
27.	Sanitary conditions and drinking water facilities	12 (5.94)	129 (63.86)	61 (30.2)
28.	Healthcare amenities for special children within the school	0	118 (58.42)	84 (41.58)
29.	School transport facilities for disabled students	39 (19.31)	75 (37.13)	88 (43.56)
30.	Library with current books related to special education	163 (80.69)	39 (19.31)	0

Note: Number mentioned in the brackets are in percentage

schools, since independence the Government of India is trying to provide adequate ISF in the form of perfect buildings and other amenities within the school premises apart from providing better trained human and material resources to facilitate the instructional process to make every child to be more inclusive in the classrooms. Here, one should note that it is not the facility that is created only by the Government or the school but the initiation taken by the individual teacher or the teachers together that makes the classroom/school to be friendlier and barrier free not only to the disabled child but also to the able one. This principle is more applicable to the special schools where the programme are independent and require co-operative efforts to achieve the objectives of the special education programme whether it is for HI, VI, MR or persons with multiple disabilities. In this respect, one should note that the quality of instruction in special education not only depends on the quantum of ISF available, but also on the quality and the extent of utilization apart from sharing of resources effectively by the teachers and the schools, which requires 'whole school approach'. Experiments in western world and other parts of the globe have proved the same. In any special school, one can not find only a particular category of the disabled child, but more than one category or multiple disabilities in a child can be observed. If it is the case, the school need not confine to its physical and instructional resources to one category but, geared up to meet the requirements of the disabled child. As such it is inferred that a school must have the resources that cater to the needs of the children with multiple disabilities, thereby better inclusiveness can be achieved atleast within the disabled children and keeping this in view, the investigator developed the ISF tool comprising the facilities needed not only to a particular category, but also all the categories of children in general. Further, the availability of ISF has been assessed by the perception of teachers working in these schools only because they are the people who are seeing, experiencing and using the facilities at every minute in discharging their roles in making the special needs children to be more dependent. Here it is to be noted that the facility may be available but may not be useful, because the facility may not be in good condition or the facility may not be available in reality or facility may be available in good condition but, incompetence of teachers may affect utilization of the facility properly. In some cases, facility available but not in adequate quantity and the centralized control over the utilization of that facility may not be upto the mark. In other sense, the issue is multifaceted, where the teachers are the better judges to say either the facility is available in good, moderate or in poor levels. Hence, the investigator has taken teachers perception as a yardstick to assess the availability of ISF in special schools.

Table 5.15 shows the number and percentage of teachers, who perceived the infrastructural facilities (ISF) in their special school as poor, moderate and good. From the table, it is noted that out of 30 ISF, 24 facilities are related to the teaching-learning process that helps the teachers to carryout their instructional procedures efficiently. Further, the ISF helps the students with disabilities too for reading, writing and learning the curriculum instructed. Each of these facilities will be made useful in one way or the other way. Braille slate and stylus (S.No.1) which are writing media for the visually impaired children are available in good level as perceived by 25 per cent of the teachers; whereas 67 and 7 per cent of teachers perceived that the same is available in poor and moderate levels respectively. The students having low vision have trouble in reading the normal print. In order to read the books, they use magnifying (enlarge) devices like stand magnifiers, hand held magnifiers etc., and lenses accordingly. It is found that out of 202 teachers, 125 teachers sensed the poor availability of magnifying devices and lenses (S.No.2), while 37 and 40 teachers felt that the same are available in their schools in good and moderate levels. Large print and coloured print materials (S.No.3) are used by children having poor/low vision children having distraction. 69 per cent of teachers figured out that the same material is available in their schools in poor form and 18 per cent told that it is in good form and the remaining 13 per cent told that it is available in moderate levels in their schools. Embossed teaching-learning materials are used by the teachers and visually impaired student to teach and learn the science related concepts, diagrams, maps etc., 18 per cent of teachers felt that their school possessed embossed teaching-learning materials (S.No.4) in good form; whereas, 21 and 61 per cent of teachers felt that the same is available in moderate and poor levels. Audio-video instructional materials and sensory training materials which make the teaching learning process more interesting are useful to teachers to teach concepts using multi-sensory approach like VAKT-Visual, Auditory, Kinesthetic and Tactile approach. More than 80 per cent of special education teachers comprehended that the availability of the audio-video instructional materials (S.No. 5) and the sensory training materials (S.No. 17) are in poor and moderate levels; whereas, the remaining 14 per cent of teachers felt the availability of the same in good form in their schools. 41 per cent of special education teachers figured out that their school had poor orientation and mobility materials (S.No.6); whereas, 33 and 27 per cent of special educators felt that their school possess moderate and good level of the same facility. This orientation and mobility materials make the students with disabilities to better utilize their fine and gross motor skills to move around within and outside the school independently. The availability of hearing aids and group hearing aids (S.No.8) that are used to utilize the residual hearing of the hearing impaired children is available in good form in the special schools as observed by 24 per cent of special education teachers and the availability of the same aid is in poor and moderate form in the special schools as observed by 72 and 4 per cent of special education teachers respectively.

The facilities like ramps/rails and special toilets (S.No.7) allow the children with disabilities to access the classrooms, corridors, grounds, toilets, entire school buildings effectively. Over 60 per cent of schools across India do not have toilet facilities (*The Hindu*–Young World, 21st March 2008). Only 16 per cent of teachers felt that these facilities are available in good form; whereas, the same is available in poor and moderate level for about 84 per cent of the teachers. Majority (i.e. 94%) of teachers felt that the availability of false roofing that facilitates to curtail extra noise (S.No.9) is in poor form in their schools; whereas, 6 per cent of teachers felt that the same is available moderately. 75 per cent of teachers were aware of the availability of overhead projector (OHP) (S.No.10) in their special schools in poor form, while 11 and 13 per cent of teachers were aware of the availability of the OHP in the schools at moderate and good levels respectively. Computer assisted instruction-CAI (S.No.11) which is used for the acquisition of the vocabulary and basic concepts, management of behaviour and learning and solve the perceptual, motivational, communication and behavioural problems, is in poor form in special schools as felt by 25 per cent of the special education teachers. 66 and 9 per cent of the special education teachers felt that the CAI is available at moderate and good form in their schools. Physiotherapy enhances the motor development while the occupational therapies are essential to strengthen the fine motor skills like writing, cutting etc., Even though these facilities are essential and can be used in multiple situations, unfortunately, these materials are limited in nature as perceived by majority of the teachers (68%). Proper lightning arrangements are essential for better visibility and it is a pre-requisite for learning in the classroom. Majority (51%) of the special education teachers felt that the lightning arrangements in the classroom (S.No.3) are in moderate form and at the same time 14 and 35 per cent of the teachers felt the same is available in poor and good form. The low-cost multimedia (S.No.14) like newspaper, radio, hand-made simulative aids etc., are found to be available moderately as per 70 per cent of the special education teachers. Only 8 and 11 per cent of special educators found that the same is found in poor and good levels respectively.

In normal conditions, the special child with disability may experience low self concept and self esteem. To develop better self-concept and self-esteem in children particularly in special children, the school must organize activity oriented programme like play way activities, learning by doing involving other children with the disabled child in constructing things that is cooperative learning which enhances the child's self-concept and confidence. For this, the indoor and outdoor games that are suitable to the special children should be organized by adopting the play equipments. Out of 202 teachers 123 of them felt that the accessibility to the adopted play materials for the disabled students (S.No.15) is available in poor form, while 39 teachers felt that the same was in moderate form. Many children with disabilities will have problems regarding expressive and receptive languages such as sequencing of sounds and of words, intelligibility of speech and articulation, fluency problems, usage of short phrases or long conversations etc., The materials such as mirrors, soft boards, vibro-tactile aids, tape recorder, cassettes, speech kit, photo articulation test, peabody picture vocabulary test materials etc., should be made available for better planning of the speech therapy according to the problems of each child. Unfortunately, only 4 per cent of the teachers felt that the facilities for speech therapy (S.No.16) are available in good form, while, 96 per cent of special education teachers felt that the same is in moderate and poor levels.

Equipments and materials to identify the children with different disabilities (e.g. Audiometer, Sequin form board test, Raven progressive matrices, Intelligence tests, Optical and Functional assessment items etc.) S.No.18) are available moderately as observed by 131 teachers and are poor as observed by 71 teachers. Majority (76 %) of teachers felt that the speech synthesizer which allows to convert the text sentences to voice output are available in poor grades, while 24 per cent of teachers felt that the same ISF is available in moderate grades (S.No.19). Likewise, the Braille type writers are found in good form in the special schools to meet the needs of the VI students as perceived by 27 per cent of special educators; while 56 and 17 per cent of special educators felt the same is available in poor and moderate forms. Talking calculators and books facilitates the visually impaired child to listen, hear and learn the textual materials and perform mathematical calculations at his/her own pace and time. 82 and 18 per cent of teachers felt that the talking calculators and books (S.No.21) are in poor and moderate grades.

Mathematical devices and aids like abacus, taylor frame and graphic aids (S.No.22) that help the visually impaired child to solve the mathematical problems involving addition, subtraction, multiplication, division, ratios, fractions etc., are in poor form in special education schools as perceived by 63 per cent of special education teachers, while 14 and 23 per cent of teachers felt that those devices are in good and moderate levels in their schools. Closed circuit television (CCTV) helps the special needs students to read the charts, graphs, pictures and text materials. 59 and 15 percentage of teachers figured out that the CCTV (S.No.23) is available in poor and moderate grades in the special education schools in which they are working and for 25 per cent of teachers it was available in good forms. The furniture for sitting both by the staff and the students (S.No.24) are adequate and are in good form as observed by 107 teachers and 46 per cent of the teachers felt the same facility is in poor and moderate levels. Uninterrupted power supply (S.No.25) in the school is not a problem for the majority of the special educators (50 %), while 6 per cent felt that it is a major problem. 72 per cent of teachers felt that the space and proper ventilation in class and staffrooms (S.No.26) is good; whereas, 17 per cent felt that the space and ventilation in rooms are poor.

Lack of safe water and sanitation can have severe health implications caused by diarrhoea or infections. A proper water and sanitation facility at schools would improve the special needs children's school attendance and their learning quality. It would also prevent dropout rates, especially among disabled girl children in higher classes. The sanitary conditions and drinking water facilities (S.No.27) are good in special schools as observed by 30 per cent of special educators; while 70 per cent observed the same in poor and moderate levels. Majority (58%) of special education teachers perceived that the health care amenities within the school to look after the special children (S.No.28) are in moderate levels, while 42 per cent felt the same in good form in the special schools they are working in. School transport facilities for the disabled students (S.No.29) are found to be good in the special schools as perceived by 44 per cent of teachers, while 56 per cent of teachers perceive the same facility is in poor and moderate forms in their schools. 163 special educators felt that the library facilities (S.No.30) are inadequate and are in poor grade, while 39 per cent of teachers felt that the same facility is available in moderate level.

In nutshell, it can be concluded that around 90-95 per cent of the special education teachers felt that their school is inaccessible to the facilities like false roofing that curtail extra noise, adopted play materials, equipments and materials to identify children with different disabilities, speech synthesizers for children with disabilities, talking calculators, speech therapy materials, computer assisted instruction and the library with current books related to the special education as they are available in poor and moderate levels. Likewise, more than 80 per cent of the special education teachers perceive that the ISF like magnifying devices and lenses, large print and coloured print materials, embossed teaching learning materials, audio-video materials, ramps/rails and special toilet facilities, overhead projector, physiotherapy and occupational therapy facilities, sensory training materials, mathematical devices and aids like abacus, taylor frame and graphic aids are in poor and moderate forms in the special schools they are working. Further, the facilities such as—Braille slate and stylus, orientation and mobility materials, facilities to use hearing aids and group hearing aids, low cost multimedia materials, braille typewriters, closed circuit television and the sanitary and drinking water facilities are in poor and moderate form in the special schools as observed by more than 70 to 75 per cent of the teachers working in the special education schools. In addition to these, the facilities like furniture for seating the staff and the students, uninterrupted power supply, space and proper ventilation in the classroom and the staff rooms, healthcare amenities for special children within the school and school transport services for disabled students are in moderate and good forms as perceived by around 80 to 95 per cent of the special education teachers. The present findings corroborate with the results of Reddy (2007) where only less than 50 per cent of the special education schools are with magnifying devices, large print materials, overhead projector, computer assisted instruction materials and speech synthesizer. Also, Pandey (2009) found that 80 per cent of the schools (Govt. and Public schools) did not have essential physical ISF. Further, the same study revealed that 91.9 per cent schools do not have teaching learning materials like braille papers, tactile maps, embossed diagram, large print books etc., and also 87.22 per cent government schools and 72.2 per cent public schools did not have educational aids and appliances like Braille duplicators and writers, writing devices etc., for educating children with special educational needs in inclusive classroom.

Emotional Intelligence, Occupational Stress and Job Satisfaction of Special Education Teachers based on the Infrastructure Facilities in the Special Schools

To find out the significant difference, if any, in the emotional intelligence, occupational stress and job satisfaction of special education teachers due to variations in the availability of the infrastructure facilities (ISF) in the special schools were they are working, the mean and SD of the ISF rated by each special education teacher in their schools have been calculated. Based on mean ± 1SD, the availability of ISF rated by the teachers has been grouped into three categories i.e. poor, moderate and good. Accordingly, the mean ISF scores ranging from 1.58 and below are categorized as poor, scores from 1.59 to 1.91 as moderate and the mean scores 1.92 and above are good ISF. As per this, there are 12 teachers who rated their ISF as poor in their schools, 148 teachers rated as moderate and 42 teachers rated the ISF as good in the special schools they are working in. The mean and SD of the emotional intelligence, occupational stress and job satisfaction scores of teachers coming under each category of ISF have been calculated. Based on the mean and SD, F-values has been worked out to know the significant difference, if any in the emotional intelligence, occupational stress and job satisfaction among these groups of special education teachers and are presented in Table—5.16.

The F-values presented in table 5.16 with respect to the occupational stress (9.32) and job satisfaction (4.24) of special education teachers who rated the ISF as poor, moderate and good are significant at 0.05 level. It means, there is significant difference in the occupational stress as well as the job satisfaction of special education teachers due to variations in the availability of the ISF as rated by them in special schools. In contrast to the above, the F-value with respect to the emotional intelligence (2.26) is less than the table value (1.96) at 0.05 level. It indicates that the special education teachers who rated the ISF as poor, moderate and good are similar in their emotional intelligence. *Thus the stated hypothesis 'there is a significant difference in the emotional intelligence, occupational stress and job satisfaction of special education teachers due to variations in the ISF available as rated by them in special schools they are working' is accepted only with respect to the occupational stress and job satisfaction of special education teachers.*

Further, the mean values reveal that the occupational stress of teachers who rated the ISF as poor in their schools are higher (Mean value : 3.30) followed by teachers who rated the ISF as good (Mean value : 2.72) and moderate (Mean value : 2.64). Similarly, the job satisfaction of special education teachers who rated the ISF as good in their schools are higher (Mean value : 3.56) followed by teachers who rated the ISF as moderate (Mean value : 3.50) and poor (Mean value : 3.17).

From the Table 5.16, it is inferred that the occupational stress and job satisfaction of special education teachers significantly differ due to variations in the availability of ISF as rated by them in special schools they are working in. In contrast, the emotional intelligence of special education teachers do not differ significantly due to variations in the availability of ISF as rated by them in special schools they are working in. Moreover, the occupational stress of special education teachers who rated the ISF as poor is higher followed by the teachers who rated ISF as

Table 5.16 : Mean and SD of the EI, OS and JS Scores of Teachers based on the Infrastructure Facilities (ISF) available and the Calculated F-values

	Mean and SD Scores of EI, OS and JS of special Education Teachers Based on the Level of ISF available in Special Schools as Rated by them						Calculated F-Values
	Poor ISF(n= 12)		Moderate ISF (n=148)		Good ISF (n=42)		
	Mean	SD	Mean	SD	Mean	SD	
EI	3.73	0.27	3.56	0.34	3.51	0.26	2.26@
OS	3.30	0.34	2.64	0.51	2.72	0.51	9.32**
JS	3.17	0.32	3.50	0.44	3.56	0.30	4.24*

Note : **Significant at 0.01 level;
*Significant at 0.05 level
@ Not significant at 0.05 level

good and moderate; whereas, the job satisfaction of teachers who rated the ISF as poor are lower followed by the teachers who rated the ISF as moderate and good.

Correlation Studies

One of the objectives of the study is to find out the relationship between the dimensions of emotional intelligence and occupational stress; dimensions of emotional intelligence and job satisfaction; and dimensions occupational stress and job satisfaction of special education teachers. To realize this objective, Karl Pearson's Co-efficient of Correlations has been computed based on special school teacher's emotional intelligence, occupational stress and job satisfaction dimensions. Also, the relationship between emotional intelligence, occupational stress and job satisfaction of special education teachers working in three categories of special schools (HI, MR and VI) and special schools as a whole are also worked out and presented in Tables—5.17 to 5.20.

Correlation between Emotional Intelligence and Occupational Stress Dimensions of Special Education Teachers

Table 5.17 illustrates the relationship between emotional intelligence (EI) and occupational stress (OS) dimensions of special education teachers.

From table 5.17, it is evinced that the dimensions—self management, social skills and emotional intelligence as a whole have significant and strong negative relationship with organizational structure and climate—OS_1 (–0.18, –0.18 and –0.17), personal and professional efficiency—OS_2 (–0.14, –0.23 and –0.21), intra and interpersonal interactions—OS_3 (–0.31, –0.35 and –0.32), environment factors—OS_4 (–0.15, –0.29 and –0.26) and, occupational stress as a whole (–0.25, –0.32 and –0.30); as the calculated r-values (mentioned in brackets) are significant at 0.05 level. It means, the higher the self management, social management and emotional intelligence of the special education teachers, the lower will be the occupational stress owing to OS_1, OS_2, OS_3, OS_4 and OS as a whole.

Similarly, the dimension 'self awareness' has significantly and negatively correlated with the personal and professional efficiency, environmental factors dimensions and occupational stress as a whole, as their r-values (–0.15, –0.15 and –0.16) are significant at 0.05 level. From this, it is evident that the lower the special education teachers self awareness, the higher will be the work stress caused by the personal and professional efficiency, environmental factors and occupational stress as a whole and vice versa. At the same time, self awareness of special education teachers did not correlate significantly with organizational

Table 5.17 : Correlation between Emotional Intelligence and Occupational Stress Dimensions of Teachers working in the Special Education Schools

EI \ OS	Organizational Structure and Climate (OS_1)	Personal and Professional Efficiency (OS_2)	Intra and Interpersonal Interactions(OS_3)	Environmental Factors (OS_4)	Occupational Stress as a Whole (OS)
Self Awareness (EI_1)	–0.08@	–0.15*	–0.13@	–0.15*	–0.16*
Self Management (EI_2)	–0.18*	–0.14*	–0.31**	–0.15*	–0.25**
Social Awareness (EI_3)	–0.07@	–0.13@	–0.15*	–0.22**	–0.18*
Social Skills (EI_4)	–0.18*	–0.23**	–0.35**	–0.29**	–0.32**
Emotional Intelligence as a Whole (EI)	–0.17*	–0.21**	–0.32**	–0.26**	–0.30**

Note : **Significant at 0.01 level
*Significant at 0.05 level
@Not Significant at 0.05 level

structure and climate and, intra and interpersonal interactions; as their r-values are not significant at 0.05 level.

Further, no significant relationship has been found between the EI dimension-social awareness and organizational structure and climate (OS_1) and, personal and professional efficiency (OS_2). In contrast to this, there is significant negative relationship between social awareness and intra and interpersonal interactions—OS_3 (–0.15), environmental factors-OS_4 (–0.22) and occupational stress as a whole (–0.18); as their r-values are significant at 0.05 level. These results indicate that where teachers report lower levels of social awareness, it is more likely that they will report higher levels of work stress due to intra and interpersonal interactions, environmental factors and OS as a whole.

From the Table 5.17, it is concluded that the EI dimensions-self-management, social skills and emotional intelligence as a whole are negatively correlated with each of the dimensions of occupational stress (OS) and OS as a whole. Likewise, the EI dimensions–self-awareness and social awareness are also correlated negatively with the OS dimensions-environmental factors and OS as a whole. Similarly, self-awareness of EI dimension has significant negative correlation with OS dimension-personal and professional efficiency; social awareness of EI dimension with intra and interpersonal interactions of OS dimension. In contrast, self awareness (EI_1) has not significantly correlated with organizational structure and climate (OS_1) and, Intra and Interpersonal Interactions (OS_3); social awareness (EI_3) has not significantly related with organizational structure and climate (OS_1) and, personal and professional efficiency (OS_2). It is also inferred that the lower the emotional intelligence, the higher will be the occupational stress of special education teachers.

Correlation between Emotional Intelligence and Job Satisfaction Dimensions of Special Education Teachers

Table 5.18 shows the correlations between EI and JS dimensions.

The table clearly shows that there is significant positive relationship between social skill and all the dimensions of JS i.e. organizational aspects-JS_1 (0.26), intra and interpersonal relationships—JS_2 (0.35), motivational climate—JS_3 (0.17), job security and financial status—JS_4 (0.28) and, JS as a whole (0.32). It is evinced from the results that where the special education teachers report higher levels of social skills, it is more likely that they will report higher levels of JS owing to JS_1, JS_2, JS_3, JS_4 and JS as a whole.

Table 5.18 : Correlation between Emotional Intelligence and Job Satisfaction Dimensions of Teachers working in the Special Education Schools

EI \ JS	Organizational Aspects (JS_1)	Intra and Interpersonal Relationships (JS_2)	Motivational Climate (JS_3)	Job Security and Financial Status (JS_4)	Job Satisfaction as a Whole (JS)
Self Awareness (EI_1)	0.29**	0.24**	–0.01@	0.24**	0.22**
Self Management (EI_2)	0.27**	0.26**	0.07@	0.26**	0.26**
Social Awareness (EI_3)	0.14@	0.27**	0.08@	0.19**	0.20**
Social Skills (EI_4)	0.26**	0.35**	0.17*	0.28**	0.32**
Emotional Intelligence as a Whole (EI)	0.32**	0.36**	0.10@	0.32**	0.32**

Note : **Significant at 0.01 level
*Significant at 0.05 level
@Not Significant at 0.05 level

Similarly, the EI dimensions 'self awareness, self management and emotional intelligence as a whole' are significantly and positively correlated with the dimensions of JS such as : organizational aspects JS_1 (0.29, 0.27 and 0.32), intra and interpersonal relationships—JS_2 (0.24, 0.26 and 0.36), job security and financial status—JS_4 (0.24, 0.26 and 0.32) and job satisfaction as a whole—JS (0.22, 0.26 and 0.32); as their r- values are significant at 0.05 level. The results suggest that the teachers who generally report higher levels of self awareness, self management and EI would also report higher levels of job satisfaction because of JS_1, JS_2, JS_4 and JS as a whole.

In contrast, the r- values report that there is no significant relationship between the motivational climate (dimension of JS) and self awareness-EI_1 (–0.01), self management—EI_2 (0.07), social awareness—EI_3 (0.08) and EI as a whole—EI (0.10). The special education teachers who reported higher level of social awareness enjoyed higher levels of job satisfaction due to intra and interpersonal relationships (JS_2), job security and financial status (JS_4) and, job satisfaction as a whole (JS). Further, the social awareness as a dimension of EI was significantly and positively related with intra and interpersonal relationships (0.27), job security and financial status (0.19) and JS as a whole (0.20); as their calculated r-values are significant at 0.01 level. At the same time, social awareness (EI_3) did not correlate significantly with the organizational aspects (JS_1) as their r-value 0.14 is not significant at 0.05 level.

From the above, it is summed up that the EI dimensions–self-awareness, self-management and EI as a whole are positively related with the dimensions of job satisfaction—'organizational aspects (JS_1)', 'intra and interpersonal relationships (JS_2)' and 'job security and financial status (JS_4)' except, the dimension 'motivational climate (JS_3)'. Likewise, the emotional intelligence dimensions-social awareness is positively related with the JS dimensions-intra and interpersonal relationships (JS_2), job security and financial status (JS_4) and job satisfaction as a whole, except the JS dimensions organizational aspects (JS_1) and motivational climate (JS_3). Moreover, the EI dimension 'social skill' has significantly and positively related with each of the job satisfaction dimensions and JS as a whole. It is also evident that the higher the emotional intelligence, the higher will be the job satisfaction of special education teachers and vice-versa.

Correlation between Occupational Stress and Job Satisfaction Dimensions of Special Education Teachers

Table 5.19 demonstrates the relationship between OS and JS dimensions of teachers working in the special schools.

Table 5.19 : Correlation between Occupational Stress and Job Satisfaction Dimensions of Teachers working in the Special Education Schools

OS \ JS	Organizational Aspects (JS_1)	Intra and Interpersonal Relationships (JS_2)	Motivational Climate (JS_3)	Job Security and Financial Status (JS_4)	Job Satisfaction as a Whole (JS)
Organizational Structure and Climate (OS_1)	−0.22**	−0.42**	−0.33**	−0.21**	−0.36**
Personal and Professional Efficiency (OS_2)	−0.14*	−0.18**	−0.10@	−0.12@	−0.17*
Intra and Interpersonal Interactions (OS_3)	−0.30**	−0.33**	−0.19**	−0.38**	−0.36**
Environmental Factors (OS_4)	−0.26**	−0.32**	−0.09@	−0.40**	−0.31**
Occupational Stress as a Whole (OS)	−0.29**	−0.40**	−0.23**	−0.35**	−0.38**

Note : **Significant at 0.01 level
*Significant at 0.05 level
@Not Significant at 0.05 level

The results of the correlations show that the dimensions of occupational stress-organizational structure and climate—OS_1, intra and interpersonal interactions—OS_3 and occupational stress as a whole—OS are strongly and negatively correlated to job satisfaction dimensions-organizational aspects—JS_1 (–0.22, –0.30 and –0.29), intra and interpersonal relationships—JS_2 (–0.42, –0.33 and –0.40), motivational climate—JS_3 (–0.33, –0.19 and –0.23), job security and financial status—JS_4 (–0.21, –0.38 and –0.35) and job satisfaction as a whole—JS (–0.36, –0.36 and –0.38); as their r-values are significant at 0.01 level. From these results, it is observed that the teachers reporting high work stress owing to OS_1, OS_3 and OS as a whole will report lower level of job satisfaction because of JS_1, JS_2, JS_3, JS_4 and JS as a whole.

Furthermore, the OS dimension 'environmental factor' is significantly and negatively correlated with organizational aspects—JS_1 (–0.26), intra and interpersonal relationships—JS_2 (–0.32), job security and financial status—JS_4 (–0.40) and JS as a whole—JS (–0.31) as their r- values are significant at 0.01 level. It indicates that the teachers reporting higher levels of stress due to environmental factors report lower levels of JS due to organizational aspects, intra and interpersonal relationships, job security and financial status and, job satisfaction as a whole. The relationship between the JS dimension - motivational climate and the OS dimension - personal and professional efficiency (OS_2) and, environmental factors (OS_4) were not found to be significant.

With regard to the OS dimension- personal and professional efficiency (OS_2) is significantly and negatively related with organizational aspects—JS_1 (–0.14), intra and interpersonal relationships—JS_2 (–0.18) and job satisfaction as a whole—JS (–0.17). It shows that the special education teachers experiencing higher levels of stress due to personal and professional efficiency will report lower levels of job satisfaction due to organizational aspects, intra and interpersonal relationships and job satisfaction as a whole and vice versa. The relationship between personal and professional efficiency (OS_2) and, job security and financial status (JS_4) is not found to be significant as the r-values are not significant (–0.09) at 0.05 level.

The OS dimensions – organizational structure and climate (OS_1), intra and interpersonal interactions (OS_3) and OS as a whole (OS) are significantly and negatively correlated with each of the JS dimensions and JS as whole. Likewise, the environmental factors (dimension of OS) are significantly and negatively correlated with each of the JS dimensions 'organizational aspects (JS_1)', 'intra and interpersonal relationships (JS_2)' 'job security and financial status (JS_4)' and JS as a whole, except the dimension 'motivational climate (JS_3)'. Similarly, the OS dimension 'personal and professional efficiency (OS_2)' has significantly and negatively correlated to the JS dimensions—JS_1, JS_2 and JS as a whole, except the JS dimensions-motivational climate (JS_3) and, job security and financial status (JS_4). Also, the higher the occupational stress, the lower will be the job satisfaction of special education teachers.

Correlation between Emotional Intelligence, Occupational Stress and Job Satisfaction of Special Education Teachers

Table 5.20 presents the correlations between emotional intelligence, occupational stress and job satisfaction of teachers working in the schools for HI, MR, VI and special schools as a whole.

Table 5.20 : Correlation between on Emotional Intelligence, Occupational Stress and Job Satisfaction of Teachers Working in the Special Education Schools for HI, MR and VI

Nature of School	Emotional Intelligence Vs Occupational Stress	Emotional Intelligence Vs Job Satisfaction	Occupational Stress Vs Job Satisfaction
Hearing Impaired	–0.35**	0.27*	–0.27*
Mentally Retarded	–0.59**	0.48**	–0.31*
Visually Impaired	–0.20@	0.27*	–0.60**
Schools as a Whole	–0.30**	0.32**	–0.38**

Note : ** Significant at 0.01 level
* Significant at 0.05 level

From the table, it is observed that the r-values with respect to the emotional intelligence and occupational stress of teachers working in the schools for HI (-0.35), MR (–0.59) and special schools as a whole (–0.30) are significant at 0.05 level. This shows that there is significant negative relationship between the special education teacher's emotional intelligence and occupational stress. It means, the higher the emotional intelligence, the lower will be the occupational stress of special education teachers and vice-versa. *Hence the formulated hypothesis, 'there is a significant relationship between emotional intelligence and occupational stress of special education teachers working in the special schools for HI, MR and special schools as a whole' is accepted only.* The results of Gardner (2005), Nikolaou and Tsaousis (2002) and, Suresh and Joshith (2008) supported the present findings, where significant negative relationship was found between emotional intelligence dimensions and occupational stress of teachers, professionals in mental health institutions and student teachers respectively. Results of the studies by Brand (2007) and, Slaski and Cartwright (2002) also support the present findings where they found significant negative relationship between occupational stress and emotional intelligence of the nurses and retail managers respectively.

On the other hand, the r-value with respect to the emotional intelligence and occupational stress of teachers working in the schools for VI (–0.20) is not significant at 0.05 level. It indicates the non-existence of significant relationship between emotional intelligence and occupational stress of special education teachers working in the schools for VI.

The table also reveals that the r-value with respect to the emotional intelligence and job satisfaction of special education teachers working in the schools for MR (0.48) and special schools as a whole (0.32) are significant at 0.01 level; and for HI (0.27) and VI (0.27) are significant at 0.05 levels. This shows the existence of positive relationship between emotional intelligence and job satisfaction. It means, the higher the emotional intelligence, the higher will be the job satisfaction of teachers and vice-versa working in all the three categories of schools separately and special schools as a whole. The corresponding nature of results has been demonstrated by the findings of the studies by Iordanoglou (2007), Wong et al. (2010) and Platsidou (2010) where the emotional intelligence of primary education teachers, school teachers and primary special education teachers respectively are positively related to their job satisfaction. *Thus the formulated hypothesis, 'there is a significant relationship between emotional intelligence and job satisfaction of special education teachers working in the special schools for HI, MR, VI and special schools as a whole' is accepted.*

Further, there exists significant negative relationship between the occupational stress and job satisfaction of teachers working in all the three categories of schools and special schools as a whole. This can be observed with the r-values of the teachers working in the schools of HI (–0.27), MR (–0.31), VI (–0.60) and schools as a whole (–0.38), as these values are significant at 0.05 level. This means, higher the occupational stress, lower will be the job satisfaction and vice-versa. *Thus the formulated hypothesis, 'there is a significant relationship between occupational stress and job satisfaction of special education teachers working in the special schools for HI, MR, VI and special schools as a whole' is accepted.* The analogous findings are verified by the results of the studies by Suryanarayana (2009) and Reddy (2007) where the occupational stress of teachers and special education teachers teaching VI children respectively are negatively related to their job satisfaction.

Thus from the above findings, it can be concluded that there is a significant negative relationship between emotional intelligence and occupational stress of teachers working in the schools for HI, MR and special schools as a whole and, no significant relationship between the EI and OS of teachers working in the schools for VI. Similarly, there is a significant negative relationship between occupational stress and job satisfaction of teachers working in all the categories of special schools. The results reveal that higher the emotional intelligence, the lower will be the occupational stress and; the higher the occupational stress, lower will be the job satisfaction of special education teachers and vice-versa. Moreover, it is noted that there is significant positive relationship between emotional intelligence and job satisfaction of teachers working in all categories of special schools. Here, the higher the emotional intelligence, the higher will be the job satisfaction of special education teachers and vice-versa.

Step-wise Multiple Regression Analysis

It is understood that several variables either independently or together influence the special education teacher's emotional intelligence, occupational stress and job satisfaction. The task of scientific evaluation involves in establishing how much and how well a set of independent variables having logical bearing on the dependent variable facilitates accurate prediction. This can be accomplished by applying stepwise multiple regression analysis.

Prediction of Independent Variables (age, community, educational qualification, training received in special education........) to the Dependent Variables (EI, OS and JS) of Special Education Teachers

As, one of the objectives of the study is to know how far and to what extent the independent variables (age, community, educational qualification, training in special education....) predict the dependent variables (emotional intelligence, occupational stress and job satisfaction) of special education teachers working in the special schools for HI, MR, VI and special schools as a whole, step wise multiple regression analysis has been carried out separately for each special school and the results are presented in tables 5.21 to 5.24.

The percentage wise contribution of the independent variables to the emotional intelligence (EI), occupational stress (OS) and job satisfaction

(JS) of teachers working in the schools for hearing impaired children are presented in table- 21 along with the β Coefficient.

Table 5.21: Prediction of Independent Variables to the EI, OS and JS of Teachers Working in the Schools for Hearing Impaired

Dependent Variables	Independent Variables	β Coefficient	Individual Contribution of the Variable (R^2)	% Wise Individual Contribution
EI	Nature of Job	–0.393	0.230	23.0
	Salary	0.263	0.292	29.2
OS	Level of Classes Handled	–0.340	0.075	7.5
	Training in Special Education	–0.277	0.130	13.0
	Salary	–0.250	0.191	19.1
JS	Salary	0.533	0.242	24.2
	Years of Experience	–0.219	0.289	28.9

From Table—5.21, it is noted that the independent variables 'monthly salary' has contributed 29 per cent followed by the variable 'nature of job' with 23 per cent to the emotional intelligence of the special education teachers working in the schools for HI. At the same time, the variable 'salary' contributes 19.1 per cent followed by the variable 'training in special education' with 13 per cent and the 'level of class handled' with 7.5 per cent to the occupational stress of the teachers working in the special schools for HI. In case of job satisfaction of teachers working in the schools for HI, the teacher's salary and the years of experience have predicted 24.2 and 28.9 per cent of their job satisfaction.

From the above finings, it is concluded that the variable 'salary' has contributed significantly to the emotional intelligence, occupational stress and job satisfaction of special education teachers working in the schools for HI, to a greater extent. The other independent variable 'nature of job' has also contributed significantly to the emotional intelligence of teachers working in the schools for HI, whereas the teachers occupational stress is predicted by the variable 'level of classes handled' and 'training received in special education' by the special education teachers working in the schools for HI. In addition to the variable, 'salary', the variable 'years of experience' has also significantly contributed to the teacher's job satisfaction to a greater extent.

Table 5.22 shows the percentage wise contribution of the independent variables to the emotional intelligence, occupational stress and job satisfaction of teachers working in the schools for mentally retarded children.

From the table, it is found that, the variable 'salary' contributes 43.7 per cent, followed by the variable 'level of classes handled' with 37.4 per cent and 'nature of job' with 23.1 per cent to the emotional intelligence of teachers working in the schools for MR children; whereas, 19.7 per cent contribution by the variable 'nature of job' to the occupational stress and 6.8 per cent contribution by community to the job satisfaction of the special education teachers working in the schools for MR children.

Table 5.22 : Prediction of Independent Variables to the EI, OS and JS of Teachers Working in the Schools for Mentally Retarded

Dependent Variables	Independent Variables	β Coefficient	Individual Contribution of the Variable (R^2)	% Wise Individual Contribution
EI	Nature of Job	–0.345	0.231	23.1
	Level of Classes Handled	0.326	0.374	37.4
	Salary	0.268	0.437	43.7
OS	Nature of Job	0.443	0.197	19.7
JS	Community	–0.261	0.068	6.8

From the above, it is summed up, that the variable 'salary' is the major predictor contributing more to the emotional intelligence of teachers working in the schools for MR followed by the other variables 'nature of job' and 'level of classes handled'. Further, it is noted that the variables 'nature of job' and 'community' are the significant predictors to the occupational stress and job satisfaction of special education teachers respectively to a greater extent.

Table 5.23 illustrates the percentage wise contribution and the â coefficient of the independent variables to the emotional intelligence, occupational stress and job satisfaction of teachers working in the schools for visually impaired children.

From table 5.23, it is interesting to note that only a single independent variable i.e. 'training in special education' has predicted 7.3 and 9 per cent to the occupational stress and job satisfaction of the teachers working in the schools for VI respectively. This means, the training received by the special education teachers in special education has significantly contributed to their occupational stress and job satisfaction. From the above, it is concluded that the independent variable 'training in special education' is the significant contributor to the occupational stress and job satisfaction of teachers working in the schools for VI.

Table 5.23 : Prediction of Independent Variables to the EI, OS and JS of Teachers Working in the Schools for Visually Impaired

Dependent Variables	Independent Variables	β Coefficient	Individual Contribution of the Variable (R^2)	% Wise Individual Contribution
OS	Training in Special Education	–0.270	0.073	7.3
JS	Training in Special Education	0.300	0.090	9.0

Table 5.24 illustrates the percentage-wise contribution of the independent variables to the dependent variables- emotional intelligence, occupational stress and job satisfaction of teachers working in the special education schools as a whole.

Table 5.24 : Prediction of Independent Variables to the EI, OS and JS of Teachers Working in Special Education Schools as a Whole

Dependent Variables	Independent Variables	β Coefficient	Individual Contribution of the Variable (R^2)	% Wise Individual Contribution
EI	Level of Classes Handled	0.136	0.229	22.9
	Nature of Job	–0.312	0.139	13.9
	Salary	0.180	0.189	18.9
	Nature of School	–0.144	0.211	21.1
OS	Level of Classes Handled	–0.187	0.116	11.6
	Training in Special Education	–0.190	0.182	18.2
	Salary	–0.208	0.146	14.6
	Nature of School	–0.298	0.068	6.8
JS	Salary	0.202	0.041	4.1

From table 5.24, it is observed that the variable 'level of classes handled' contributes 22.9 per cent, followed by the variable 'nature of school' with 21.1 per cent, 'salary' with 18.9 per cent and 'nature of job' with 13.9 per cent to the dependent variable 'emotional intelligence' of the special education teachers. In case of the occupational stress, the variable 'training in special education', contributes to 18.2 per cent followed by the variable 'salary' with 14.6 per cent, 'level of classes handled' with 11.6 per cent and 'nature of school' with 6.8 per cent. The corresponding results were confirmed by the results of Reddy (2007) where the independent variable 'nature of school working' has predicted occupational stress of special education teachers. Further, it is noted that among the independent variables taken in to account for the study, only the variable 'salary' has contributed 4.1 per cent to the job satisfaction of the special education teachers. The results of the study by Reddy (2007) substantiate the present findings where the variable 'salary' of the special education teachers emerged as a major predictor of their job satisfaction.

From the above, it is concluded that the independent variables 'level of classes handled', 'nature of school', 'salary' and 'nature of job' are the significant contributors to the emotional intelligence, whereas the variable 'training in special education', 'salary', 'level of classes handled' and 'nature of school' have contributed significantly to the occupational stress of special education teachers. Further, the variable 'salary' has contributed to the job satisfaction of special education teachers to certain extent.

Prediction of Independent Variable (EI dimensions) to the Dependent Variables (OS and JS) and, Independent Variable (OS dimensions) to the Dependent Variable (JS)

In order to explore which of the specific dimensions of the independent variable (EI) are the important predictors of occupational stress and job satisfaction, step-wise multiple regression analysis is undertaken with occupational stress and job satisfaction as the dependent variables and each of the dimensions of emotional intelligence as the independent variables. Further, to identify which of the dimensions of the independent variable (occupational stress—OS) is the important predictor of the dependent variable (job satisfaction—JS), step-wise regression analysis is carried out. The step-wise multiple regression analysis is worked out separately for the special education teachers working in the schools for HI, MR, VI and special schools as a whole. The results of the analysis are presented in table 5.25.

Table 5.25: Prediction of Independent Variable (EI dimensions) to the Dependent Variables (OS and JS), and Independent Variable (OS dimensions) to the Dependent Variable (JS) of the Special Education Teachers Working in the Schools for HI, VI, MR and Special Schools as a Whole

Dependent Variables	Independent Variables	β Coefficient	Individual Contribution of the Variable (R^2)	% Wise Individual Contribution
Schools for Hearing Impaired—HI				
OS	Social Skills (EI_4)	–.367	.135	13.5
JS	Social Skills (EI_4)	–.278	.077	7.0
JS	Intra and Interpersonal Interactions (OS_3)	–.401	.160	16.0
Schools for Visually Impaired—VI				
OS	-	-	-	-
JS	Self awareness (EI_1)	.335	.112	11.2
JS	Intra and Interpersonal Interactions (OS_3)	–.650	.422	42.2
Schools for Mentally Retarded—MR				
OS	EI as a Whole (EI)	–.592	.351	35.1
JS	EI as a Whole (EI)	.480	.230	23.0
JS	Organizational Structure and Climate (OS_1)	–.438	.192	19.2
Special Schools as a Whole				
OS	Social Skills (EI_4)	–.323	.104	10.4
JS	EI as a Whole (EI)	–.323	.105	10.5
JS	O.S Whole (OS)	–.700	.146	14.6
	Personal and Professional Efficiency (OS_2)	.397	.202	20.2

From table 5.25, it is evident that the EI dimension 'social skill' has contributed 13.5 per cent and 7 per cent to the dependent variables-occupational stress (OS) and job satisfaction (JS). Further, the OS_3 dimension 'intra and interpersonal interactions' has contributed 16 per cent to the job satisfaction of special education teachers working in the schools for HI.

For the special education teachers working in the schools for VI, the emotional intelligence (EI) dimension 'self awareness' has contributed 11.2 per cent to their JS. The OS dimension 'intra and interpersonal interactions' has accounted for 42.2 per cent to their JS. Further, none of the EI dimensions had contributed significantly to the OS.

When OS and JS of the special education teachers (working in the schools for MR) is taken as a dependent variable and the dimension of EI as dependent variable, EI as a whole accounted for 35.1 per cent and 23 per cent to OS and JS respectively. When the dimensions of OS are taken as independent variables and JS as dependent variable, the dimension 'organizational structure and climate—OS_1' contributed 19.2 per cent to the JS of teachers working in the schools for MR.

When special education teachers as a whole is taken into account, the emotional intelligence dimension 'social skill' emerged as a significant contributor to OS, as it accounts for 10.4 per cent of variance in OS. The results of the study by Adeyemo and Ogunyemi (2007) and Gardner (2005) concurred with the present findings where the dimensions of emotional intelligence emerges as significant predictors of occupational stress of university academic staff and teachers respectively. With regard to the dependent variable JS, the independent variable EI as a whole contributed to 10.5 per cent. Similar results are noticed in the findings of the study by Kafetsics and Loumakou (2007) where the interpersonal branch of EI has predicted job satisfaction of teachers. On the other hand, when OS was taken as independent variable, its dimension 'personal and professional efficiency' contributed 20.2 per cent followed by OS as a whole for 14.6 per cent to the dependent variable (job satisfaction).

From the above, it is summed up that, the independent variable EI dimension 'social skill' is the significant contributor to the OS of teachers working in the schools for HI and special schools as a whole. The 'EI as a whole' contributed significantly to OS and JS of teachers working in the schools for MR and, to the JS of teachers working in special schools as a whole. Further, the OS dimension 'intra and interpersonal interactions' which acted as independent variable emerged as significant contributor to the JS of teachers working in the schools for HI and VI. The EI dimension 'self-awareness' is the significant contributor to the JS of teachers working in the schools for VI children. Also, the independent variable of OS dimension 'organizational structure and climate' is another significant contributor to the JS of teachers working for MR children. Similarly, the dependent variable 'job satisfaction' is predicted by two of the independent variables 'OS as a whole and personal and professional efficiency' of OS dimensions.

Summary of the Results and Discussion

The results of the descriptive analysis in Part—I and differential analysis in Part—II reveals the following:

Part—I : Descriptive Analysis

1. More than 85 per cent of the teachers working in the special education schools possess moderate and low level of emotional intelligence, whereas 86 per cent of special education teachers experience moderate and high level of occupational stress. Likewise, more than 88 per cent of teachers are with moderate and low level of job satisfaction irrespective of the special schools they are working in (refer table-5.2).
2. Out of 28 personal competencies listed under *self-awareness* and *self management* dimensions of emotional intelligence (EI), the special education teachers possess moderate level of EI in 20 aspects, whereas they exhibit only low level of EI in four aspects and high level of EI in the rest of the four aspects. Likewise, in social competencies, out of 30 aspects mentioned under the dimensions of *social awareness* and *social skills*, the special education teachers demonstrated moderate level of EI in 19 aspects and low level of EI in four aspects. Contrary to this, on seven aspects, their EI is at high level (refer table 5.3).
3. In the dimension *'organizational structure and climate'*, out of 16 stressors the teachers experience high level of stress due to seven stressors. The remaining nine stressors have generated only moderate level of stress. Further, the eight aspects in *'personal and professional efficiency'* dimension have evoked moderate level of stress. Only one stressor has generated low level of stress in special education teachers. In contrast, the three stressors have emerged as potential sources that triggered high level of stress in them. Correspondingly, the six stressors mentioned under *'intra and interpersonal interactions'* dimension have generated moderate level of stress, whereas the remaining six stressors have evoked only low level of stress. In the dimension of *'environmental factors'*,

the two aspects have evoked high level of stress, while in seven aspects the teachers experience moderate level of stress. In the remaining three aspects the teachers experience low level of stress (refer table 5.4).

4. In job satisfaction, the teachers are moderately satisfied in all the 12 organizational aspects. Similarly, in the second dimension i.e. intra and interpersonal relationships, out of ten aspects the teachers are moderately satisfied in eight aspects, while highly satisfied in the remaining two aspects. In the dimension 'motivational climate' the teachers are least satisfied in four aspects, moderately satisfied in six aspects and, highly satisfied in four aspects. In 'job security and financial status' dimension, out of ten aspects the teachers are least satisfied with two aspects and in the remaining eight aspects, their satisfaction is at moderate level (refer table 5.5).

Part—II : Differential Analysis

5. The variable 'nature of job' and 'salary' has significant influence on the emotional intelligence, whereas, the variable 'level of classes handled' influence occupational stress and the variable 'salary' has significant bearing on the job satisfaction of special education teachers working in the schools for HI children. The teachers in permanent position and receiving higher salary (₹ 20,001 and above) possess higher levels of emotional intelligence than their counterparts with temporary position and receiving low salary (₹ 10,000 and below and ₹ 10,001 and 20,000). Also, the teachers teaching primary classes experience more stress than their counterparts teaching higher secondary and secondary classes. Moreover, the higher the salary the teacher receives, the higher will be the job satisfaction and vice-versa (refer tables 5.6 to 5.14).
6. The variable 'training in special education' has significantly influenced the occupational stress and job satisfaction of special education teachers working in the schools for visually impaired. The teachers working in the schools for VI, who received higher order of professional training like B.Ed. in Special Education have lower occupational stress and enjoy higher job satisfaction than their counterparts who have received training only in Diploma Special Education (refer tables 5.6 to 5.14).
7. Except the variable 'training in special education', all the other variables have significantly influenced the emotional intelligence of special education teachers working in the schools for MR

children. The teachers belonging to 46 and above years of age group, BC category, graduation with B.Ed. and M.Ed. qualification, handling higher secondary classes, holding permanent position, receiving ₹ 20,001 and above salary and, 20 years and above years of experience showed higher levels of emotional intelligence than their counterparts belonging to 30 and below years of age group, OC category, having only teacher training qualification, handling primary classes, holding temporary position, receiving ₹ 10,000 and below salary and having ten and below years of experience. Further, the two independent variables 'nature of job and salary' have significant bearing on their occupational stress. The teachers holding temporary position and receiving low salary (₹ 10,000 and below) are higher in occupational stress than their counterparts in permanent position and receiving high salary (₹ 20,001 and above) respectively. Likewise, the variable 'salary' has significantly influenced their job satisfaction. The higher the salary the teacher receives, the higher will be the job satisfaction of teachers working in the schools for MR children and vice-versa (refer tables 5.6 to 5.14).

8. The independent variables 'educational qualification, nature of special school the teachers working, level of classes handled, nature of job and, salary' of special education teachers have significantly influenced their emotional intelligence. On the other hand, the variables 'age, nature of special school working, training in special education, level of classes handled and, nature of job' has significantly influenced the special education teachers occupational stress. Further, the variable 'salary' has significant bearing on the job satisfaction of teachers working in the special schools together. The mean values indicates that the EI of teachers : possessing graduation with B.Ed. and M.Ed. qualification, working in the schools for VI children, teaching higher secondary classes, holding permanent position and, receiving high salary ₹ 20,001 and above are higher than their counterparts possessing teacher training and graduation with B.Ed. qualification, working in the schools for HI and MR children, teaching secondary and primary classes, holding temporary position and, receiving low salary ₹ 10,001-20,000 and ₹ 10,000 and below respectively. Like-wise, the occupational stress of teachers belonging to 30 and below years of age group, working in the schools for VI children, who received low order of professional training like Diploma in special education, handling

primary classes, holding temporary position are higher than the teachers belonging to 46 and above years and 31-45 years of age group, working in the schools for MR and HI children, who received high professional training like B.Ed. special education, handling secondary and higher secondary classes and holding permanent position respectively. Further, the teachers receiving high salary ₹ 20,001 and above are more satisfied in their job than the teachers receiving low salary ₹ 10,001-20,000 and ₹ 10,000 and below (refer tables 5.6 to 5.14).

9. Around 90 - 95 per cent of the special education teachers felt that their school is inaccessible to the facilities like false roofing that curtail extra noise, adopted play materials, equipments and materials to identify children with different disabilities, speech synthesizers for children with disabilities, talking calculators, speech therapy materials, computer assisted instruction and the library with current books related to the special education as they are available in poor and moderate levels. Likewise, more than 80 per cent of the special education teachers perceive that the ISF like magnifying devices and lenses, large print and colored print materials, embossed teaching learning materials, audio-video materials, ramps/rails and special toilet facilities, overhead projector, physiotherapy and occupational therapy facilities, sensory training materials, mathematical devices and aids like abacus, taylor frame and graphic aids are in poor and moderate forms in the special schools they are working. Further, the facilities such as—Braille slate and stylus, orientation and mobility materials, facilities to use hearing aids and group hearing aids, low cost multimedia materials, braille typewriters, closed circuit television and the sanitary and drinking water facilities are in poor and moderate form in the special schools as observed by more than 70 to 75 per cent of the teachers working in the special education schools. In addition to these, the facilities like furniture for seating the staff and the students, uninterrupted power supply, space and proper ventilation in the classroom and the staff rooms, healthcare amenities for special children within the school and school transport services for disabled students are in moderate and good forms as perceived by around 80 to 95 per cent of the special education teachers (refer table 5.15).

10. The occupational stress and job satisfaction of special education teachers significantly differ due to variations in the availability of ISF as rated by them in special schools they are working. In

contrast, the emotional intelligence of special education teachers do not differ significantly due to variations in the availability of ISF as rated by them in special schools they are working. Moreover, the occupational stress of special education teachers who rated the ISF as poor is higher followed by the teachers who rated ISF as good and moderate; whereas, the job satisfaction of teachers who rated the ISF as poor are lower followed by the teachers who rated the ISF as moderate and good (refer table 5.16).

11. The EI dimensions—self management, social skills and emotional intelligence as a whole are negatively correlated with each of the dimensions of occupational stress (OS) and OS as a whole. Like-wise, the EI dimension—self-awareness and social awareness are also correlated negatively with the OS dimensions - environmental factors and OS as a whole. Similarly, self-awareness of EI dimension has significant negative correlation with OS dimension-personal and professional efficiency; social awareness of EI dimension with intra and interpersonal interactions of OS dimension. In contrast, self awareness (EI_1) has not significantly correlated with organizational structure and climate (OS_1) and, Intra and Interpersonal Interactions (OS_3); social awareness (EI_3) has not significantly related with organizational structure and climate (OS_1) and, personal and professional efficiency (OS_2). It is also inferred that lower the emotional intelligence, the higher will be the occupational stress of special education teachers (refer table 5.17).

12. The EI dimensions—self-awareness, self management and EI as a whole are positively related with the dimensions of job satisfaction—'organizational aspects (JS_1)', 'intra and interpersonal relationships (JS_2)' and 'job security and financial status (JS_4)' except, the dimension 'motivational climate (JS_3)'. Like-wise, the emotional intelligence dimension-social awareness is positively related with the JS dimensions - intra and interpersonal relationships (JS_2), job security and financial status (JS_4) and job satisfaction as a whole, except the JS dimensions organizational aspects (JS_1) and motivational climate (JS_3). Moreover, the EI dimension 'social skill' has significantly and positively related with each of the job satisfaction dimensions and JS as a whole. It is also evident that higher the emotional intelligence, higher will be the job satisfaction of special education teachers and vice-versa (refer table 5.18).

13. The OS dimensions-organizational structure and climate (OS_1), intra and interpersonal interactions (OS_3) and OS as a whole (OS) are significantly and negatively correlated with each of the JS dimensions and JS as whole. Like-wise, the environmental factors (dimension of OS) are significantly and negatively correlated with each of the JS dimensions 'organizational aspects (JS_1)', 'intra and interpersonal relationships (JS_2)' 'job security and financial status (JS_4)' and JS as a whole, except the dimension 'motivational climate (JS_3)'. Similarly, the OS dimension 'personal and professional efficiency (OS_2)' is significantly and negatively correlated to the JS dimensions - JS_1, JS_2 and JS as a whole, except the JS dimensions - motivational climate (JS_3) and, job security and financial status (JS_4). Also, the higher the occupational stress, the lower will be the job satisfaction of special education teachers (refer table 5.19).
14. There is a significant negative relationship between emotional intelligence and occupational stress of teachers working in the schools for HI, MR and special schools as a whole and, no significant relationship between the EI and OS of teachers working in the schools for VI. Similarly, there is a significant negative relationship between occupational stress and job satisfaction of teachers working in all the categories of special schools. The results reveal that the higher the emotional intelligence, the lower will be the occupational stress and; the higher the occupational stress, the lower will be the job satisfaction of special education teachers and vice-versa. Moreover, it is noted that there is significant positive relationship between emotional intelligence and job satisfaction of teachers working in all categories of special schools. Here, the higher the emotional intelligence, the higher will be the job satisfaction of special education teachers and vice-versa (refer table 5.20).
15. The variable 'salary' has contributed significantly to the emotional intelligence, occupational stress and job satisfaction of special education teachers working in the schools for HI, to a greater extent. The other independent variable 'nature of job' has also contributed significantly to the emotional intelligence of teachers working in the schools for HI, whereas the teachers occupational stress is predicted by the variable 'level of classes handled' and 'training received in special education' by the special education teachers working in the schools for HI. In addition to the variable, 'salary', the variable 'years of experience' has also significantly contributed to the teacher's job satisfaction to a greater extent (refer table 5.21).

16. The variable 'salary' is the major predictor contributing more to the emotional intelligence of teachers working in the schools for MR followed by the other variables 'nature of job' and 'level of classes handled'. Further, it is noted that the variables 'nature of job' and 'community' are the significant predictors to the occupational stress and job satisfaction of special education teachers respectively to a greater extent (refer table 5.22).
17. The independent variable 'training in special education' is the significant contributor to the occupational stress and job satisfaction of teachers working in the schools for VI (refer table 5.23).
18. The independent variables 'level of classes handled', 'nature of school', 'salary' and 'nature of job' are the significant contributors to the emotional intelligence, whereas the variable 'training in special education', 'salary', 'level of classes handled' and 'nature of school' have contributed significantly to the occupational stress of special education teachers. Further, the variable 'salary' has contributed to the job satisfaction of special education teachers working in the special schools together (refer table 5.24).
19. The independent variable EI dimension 'social skill' is the significant contributor to the OS of teachers working in the schools for HI and special schools as a whole. The 'EI as a whole' contributed significantly to OS and JS of teachers working in the schools for MR and, to the JS of teachers working in special schools as a whole. Further, the OS dimension 'intra and interpersonal interactions' which acted as independent variable emerged as significant contributor to the JS of teachers working in the schools for HI and VI. The EI dimension 'self-awareness' is the significant contributor to the JS of teachers working in the schools for VI children. Also, the independent variable of OS dimension 'organizational structure and climate' is another significant contributor to the JS of teachers working for MR children. Similarly, the dependent variable 'job satisfaction' is predicted by two of the independent variables 'OS as a whole and personal and professional efficiency' of OS dimension (refer table 5.25).

The summary and suggestions of the study are presented in next chapter-VI.

CHAPTER 6

Summary and Suggestions

Introduction

Researches in the field of special education are scanty in India. Most of the researches in the field of special education are centered on special child. The problems associated with the teacher who is the pivotal point in the special education field are neglected. The multiple roles played by the special education teacher demands intra and interpersonal skills and exert lot of stress and strain in them. Research evidence on occupational stress suggests the teaching is among one of the most stressful occupations (Boyle et al., 1995; Doune, 1999; Hui and Chan, 1996; Schonfeld, 2001). As far as the social welfare occupations are concerned, it has been claimed that in fact, teachers experience the highest levels of stress (Travers and Cooper, 1993). The job of special school teachers is thus much more demanding of experimentation with novel activities. The increased demands and changes in special education field makes the special education teachers to play diverse and challenging roles while: planning and organizing the educational programme for the students with disabilities, teaching and transacting the framed curriculum, training the students in plus-curricular activities, guiding and counselling the students, parents and colleagues, and intra and interpersonal interactions with the para-professionals and the stakeholders.

The need for flexibility, autonomy and novelty makes their job definitions inherently ambiguous making room for more role conflicts. Also, the complexity of their roles creates stress and strain in them that ultimately leads to their job dissatisfaction. The challenge of overcoming stress and performing the tasks in special school is such that they need high degree of emotional strength, flexibility of procedures and routines, freedom to act according to the student needs and collegial support. Payne (2005) observed that special education teachers lack the leadership qualities that heighten the ability for them to deal with the demands of the job. Payne also noted that special education teachers must develop leadership skills that will assist in becoming effective advocates in the field of education. In simple terms, special education teachers need to be (*a*) self aware of abilities and skills required for the range of the roles, responsibilities and demands of their work; (*b*) manage emotional reactions to specific situations and people; (*c*) accurately pick up on emotions in other people and react to others emotions and understanding others needs; and (*d*) socially skilled enough to use awareness of one's own emotions and the emotions of others to manage interactions successfully. In this context, the present study aimed to identify the emotional intelligence, occupational stress and job satisfaction of special education teachers.

Title of the Problem

'Emotional Intelligence, Occupational Stress and Job Satisfaction of Special Education Teachers'.

Objectives of the Study

The following objectives have been framed for the present study :

1. To develop a tool to assess the level of emotional intelligence (EI) of teachers working in the special education schools;
2. To develop a tool to assess the level of occupational stress (OS) of teachers working in the special education schools;
3. To identify the level of job satisfaction (JS) of teachers working in the special education schools;
4. To find out the significant differences, if any, in the emotional intelligence, occupational stress and job satisfaction of special education teachers due to variations in their age, community, educational qualification, nature of special schools the teachers working in, training received in special education, level of classes handled, nature of job, years of experience and salary they receive;
5. To develop a tool to assess the level of infrastructure facilities (ISF) available in the special education schools, rated by the special education teachers;

to assess the emotional intelligence and occupational stress of special education teachers. The job satisfaction scale developed by Reddy (2007) has been adopted and slightly modified the same to identify the factors influencing the job satisfaction of special education teachers.

As resource inadequacy is a major problem faced by the special education teachers in transacting the curriculum, the study attempts to explore into the infrastructure facilities available in the special education schools using the infrastructure facilities rating scale developed by the investigator. Also, the study intends to find out the significant differences, if any, in the emotional intelligence, occupational stress and job satisfaction of the special education teachers due to variations in their age, community, educational qualification, nature of special schools the teachers working in, training in special education, level of classes handled, nature of job, years of experience, salary they receive and the infrastructure facilities available in the special education schools.

Further, the study deliberated the relationship between emotional intelligence and occupational stress, emotional intelligence and job satisfaction and, occupational stress and job satisfaction of special education teachers. Also, the study focussed on how far and to what extent the personal variables i.e. age, community, educational qualification, nature of special schools the teachers working in, training in special education, level of classes handled, nature of job, years of experience and salary they receive are contributing to the dependent variables i.e. emotional intelligence, occupational stress and job satisfaction of special education teachers. In addition, it also focuses its attention on the contribution of emotional intelligence dimensions to the occupational stress and job satisfaction; occupational stress dimensions to the job satisfaction of special education teachers working in different types of special schools.

Need and Importance of the Study

Any special education programme, whether it is for physically challenged, intellectually impaired, emotionally disturbed and talented should focus on the innate abilities of the child rather than expecting the child to do extraordinary things. In other words, what is available in the child is more important rather than the things which are not available within the child. The human personality should be developed in-terms of the minimum knowledge, skills and capabilities required to perform the functions for healthy living. In this context, a special education teacher is one who should know the innate abilities of the child and compensate the disabilities of the child by promoting the inner strengths of the individual. For this, a special education teacher's role is not just information provider but a facilitator to the child in every walk of life. The need for flexibility, autonomy and novelty makes their job definitions inherently ambiguous making room for more role conflicts. Also, the complexity of their roles creates stress and strain in them that ultimately leads to their job dissatisfaction.

Further, it is clear from the literature reviewed in chapter—II, the special education teachers in both India and west are experiencing occupational stress and they are in need of emotional stability to face the challenges that are ahead in their way. A critical view at the research studies reviewed in chapter—II indicates that the research on the combination of the three variables i.e. emotional intelligence, occupational stress and job satisfaction of special education teachers are limited and sporadic in nature. Further, the available studies are of foreign origin and the Indian scene is wide open for the researchers. A comprehensive study on emotional intelligence, occupational stress and job satisfaction of special education teachers will give clear cut picture about the emotional intelligence, occupational stress and job satisfaction, and the relationship among these three. Infact, researches in this area provide better insights to create effective organizational environment, healthy intra and inter-personal relations, professional interactions, strengthening of the professional training components, the ways and means to equip teachers with instructional assignments and arrangements to meet the needs of the global society. Similarly, the studies on emotional intelligence, occupational stress and job satisfaction of teachers facilitate to know what factors contribute to job satisfaction/dissatisfaction among the special education teachers. Also, such studies will give better insight into the influence of personal variables of teachers on their emotional intelligence, occupational stress and job satisfaction which can provide for better policy planning, policy development and implementation in education, selection and training of special education teachers.

Methodology used in the Study

Method

Survey method is used in the study.

Tools used in the Study

The prime objective of the investigation is to identify the emotional intelligence, occupational stress and the job satisfaction of the special education teachers. To achieve the above stated objectives, the researcher developed and adopted the following tools:

(*i*) Rating Scale to assess the Emotional Intelligence of the Special Education Teachers (developed by the investigator);

(*ii*) Rating Scale to assess the Occupational Stress of the Special Education Teachers (developed by the investigator);

(*iii*) Rating Scale to assess the Job Satisfaction of the Special Education Teachers (adopted and modified from Reddy, 2007);

(*iv*) Rating Scale to assess the Infrastructure Facilities available in the Special Education Schools (developed by the investigator).

Validity and Reliability of the Research Tools

The developed tools were given to a panel of experts in the field concerned. Based on their suggestions certain statements in the tools were retained, modified and deleted. The content validity and face validity of the tools were examined by the subject experts. The intrinsic validity of the tools are EIS - 0.93, OSS - 0.98 and JSS - 0.96). The reliability of the tools was determined by Split-half Method. The detailed procedure adopted to establish the reliability and validity of the tools are explained in chapter—IV i.e. Methodology. The obtained reliability values for the tools are presented hereunder :

Name of the Tool	Reliability value through Split-half Method	
	Half test reliability	Whole test reliability
Emotional Intelligence Rating Scale	0.78	0.88
Occupational Stress Rating Scale	0.95	0.97
Job Satisfaction Rating Scale	0.84	0.92
Infrastructure Facilities Rating Scale	0.76	0.86

Locale and Sample of the Study

The area of the study encompasses Chennai City of the Tamil Nadu State. As per the Directory of the Office of the State Commissioner for the Disabled, Tamil Nadu State and the District Disabled Rehabilitation Office, Chennai, totally there are forty six special education schools functioning for the visually impaired (15), hearing impaired (15) and the mentally retarded (16) and are recognized by the Government. For the purpose of the study, the investigator randomly selected 12 special education schools (4 schools for visually impaired, 4 schools for hearing impaired and 4 schools for mentally retarded i.e. 26 per cent of the total schools available) by using Simple Random Sampling Technique. There are totally 226 teachers working in these schools. All the teachers working in these schools were considered for the study. But due to absence and non-response of some teachers, 202 special education teachers formed the sample of the present study.

Data Collection

The developed tools were administered to the special education teachers after establishing good rapport with the school heads and teachers. The teachers were directed to go through the instructions before rating the statements in the respective tools.

Statistical Techniques used in the Study

The collected data were analyzed by using appropriate statistical techniques such as : number and percentage, mean, SD, t-test, F-test, correlations and step-wise multiple regression analysis. To find out the number and percentage of special education teachers coming under low, moderate and high levels of Emotional Intelligence (EI), Occupational Stress (OS) and Job Satisfaction (JS), mean and standard deviation of the EI, OS and JS scores have been computed for each special education teacher. By using mean ± 1 SD, the number and percentage of teachers coming under low, moderate and high EI, OS and JS were identified by category wise special schools (i.e. VI, HI and MR) as well as special schools together. To identify the level of EI, OS and JS in special education teachers, mean and SD of the EI, OS and JS scores has been computed for each statement. Mean ± 1 SD was used to categorize the statements into low, moderate and high level of EI, OS and JS. Further, to find out the significant difference, if any, in the EI, OS and JS due to variations in the independent variables (age, community, educational qualification, nature of special schools the teachers working in, training received in special education, level of classes handled, nature of job, salary per month and years of experience of special education teachers; mean, SD has been worked out for each group in a variable. Based on these mean and SD scores, t / F-tests have been calculated appropriately. To find out the infrastructure facilities (ISF) available in the special education schools, the number and percentage of special education teachers working in the schools with poor, moderate and high infrastructure facilities (ISF), as rated by them were calculated. Further, mean ± 1 SD were calculated to categorize the teachers coming under poor, moderate and good level of ISF based on the mean and SD scores. The mean and SD of EI, OS and JS scores of the respective categories of teachers have been worked out to find out significance difference if any, in the emotional intelligence, occupational stress and job satisfaction of special education teachers due to variations in the availability of the ISF's.

Correlations were computed to find out the relationship between emotional intelligence and occupational stress, occupational stress and job satisfaction, emotional intelligence and job satisfaction of special education teachers. Step-wise multiple regression analysis was carried out to find out the contribution of the independent variables (age, community...) to the dependent variables (EI, OS and JS) of the special education teachers. Also, contribution of EI dimensions to the OS and JS; OS dimensions to JS of special education teachers were found using step-wise multiple regression analysis.

Findings of the Study

The results of the descriptive analysis in Part—I and differential analysis in Part—II reveals the following :

Part—I : Descriptive Analysis

1. More than 85 per cent of the teachers working in the special education schools possess moderate and low level of emotional intelligence, whereas 86 per cent of special education teachers experience moderate and high level of occupational stress. Likewise, more than 88 per cent of teachers are with moderate and low level of job satisfaction irrespective of the special schools they are working in.

2. The special education teachers possess moderate level of EI in 9 aspects of the self awareness dimension i.e. identifying and separating their emotions, knowing their own feelings and their impact on actions, acknowledging their own strengths and weaknesses, self-evaluating to overcome difficult situations, continuing to act on their beliefs under criticism, feeling good about themselves while looking at their both good and bad points and feeling confident in delivering the goods upto the expectations in their job. Furthermore, they possess low level of EI in defending while receiving negative feedback. Contrary to this, in knowing their priorities and being happy while looking at the things, the teachers evince high level of EI. Overall, special education teachers possess moderate level of self-awareness.

The teachers exhibit moderate level of self-management skills in 11 aspects such as—controlling their anger, being patient, presence of mind, ability in changing ideas and goals based on new information, behaving gently in stressful situations, maintaining the standards of honesty and integrity, taking calculated risks to reach the goals, initiating action to create possibilities for the future, showing optimistic behaviour, achieving small goals and in acting on their own values in risk-full situations. Also, they possess high level of self managing skills in doing their duties with responsibility and commitment and, in organizing the work environment. Contrary to this, the special education teachers exhibit low level of emotional skills in three EI competencies i.e. feeling easy on occasions where new ideas and information are to be accepted, admitting the mistakes publicly and in exhibiting initiative skills in taking up new assignments.

In the dimension 'social awareness', the special educators have moderate level of social awareness skills in majority of the EI competencies such as—being sensitive to the feelings of others, empathetic feeling, ability of interfering in others feeling and helping others to overcome the problem, working by understanding the organizational financial constraints and acting, the ability to understand the organizational values and un-spelt out rules, recognizing the forces in the school and working to meet the requirements of the job and being aware of the infrastructure facilities available in the schools. Furthermore, the teachers demonstrate high level of social awareness by listening attentively to the school needs, using equipments to cater to the needs of the students with special needs and being oriented to their duty. Contrary to this, in aspects such as—confronting with the un-ethical actions of others and making the curriculum to meet the diverse background of special needs students, the teachers show low level of social awareness.

In the aspects such as—encouraging colleagues, providing on going mentoring/coaching to colleagues, getting along with others easily in work situations, seeking help from others, teaching others by setting an example, having clear ideas to realize the vision of the school, being active partner in solving the conflicts, trying new methods and techniques in teaching-learning process, believing in team work, avoiding quarrel, establishing and maintaining close relationship with other professionals at work and, convincing the students and parents interest, the special educators possess moderate level of social skills. Moreover, teachers have high level of social skills in appreciating others for their success, maintaining good relations and co-operating with the school personnel, interacting well with the students and parents, providing guidance and counselling and making friends easily. In contrast, they evince only low level of social skills in two aspects i.e. insisting students to learn what they lack and being away from the conflict situations.

3. The potential occupational stressors in the dimension 'organizational structure and climate' causing high level of stress in special educators are long working hours and expectations to do more work, carrying multiple responsibilities, role conflict in their profession, problematic individualized educational plan for pupils with multiple disabilities, large class size with diverse needs students, lack of time to pay individual attention and taking responsibilities of others. The remaining stressors—lack of information in carrying out the professional responsibilities, working on assignments that are unnecessary to their profession, lack of equipments and teaching-learning materials, inadequate supportive staff and trained human resources, non-involvement in decision making process in their profession, lack of opportunities for promotion, inadequate salary and stringent rules and regulations in the school have evoked moderate level of stress in special education teachers.

The stressors such as—lack of opportunities for professional enhancement in the form of participation in professional meetings/ seminars/conferences, inadequate knowledge in using aids and appliances and thrust on the development of curricular innovations and materials have evoked high level of stress in teachers. Contrast to this, lack of commitment and interest to perform the job has generated only low level of stress in teachers. Further, inadequate training in special education, being overqualified to perform the job, problem in identification and assessment procedures, difficulty in managing students, difficulty in solving the problems, facing problems in decision making process, difficulty in completing the task within a stipulated period of time and difficulty in implementing new procedures and policies are the aspects that generated moderate level of occupational stress in teachers because of inadequacy in their personal and professional efficiency.

Teachers felt that stressful interactions and inadequate support from the parents, lack of team work and professional collaboration to meet the divergent needs of children, being angry with the students for their continuous failure, difficult to satisfy the requirements of the management, poor quality of feedback and supervision that address teacher concerns and problems in discussing the failure of students with their parents as stressors causing moderate level of stress. The aspects—difficult in adjusting with the colleagues, lack of healthy interactions among the teachers, inadequate knowledge to provide guidance and counselling to the students and parents, understanding the behaviour of the students, misunderstanding the organizational values and goals and lack of pro-active communication with the school management has created only low level of occupational stress among the special education teachers.

Out of 12 stressors arising out of the dimension 'environmental factors', two stressors i.e. seldom opportunity to utilize the abilities and experience independently and seldom reward for the hard labour have evoked high level of stress in special educators. Furthermore, the teachers experience moderate level of occupational stress because of the complaints made by the students, bullying and frightening by the students inside and outside the school, complaints by the staff members, lack of respect for the special education profession by the pupils, parents and the society, theft and damage of property by the students, students indiscipline apart from students drug abuse. The teachers experience low level of stress in the remaining stressors i.e. fraud and financial mismanagement within the school, polluted working environment and problem in solving students disputes.

4. The job satisfaction of the special education teachers is observed to be moderate in all the organizational aspects such as: comfortable working environment, conflicts in the school, in-service training received by the teachers, freedom to express their ideas, lack of proper facilities to prepare materials, inadequate classroom facilities, leave rules in the schools, sufficient time they received for rest and recreation, excess workload, non-participation in the policy formulation, trouble in maintaining discipline in the classroom and opportunities for promotion in the school.

The special educators are highly satisfied in intra and interpersonal relationships maintained with the job personnel's and students. In other aspects such as—principals helping tendency in improving the personal skills and their relationship, misunderstanding the teacher in workplace by others, students approach to discuss their difficulties, making adjustments in their job as a special education teacher, co-operation and support from the colleagues, believing people in the job to discuss the confidential issue, emotional support provided by the colleagues and subordinates, students respect and their attention, the special education teachers possess moderate level of job satisfaction.

The special education teachers are highly satisfied in their job due to the motivational aspects such as—teacher's optimistic attitude towards their job, personal satisfaction with the service they are rendering, interest in their job and, the nature of job they have selected. Also, they are moderately satisfied with their job as they are not often motivated by their school management, receive inadequate feedback from their principal for their improvement, inadequate opportunities for the advancement and growth, job involvement, lack of appreciation for the academic knowledge and abilities from the seniors and in executing their work. At the same time the teachers are least satisfied with their job as they are not given any rewards for the individual work from the school, the rewards given have not motivated them, feel tired after returning from their schools and are not given any perks for their achievement.

In the dimension 'job security and financial status', the special education teachers are least satisfied because of inadequate grants for the development of the school and inadequate salary received in special education field while comparing with the salary of the general educators. Moreover, they are moderately satisfied in the remaining aspects i.e. self-respect from their profession, salary they are receiving, temporary nature of the job, earnings in their profession compared to the earnings in other profession, job security and, freedom of exposing their talents and skills in their job.

Part—II : Differential Analysis

5. The variations in the age group has not significantly influenced the emotional intelligence, occupational stress and job satisfaction of special education teachers and teachers working in special schools as a whole, except the teachers working in the schools for MR with respect to emotional intelligence and teachers working in special schools as a whole with respect to occupational stress only. Further, lower the age group, lower will be the emotional intelligence of teachers working in the schools for MR children. The teachers of 30 years and below age group experience higher levels of occupational stress followed by teachers belonging to 46 years and above and 31 to 45 years age group.
6. The variable 'community' has not significantly influenced the emotional intelligence, occupational stress and job satisfaction of special education teachers, except the emotional intelligence of teachers working in the schools for MR children. The BC community teachers demonstrated higher levels of EI than their counterparts with OC and MBC / SC & ST communities.
7. The variable 'educational qualification' of teachers has significantly influenced the emotional intelligence of teachers working in the schools for MR and special schools as a whole. On the other hand, it has not significantly influenced the emotional intelligence of teachers working in the schools for HI and VI. Higher the educational qualifications, higher will be the emotional.

intelligence of teachers working in the schools for MR. Contrary to the above, the variation in the educational qualification of teachers working in all types of special schools has not significantly influenced their occupational stress and job satisfaction.

8. The variable 'nature of special schools the teachers working in' has significant influence on their emotional intelligence, occupational stress and job satisfaction. Further, the teachers working in the schools for VI children possess high emotional intelligence and experience more occupational stress than their counterparts working in the schools for HI and MR. On the other hand, the teachers working for HI children have higher levels of job satisfaction than their counterparts working in the schools for VI and MR.
9. The variable 'training received in special education' by the teachers working in all types of special schools has not significantly influenced their emotional intelligence; whereas, it has significantly influenced the occupational stress of teachers working in the schools for VI and special schools as a whole, but not the teachers working in the schools for MR and HI. Similarly, the job satisfaction of teachers working in the schools for VI differed significantly because of the training they received in special education; whereas, it has not influenced the job satisfaction of teachers working in the schools for HI, MR and special schools as a whole. Further, the teachers working in the schools for VI, who received higher order of professional training like B.Ed. in Special Education has lower occupational stress and enjoys higher job satisfaction than their counterparts who possess only Diploma in Special Education.
10. The variable 'level of classes handled' has significantly influenced the emotional intelligence of teachers working in the schools for MR and special schools as a whole and occupational stress of teachers working in the schools for HI and special schools as a whole. Contrary to this, the emotional intelligence of teachers working in the schools for HI and VI, occupational stress of teachers working in the schools for VI and MR and the job satisfaction of teachers working in all the categories of special schools has not differed significantly due to variations in the level of classes handled by them. Also, the teachers handling higher secondary classes possess higher level of emotional intelligence and experience lower rates of occupational stress than their counterparts who handle secondary and primary level classes.

11. The variable 'nature of job' has significantly influenced the emotional intelligence of teachers working in the schools for HI, MR and special schools as a whole and, the occupational stress of teachers working in the schools for MR and special schools as a whole. Contrary to this, it has not influenced the emotional intelligence of teachers working in the schools for VI, occupational stress of teachers working in the schools for HI and VI and, job satisfaction of teachers working in all the categories of special schools. The teachers serving in permanent position possess more emotional intelligence and low level of occupational stress and vice-versa.
12. The variable 'salary of the teachers' has significantly influenced the emotional intelligence of teachers working in the schools for HI, MR and special schools as a whole; whereas, it has not influenced the emotional intelligence of teachers working in the schools for VI. The teachers receiving higher salary possess high level of emotional intelligence and vice-versa. Likewise, the occupational stress of teachers working in the schools for MR is significantly influenced by their salary. On the other hand, it has not influenced the occupational stress of teachers working in the schools for HI, VI and special schools as a whole. The teachers receiving more than ₹ 10,001 to 20,000 as a monthly salary have low occupational stress rates than their counterparts receiving salary of ₹ 20,001 and above and, ₹ 10,000 and below. The job satisfaction of teachers working in the schools for HI, MR and special schools as a whole is significantly influenced by their salary; whereas, it has not made any significant difference in the job satisfaction of teachers working in the schools for VI. Moreover, the higher the teacher's salary, the better is the job satisfaction of teachers and vice versa.
13. The variable 'years of experience' has significantly influenced the emotional intelligence of teachers working in the schools for MR; while the same has not influenced the emotional intelligence of teachers working in the schools for HI, VI and special schools as a whole. The teachers with more years of experience possess higher emotional intelligence than their counterparts with less years of experience. The occupational stress and job satisfaction of teachers working in all the categories of schools have not differed significantly due to variations in their years of experience.
14. Around 90-95 per cent of the special education teachers felt that their school is inaccessible to the facilities like false roofing that

curtail extra noise, adopted play materials, equipments and materials to identify children with different disabilities, speech synthesizers for children with disabilities, talking calculators, speech therapy materials, computer assisted instruction and the library with current books related to the special education, as they are available in poor and moderate levels. Likewise, more than 80 per cent of the special education teachers perceive that the ISF like magnifying devices and lenses, large print and coloured print materials, embossed teaching learning materials, audio-video materials, ramps/rails and special toilet facilities, overhead projector, physiotherapy and occupational therapy facilities, sensory training materials, mathematical devices and aids like abacus, taylor frame and graphic aids are in poor and moderate forms in the special schools they are working. Further, the facilities such as—Braille slate and stylus, orientation and mobility materials, facilities to use hearing aids and group hearing aids, low cost multimedia materials, braille typewriters, closed circuit television and the sanitary and drinking water facilities are in poor and moderate form in the special schools as observed by more than 70 to 75 per cent of the teachers working in the special education schools. In addition to these, the facilities like furniture for seating the staff and the students, uninterrupted power supply, space and proper ventilation in the classroom and the staff rooms, health care amenities for special children within the school and school transport services for disabled students are in moderate and good forms, as perceived by around 80 to 95 per cent of the special education teachers.

15. The occupational stress and job satisfaction of special education teachers significantly differ due to variations in the availability of ISF as rated by them in special schools where they are working. In contrast, the emotional intelligence of special education teachers do not differ significantly due to variations in the availability of ISF as rated by them in special schools where they are working. Moreover, the occupational stress of special education teachers who rated the ISF as poor is higher followed by the teachers who rated ISF as good and moderate; whereas, the job satisfaction of teachers who rated the ISF as poor are lower followed by the teachers who rated the ISF as moderate and good.

16. The EI dimensions—self management, social skills and emotional intelligence as a whole are negatively correlated with each of the dimensions of occupational stress (OS) and OS as a whole.

Likewise, the EI dimensions—self awareness and social awareness are also correlated negatively with the OS dimensions— environmental factors and OS as a whole. Similarly, the self awareness of EI dimension has significant negative correlation with OS dimension—personal and professional efficiency; social awareness of EI dimension with intra and interpersonal interactions of OS dimension. In contrast, self awareness (EI_1) has not significantly correlated with organizational structure and climate (OS_1) and, intra and interpersonal interactions (OS_3); social awareness (EI_3) has not significantly related with organizational structure and climate (OS_1) and, personal and professional efficiency (OS_2). It is also inferred that the lower the emotional intelligence, the higher will be the occupational stress of special education teachers.

17. The EI dimensions—self awareness, self management and EI as a whole are positively related with the dimensions of job satisfaction—'organizational aspects (JS_1)', 'intra and interpersonal relationships (JS_2)' and 'job security and financial status (JS_4)' except, the dimension 'motivational climate (JS_3)'. Likewise, the emotional intelligence dimensions—social awareness is positively related with the JS dimensions—intra and interpersonal relationships (JS_2), job security and financial status (JS_4) and job satisfaction as a whole, except the JS dimensions—organizational aspects (JS_1) and motivational climate (JS_3). Moreover, the EI dimension 'social skill' has significantly and positively related with each of the job satisfaction dimensions and JS as a whole. It is also evident that the higher the emotional intelligence, the higher will be the job satisfaction of special education teachers and vice-versa.
18. The OS dimensions—organizational structure and climate (OS_1), intra and interpersonal interactions (OS_3) and OS as a whole (OS) are significantly and negatively correlated with each of the JS dimensions and JS as whole. Likewise, the environmental factors (dimension of OS) are significantly and negatively correlated with each of the JS dimensions—'organizational aspects (JS_1)', 'intra and interpersonal relationships (JS_2)' 'job security and financial status (JS_4)' and JS as a whole, except the dimension 'motivational climate (JS_3)'. Similarly, the OS dimension 'personal and professional efficiency (OS_2)' is significantly and negatively correlated to the JS dimensions—JS_1, JS_2 and JS as a whole, except the JS dimensions—motivational climate (JS_3) and, job security

and financial status (JS_4). Also, the higher the occupational stress, the lower will be the job satisfaction of special education teachers.

19. There is a significant negative relationship between emotional intelligence and occupational stress of teachers working in the schools for HI, MR and special schools as a whole and, no significant relationship between the EI and OS of teachers working in the schools for VI. Similarly, there is a significant negative relationship between occupational stress and job satisfaction of teachers working in all the categories of special schools. The results reveal that the higher the emotional intelligence, the lower will be the occupational stress and; the higher the occupational stress, the lower will be the job satisfaction of special education teachers and vice-versa. Moreover, it is noted that there is significant relationship between emotional intelligence and job satisfaction of teachers working in all categories of special schools. Here, the higher the emotional intelligence, the higher will be the job satisfaction of special education teachers and vice-versa.
20. The variable 'salary' has contributed significantly to the emotional intelligence, occupational stress and job satisfaction of special education teachers working in the schools for HI, to a greater extent. The other independent variable 'nature of job' has also contributed significantly to the emotional intelligence of teachers working in the schools for HI, whereas the teachers occupational stress is predicted by the variable 'level of classes handled' and 'training received in special education' by the special education teachers working in the schools for HI. In addition to the variable, 'salary', the variable 'years of experience' has also significantly contributed to the teacher's job satisfaction to a greater extent.
21. The variable 'salary' is the major predictor contributing more to the emotional intelligence of teachers working in the schools for MR followed by the other variables 'nature of job' and 'level of classes handled'. Further, it is noted that the variables 'nature of job' and 'community' are the significant predictors to the occupational stress and job satisfaction of special education teachers respectively to a greater extent.
22. The independent variable 'training in special education' is the significant contributor to the occupational stress and job satisfaction of teachers working in the schools for VI.
23. The independent variables 'level of classes handled', 'nature of school', 'salary' and 'nature of job' are the significant contributors to the emotional intelligence, whereas the variables 'training in

special education', 'salary', 'level of classes handled' and 'nature of school' have contributed significantly to the occupational stress of special education teachers. Further, the variable 'salary' has contributed to the job satisfaction of special education teachers to certain extent.

24. The independent variable EI dimension 'social skill' is the significant contributor to the OS of teachers working in the schools for HI and special schools as a whole. The 'EI as a whole' contributed significantly to OS and JS of teaches working in the schools for MR and, to the JS of teachers working in special schools as a whole. Further, the OS dimension 'intra and interpersonal interactions' which acted as independent variable emerged as significant contributor to the JS of teachers working in the schools for HI and VI. The EI dimension 'self-awareness' is the significant contributor to the JS of teachers working in the schools for VI children. Also, the independent variable of OS dimension 'organizational structure and climate' is another significant contributor to the JS of teachers working for MR children. Similarly, the dependent variable 'job satisfaction' is predicted by two of the independent variables 'OS as a whole and personal and professional efficiency of OS dimensions.

Implications of the Study

1. As the results revealed that around 90 per cent of the teachers encompass only low and moderate level of emotional intelligence, there is a need for training in emotional intelligence to the special education teachers both at pre-service and in-service levels. Also, while designing the curriculum for the teacher educators/special educators, Rehabilitation Council of India and National Council for Teacher Education should include the emotional intelligence components along with the other skills. Further, the principal/head teachers should give due recognition to the teachers working under them in order to facilitate good interpersonal skills. They should be given due opportunity while making important decisions. In addition, the school management should assess the actual schools needs, the competencies needed to handle those needs and also should assess the teacher's strength and weaknesses by providing adequate feedback. Also, the head teachers should encourage teachers to use the emotional intelligence skills in their job and they should provide flexible environment that enhance teachers insightfulness. This facilitates them to utilize their emotional intelligence more effectively in

the work place and to deal effectively with the negative emotions that arise from their work situations.

2. The study revealed that more than 80 per cent of the special education teachers experience high and moderate level of occupational stress. This trend indicates that there is a need for strengthening the organizational structure and climate of the special education schools, providing opportunities for professional enhancement in the form of participation in professional meetings and seminars, promoting situations for healthy professional interactions and making the working environment more flexible to work. This may be carried out by developing responsive induction programmes to support the beginning special educators, creating positive work environments and systems of support by giving adequate supportive resources, increasing the level and quality of administrative support, fostering professional development to encourage teacher effectiveness, structuring teachers roles to focus on student learning and, paying reasonable salaries as incentives. Further, Mokdad (2005) suggested that the teaching work needs to be ergonomically designed in order to combat occupational stress. Educational ergonomics refers to the application of theories, models, laws and methods of ergonomics to the educational settings. Educational ergonomics are : teaching (teaching methods, teaching aids, increasing learners motivation); academic curricula (design, development, enrichment, evaluation); assessment of academic performance (developing evaluation tools, assessing evaluation tools, academic achievement tests, exams); development of individuals (students, teachers, administrators); the design of context design (study place, the design of classrooms and amphitheaters, computer stations, the physical environment); and the legislative framework (laws and regulations). The same should be carried out in special education profession to overcome stress in special educators. Furthermore, the school management should arrange for cognitive behavioural programme to enhance teachers stress management resources.

3. As more than 88 percent of special education teachers enjoy only low and moderate levels of job satisfaction, it is essential to provide favourable working environment, favourable fiscal policy towards special education teachers in-terms of increased salaries and benefits, terms and conditions of employment, recognize special education profession as valuable and sensitize the society

to be more understanding and helpful, improve planning and programming including personnel, time and resource allocation, protect teachers rights and their economic and social interests, respond to the demands of special education, and should allow for equipment improvements and modern communication tools related to special education profession. Extrinsic rewards will also go a long way to motivate the special education teachers for their creative activities. The school system should confer special education teachers for doing the job well. The head teachers should give adequate supportive hand to improve the professional skills and provide opportunities for teachers to interact and be supportive to one another. Also, the head teachers should involve them in group discussion while making decisions.

4. The study revealed that the EI of teachers :possessing graduation with B.Ed. and M.Ed. qualification, working in the schools for VI children, teachers teaching higher secondary classes, holding permanent position and, receiving high salary ₹ 20,001 and above are higher than their counterparts possessing teacher training and graduation with B.Ed. qualification, working in the schools for HI and MR children, teaching secondary and primary classes, holding temporary position and, receiving low salary ₹ 10,001-20,000 and ₹ 10,000 and below respectively. This trend indicates that while giving training in emotional intelligence, these categories of teachers should be given due importance. In-order to enhance emotional intelligence among special education teachers, the curriculum at pedagogical level should be tuned to include emotional skills and activities. They should be involved in group discussions and group meetings to understand and solve the problems effectively. Also, while recruiting teachers for special education profession, the group of special education teachers disclosing high emotional intelligence should be given prior importance and should also be assessed for emotional competencies for appropriate placements to handle classes. At the same time, the variables, 'level of classes handled', 'nature of special school the teachers working in', 'salary' and 'nature of job' have significantly contributed to the emotional intelligence. Here, the special education teachers handling various levels of classes, working in different types of special schools, range of salary they are drawing, and nature of position holding decided the emotional intelligence to certain extent, so these variables should be given due importance while selecting, training and placement of the special education teachers. Also, the policy

makers should bear these independent variables of teachers that has influenced and contributed to the EI, while structuring the framework for special education profession.

5. At the same time, the occupational stress of teachers belonging to 30 and below years of age group, working in the schools for VI children, who received lower order of professional training like Diploma in special education, handling primary classes, holding temporary position are higher than the teachers belonging to 46 and above years and 31-45 years of age group, working in the schools for MR and HI children, who received high professional training like B.Ed. special education, handling secondary and higher secondary classes and holding permanent position respectively. It is apt to give due importance to these group of teachers while giving stress management programmes. Also, the special education teachers belonging to lower age group should be oriented towards the problems and prospects of the special education profession in order to cope with the stress and strain arising due to various sources of stressors. Also, the beginning special educators should be given in-service training programme from time to time. Further, the special education teachers handling primary classes should be altered from time to time to teach/handle higher secondary classes to overcome stress. Furthermore, the variables 'training in special education', 'salary', 'level of classes handled' and 'nature of special schools the teachers working in' have contributed significantly to the occupational stress of special education teachers. This suggests that the training of the special education teachers in various special education aspects should be made mandatory; salary of the special education teachers should be framed without any prejudice on par with regular school teachers, special education teachers should be allowed to handle classes according to their skills and interests and; stress management programmes to be structured should meet the specific requirements and demands of the special education teachers working in different types of special schools to combat stress.

6. The variable 'salary' has influenced and contributed to the job satisfaction of special education teachers. This result entails that salary of the special education teachers should be enhanced on par or even more than the salary of the general education teachers/other professionals as their work demands are tough to accomplish in their profession. Further, the salary structure

should be fixed to the special education teachers irrespective of the different types of special schools they are working in.

7. The correlation studies revealed that there is a significant negative relationship between EI and OS; OS and JS and positive relationship between EI and JS. These results further confirm the need to inculcate emotional intelligence skills in special education teachers to reduce the severity of occupational stress and enhance their job satisfaction.

8. The results based on the step wise multiple regression analysis showed that the dimension 'social skill' (EI dimension) contributed to the occupational stress of special education teachers. This recommends that social skill as important ability to be considered while dealing with occupational stress of special education teachers. In other words, while planning for stress management programme, social skills of the special education teachers should be taught and should be included in the pre and in-service training programmes. In case of job satisfaction of special education teachers, total emotional intelligence i.e all the four dimensions—self awareness, self- management, social awareness and social skills have contributed to their job satisfaction indicating once-again, the need for emotional intelligence competencies through EI training to special education teachers so as to enjoy utmost satisfaction in their profession. Further, the occupational stress dimension—'personal and professional efficiency' and 'occupational stress as a whole' have significantly contributed to the special education teachers job satisfaction indicating the need for improvement in the organizational structure and climate, personal and professional efficiency of teachers, intra and interpersonal interactions and environmental factors to bring job satisfaction.

9. Majority of special education teachers felt that their special schools are inaccessible to many of the infrastructural facilities. It is obligatory on the part of the school management to provide the facilities to transact the curriculum into practice in an effective way to enhance teaching –learning process thereby bringing quality special education programme. Further, the Govt., and NGO's shall allot funds to procure the infrastructural facilities that are lacking in special education schools. Also, the school management should be aware of the schemes available and should make use of those schemes to enhance the infrastructural facilities in schools. This may be done through awareness and orientation programmes to the school heads or management.

10. Furthermore, the availability of infrastructure facilities as rated by special education teachers in special schools they are working have significant bearing on their occupational stress and job satisfaction. It is noted that the teachers who rated the ISF as poor exhibit high level of occupational stress and low levels of job satisfaction. This trend indicates that there is a need to enhance ISF in special schools in order to reduce occupational stress and increase job satisfaction among special education teachers.

Delimitations of the Study

1. The emotional intelligence, occupational stress and job satisfaction of special education teachers have been assessed only based on the self-ratings of the special education teachers.
2. The study is confined to Chennai city of Tamilnadu State.
3. The study is limited only to the special education teachers working in the schools for hearing impaired, mentally retarded and visually impaired children.
4. Rating scale is the only tool used to assess the emotional intelligence, occupational stress and job satisfaction of the special education teachers.
5. The dimension 'home-work interface', which is one of the sources of the occupational stress, is not included in the tool, as the investigator concentrated only on the work environment of the special education teachers.
6. The infrastructure Facilities Rating Scale is rated by the special education teachers only.
7. The effect of only a few personal variables on EI, OS and JS has been studied.

Suggestions for Further Research

1. Studies can be conducted to identify the emotional intelligence, occupational stress and job satisfaction of special education teachers working in the schools for orthopedic handicapped, learning disabled, multiple disabled, autism etc.,
2. Studies can be attempted to identify the emotional intelligence, occupational stress and job satisfaction of special education teachers working in inclusive education setup.
3. Studies can be conducted to assess the emotional intelligence, occupational stress and job satisfaction using multiple tools.

4. Similar studies can be conducted covering the special schools functioning in other Districts of Tamil Nadu State and other parts of India.
5. Studies can be attempted to identify the effectiveness of emotional intelligence training and stress coping strategies.
6. Studies can be conducted to identify the emotional intelligence, occupational stress and job satisfaction of principals/head teachers in special education and inclusive schools.
7. Studies can be done to identify the emotional intelligence of parents of children with disabilities.
8. Studies can be undertaken to identify the stress patterns of parents of children with disabilities.
9. Separate studies can be undertaken to identify the infrastructure facilities available in special education schools and regular schools to meet the needs of the special needs children.
10. Studies can be attempted to find out how far and to what extent the other variable that are not covered in the present study influence the dependent variables i.e. EI, OS and JS of special education teachers.

Bibliography

Abd-El-Fattah, S.M. (2010) 'Longitudinal Effects of Pay Increase on Teachers Job Satisfaction: A Motivational Perspective', *The Journal of International Social Research,* Vol. 3, No. 10, pp. 11-21, Winter.

Abel, M. H. and Sewell, J. (1999) 'Stress and Burnout in Rural and Urban Secondary School Teachers', *The Journal of Educational Research,* Vol. 92, No.5, pp. 287-293, May-June.

Adams, J.S. (1965) *'Advances in Experimental Social Psychology',* In L. Berkowitz Inequity in Social Exchange, (2nd ed.), Academic Press, New York.

Adeyemo, D.A. and Ogunyemi, B. (2007) 'Emotional intelligence and Self-Efficacy as Predictors of Occupational Stress Among Academic Staff in Nigerian University', *E- Journal of Organizational Learning and Leadership,* Vol. 7, No. 2, Fall & Winter.

Adler, D.A., McLaughlin, T.J., Rogers, W.H., Chang, H., Lapitsky, L. and Lerner, D. (2006) 'Job Performance Deficits Due to Depression', *The American Journal of Psychiatry,* Vol. 163, pp. 1569-1576.

Ahghar, G. (2008) 'The Role of School Organizational Climate in Occupational Stress Among Secondary School Teachers in Tehran', *International Journal of Occupational Medicine and Environmental Health,* Vol. 21, No. 4, pp. 319-329.

Al Khateeb, J.M. and Hadidi, M. S. (2009) 'Teachers and Mothers Satisfaction with Resource Room Programmes in Jordan', *Journal of the International Association of Special Education*, Vol. 10, No. 1, pp. 56-59, Spring.

Al-Fudail, M. and Mellar, H. (2008) 'Investigating Teacher Stress When Using Technology', *Computers and Education*, Vol. 51, No. 3, pp.1103-1110, November.

Allen, D. (2001) *'Getting Things Done: The Art of Stress-free Productivity'*, Penguin Books, New York.

Aluja, A., Blanch, A. and Garcia, L.F. (2005) 'Dimensionality of Maslach Burnout Inventory in School Teachers : A Study of Several Proposals', *European Journal of Psychological Assessment*, Vol. 21, No. 1, pp. 67-76.

Amaladoss Xavier, S.J. (2009) 'Relationship Between Job Satisfaction and Teaching Competency', *Research and Reflections on Education*, Vol. 7, No. 2, pp. 22-24, April-June.

Amirtagowri, R. and Thiagarajan, A.P. (2005) 'Occupational Dilemmas of Educational Women—An Analysis', *Perspectives in Education*, Vol. 21, No.3, pp. 175-183.

Amirtha, A. and Kadhiravan, S. (2006) 'Influence of Personality on the Emotional Intelligence of Teachers', *EduTracks*, Vol. 5, No. 12, pp. 25-29, August.

Andrews, L., Evans, S. and Miller, N. (2002) 'How Can We Prepare and Retain Effective Special Education Teachers ? ', *Academic Exchange Quarterly*, Vol. 6, No. 2, pp. 36.

Angerer, J.M. (2003) 'Job Burnout', *Journal of Employment Counselling*, Vol. 40, No.3, pp. 98-107.

Antoniou, A.-S., Polychroni, F. and Vlachakis, A.-N. (2006) 'Gender and Age Differences in Occupational Stress and Professional Burnout Between Primary and High School Teachers in Greece', *Journal of Managerial Psychology*, Vol. 21, No. 7, pp. 682-690.

Antoniou, A.-S., Polychroni, F. and Kotroni, C. (2009) 'Working with Students with Special Educational Needs in Greece: Teachers Stressors and Coping Strategies', *International Journal of Special Education*, Vol. 24, No.1, pp. 100-111.

Arora, S. and Hussain, M.I. (2008) 'Work Alienation Among Primary School Teachers', *Journal of Teacher Education and Research*, Vol. 3, No. 1, pp. 1-14, June.

Ashcraft, D.M. (1992) *'Health in the Workplace'*, In K. Kelly (ed.), Issues, Theory and Research in Industrial/Organizational Psychology, pp. 259-283, Elsevier Science Publications B.V., Amsterdam.

Ashford, S.J., Lee, C. and Bobko, P. (1989) 'Content, Causes, and Consequences of Job Insecurity: A Theory-based Measure and Substantive Test', *Academy of Management Journal*, Vol. 32, pp. 803-829.

Ashforth, B.E. and Humphrey, R.H. (1995) 'Emotion in the Workplace: A Reappraisal', *Human Relations*, Vol. 48, pp. 97-124.

Astin, A. W. (1993) *'What Matters in College? : Four Critical Years Revisited'*, Jossey—Bass, San Francisco.

Austin, D.A. (1981) 'The Teacher Burnout Issue', *Journal of Physical Education, Recreation and Dance*, Vol. 52, No. 9, pp. 35-36.

Australian Teaching Council, (1995) *'What Do Teachers Think ?'*, A Report of Market Research Commissioned by the Australian Teaching Council, Australian Teaching Council, Leichhardt, N.S.W. 2040.

Axup, T. and Gersch, I. (2008) 'The Impact of Challenging Student Behaviour Upon Teachers' Lives in a Secondary School: Teacher's Perceptions', *British Journal of Special Education*, Vol. 35, No.3, pp.144-151, September.

Bakker, A.B., Demerouti, E., De Boer, E. and Schaufeli, W. B. (2003) 'Job Demands and Job Resources as Predictors of Absence Duration and Frequency', *Journal of Vocational Behaviour*, Vol. 62, pp. 341–356.

Balabaskar, K. (2009) 'Job Satisfaction of Special Educators Teaching Children with Special Needs : A Comparative Study', *Indian Journal of Research in Education and Extension*, Vol.1, No.1, pp. 74-86, Jan – Jun.

Balabaskar, K. (2010) 'Impact of Occupational Stress on Special Educators Working in Special Schools', *Disabilities and Impairments*, Vol. 24, No.1, pp. 13-22.

Bansibihari, P. and Pathan, Y. G. (2004) 'Emotional Intelligence of Secondary Teachers in Relation to Gender and Age', *Asian Journal of Psychology and Education*, Vol. 39, No. 5 & 6, pp. 18-21.

Barnes, B.L., Agago, M.O. and Coombs, W. T. (1998) 'Effects of Job-related Stress on Faculty Intension to Leave Academic', *Research in Higher Education*, Vol. 39, No. 4, pp. 457- 468.

Bar-On, R. (1997) 'Bar-On Emotional Quotient Inventory: A Measure of Emotional Intelligence, *Technical Manual* (ed.), Multi-health Systems, Toronto.

Bar-On, R. (2003) 'How Important is it to Educate People to be Emotionally and Socially Intelligent, and Can It Be Done?', *Perspectives in Education*, Vol. 21, No. 4, pp. 3-13.

Bar-On, R. (2005) *'The Bar-On Model of Emotional-Social Intelligence'*, In P. Farnandez-Berrocal and N. Extremera (Guest Editors), Special Issue on emotional intelligence, *Psichotema*, Vol. 17.

Basu, J., Mitra, S.K. and Bhattacharyya, P. (2004) 'Mothering the Mentally Challenged Child: A Qualitative Exploration of the Stress and Strengths', *Journal of Community Guidance and Research*, Vol. 21, No.3, pp. 282-292, November.

Baumann, M. R., Sniezek, J. A., and Buerkle, C. A. (2001) *'Self-evaluation, Stress, and Performance: A Model of Decision-making Under Acute Stress'*, In E. Salas and G. Klein (eds.), Linking Expertise and Naturalistic Decision-making (pp. 139 -158), Lawrence Erlbaum Associate, Mahwah, NJ.

Bayer, E. and Chauvet, N. (1980) *'Libertes et Constraints de I'Exercise pedagogique'*, Faculte de Psychologie et Sciences de I'Education, Geneve.

Beegam, N.H.L. and Dhamangadan, B. (2000) 'Sex Difference in Job Satisfaction of College Teachers in Kerala State', *Indian Journal of Psychometry and Education*, Vol.31, No.1, pp. 67-71.

Beehr, T.A. and Franz, T.M. (1986) *'The Current Debate About the Meaning of Job Stress'*, In J.M. Ivancevich and D. C. Ganster (eds.), Job Stress: From theory to suggestion (pp. 5-18), Haworth Press, New York.

Beehr, T.A., Walsh, J.T. and Taber, T.D. (1976) 'Relationship of Stress to Individually and Organizationally Valued States: Higher Order Needs as a Moderator', *Journal of Applied Psychology*, Vol. 61, pp. 41-47.

Beer J. and Beer J. (1992) 'Burnout and Stress, Depression and Self-esteem of Teachers', *Psychological Reports*, Vol. 71, pp. 1331-1336.

Belasco, J.A. and Alutto, J.A. (1972) 'Decisional Participation and Teacher Satisfaction', *Educational Administration Quarterly*, Vol. 8, pp. 44-58.

Belcastro, P.A. and Gold, R.S. (1983) 'Teacher Stress and Burnout: Implications for School Health Personnel', *Journal of School Health*, Vol. 53, pp. 404-407.

Benmansour, N. (1998) 'Job Satisfaction, Stress and Coping Strategies Among Moroccan High School Teachers', *Mediterranean Journal of Educational Studies*, Vol. 53, No.2, pp. 223-246.

Bensky, J.M., Shaw, S.F., Gouse, A.S., Bates, H., Dixon, B. and Beane, W.E. (1980) 'Public Law 94 -142 and Stress : A Problem for Educators of Exceptional Children', *Exceptional Children*, Vol. 47, pp. 24-29.

Best, J.W. (1989) *'Research in Education'*, Prentice Hall of India Pvt. Ltd., New Delhi.

Betancourt-Smith M., Inman D. and Marlow L. (1994) *'Professional Attrition: An Examination of Minority and Non-minority Teachers At-risk'*, Paper Presented at the Annual Meeting of the Mid-South Educational Research Association, Nashville, TN.

Betoret, F. D. (2006) 'Stressors, Self-efficacy, Coping Resources and Burnout Among Secondary School Teachers in Spain', *Educational Psychology*, Vol. 26, No. 4, pp. 519-539, August.

Betoret, F. D. (2009) 'Self-efficacy, School Resources, Job Stressors and Burnout Among Spanish Primary and Secondary School Teachers: A Structural Equation Approach', *Educational Psychology*, Vol. 29, No. 1, pp. 45-68, January.

Beverly, A. (2009) *'An Analysis of Job Satisfaction for Special Educators Who Instruct Students with Emotional / Behavioral Disorders: How Working Conditions Impact Commitment'*, Ph.D. Thesis Submitted to the University of North Texas Retrieved from http://gradworks.umi.com/33/99/3399384. html on 08.08.10.

Bhandari, R. A. and Patil, N.H. (2009) 'Job Satisfaction of Women Teachers', *EduTracks*, Vol.8, No. 11, July.

Billingsley, B. S. (2003) *'Special Education Teacher Retention and Attrition: A Critical Analysis of the Literature'*, (COPSSE Document No. RS-2), Center on Personnel Studies in Special Education, University of Florida, Gainesville, FL.

Billingsley, B. S. and Cross, L. H. (1992) 'Predictors of Commitment, Job Satisfaction, and Intent to Stay in Teaching: A Comparison of General and Special Educators', *The Journal of Special Education*, Vol. 25, No. 4, pp. 453-471.

Billingsley, B.S. (1993) 'Teacher Retention and Attrition in Special and General Education: A Critical Review of the Literature', *The Journal of Special Education*, Vol. 27, pp. 137-174.

Billingsley, B.S. (2002) 'Improving Special Education Teacher Retention: Implications from a Decade of Research', *Journal of Special Education Leadership*, Vol. 15, No. 2, pp. 60-68, November.

Bindhu, C. M. (2006) 'Relationship Between Job Satisfaction and Stress Coping Skills of Primary School Teachers', *EduTracks*, Vol. 6, No. 5, pp. 34 -36, January.

Bishay, A. (1996) 'Teacher Motivation and Job Satisfaction: A Study Employing the Experience Sampling Method', *Journal of Undergraduate Studies*, Vol. 3, pp. 147-154, Fall.

Blai, B. (1982) 'Predicting Job Satisfaction', *ERIC*, Vol. 17, No. 5, ERIC Document Reproduction Service No. ED 210582.

Blum, M.L. and Naylor, J.C. (1968) *'Industrial Psychology'*, Harper and Row, New York, pp. 364-386.

Bobbitt, S.A., Leich, M.C., Whitener, S.D. and Lynch, H.F. (1994) *'Characteristics of Stayers, Movers, and Leavers: Results from the Teacher follow-up Survey*', Department of Education, Office of Educational Research and Improvement, National Centre For Education Statistics, NCES 94-337, Washington, DC, U.S.

Boe, E.E. and Gilford, D.M. (1992) '*Teacher Supply, Demand and Quality*', National Research Council, National Academy Press, Washington, DC, p. 36.

Bogler, R. (2001) 'The Influence of Leadership Style on Teacher Job Satisfaction', *Educational Administration Quarterly*, Vol. 37, No. 5, pp. 662-683.

Boomer, L. and King, T. (1981) 'Teacher Identification of Behaviour Problems Among Junior High School Students: A Preliminary Study', *Behavioural Disorders*, Vol. 6, pp. 219-222.

Borg, M. (1990) 'Occupational Stress in British Educational Settings: A Review', *Educational Psychology*, Vol. 10, pp. 103-126.

Borg, M.G. and Falzon, J. M. (1991) 'Sources of Teachers Stress in Maltese Primary Schools', *Research in Education*, Vol. 46, pp. 1-15.

Borg, M.G., Riding R. J. and Falzon J. M. (1991) 'Stress in Teaching: A Study of Occupational Stress and its Determinants, Job Satisfaction and Career Commitment Among Primary School Teachers', *Educational Psychology, Vol. 11*, pp. 59-75.

Boutskou, E. (2007) 'The Role of Special Education Teachers in Primary Schools in Greece', *International Studies in Sociology of Education*, Vol. 17, No. 3, pp. 289-302, September.

Bowman, G. (1998) '*Some Commonly Asked Questions About Stress*', Retrieved from http://www.hsc.edu/stu/counseling/stress.html on 02.05.2009.

Boyatzis, R.E., Goleman, D. and Rhee, K. (2000) '*Clustering Competence in Emotional Intelligence: Insights from the Emotional Competence Inventory (ECI)*', In R. Bar-On and J.D. A. Parker (eds.), The Handbook of Emotional Intelligence : Theory, Development, Assessment and Application at Home, School and in the Workplace (pp. 343-362), Jossey-Bass, San Francisco.

Boyle. G. J., Borg, M.G., Falzon, J.M., and Baglioni, A.J. (1995) 'A Structural Model of the Dimensions of Teacher Stress', *British Journal of Educational Psychology*, Vol. 65, pp. 49-67.

Brackett, M.A., Palomera, R., Mojsa-Kaja, J., Reyes, M.R. and Salovey, P. (2010) 'Emotion-regulation Ability, Burnout, and Job Satisfaction Among British Secondary School Teachers', *Psychology in the Schools*, Vol. 47, No. 4, pp. 406-417.

Bradberry, T. and Greaves, J. (2009) '*Emotional Intelligence 2.0*', Publishers Group West, San Francisco.

Brahmaiah, T. and Rao, D.B. (2009) '*Stress of Student Teachers*', Discovery Publishing House, New Delhi.

Brand, T. (2007) '*Exploration of the Relationship Between Burnout, Occupational Stress and Emotional Intelligence in the Nursing Industry*', MA Dissertation (Industrial Psychology), Submitted to the University of Stellenbosch, Western Cape, South Africa.

Brenner, S.D., Sorbom, D. and Wallius, E. (1985) 'The Stress Chain : A Longitudinal Study of Teacher Stress, Coping and Social Support', *Journal of Occupational Psychology*, Vol. 58, pp. 1-14.

Breuse, E. (1984) '*Identification de las Fuentes de Tension en al Trabajo Professional del Enseniante*', In J.M. Esteve (ed.) Professors en Conflicto, Narcea, Madrid, pp. 78-85.

Brodinsky, B. (1984) 'Teacher Morale: What Build it, What Kills It', *Instructor*, Vol. 5, pp. 36-40.

Brokke, D. (2002) '*Determinants of Job Satisfaction and job Dissatisfaction of Administrators in the American Association of Christian Schools*', Congress on Christian School Education Grace Christian School, Huntington, West Virginia, pp. 175-179.

Brouwers A., Evers W. J. G. and Tomic W. (2001) 'Self-efficacy in Eliciting Social Support and Burnout Among Secondary School Teachers', *Journal of Applied Social Psychology, Vol. 31*, pp. 1474-1491.

Brown, M. and Ralph, S. (1992) 'Towards the Identification of Stress in Teachers', *Research in Education*, Vol. 48, pp. 103-110.

Brown, S., and Nagel, L. (2004) 'Preparing Future Teachers to Respond to Stress: Sources and Solutions', *Action in Teacher Education*, Vol. 26, pp. 34-42.

Brownell, M. T. and Smith, S. W. (1993) 'Understanding Special Education Teacher Attrition: A Conceptual Model and Implications for Teacher Educators', *Teacher Education and Special Education*, Vol. 16, No. 3, pp. 370-382.

Bruce, K. and Cacciope, R. (1989) 'A Survey of why Teachers Resigned from Government Secondary Schools in Western Australia', *Australian Journal of Education*, Vol. 33, No. 1, pp. 68-82.

Brundage, G.C. (2007) '*EFL Foreign Teacher Stress in Korea: Causes and Coping Mechanisms*', Education Resources Information Centre, Retrieved from www.eric.ed.gov/ERICWebPortal/recordDetail?accno-ED502354 on 07.12.09.

Brunetti, G. J. (2001) 'Why Do They Teach? : A Study of Job Satisfaction Among Long-term High School Teachers', *Teacher Education Quarterly*, Summer, Retrieved from http://findarticles.com/p/articles/mi_qa3960/is_200107/ai_n8974684 on 12.11.09.

Buckhalt, J.A., Marchetti, A. and Bearden, L.J. (1990) 'Source of Job Stress and Job Satisfaction Reported by Direct Care Staff of Large Residential Mental Retardation Facilities', *Education and Training in Mental Retardation*, Vol. 25, pp. 344-351.

Burgstahler, S. (2003) 'The Role of Technology in Preparing Youth with Disabilities for Postsecondary Education and Employment' *Journal of Special Education Technology*, Vol. 18, No. 4, pp. 7-19.

Burke R. J. and Greenglass E. R. (1995) 'A Longitudinal Examination of the Cherniss Model of Psychological Burnout', *Social Science and Medicine, Vol. 40*, pp. 1357-1363.

Burke R. J., Greenglass E. R. and Schwarzer R. (1996) 'Predicting Teacher Burnout Over Time: Effects of Work Stress, Social Support, and Self-Doubts on Burnout and its Consequences', *Anxiety, Stress and Coping: An International Journal, Vol. 9*, pp. 261-275.

Burke, E. and Dunham, J. (1982) 'Identifying Stress in Language Teaching', *British Journal of Language Teaching*, Vol. 20, pp. 149-52.

Burke, R.J. and Greenglass, E. (1994) 'A Longitudinal Study of Psychological Burnout in Teachers', *Human Relations*, Vol. 47, No.3, pp. 1-15.

Busch, T., Fallan, L. and Petterson, A. (1998) 'Disciplinary Differences in Job Satisfaction, Self-efficacy, Goal Commitment and Organizational Commitment Among Faculty Employees in Norwegian Colleges : An Empirical Assessment of indicators of Performance', *Quality in Higher Education*, Vol. 4, No. 2, pp. 137-157.

Butler, J.K. (1991) 'Toward Understanding and Measuring Conditions of Trust: Evolution of a Condition of Trust Inventory', *Journal of Management*, Vol. 17, pp. 643-663.

Cameron, A. (2003) '*Work Profile Questionnaire: Emotional Intelligence*', In B. S. Blake, J. C. Impara, and R. A. Spies (eds.), The Fifteenth Mental Measurements Yearbook, Buros Institute of Mental Measurements, Lincoln, NE.

Camilli, K.A. (2004) '*Teacher Job Satisfaction and Teacher Burnout as a Product of Years of Experience in Teaching*', Thesis Submitted to the Rowan University.

Caputo, J.S. (1991) '*Stress and Burnout in Library Service*', Oryx Press, Phoenix.

Carbonneau, N., Vallerand, R. J., Fernet, C. and Guay, F. (2008) 'The Role of Passion for Teaching in Intrapersonal and Interpersonal Outcomes', *Journal of Educational Psychology*, Vol. 100, No.4, pp. 977-987, November.

Cartwright, S. and Cooper, C.L. (1997) *'Managing Workplace Stress'*, Thousand Oaks, Sage Publications, California.

Caton, D., Grossnickle, W., Cope, J., Long, T. and Mitchell, C. (1998) Burnout and Stress Among Employees at an Institution for Mentally Retarded Persons, *American Journal on Mental Retardation*, Vol. 93, 300-304.

Certo, J. L. and Fox, J. E. (2002) 'Retaining Quality Teachers', *High School Journal*, Vol. 86, No. 1, 57-75.

Ceyanes, J. W. (2004) *'Analyses Between Teachers trust in the Principal and Teacher Burnout as Identified by Teachers in Selected Texas Public Schools'*, Thesis Submitted to the Office of Graduate Studies of Texas A & M University.

Chambers, C. (2008) 'Special Education's Challenges', *District Administration*, Vol. 44, No.13, pp. 27-29, December.

Chamundeswari, S. and Vasanthi, S. (2009) 'Job Satisfaction and Occupational Commitment Among Teachers', *EduTracks*, Vol. 8, No. 6, pp. 29-31, February.

Chan D. W. and Hui E. K. P. (1998) 'Stress, Support and Psychological Symptoms Among Guidance and Non-guidance Secondary School Teachers in Hong Kong', *School Psychology International*, Vol. 19, pp. 169-178.

Chan, A.H.S., Chen, K. and Chong, E.Y.L. (2010) *'Work Stress of Teachers from Primary and Secondary Schools in Hong Kong'*, Proceedings of the International Multi-conference of Engineers and Computer Scientists 2010, Vol. III, IMECS, March 17-19, 2010, Hong Kong.

Chan, D. W. (2003) 'Hardiness and Its Role in the Stress-burnout Relationship Among Prospective Chinese Teachers in Hong Kong', *Teaching and Teacher Education*, Vol. 19, No. 4, pp. 381.

Chan, D.W. (2008) 'Emotional Intelligence, Self-efficacy, and Coping Among Chinese Prospective and In-service Teachers in Hong Kong', *Educational Psychology*, Vol. 28, No. 4, pp. 397-408, July.

Chan, D.W. and Hui, E.K.P. (1995) 'Burnout and Coping Among Chinese Secondary School Teachers in Hong Kong', *British Journal of Educational Psychology*, Vol. 65, pp. 15-25.

Chandraiah, K. (1993) *'Occupational Stress, Job Satisfaction, Job Involvement and Locus of Control Among Public and Private College Teachers in Different*

Age levels', Ph. D. Thesis submitted to Sri Venkateswara University, Tirupati.

Chaplain, R. (1995) 'Stress and Job Satisfaction: A study of English Primary School Teachers', *Educational Psychology,* Vol. 15, No. 4, pp.473- 489.

Chaplain, R.P. (2001) 'Stress and Job Satisfaction Among Primary Head Teachers', *Educational Management Administration and Leadership,* Vol. 29, No. 2, pp. 197-215.

Chaturvedi, M. and Purushothaman, T. (2009) 'Coping Behaviour of Female Teachers: Demographic Determinants', *Indian Psychiatry Journal,* Vol. 18, No. 1, pp. 36-38.

Chen M. and Miller, G. (1997) *'Teacher Stress: A Review of the International Literature'*, ERIC Document Reproduction Service No. ED 410 187.

Chen, J. (2010) 'Chinese Middle School Teacher Job Satisfaction and Its Relationships with Teacher Moving', *Asia Pacific Education Review,* Retrieved from http://www.springerlink.com/content/d5058j601h030g 36/fulltext.pdf on 07.08.10, DOI 10.1007/s12564-010-9085-1.

Chopra, R. and Gartia, R. (2009) 'Accountability of Secondary School Teachers in Relation to Their Occupational Stress', *EduTracks,* Vol. 8, No. 7, pp. 41-43, March.

Choy, S.P., Bobbitt, S.A., Henke, R.R., Medrich, E.A., Horn, L.J. and Lieberman, J. (1993) *'America's Teachers: Profile of a Profession'*, Department of Education, National Centre for Education Statistics (NCES 93-025), Washington, DC: U.S.

Christina M.L., Thomas H. H. and Singh, K. (2004) 'The Relationship of Occupational Stress, Psychological Strain, and Coping Resources to the Turnover Intentions of Rehabilitation Counsellors', *Rehabilitation Counselling Bulletin,* Vol. 48, No. 1, pp. 19-30.

Chubb J. E. (1988) 'Why the Current Wave of School Reform Will Fail', *Public Interest,* Vol. 90, pp. 28-49.

Ciarrochi, J., Chan, A. and Bajgar, J. (2001) 'Measuring Emotional Intelligence in Adolescents', *Personality and Individual Differences,* Vol. 31, pp. 1105-1119.

Ciarrochi, J., Chan, A. and Caputi, P. (2000) 'A Critical Evaluation of the Emotional Intelligence Construct', *Personality and Individual Differences,* Vol. 28, pp. 539-561.

Cinamon, R.G., Rich, Y. and Westman, M. (2007) 'Teacher's Occupation-Specific Work-family Conflict', *Career Development Quarterly,* Vol. 55, No. 3, pp. 249-261, March.

Clark, E.H. (1980) *'An Analysis of Occupational Stress Factors as Perceived by Public School Teachers'*, Doctoral Dissertation, Auburn University.

Clunies-Ross, P., Little, E. and Kienhuis, M. (2008) 'Self-reported and Actual Use of Proactive and Reactive Classroom Management Strategies and Their Relationship with Teacher Stress and Student Behaviour', *Educational Psychology*, Vol. 28, No. 6, pp. 693-710, October.

Colangelo, T. M. (2004) *'Teacher Stress and Burnout and the Role of Physical Activity and Parent Involvement'*, MA Dissertation, Dept. of Psychology, Central Connecticut State University, New Britain, Connecticut.

Collins Dictionary (2005) *'Collins English Dictionary'*, *Harper Collins Publishers*, New York, USA.

Connors, S.A. (1983) 'The School Environment : A Link to Understanding Stress', *Theory in Practice*, Vol. 22, No. 1, pp. 15-20.

Cook, J.M. and Leffingwell, R.J. (1982) 'Stressors and Remediation Techniques for Special Educators', *Exceptional Children*, Vol. 49, pp. 54-59.

Cooper, C. L. and Travers, C. (1996) *'Teachers Under Pressure: Stress in the Teaching Profession'*, Routledge, London.

Cooper, C. L., Cooper, R.D. and Eaker, L.H. (1988a) *'Living with Stress'*, Penguin Health, London.

Cooper, C. L., Dewe, P. J. and O'Driscoll, M. P. (2001) *'Organizational Stress: A Review and Critique of Theory, Research and Applications'*, Sage Publications, Thousand Oaks, California.

Cooper, C. L., Sloan, S. J. and Williams, S. (1988) *'Occupational Stress Indicator Management Guide'*, NFER-Nelson, Windsor.

Cooper, C., U. Rout and B. Faragher (1989) 'Mental Health, Job Satisfaction, and Job Stress Among General Practitioners', *B Medical Journal*, Vol. 298, pp. 366-370.

Cooper, C.L. and Marshall, J. (1978) *'Sources of Managerial and White Collar Stress'*, In C.L. Cooper and R. Payne (eds.), Stress at Work, John Wiley & Sons, Chichester, pp. 81-105.

Corcoran, T. B., Walker, L. J. and White, J. L. (1988) *'Working in Urban Schools'*, Institute for Educational Leadership, Washington, DC.

Cox T. (1977) *'The Nature and Management of Stress in Schools in Clywd Country Council'*, (ed.) The Management of Stress in Schools (Conference Report Prepared by Clywd Country Council Department of Education), In T. Cox and T. Brockley (1984), 'The Experience and Effects of Stress in Teachers', *British Educational Research Journal*, Vol. 10, No. 1, pp. 83-87.

Crane, S.J. and Iwanicki, E.F. (1986) 'Perceived Role Conflict, Role Ambiguity and Burnout Among Special Education Teachers', *Remedial and Special Education*', Vol. 7 No.2, pp. 24 - 31.

Cross, L. H. and Billingsley, B. (1994) 'Testing a Model of Special Educator's Intent to Stay in Teaching', *Exceptional Children*, Vol. 60, No. 5, pp. 411-421.

Crossman, A. and Harris, P. (2006) 'Job Satisfaction of Secondary School Teachers', *Educational Management Administration and Leadership*, Vol. 34, No. 1, pp. 29-46.

Cruz, O. A., Pole, C. J. and Thomas, S. M. (2007) 'Chairs of Academic Departments of ophthalmology', *Ophthalmology*, Vol.114, No.12, pp. 2350-2355, December.

Cummins R.C. (1990) 'Job Stress and the Buffering Effort of Supervisory Support', *Group and Organizational Studies*, Vol. 15, No. 1, pp. 92-104.

Currie, P. and Rotatori, A. (1987) '*Stressors and Reactions Experience by Special Education Professionals*', In A. Rotatori, M. Banbury and R. Fox (eds), Issues in Special Education (pp. 99 -112), Mayfield Mountain View, CA.

Date, S.S. (2006) 'Emotional Maturity of Male and Female Secondary School Teachers of Dhule District', *Journal of Community Guidance and Research*, Vol. 23, No.1, pp. 8-10.

David, R.S. and Roy, R. (2010) 'Relationship Between Emotional Intelligence and Teachers Competency', *Journal of Community Guidance and Research*', Vol. 27, No.2, pp. 191-201, July.

Davis J. and Wilson S. M. (2000) 'Principal's Efforts to Empower Teachers: Effects on Teacher Motivation and Job Satisfaction and Stress', *The Clearing House*, Vol. 73, pp. 349-353.

Davis, K. (1972) '*Human Behaviour at Work : Human Relations and Organizational Behaviour*', 4th Edition, McGraw Hill Book Company, New York, pp. 52-79.

Davis, M. E. (2009) '*The Association Between Change Styles and Job Satisfaction Among Teachers Working in International Schools*', Ph.D Thesis Submitted to the University of Southern Queensland.

De Nobile, J. and McCormick, J. (2005) '*Job Satisfaction and Occupational stress in Catholic Primary Schools*', Paper Presented at the Annual Conference of the Australian Association for Research in Education, Sydney.

Dedrick, C.V.L. and Raschke, D.B. (1980) '*The Special Education and Stress*', National Education Association, Washington, DC.

Demerouti, E., Bakker, A. B., Nachreiner, F. and Schaufeli, W. B. (2001) 'The Job Demands–Resources Model of Burnout', *Journal of Applied Psychology*, Vol. 86, pp. 499-512.

Dhar, S., Dhar, U. and Srivastava, D.K. (2001) *'Manual for Job Involvement Scale'*, Ankur Psychological Agency, Lucknow.

Dinham, S. (1993) 'Teachers Under Stress', *Australian Educational Researcher*, Vol. 20, No.3, pp.1-16.

Dixit, M. (1993) *'Manual for Job Satisfaction Scale for Primary and Secondary Teachers'*, National Psychological Corporation, Agra.

Dominguez-Cruz, G. (2003) *'Relationship of Leadership Orientations to Emotional Intelligence of Public Elementary, Intermediate and High School Principals in Puerto Rico'*, Ph.D. Thesis Submitted to Dowling College.

Dorman J. P. (2003) 'Relationship Between School and Classroom Environment and Teacher burnout: A LISREL analysis', *Social Psychology of Education, Vol. 6*, pp. 107-127.

Dunham, J. (1976) *'Stress Situations and Responses'*, In NAS/UWT (1976), Stress in schools, Hemel Hempstead.

Dunham, J. (1980) 'An Exploratory Comparative Study of Staff Stress in English and German Comprehensive Schools', *Educational Review*, Vol. 32, pp. 11-20.

Dunham, J. (1992) *'Stress in Teaching'*, Routledge, New York.

Dussault M., Deaudelin C., Royer N. and Loiselle J. (1999) 'Professional Isolation and Occupational Stress in Teachers', *Psychological Reports, Vol. 84*, pp. 943-946.

Dworkin, A.G., Haney, C.A., Dworkin, R.J. and Telschow, R.L. (1990) 'Stress and Illness Behaviour Among Urban Public School Teachers', *Educational Administration Quarterly*, Vol. 26, No. 1, pp. 60-72.

Eichinger, J. (2000) 'Job Stress and Satisfaction Among Special Education Teachers', *Psychological Abstracts International*, Vol. 88, No. 3, pp. 1184, March.

Eisenman, G. and Thornton, H. (1999) 'Tele-mentoring: Helping New Teachers Through the First Year', *T.H.E. Journal*, Vol. 26, No. 9, pp. 79.

Ellis, T.I. (1984) *'Motivating Teachers for Excellence'*, ERIC Clearing House on Educational Management: ERIC Digest No. 6, ERIC Document Reproduction No. ED259449, pp. 21.

Embich, J. L. (2001) 'The Relationship of Secondary Special Education Teacher's Role and Factors that lead to Professional Burnout', *Teacher Education and Special Education*, Vol. 24, No. 1, pp. 58-69.

Engelbrecht, P., Swart, E. and Eloff, I. (2001) 'Stress and Coping Skills of Teachers with a Learner with Down's Syndrome in inclusive Classrooms', *South African Journal of Education*, Vol. 21, No 4, pp. 256-259.

Epstein, S. (1998) *'Constructive Thinking: The Key to Emotional Intelligence'*, Prager, Westport, CT.

Epstein, S. R. (1990) 'Staff burnout in Shelters for Battered Women : A Change for the 90's', *Responses to Victimization of Women and Children*, Vol. 13, No.1, pp. 9-12.

Evers, W. J. G., Tomic, W., and Brouwers, A. (2004) 'Burnout Among Teachers: Students and Teachers Perceptions Compared', *School Psychology International*, Vol. 25, No. 2, pp. 131-148.

Extremera, N. and Fernandez-Berrocal, P. (2005) 'Perceived Emotional Intelligence and Life Satisfaction : Predictive and Incremental Validity Using the Trait Meta Mood Scale', *Personality and Individual Differences*, Vol. 39, pp. 937-948.

Fairbrother, K. and Warn, J. (2003) 'Workplace Dimensions, Stress and Job Satisfaction', *Journal of Managerial Psychology*, Vol. 18, No. 1, pp.8-21.

Farber, B.A. (1991) *'Crisis in Education: Stress and Burnout in the American Teachers'*, Jossey Bass, San Francisco.

Fernandez-Berrocal, P. and Extremera, N. (2006) 'Emotional intelligence : A Theoretical and Empirical Overview of Its First 15 Years of History', *Piscothema*, Vol. 18, pp. 7-12.

Fernandez-Berrocal, P., Alcaide, R., Extremera, N. and Pizarro, D. (2006) 'The Role of Emotional Intelligence in Anxiety and Depression among Adolescents', *Individual Differences Research*, Vol. 4, No.1, pp. 16-27.

Fimian, M.J. (1985) 'Organizational Variables Related to Stress and Burnout in Community Based Programmes', *Education and Training of the Mentally Retarded*, Vol. 19, pp. 201-209.

Fimian, M.J. (1986) 'Social Support and Occupational Stress in Special Education', *Exceptional Children*, Vol. 52, pp. 436-442.

Fimian, M.J. (1986a) 'Social Support, Stress and Special Education: Improving the Work Situation', *Pointer*, Vol. 31, No.1, pp. 49-53.

Fimian, M.J. and Blanton, L. P. (1986) 'Variables Related to Stress and Burnout in Special Education Teacher Trainees and First-year Teachers', *Teacher Education and Special Education: The Journal of the Teacher Education*, Division of the Council for Exceptional Children, Vol. 9, No. 1, pp. 9-21.

Fimian, M.J. and Santoro, T.M. (1983) 'Sources and Manifestations of Occupational Stress as Reported by full- time Special Education Teachers', *Exceptional Children*, Vol. 46, No. 6, pp. 540–543.

Fletcher, J.B. and Payne, R. 1980) 'Stress and work: A Review and a Theoretical Framework- Part 1', *Personnel Review*, Vol. 9, pp. 1-20.

Fordasz, H. and Leder, G. (2006) 'Work Patterns and Stressors of Experienced and Novice Mathematics Teachers', *Australian Mathematics Teacher*, Vol. 62, No. 3, pp. 36-40.

Forlin, C. (1997) 'Inclusive Education in Australia', *Special Education Perspectives*, Vol. 6, No. 1, pp. 21-26.

Forlin, C. (2001) 'Inclusion: Identifying Potential Stressors for Regular Class Teachers', *Educational Research*, Vol. 43, pp. 235-245.

Frank, A. and Mckenzie, R. (1993) 'The Development of Burnout Among Special Educators', *Teacher Educator and Special Education*, Vol. 16, pp. 161 -170.

French, J.R.P. and Caplan, R.D. (1970) 'Psychosocial Factors in Coronary Heart Disease', *Industrial Medicine*, Vol. 39, pp. 383- 397.

French, J.R.P. and Caplan, R.D. (1973) '*Organisational Stress and Individual Strain*', In A. J. Marrow (ed.), The Failure of Success, John Wiley, New York.

French, J.R.P., Israel, J., and As, D. (1960) 'An Experiment on Participation in a Norwegian Factory : Interpersonal Dimensions of Decision Mking', *Human Relations*, Vol. 13, No.1, pp. 3-19.

Friedlander, F. and Margulies, N. (1969) 'Multiple Inputs of Organizational Climate and Individual Value System Upon Job Satisfaction', *Personnel Psychology*, Vol. 22, pp. 171-183.

Friedman, I. (1995) 'Student Behaviour Patterns Contributing to Teacher Burnout', *Journal of Educational Research*, Vol. 88, No. 5, pp. 281-290.

Frone, M.R. and Yardley, J.K. (1996) 'Workplace Family-supportive Programmes: Predictors of Employed Parent's Importance Ratings', Journal *of Occupational and Organizational Psychology*, Vol. 69, pp. 351-366.

Frone, M.R., Russell, M. and Cooper, M. (1992) 'Prevalence of Work-Family Conflict: Are Work and Family Boundaries Asymmetrically Permeable ?', *Journal of Organizational Behaviour*, Vol. 13, pp. 723-729.

Gakhar, S.C., Sukhjiwan, K. and Kaur, N. (2005) 'Job Satisfaction of Scheduled Caste and Non-scheduled Caste Teachers in Relation to Self-concept, Anxiety and Attitude Towards Teaching', *Asian Journal of Psychology and Education*, Vol. 38, No. 1-2, pp. 9-12.

Gannon, M.J. (1977) '*Management : An Organizational Perspective*', Little Brown & Company, Boston Toronto, pp. 207-217.

Ganzach, Y. (2003) 'Intelligence, Education, and Facets of job Satisfaction', *Work and Occupations*, Vol. 30, No. 1, pp. 97-122.

Gardner, H. (1983) '*Frame of Mind: The Theory of Multiple Intelligences*', Basic Books, New York.

Gardner, L. (2005) '*Emotional Intelligence and Occupational Stress*', Ph.D. Thesis Swinburne University, September.

Garrett, E.H. and Woodsworth, R.S. (1981) '*Statistics in Psychology and Education*', Vakkils, Feffer and Simons Ltd., Bombay.

Garrett, H.E. (1966) '*Statistics in Psychology and Education*', David Mckey Company, Inc. and Longman Group Ltd.

George, N. L., George, M. P., Gersten R. and Grosenick, J. K. (1995) 'To Leave or to Stay: An Exploratory Study of Teachers of Students with Emotional and Behavioural Disorders', *Remedial and Special Education*, Vol. 16, pp. 227-236.

Gersten, R., Keating T., Yovanoff, P. and Harniss, M. K. (2001) 'Working in Special Education: Factors that Enhance Special Educator's Intent to stay', *Exceptional Children, Vol. 67*, No. 4, pp. 549-567.

Geving, A.M. (2007) 'Identifying the Types of Student and Teacher Behaviours Associated with Teacher Stress', *Teaching and Teacher Education: An International Journal of Research and Studies*, Vol. 23, No. 5, pp. 624-640, July.

Ghazi, S. R. (2004) '*Job satisfaction of Elementary School Head Teachers (Toba Tek Singh) in Punjab*', Ph.D. Thesis Submitted to National University for Modern Languages, Islamabad.

Gillespie, N.A., Walsh, M., Winefield, A.H., Dua, J. and Stough, C. (2001) 'Occupational Stress in Universities: Staff Perceptions of the Causes, Consequences and Moderators of Stress', *Work & Stress*, Vol. 15, No. 1, pp. 53-72.

Gil-Olarate, P., Palomera, R. and Brackett, M.A. (2006) 'Relating Emotional Intelligence to Social Competence and Academic Achievement Among High School Students', *Piscothema*, Vol. 18 (Suppl.), pp. 118-123.

Glowinkowski, S.P. and Cooper, C.L. (1985) 'Current Issues in Organizational Stress Research', *Bulletin of the British Psychological Society*, Vol. 38, pp. 212 - 216.

Gmelch, W. H., Wilke, P. K. and Lorrich, N. P. (1986) 'Dimensions of Stress Among University Faculty: Factor Analytic Results from National Study', *Research in Higher Education*, Vol. 24, pp. 266-286.

Hawkes, R.R. and Dedrick, C.V. (1988) 'Teacher Stress : Phase II of a Descriptive Study', *National Association of Secondary School Principals Bulletin*, Vol. 67, No. 461, pp. 78-83.

Hay/McBer (2000) *'Research Into Teacher Effectiveness: A Model of Teacher Effectiveness'*, Report by HayMcBer to the Department for Education and Employment, Retrieved from http://www.dfee.gov.uk/teachingreforms/mcber/ on 2.06.08.

Hedges, J. (1973) 'New Patterns of Working Time', *Monthly Labour Review*, Vol. 96, pp. 3-8.

Herzberg, F. (1966) *'Work and the Nature of Man'*, World Publishing Co, Cleveland.

Herzberg, F., Mausner, B. and Synderman, B. (1959) *'The Motivation to Work'*, John Wiley & Sons Inc., New York.

Hinkle, L.E. (1977) *'The Concept of Stress in the Biological and Social Sciences'*, In Z. J. L. D. R. and W. P. C. Lipowski (ed.), Psychosomatic Medicine: Current Trends and Clinical Implications, Oxford University Press, New York.

Hock and Roger (1996) 'Professional Burnout Among Public School Teachers', *Public Personnel Management*, Vol. 101, pp. 167-189.

Hollifield, S.T. (2005) *'An Examination of Teacher Job Satisfaction, Work-related Stress and Organizational Culture in Three School Districts'*, ETD Collection for Wayne State University, Paper AAI3196204, Retrieved from http://digitalcommons.wayne.edu/dissertations/AAI3196204 on 07.12.09.

Hopkins, M. M., and Bilimoria, D. (2008) 'Social and Emotional Competencies Predicting Success for Male and Female Executives', *Journal of Management Development*, Vol. 27, No. 1, pp. 13-35.

Hopkins, M.M., O'Neil, D.A., and Williams, H.W. (2007) 'Emotional Intelligence and Board Governance: Leadership Lessons from the public Sector', *Journal of Managerial Psychology*, Vol. 22, No. 7, pp. 683-700.

Hoppock, R. (1935) *'Job Satisfaction'*, Harper, New York, pp. 47.

Hourani, L.L., Williams, T.V. and Kress, A.M., (2006) 'Stress, Mental Health and Job Performance Among Active Duty Military Personnel: Findings from the 2002 Department of Deference Health-related Behaviours Survey', *Military Medicine*, Vol. 171, No. 9, pp. 849-856

Hoy, W. K. and Miskel, C.G. (1987) *'Educational Administration Theory, Research and Practice'*, 3 ed., Random House, New York.

Hsieh, H-L., Huang, L-C. and Su, K-J. (2004) 'Work Stress and Job Performance in the Hi-tech Industry: A Closer View for Vocational

Education', *World Transactions on Engineering and Technology Education*, Vol. 3, No. 1, pp. 147-150.

Hughey, M.L. and Murphy, P.J. (1982) 'Are Rural Teachers Satisfied with the Quality of Their Work Life ?', *Education*, Vol. 104, pp. 56-66.

Hui, E. K. P. and Chan, D. W. (1996) 'Teacher Stress and Guidance Work in Hong Kong Secondary School Teachers' *British Journal of Guidance and Counselling*, Vol. 24, pp. 199-211.

Hurren, B. L. (2006) 'The Effects of Principal's Humour on Teacher's Job Satisfaction', *Educational Studies*, Vol. 32, No. 4, pp. 373-385, December.

Hyde, A., Pattie, S. and Dhar, U. (2002) *'Manual for Emotional Intelligence Scale'*, Vedant Publications, Lucknow.

ILO Report (1981) *'Employment and Conditions of Works of Teachers in Geneva'*. International London's Office, London.

Indu, H. (2009) 'Emotional Intelligence of Secondary Teacher Trainees', *EduTracks*, Vol. 8, No. 9, pp. 34-36, May.

Ingersoll R. M. (1996) 'Teacher's Decision-making Power and School Conflict', *Sociological Quarterly, Vol. 69, pp.* 159-176.

Ingham, G. (1970) *'Size of Industrial Organization and Work Behaviour'*, Cambridge University Press, Cambridge England.

Iordanoglou, D. (2007) 'The Teacher as Leader: The Relationship Between Emotional Intelligence, Leadership Effectiveness, Commitment and Satisfaction', *Journal of Leadership Studies*, Vol. 1, No. 3, pp. 57-66.

Ismail, A., Yao, A., Yeo, E., Lai-Kuan, K. and Soon-Yew, J. (2010) 'Occupational Stress, Emotional Intelligence and Job Satisfaction : An Empirical Study in Private Institutions of Higher Learning', *Scientific e-journal of Management Science*, Vol. 16, No. 5, pp. 5-33, Retrieved form www.revistanegotium.org.ve on 27.07.10.

Jackson, S.E., Schwab, R.L. and Schuler, R.S. (1986) 'Towards an Understanding of the Burnout Phenomenon', *Journal of Applied Psychology*, Vol. 71, No. 4, pp. 630-640.

Jamal, S., Hasan, A. and Raheem, A. (2007) 'Predictors of Organizational Commitment of Secondary School Teachers', *EduTracks*, Vol. 6, No. 8, pp. 36- 40, April.

James, K. (1999) 'Rethinking Organisational Stress: The Transition to the New Employment Age', *Journal of Managerial Psychology*, Vol. 14, No.7, pp. 545-557.

Jarvis, M. (2002) 'Teacher Stress: A Critical Review of Recent Findings and Suggestions for Future Research Directions', *Teacher Support Network*, Vol. 14, No. 1.

Jayanthi and Agarwal, R. (2006) 'A Study of the Socio-emotional Climate of the Classroom in Respect of Teaching Experience, Total Income, Age, Teaching Subject and Sex of Secondary School Teachers', *Asian Journal of Psychology and Education*, Vol. 39, No. 7 and 8, pp. 2-11.

Jayaprabha, R. (2003) '*Metacognitive and Cognitive Strategies to Overcome Behaviour Difficulties in Children*', Ph.D. Thesis, Alagappa University, Karaikudi.

Jex, S. M. (1998) '*Stress and Job Performance: Theory, Research and Implications for Managerial Practice*', Sage Publications, Thousand Oaks, CA.

John. B. (2007) '*Occupational Stress of Teachers Working in the Schools for Visually Impaired Children in the Malabar Region of Kerala*', M.Phil. Dissertation submitted to the Department of Education, Alagappa University.

Johnson, A.B., Gold, V. and Vickers, L.L. (1982) 'Stress and Teachers of the Learning Disabled, Behaviour Disordered and Educable Mentally Retarded', *Psychology in the Schools*, Vol. 19, pp. 552-557.

Johnson, T.W. and Stinson, J.E. (1975) 'Role Ambiguity, Role Conflict and Satisfaction : Moderating Effects of Individual Differences', *Journal of Applied Psychology*, Vol. 60, pp. 329-333.

Joolideh, F. and Yeshodhara, K. (2008) 'Organizational Commitment Among High School Teachers in India and Iran', *EduTracks*, Vol. 7, No. 10, pp. 38- 41, June.

Joshi, C.P. and Singhvi, M.K. (2000) 'A Study of Burnout in College Teachers', *Indian Journal of Clinical Psychology*', Vol. 27, No. 1, pp. 144-148.

Kafetsios, K. and Loumakou, M. (2007) 'A Comparative Evaluation of the Effects of Trait Emotional Intelligence and Emotion Regulation on Affect at Work and Job Satisfaction', *International Journal of Work Organisation and Emotion*, Vol. 2, No.1, pp. 71-87.

Kafetsios, K., and Zampetakis, L. A. (2008) 'Emotional Intelligence and Job Satisfaction: Testing the Mediatory Role of Positive and Negative Affect at Work', *Personality and Individual Differences*, Vol. 44, No. 3, pp. 710-720.

Kahn, R., Wolfe, D., Quinn, R. and Snoek, J. (1964) '*Organizational stress: Studies in Role Conflict and Ambiguity*', (ed.), John Wiley, New York.

Kalker, P. (1984) 'Teacher Stress and Burnout : Causes and Coping Strategies', *Contemporary Education*, Vol. 56, No. 1, pp. 16-19.

Kalliath, T.J. and Beck, A. (2001) 'Is the Path to Burnout and Turnover Paved by a Lack of Supervisory Support ?', *New Zealand Journal of Psychology*, Vol. 30, No.2, pp. 72-78.

Kaplan, F. (2003) '*Educating the Emotions: Emotional Intelligence Training for Early Childhood Teachers and Caregivers*', Ph.D. Thesis submitted to Cardinal Stritch University.

Karasek, R.A. (1979) 'Job Demands, Job Decision Latitude, and Mental Strain: Implications for Job Redesign', *Administrative Science Quarterly*, Vol. 24, pp. 285-306.

Karasek, R.A. and Theorell, (1990) '*Healthy Work: Stress, Productivity and the Reconstruction of Working Life*', Basic Books, New York.

Kaufhold, J.A., Alverez, V.G. and Arnold, M. (2006) 'Lack of School Supplies, Materials and Resources as an Elementary Cause of Frustration and Burnout in South Texas Special Education Teachers', *Journal of Instructional Psychology*, Vol. 33, No. 3, pp. 159-161, September.

Kaur, S. (2008) 'Occupational Stress in Relation to Teacher Effectiveness Among Secondary School Teachers', *EduTracks*, Vol. 7, No. 10, pp. 27-29, June.

Keller, R.T. (1975) 'Role Conflict and Ambiguity : Correlates with Job Satisfaction and Values', *Personnel Psychology*, Vol. 28, pp. 57-64.

Kelly A. L. and Berthelsen D.C. (1995) 'Preschool Teacher's Experience of Stress', *Teaching and Teacher Education, Vol. 11, pp.* 345-357.

Khalid, T. and Kausar, R. (2008) 'Depression and Quality of Life Among Caregivers of People Affected by Stroke', *Asia Pacific Disability Rehabilitation Journal*, Vol.19, No.2, pp.103-109.

Khan, M.A. and Kumar, A. (2008) 'Relationship Between Emotional Intelligence and Achievement Motivation Among Women Teachers of Secondary Schools of Delhi', *Journal of Teacher Education and Research*, Vol. 3, No. 1, pp. 15-18, June.

Kim, 1. and Loadman, W. (1994) '*Predicting Teacher Job Satisfaction*', ERIC Document Reproduction Service No. ED 383 707.

Kitle, F. and Leynen, F. (2003) 'A Study of Work Stressors and Wellness/ Health Outcomes Among Belgian School Teachers', *Psychological Abstracts International*, Vol. 90, No. 3, pp. 3096, September.

Klassen, R.M. and Anderson, C.J.K. (2009) 'How Times Change: Secondary Teachers' Job Satisfaction and Dissatisfaction in 1962 and 2007', *British Educational Research Journal*, Vol. 35, No.5, pp. 745-759, October.

Klassen, R.M., Foster, R.Y., Rajani, S. and Bowman, C. (2009) 'Teaching in the Yukon: Exploring Teachers' Efficacy Beliefs, Stress, and Job Satisfaction in a Remote Setting', *International Journal of Educational Research*, Vol. 48, No. 6, pp. 381-394, Retrieved from www.science direct.com on 08.08.10.

Kluemper, D. H. (2008) 'Trait Emotional Intelligence: The Impact of Core-self Evaluations and Social Desirability', *Personality and Individual Differences*, Vol. 44, No. 6, pp. 1402-1412.

Kokkinos, C. M., Panayiotou, G. and Davazoglou, A. M. (2005) 'Correlates of Teacher Appraisals of Student Behaviours', *Psychology in the Schools*, Vol. 42, pp. 79-89.

Koslowski, M. (1998) *'Modelling the Stress-strain Relationship in Work Settings'*, Routledge, London.

Kumar, C. J. and Rao, D. B. (2007) *'Job Satisfaction of Teachers'*, Discovery Publishing House, New Delhi.

Kumar, N. (2007) *'Influence of Certain Psycho-sociological Factors on the Occupational Stress Among the Public and Private School Teachers of Orissa'*, Ph.D. Thesis submitted to Utkal University.

Kumaraan, D. (2003) 'Organizational health and academic performance', *Perspectives in Education*, Vol.19, No.4, pp. 221-234.

Kumaraswamy, T. and Sarma, P.S. (2005) 'Job involvement of secondary school teachers', *International Educator*, Vol. 17, No. 2, pp. 18-20, December.

Kyriacou, C. (1987) 'Teacher stress and burnout: An international review', *Educational Research*, Vol. 29, No. 2, pp.146-152.

Kyriacou, C. (1989) *'The nature and prevalence of teacher stress'*, In M. Cole and S. Walker (eds), Teaching and stress (pp. 26-34), Open University Press, Milton Keyness.

Kyriacou, C. (1997) *'Effective teaching in schools'*, 2nd eds., Stanley Thorne, Cheltenham, pp. 156.

Kyriacou, C. (2001) 'Teacher Stress: Direction for Future Research', *Educational Review*, Vol. 53, No. 1, pp. 27-35.

Kyriacou, C. and Chien, P.Y. (2004) 'Teacher Stress in Taiwanese Primary Schools', *Journal of Educational Enquiry*, Vol. 5, No.2, pp. 86-103.

Kyriacou, C. and Sutcliff, J. (1978) 'A model of Teacher Stress', *Educational Studies*, Vol. 4, pp. 1-6.

Kyriacou, C. and Sutcliffe, J. (1977) 'Teacher Stress: A Review', *Educational Review*, Vol. 24, No. 4, pp. 299-306.

Kyriacou, C. and Sutcliffe, J. (1978a) 'Teacher Stress : Prevalence, Sources and Symptoms', *British Journal of Educational Psychology*, Vol. 48, No. 2, pp. 159-167, June.

Kyriacou, C. and Sutcliffee, J. (1979) 'Teacher Stress and Satisfaction', *Educational Research*, Vol. 21, No. 2, pp. 89-96.

Landsbergis, P.A. (1988) 'Occupational Stress Among Healthcare Workers: A Test of the Job Demands-control Model', *Journal of Organizational Behaviour*, Vol. 9, pp. 217-239.

Langdon, C.A. (1996) 'The Third Phi Delta Kappa Poll of Teacher's Attitudes Toward the Public Schools', *Phi Delta Kappan*, Vol. 78, No. 3, pp. 244-250.

Latha, A., Sangeetha, R. and Anantha Sayanam, R. (2005) 'Study of Emotional Intelligence and Its Effects on Teacher Effectiveness Among School Teachers', *Journal of Educational Research and Extension*, Vol. 42, No. 3, pp. 20-29.

Laughlin, A. (1984) 'Teacher Stress in Australian Setting: The Role of Biographical Mediators', *Educational Studies*, Vol. 10, No.1, pp. 7-22.

Lawrenson, G. M. and McKinnon, A. (1982) 'A Survey of Classroom Teachers of the Emotionally Disturbed: Attrition and Burnout Factors', *Behavioural Disorders*, Vol. 8, pp. 41- 49.

Lazarus, R S, (1974) 'Psychological Stress and Coping in Adaptation and Illness', *International Journal of Psychiatry in Medicine*, Vol. 5, pp. 321-333.

Lazarus, R. (1976) *'Patterns of Adjustment'*, 3rd ed, McGraw-Hill, New York.

Lazarus, R. S. (1999) *'Stress and Emotion: A New Synthesis'*, Springer Publishing Company, New York.

Lazarus, R.S. (1966) *'Psychological Stress and the Coping Process'*, McGraw-Hill, New York.

Lee, F. M. (2003) *'Conflict Management Styles and Emotional Intelligence of Faculty and Staff at a Selected College in Southern Taiwan (China)'*, Ed.D. Degree submitted to the University of Florida.

Lee, R., and Ashforth, B. (1996) 'A Meta-analytic Examination of the Correlates of the Three Dimensions of Job Burnout', *Journal of Applied Psychology*, Vol. 81, pp. 123-133.

Lee, V.E., Dedrick, R.F. and Smith, J.B. (1991) 'The Effects of the Social Organization of Schools on Teachers', *Sociology of Education*, Vol. 64, pp. 190-208.

Lees, A and Barnard, D. (1999) *'Highly Effective Head Teachers: An Analysis of a Sample of Diagnostic Data from the Leadership Programme for Serving Head Teachers'*, Report prepared for Hay/McBer.

Leka, S., Griffiths, A. and Cox, T. (2004) *'Work Organization and Stress'*, World Health Organization, Nottingham: UK.

Leung, S.S.K., Mak, Y.W., Chui, Y.U., Chiang, V.C. and Lee, A.C. (2009) 'Occupational Stress, Mental Health Status and Stress Management Behaviours Among Secondary School Teachers in Hong Kong', *Health Education Journal*, Vol. 68, No. 4, pp. 328-343.

Levinson, H. (1978) 'The Abrasive Personality', *The Harvard Business Review*, Vol. 56, pp. 86-94, May-June.

Lewin, K., Lippitt, R. and White, R.K. (1939) 'Patterns of Aggressive Behaviour in Experimentally Created Social Climates', *Journal of Social Psychology*, Vol. 10, pp. 271-99.

Lewis, S. and Cooper, C.L. (1989) '*Career Couples*', Unwin, London.

Lin, J-D., Lee, T-N., Yen, C-F., Loh, C-H., Hsu, S-W., Wu, J-L. and Chu, C. M. (2009) 'Job Strain and Determinants in Staff Working in Institutions for People with Intellectual Disabilities in Taiwan: A Test of the Job Demand-control-support Model', *Research in Developmental Disabilities: A Multidisciplinary Journal*, Vol. 30, No.1, pp.146-157, Jan-Feb.

Ling-feng, W. (2005) 'Stress and Mental Health of the Kindergarten Teachers in Huzhou', *Chinese Journal of School Health*, Retrieved from http://en.cnki.com.cn/Article_en/CJFDTOTAL-XIWS200511011.htm on 4.3.09.

Lingfeng, W. (2008) 'An Investigation into the Professional Stress of Special Education Teachers', *Chinese Journal of Special Education*, Retrieved from http://en.cnki.com.cn/Article_en/CJFDTOTAL-ZDTJ200908012.htm on 12.07.09.

Littrell, P., Billingsley, B and Cross, L. (1994) 'The Effects of Principal Support on Special and General Educator's Stress, Job Satisfaction, School Commitment, Health, and Intent to Stay in Teaching', *Remedial and Special Education*, Vol. 15, No. 5, 297-310.

Locke, E.A. (1973) 'Satisfiers and Dissatisfiers Among White Collar and Blue Collar Employee', *Journal of Applied Psychology*, Vol. 58, pp. 67-76.

Locke, E.A. (1976) '*Handbook of the Industrial and Organizational Psychology*', In M.D. Dunnette (ed.), The Nature and Causes of Job Satisfaction, Chicago and McNally, pp. 1297-1349.

Lodahl, T. and Kejner, M. (1965) 'The Definition and Measurement of Job Involvement', *Journal of Applied Psychology*, Vol. 49, pp. 24-33.

Lopes, P.N., Brackett, M.A., Netzlek, J.B., Schutz, S.I. and Salovey, P. (2004) 'Emotional Intelligence and Social Interaction', *Personality and Social Psychology Bulletin*, Vol. 30, No. 8, pp. 1018 -1034.

Lopes, P.N., Salovey, P. and Straus, R. (2003) 'Emotional Intelligence, Personality and the Perceived Quality of Social Relationships', Personality *and Individual Differences*, Vol. 35, pp. 641-658.

Lopes, P.N., Salovey, P. Cote, S. and Beers, M. (2005) 'Emotion Regulation Ability and the Quality of Social Interaction', *Emotion*, Vol. 5, pp. 113-118.

Low, G. (2000) *'Quantifying Emotional Intelligence: Positive Contributions of the Emotional Mind'*, Annual Faculty Lecture, Texas A & M University-Kingsville.

Luthans, F. (1998) *'Organizational Behaviour'*, 8th ed., Irwin / McGrawhill, Boston, pp. 173-187.

Luthans, F. (2002) *'Organizational Behaviour'*, 9th ed., New York, McGraw-Hill.

Ma, X. and MacMillan, R.B. (1999) 'Influences of Workplace Conditions on Yeachers' Job Satisfaction', *The Journal of Educational Research*, Vol. 93, No. 1, pp. 39-47, Sep.-Oct.

Makinen R. and Kinnunen U. (1986) 'Teacher Stress Over a School Year', *Scandinavian Journal of Educational Research*, Vol. 30, pp. 55-70.

Male, D. B. and May, D. (1997) 'Stress, Burnout and Workload in Teachers of Children with Special Educational Needs', *British Journal of Special Education*, Vol. 24, No. 3, pp. 133-140.

Manassero M., Garcia-Buades E., Torrens G., Ramis C., Vazquez A. and Ferrer V.A. (2006) 'Teacher Burnout: Attributional Aspects', *Psychology in Spain, Vol. 10, pp. 66-74.*

Manjunathaiah, B.N. (2003) *'Personality Adjustment and Job Satisfaction of Teachers Working in Schools for Visually Impaired Children'*, Ph.D. Thesis submitted to the Dept. of Education, Mysore University.

Manoj Kumar, K. (2006) *'Occupational Stress and Coping Styles of High School Teachers in Nellore Dist*rict', M.Phil Dissertation submitted to Madurai Kamaraj University.

Manthei, R. and Gilmore, A. (1996) 'Teacher Stress in Intermediate Schools', *Educational Research*, Vol. 38, No.1, pp.3-19.

Maolin, Z. and Xiaoxin, D. (2008) 'A Study on the Job Stress and Coping Strategies of Special School Teachers', *Chinese Journal of Special Education*, Retrieved from http://en.cnki.com.cn/Article_en/ CJFDTOTAL - ZDTJ200811003.htm on 3.6.09.

Margolis, B.L., Kroes, W.H. and Quinn, R.P. (1974) 'Job Stress : An Unlisted Occupational Hazard', *Journal of Occupational Medicine*, Vol. 1. No. 16, pp. 654-661.

Markham, P.L. (1999) 'Stressors and Coping Strategies of ESL Teachers', *Journal of Instructional Psychology*, Vol. 26, No. 4, pp. 268-279.

Marmot, M., Siegrist, J., Theorell, T. and Feeney, A. (1999) *'Health and the Psycho-social Environment at Work'*, In M. Marmot and R.G. Wilkinson (eds.), Social Determinants of Health, Oxford University Press, Oxford, pp. 105-131.

Marston, S., Courtney, V. and Brunetti, G. (2006) 'Voices of Experienced Elementary Teachers: Their Insights About the Profession', *Teacher Education Quarterly,* Retrieved from findArticles.com on 7.12.2009.

Maslach, C. (1982) 'Understanding Burnout : Definitional Issues in Analyzing a Complex Phenomenon', In W.S. Paine (ed.), Job Stress and Burnout (pp.29-40), Sage, Beverly Hills.

Maslach, C. and Jackson, S.E. (1981) 'The Measurement of Experienced Burnout', *Journal of Occupational Behaviour,* Vol. 2, pp. 99-113.

Maslach, C., Schaufeli, W. B. and Leiter, M.P. (2001) 'Job Burnout', *Annual Review of Psychology,* Vol. 52, pp. 397-422.

Maslow, A.H. (1943) '*Motivation and Personality*', Harper and Row, New York.

Mathew, L. (2005) '*Sources Effects and the Coping Strategies of Occupational Stress Among Special Education Teachers in India*', Thesis submitted to the Dept., of Psychology, Calicut University, Kerala.

Mayer, J.D. and Salovey, P. (1997) '*What is Emotional Intelligence ?*', In P. Salovey and D. Sluyter (eds.), Emotional Development and Emotional Intelligence: Implications for Educators, Basic Books, New York, pp. 3-31.

Mayer, J.D., Caruso, D.R. and Salovey, P. (1999) 'Emotional Intelligence Meets Traditional Standards for an Intelligence', *Intelligence,* Vol. 27, pp. 267-299.

Mayer, R.C. and Davis, J.H. (1999) 'The Effect of the Performance Appraisal System on Trust for Management: A Field Quasi-experiment', *Journal of Applied Psychology,* Vol. 84, pp. 123-136.

Mc Grath, J.E. (1976) '*Stress and Behaviour in Organizations*', In M.D. Dunnette, (ed.), 1976 Handbook of Industrial and Organizational Psychology, C.A. Palto, Counselling Psychological Stress.

McCarthy, C. J., Lambert, R.G., O'Donnell, M. and Melendres, L.T. (2009) 'The Relation of Elementary Teacher's Experience, Stress, and Coping Resources to Burnout Symptoms', *Elementary School Journal,* Vol. 109, No. 3, pp. 282-300, January.

McCormick, J. (1997) 'Occupational Stress of Teachers: Biographical Differences in a Large School System', *Journal of Educational Administration,* Vol. 35, No. 1, pp. 18-38.

McCormick, J. (1997a) 'An Attribution Model of Teacher's Occupational Stress and Job Satisfaction in a Large Educational System', *Work and Stress,* Vol. 11, No.1, pp. 17-32.

McEwen, A. and Thompson, W. (1997) 'After the National Curriculum: Teacher Stress and Morale', *Research in Education*, Vol. 57, pp. 57-67.

McManus, M. E., and Kauffman, J. M. (1991) 'Working Conditions of Teachers of Students with Behaviour Disorders: A National Survey', *Behavioural Disorders*, Vol. 16, pp. 247-259.

Mehrotra, A. (2002) *'A Comparative Study of Leadership Styles of Principals in Relation to Job Satisfaction of Teachers and Organizational Climate in Government and Private Senior Secondary School of Delhi'*, Ph.D. Thesis in Education submitted to the Jamia Millia Islamia, A Central University.

Meijer, J. (2001) 'Stress in the Relationship Between Trait and State Anxiety', *Psychological Reports*, Vol. 88, pp. 947-964.

Mertler, C. A. (2001) *'Teacher Motivation and Job Satisfaction in the New Millennium'*, Paper presented at the Annual Meeting of the Mid-Western Educational Research Association (Chicago, IL, October 24-27, 2001), ERIC Reproduction No. ED461649.

Michaelowa, K. (2002) *'Teacher Job Satisfaction, Student Achievement, and the Cost of Primary Education in Francophone Sub-Saharan Africa'*, Hamburgisches Welt-Wirtschafts-Archiv (HWWA) Discussion paper, No. 188, Hamburg Institute of International Economics. Retrieved from http://purl.umn.edu/26273 on 25.01.10

Michelle, L. (2009) *'Factors of Teacher Induction Which Impact Job Satisfaction and Attrition in Teachers'*, Thesis Submitted to the Mississippi State University.

Milkovich, G.T. and Boudreau, J. (1988) *'Personnel Human Resource Management : A Thiagnostic Approach'*, 5th ed., Business Publications Inc., U.S.A., pp. 165-177.

Miller, M. D., Brownell, M. and Smith, S. W. (1999) 'Factors that Predict Teachers Staying in Leaving, or Transferring from the Special Education Classroom' *Exceptional Children*, Vol. 65, No. 2, pp. 201-218.

Mills, V. K. F. (1995) *'Occupational Stress and Coping in Women Managers: Individual and Organizational Outcomes'*, Ph.D. Thesis, University of Denver, United States of America.

Minkler, M. and Biller, R.P. (1979) 'Role Shock : A 1001 Foe Conceptualizing Stresses Accompanying Disruptive Role Transitions', *Human Relations*, Vol. 29, No. 2, pp. 125-40.

Mishra, P.K. (1996) *'Role Stress in Special Groups'*, In D.M. Pestonjee (ed.), Stress and Coping : The Indian Experience (2nd ed.-pp.137-215), New Delhi, Sage Publications.

Misra, (1986) *'A Study of Meaning in Life, Stress and Burnout of Secondary School Teachers of Calcutta'*, Ph.D. Thesis, Centre of Advanced Studies in Education, M.S. University, Baroda.

Misshawk, M.J. (1971) 'Supervisory Skills and Employee Satisfaction', *Personnel Administration*, Vol. 34, pp. 29-33.

Mohammadyfar, M.A., Khan, M.S. and Tamini, B.K. (2009) 'The effect of Emotional Intelligence and Job Burnout on Mental and Physical Health', *Journal of the Indian Academy of Applied Psychology*, Vol. 35, No. 2, 219-226, July.

Mokdad, M., (2005) 'Occupational Stress Among Algerian Teachers', *African Newsletter on Occupational Health and Safety*, Vol.15, pp. 46-47.

Moos, R.H. and Insel, P.N. (1974) *'Moos Work Environment Scale'*, Consulting Psychologists Press, Palo Alto, CA.

Motseke, M. J. (1998) *'Factors Contributing to Teacher's Stress in Township Secondary Schools'*, Master's Thesis in Psychology of Education, University of South Africa, Pretoria.

Moulay, G.J. (1964) *'The Science of Educational Research'*, American Book Company, New York, p. 3.

Muchinsky, P.M. (2000) *'Psychology Applied to Work'*, 6th ed., Belmont, Wadsworth.

Muchinsky, P.M. (2000a) 'Emotions in the Workplace: The neglect of Organizational Behaviour', *Journal of Organizational Behaviour*, Vol. 21, pp. 801-805.

Mudgil, Y., Muhar, I.S. and Bhatia, P. (1991) *'Manual for Teacher's Job Satisfaction Scale'*, National Psychological Corporation, Agra.

Musthafa, M.A. and Jaseena, M.J. (2008) 'Job satisfaction of pre-school teachers of Kerala', *International Educator*, Vol. 20, No. 2, pp. 1-7.

Mykletun, R.J. (1984) 'Teacher Stress : Perceived and Objective Sources and Quality of Life', *Scandinavian Journal of Educational Research*, Vol. 28, No.1, pp. 17-45.

Nagel, L. and Brown, S. (2003) 'The ABCs of Managing Teacher Stress', *The Clearing House*, Vol. 76, pp. 255-258.

Nahavandi, A. and Malekzadeh, A. R. (1999) *'Organizational Behaviour: The Person - Organization Behaviour'*, Prentice-Hall, Upper Saddle River, New Jersey.

Nance, E. and Calabrese, R.L. (2009) 'Special Education Teacher Retention and Attrition: The Impact of Increased Legal Requirements', *International Journal of Educational Management*, Vol. 23, No.5, pp. 431-440.

Natale, J. (1993) 'Why Teachers Leave', *Executive Educator*, Vol. 15, No. 7, pp. 14-18, July.

Natarajan, P. (2001) 'School Organizational Climate and Job Satisfaction of Teachers', *Journal of Indian Education*, Vol. XXVII, No. 2, August.

National Center for Education Statistics— NCES (1997), *'Dropout rates in the United States: 1996', Retrieved from* http://nces.ed.gov/pubs98/dropout/index.html on 20.03.08

Nazar, N.A. and Ahmad, S.F. (1998) 'Sources of Satisfaction and Dissatisfaction Among Teachers (A test of two factor theory)', *Indian Journal of Training and Development*, Vol. 28, No.4, pp. 77-92.

Needle, R.H., Griffin, T., Svendsen, R. and Berney, C. (1980) 'Teacher Stress: Sources and Consequences', *Journal of School Health*, Vol. 50, No. 2, pp. 96-99.

Neelakandan, R. (2007) 'Emotional Competence of Primary School Teachers', *EduTracks*, Vol. 6, No. 9, pp. 30-33, May.

Neelakandan, R. and Rajendran, K. (2007) 'Job Satisfaction of Public Sector Employees', *Journal of Community Guidance and Research*, Vol. 22, No.1, pp. 76-80, March.

Neetha, A.J. (2008) *'An Interaction Effect of Language Proficiency, Emotional Intelligence and Reasoning Ability on Teaching Competency of D.Ed. Students'*, Ph.D. Thesis, Dept. of PG Studies and Research in Education, Kuvempu University.

Nelson, D. and Low, G. (1999) *'Exploring and Developing Emotional Intelligence Skills'*, EI Learning Systems, Kingsville, TX.

Nelson, D. and Low, G. (2003) *'Emotional Intelligence: Achieving Academic and Career Excellence'*, Prentice-Hall, Upper Saddle River, NJ.

Nelson, D. and Low, G. (2005) *'Emotional Intelligence: The Role of Transformative Learning in Academic Excellence'*, Texas Study of Secondary Education, Vol. 13, pp. 7-10.

Nelson, J. R. and Roberts, M. L. (2000) 'Ongoing Reciprocal Teacher-student Interactions Involving Disruptive Behaviours in General Education Classrooms', *Journal of Emotional and Behavioural Disorders*, Vol. 8, No. 1, pp. 27–37.

Nelson, J. R., Maculan, A., Roberts, M.L. and Ohlund, B. (2001) 'Sources of Occupational Stress for Teachers of Students with Emotional and Behavioural Disorders', *Journal of Emotional and Behavioural Disorders*, Vol. 9, No. 2, pp. 123-130.

Newell, S. (2002) *'Creating the Healthy Organization: Well-being, Diversity and Ethics at Work'*, Thomson Learning, London.

Newmann F. M., Rutter R. A. and Smith M. S. (1989) 'Organizational Factors that Affect School sense of Efficacy, Community, and Expectations', *Sociology of Education, Vol. 62, pp.* 221-238.

Nikolaou, I. and Tsaousis, I. (2002) 'Emotional Intelligence in the Workplace: Exploring its Effects on Occupational Stress and Organisational Commitment', *International Journal of Organizational Analysis*, Special Issue on Emotional Intelligence, No. 10, No. 4, pp. 327-342.

Nord, W. and Costigan, R. (1973) 'Worker Adjustment to the Four-day Week : A Longitudinal Study', *Journal of Applied Psychology*, Vol. 58, pp. 60-66.

NPE (1986) *'National Policy on Education'*, Ministry of Human Resource Development, Government of India, New Delhi.

O' Driscoll, M. P. and Beehr, T. A. (1994) 'Supervisor Behaviors, Role Stressors and Uncertainty as Predictors of Personal Outcomes for Subordinates', *Journal of Organizational Behaviour*, Vol. 15, pp. 141-155.

O' Driscoll, M. P. and Cooper, C. L. (2002) *'Job-related Stress and Burnout'*, In P. Warr (ed.), Psychology at work, (5th ed.), Clays Ltd., London.

O'Connor, P.R. and Clarke, V.A. (1990) 'Determinants of Teacher Stress', *Australian Journal of Education*, Vol. 34, No. 1, pp. 41-51.

Okebukola, P.A. and Jegede, O.F. (1989) 'Determinants of Occupational Stress Among Teachers in Nigeria', *Educational Studies*, Vol. 15, No. 1, pp. 23- 36.

Oliva, K. (2003) *'Special Education Teachers and Use of Technology'*, In C. Crawford et al. (eds.), *Proceedings of Society for Information Technology and Teacher Education International Conference 2003* (pp. 3748-3751), AACE, Chesapeake, VA, Retrieved from http://www. editlib.org/p/18816.

Ololube, N.P. (2006) 'Teachers Job Satisfaction and Motivation for School Effectiveness: An Assessment', *Essays in Education*, Vol. 18, Article 9, Fall.

Organ, D.W. and Bateman, T.S. (1991) *'Organizational Behaviour'*, Irwin, Boston.

Osipow, S. H. (1998) *'Occupational Stress Inventory: Revised Edition (OSI-R): Professional Manual'*, Psychological Assessment Resources, Odessa, Florida.

Otto, R. (1986) *'Teachers Under Stress: Health Hazards in a Work-role Mode of Response'*, Melbourne, Hill of Content.

Oxford Dictionary (2003) *'Oxford Dictionary of English'*, Oxford University Press, UK.

Palmer, B., and Stough, C. (2001) '*Workplace SUEIT: Swinburne University Emotional Intelligence Test-Interim Technical Manual*', Organisational Psychology Research Unit, Swinburne University, Australia.

Palmer, B., Donaldson, C. and Stough, C. (2002) 'Emotional Intelligence and Life Satisfaction', *Personality and Individual Differences*, Vol. 33, pp. 1091-1100.

Palomera, R. and Brackett, M.A. 92006) 'Frequency of Positive Affect as a Possible Mediator Between Perceived Emotional Intelligence and Life satisfaction', *Ansiedad y Estres*, Vol. 12, No. 2-3, pp. 231-239.

Panda, A.K. (2009) 'Emotional Intelligence and Personality Traits of Pupil Teachers', *Journal of Community Guidance and Research*, Vol. 26, No.2, pp. 122-136, July.

Pandey, Y. (2009) '*A Study of Barriers in the Implementation of Inclusive Education at the Elementary Level*', Ph.D. Thesis in Education submitted to the Jamia Millia Islamia, A Central University, New Delhi.

Pareek, A. and Metha, M. (1997) '*Role Stress in Special Groups*', In D.M., Pestonjee (ed.), Stress and Coping : The Indian Experience (2nd ed. - pp.137-215), New Delhi, Sage Publications.

Parker, J.D., Hogan, M.J., Eastabrook, J.M., Oke, A. and Wood, L.M. (2006) 'Emotional Intelligence and Student Retention : Predicting the Successful Transition from High School to University', *Personality and Individual Differences*, Vol. 41, No.7, pp. 1329-1336.

Paulse, J. (2005) '*Sources of Occupational Stress for Teachers, with Specific Reference to the Inclusive education Model in the Western Cape*', Mini-thesis submitted for the Degree of Master of Atium to the Department of Industrial Psychology, University of the Western Cape.

Payne, R. (2005) 'Special Education Teacher Shortages: Barriers or Lack of Preparation ?', *The International Journal of Special Education*, Vol. 20, No.1, pp. 88-91.

Pearlin, L. (1989) 'The Sociological Study of Stress', *Journal of Health and Social Behaviour*, Vol. 30, pp. 241-256.

Pelletier, K. R. and R. Lutz (1988) 'Healthy People—Healthy Business: A Critical Review of Stress management Programmes in the Workplace,' *American Journal of Health Promotion*, Vol. 2, No. 3, pp. 5-12.

Perie, M., Bake, D.P. and Whitener, S. (1997) '*Job Satisfaction Among America's Teachers : Effects of Workplace Conditions, Background Characteristics and Teacher Compensation*', Statistical Analysis Report, American Institutes for Research, National Centre for Education Statistics, U.S. Dept. of Education, Office of Educational Research and Improvement, NCES, 97-XXX, July, pp. 3-4.

Pethe, S., Chaudhari, S. and Dhar, U. (2001) *'Manual for Organizational Climate Scale'*, National Psychological Corporation, Agra.

Petrides, K. V. and Furnham, A. (2000) 'On the Dimensional Structure of Emotional Intelligence', *Personality and Individual Differences*, Vol. 29, pp. 313-320.

Petrides, K. V. and Furnham, A. (2001) 'Trait Emotional Intelligence: Psychometric Investigation with Reference to Established Trait Taxonomies', *European Journal of Personality*, Vol. 15, pp. 425-448.

Petrides, K. V. and Furnham, A. (2004) *'Technical Manual of the Trait Emotional Intelligence Questionnaire (TEIQue)'*, Institute of Education, University of London, London.

Petrides, K. V. and Furnham, A. (2006) 'The Role of Trait Emotional Intelligence in a Gender-specific Model of Organizational Variables', *Journal of Applied Social Psychology*, Vol. 36, No. 2, pp. 552-569.

Petrides, K. V., Pita, R. and Kokkinaki, F. (2007) 'The Location of Trait Emotional Intelligence in Personality Factor Space', *British Journal of Psychology*, Vol. 98, pp. 273-289.

Phillips, B.L. and Lee, M. (1980) *'The Changing Role of the American Teacher : Current and Future Sources of Stress'*, In C.L. Cooper and J. Marshall (eds.) White Collar and Professional Stress, Wiley, Chichester.

Pithers, R. T. (1995) 'Teacher Stress Research: Problems and Progress', *British Journal of Educational Psychology*, Vol. 65, pp. 387-392.

Platsidou, M. (2009) *'Burnout, Job Satisfaction and Emotional Intelligence of Special Education Teachers'*, Paper presented in EERA Conference 2009, Retrieved from http:// www. eera-ecer. eu/ecer- programmes-and-presentations/conference /ecer- 2009 /contribution/1368/ ?no_cache=1 on 20.8.09.

Platsidou, M. (2010) 'Trait Emotional Intelligence of Greek Special Education Teachers in Relation to Burnout and Job Satisfaction', *School Psychology International*, Vol. 31, No. 1, 60-76.

Platsidou, M. and Agaliotis, I. (2008) 'Burnout, Job Satisfaction and Instructional Assignment-related Sources of Stress in Greek Special Education Teachers', *International Journal of Disability, Development and Education*, Vol. 55, No.1, pp. 61-76, March.

Porter, L, Lawler, E. and Hackman, J. (1975) *'Behaviour in Organization'*, McGraw-Hill Company, New York.

Porter, L.W., Steers, R.M., Mowday, R.T. and Boulian, P.V. (1974) 'Organizational Commitment, Job Satisfaction and Turnover Among Psychiatric Technicians', *Journal of Applied Psychology*, Vol. 59, pp. 603-609.

Prakee, B., Peet, A.V. and Wolf, K. van der (2007) 'Challenging Parents, Teacher Occupational Stress and Health in Dutch Primary Schools', *International Journal about Parents in Education*, Vol. 1, pp.36-44.

Price, W. and Terry, E. J. (2008) *'Relationship Between Small Class Size in Early Elementary Grades and Teacher Job Satisfaction in a Single School District'*, Creative Commons Attribution License, Version1:2, July 2008, Retrieved from http://creativecommons.org/licence/by/2.0/ on 12.04.09.

Pritchard, R.A. and Karasick, B.W. (1973) 'The Effects of Oraganizational Climate on Managerial Job Performance and Job Satisfaction', *Behaviour and Human Performance*, Vol. 9, pp. 126-146.

Pullis, M. (1992) 'An Analysis of the Occupational Stress of Teachers of the Behaviourally Disordered: Sources, Effects, and Strategies for Coping', *Behavioural Disorders*, Vol. 17, No. 3, pp. 191-201.

Punch K. F. and Tuettemann, E. (1990) 'Correlates of Psychological Distress Among Secondary School Teachers', *British Educational Research Journal*, Vol. 16, pp. 369-382.

Qiang, X., Zhiwen, T. and Xinxia, H. (2008) 'A Study on Relationship Between Work Stress Source and Coping Style in School Teachers', *Chinese Journal of Special Education*, Retrieved from http://en.cnki.com.cn /Article_en/CJFDTOTAL-ZDTJ200806020.htm on 17.07.09.

Raj, T. (2001) 'An Empirical Study of Correlates of Teacher Effectiveness of Secondary School Teachers', *The Educational Review*, Vol. 107, No.1, pp. 6-8.

Rajeswari, S.M., Santhanam, T., Babu, B.P. and Rao, D.B. (2008) *'Stress and Attitude of Women Teachers'*, Discovery Publishing House, New Delhi.

Ramathulasamma, K. and Rao, D.B. (2003) *'Job Satisfaction of Teachers'*, Discovery Publishing House, New Delhi.

Ramayah, T., Jantan, M. and Tadisina, S.K. (2001) *'Job Satisfaction: Empirical Evidence of Alternatives to Job Descriptive Index'*, National Decision Sciences conference, San Francisco, November.

Ranft, V.A. and Ranft, A.L. (1999) *'Rightsizing the Multi-divisional Firm : Individual Response to Change Across Divisions'* West Virginia University, Carruth Counseling Center, pp. 199.

Rao, D.B. and Sridhar, D. (2003) *'Job Satisfaction of School Teachers'*, Discovery Publishing House, New Delhi.

Ravichandran, R. and Rajendran, R. (2007) 'Perceived Sources of Stress Among the Teachers', *Journal of the Indian Academy of Applied Psychology*, Vol. 33, No.1, pp. 133-136, January.

Reddy, G.L. (2005) *'Role Performance of Special Education Teachers : Problems and Prospects'*, Discovery Publishing House, New Delhi.

Reddy, G.L. (2000) *'Role Performance of the Special Education Teachers'*, Major Research Project Report, sponsored by (ERIC-NCERT, New Delhi) Dept. of Education, Alagappa University, Karaikudi.

Reddy, G.L. (2004) *'Awareness, Attitude and Competencies Required for Special and Normal School Teachers in Dealing Children with Disabilities'*, Major Research Project Report, sponsored by Ministry of Social Justice and Empowerment, Govt. of India, New Delhi, Dept. of Education, Alagappa University, Karaikudi.

Reddy, G.L. (2007) *'Occupational Stress, Professional Burnout and Job Satisfaction of Special Education Teachers'*, Major Research Project, Ministry of Social Justice and Empowerment, Govt., of India, New Delhi.

Reddy, G.L. and Poornima, R. (2008) 'Problems Faced by the Special Education Teachers Working in the Schools for Mentally Retarded Children', *Journal of Disabilities and Impairment*, Vol. 22, No.2, pp. 111-119.

Reddy, G.L. and Poornima, R. (2009) 'A Study on Occupational Stress of Teachers Working in the Special Schools for Visually Impaired Children', *Disabilities and Impairments*, Vol. 23, No.1, pp. 7-18.

Reed, T.G. (2005) *'Elementary Principal Emotional Intelligence, Leadership Behaviour and Openness : An Exploratory Study'*, Ph.D. Thesis submitted to the Graduate School of the Ohio State University.

Remould, J. E. (2006) 'Enhancing Emotional Intelligence of Student Teachers Through Enneagram Educational Programme', *EduTracks*, Vol. 6, No.3, pp. 25-31, November.

Rieg, Sue A. Paquette, Kelli R.; Chen, Yijie (2007) 'Coping with Stress: An Investigation of Novice Teacher's Stressors in the Elementary Classroom', *Education*, Vol. 128, No.2, pp. 211-226, December.

Robbins, S., Water-Marsh, T., Caciope, R. and Millet, B. (1994) *'Organizational Behaviour Concepts, Controversies and Applications'*, Prentice Hall, Sydney, Australia.

Robinson, J., Athanasiou, R. and Head, K. (1969) *'Measures of Occupational Attitudes and Occupational Characteristics'*, Ann Arbor, University of Michigan Survey Research Center.

Rocca, A.D. and Kostanski, M. (2001) *'Burnout and Job Satisfaction Amongst Victorian Secondary School Teachers : A Comparative Look at Contract and Permanent Employment'*, Discussion paper ATEA Conference— Teacher Education : Change of Heart, Mind and Action, Melbourne, pp. 1-7.

Rogers, R.E. and McIntire, R.H. (1983) '*Organization and Management Theory*', John Wiley & Sons, New York, pp. 130-150.

Rosenblatt, Z. and Shirom, A. (2004) 'Predicting Teacher Absenteeism by Personal Background Factors', *Journal of Educational Administration*, Vol. 43, No. 2, pp. 209-225.

Rosenholtz S. J. (1985) 'Effective Schools: Interpreting the Evidence', *American Journal of Education, Vol. 93, pp.* 352-388.

Ross Azura, Z. and Normah, C. D. (2008) *'Teacher Stress: An Examination of Factors Influencing Teaching Performance in the Rural Elementary Schools'*, Simposium Sains Kesihatan Kebangsaan ke 7, Hotel Legend, Kuala Lumpur, pp. 224 - 225, 18th -19th, June 2008, Retrieved from http://www.fskb.ukm.my/penerbitan/sihat 2008/ Psikologi%20Kesihatan/Ros%20Azura%20ms%20224%20%20225.pdf.

Rout, U. R. and Rout, J. K. (2002) *'Stress Management for Primary Health Professionals'*, Kluwer Academic/Plenum Publishers, New York.

Russell, D.W., Altmaier, E. and Van Velzen, D. (1987) 'Job-related Stress, Social Support and Burnout Among Classroom Teachers', *Journal of Applied Psychology*, Vol. 72, No. 2, pp. 269-74.

Sahaya Mary, R. and Samuel, M. (2010) 'Influence of Emotional Intelligence on Attitude Towards Teaching of Student Teachers' *EduTracks*, Vol. 9, No.12, pp.42 – 46, August.

Salami, S.O. (2007) 'Relationships of Emotional Intelligence and Self-efficacy to Work Attitudes Among Secondary School Teachers in South Western Nigeria', *Essays in Education*, Vol. 20, pp. 43-56, Spring.

Salami, S.O. (2008) 'Impact of Job Satisfaction and Organizational Commitment on Organizational Citizenship behaviour : The Moderating Role of Group Cohesiveness', *Perspectives in Education*, Vol. 24, No.1, pp. 40-50.

Salo, K. (2002) *'Teachers Stress as a Longitudinal Process'*, Research Project : Teacher Work, Stress and Health', University of Jyväskylä, Jyväskylä Studies in Education, Psychology and Social Research, Finland.

Salovey, P. and Grewal, D. (2005) 'The Science of Emotional Intelligence', *Current Directions in Psychological Science*, Vol. 14 -16, pp. 281–285.

Salovey, P. and Mayer, J. (1997) 'EI Meets Traditional Standards for an Intelligence', *Intelligence*, Vol. 27, pp. 267-298.

Salovey, P. and Mayer, J.D. (1990) 'Emotional Intelligence', *Imagination, Cognition and Personality*, Vol. 9, pp. 185-211.

Salovey, P., Stroud, L.R., Woolery, A. and Epel, E.S. (2002) 'Perceived Emotional Intelligence, Stress Reactivity and Symptom Reports :

Further Explorations Using the Trait Meta-mood Scale', *Psychology and Health*, Vol. 17, pp. 611-627.

Santavirta, N., Solovieva, S. and Theorell, T. (2007) 'The Association Between Job Strain and Emotional Exhaustion in a Cohort of 1,028 Finnish Teachers', *British Journal of Educational Psychology*, Vol. 77, No. 1, pp. 213-228, March.

Santhakumari, (2003) '*Effectiveness of Meta-cognitive Strategies to Overcome Language Learning Difficulties Among Higher Secondary Students*', Ph.D. Thesis, Alagappa University, Karaikudi.

Sargent, T. and Hannum, E. (2003) '*Keeping Teachers Happy: Job Satisfaction Among Primary School Teachers in Rural China*', Paper prepared for the International Sociology Association Research Committee on Social Stratification and Mobility (RC28), August 21-23, 2003, New York University.

Sarros, J.C. and Sarros, A.M. (1992) 'Social Support and Teacher Burnout', *Journal of Educational Administration*, Vol. 30, No.1, pp. 55-69.

Saveri, Sr. (2009) 'Relationship Between Job Satisfaction and Life Satisfaction Among B.T. Assistant Teachers', *EduTracks*, Vol. 8, No.9, pp. 37-40, May.

Saxena, S.K. (1994) '*Manual for Job Satisfaction Scale for Teacher's : Form B - for School Teachers*', Agra Psychological Research Cell, Agra.

Schneider, G.T. (1984) 'Teacher Involvement in Decision Making Zones of Acceptance, Decision Condition and Job Satisfaction', *Journal of Research and Development in Education*, Vol. 18, pp. 25-32.

Schonfeld I. S. (1992) 'School Conditions Induce Teacher Depression', *Teaching and Teacher Education, Vol. 8, pp.* 151-158.

Schwab, R.L. (1983) 'Teacher Burnout : Moving Beyond Psychobabble', *Theory Into Practice*, Vol. 22. pp. 21-25.

Schwab, R.L. and Iwanicki, E.F. (1982) 'Perceived Role Conflict, Role Ambiguity and Teacher Burnout', *Education Administrative Quarterly*, Vol. 18, pp. 60-74.

Schwarzer, R. and Hallum, S. (2008) 'Perceived Teacher Self-efficacy as a Predictor of Job Stress and Burnout: Mediation Analyses', *Applied Psychology : An International Review*, Vol. 57, pp. 152–171.

Seaward, B.L. (2005) '*Managing Stress: Principals and Strategies for Health and well-being*', Sudbury, Jones & Bartlett Publishers, Massachusetts.

Selye, H. (1936). 'A Syndrome Produced by Diverse Nocuous Agents', *Nature* Vol. 138, pp. 32. Retrieved from http://www.nature.com/nature/journal /v138 /n3479/pdf /138032a0. pdf on 8.04.08.

Selye, H. (1976) *'The Stress of Life'*, McGraw-Hill, New York.

Shafeeq, N.Y. (2000) 'A Study of Job Satisfaction of Teachers Working in the Schools for Visually Impaired in Relation to Their Adjustment', *Disabilities and Impairments*, Vol.14, No. 2, pp. 115-119.

Shann, M. H. (1998) 'Professional Commitment and Satisfaction Among Teachers in Urban Middle Schools', *The Journal of Educational Research*, Vol. 92, No. 2, pp. 67-86.

Sharma, B.K. and Patnaik, S.P. (2009) 'Organizational Health of Elementary Schools and Job Satisfaction of Teachers', *EduTracks*, Vol. 8, No. 6, pp. 32-34, February.

Sharma, H.C. and Bharadwaj, R. (1995) *'Manual for the Scale of Emotional Competencies'*, Pankajan Mapan, Bal Niwas, Taj Basai, Agra.

Sharma, R. (2008) 'A Study of Art Competencies of B.Ed. Pupil Teachers as Correlates of Emotional Intelligence, Creativity and Achievement Motivation', *Journal of Teacher Education and Research*, Vol. 3, No. 1, pp. 15-18, June.

Shaw, S.F., Bensky, J.M. and Dixon, B. (1981) *'Stress and Burnout: A Primer for Special Education and Special Education Services Personnel'*, Council for Exceptional Children, Reston, VA.

Shejwal, B.R. and Mohammadi, S. (2006) 'Job Burnout and Coping Mechanisms Among High School Teachers', *Journal of Psychological Researchers*, Vol. 50, No. 1, pp. 27-33.

Shukla, A. and Trivedi, T. (2008) 'Burnout in Indian Teachers', *Asia Pacific Education Review*, Vol. 9, No. 3, pp. 320-334.

Shyamala, V. (2004) *'Effectiveness of Certain Strategies in Overcoming Antisocial Behaviour Among High School Students'*, Ph.D. Thesis, Alagappa University, Karaikudi.

Sibia, A., Misra, G. and Srivastava, A.K. (2004) 'Towards Understanding Emotional Intelligence in the Indian Context: Perspectives of Parents, Teachers and Children', *Psychological Studies*, Vol. 49, No. 2 & 3, pp. 114-123, April-July.

Siegall, M. and Cummings, L.L. (1995) 'Stress and Organizational Role Conflict', *Genetic, Social and General Psychology Monographs*, Vol. 121, No.1, pp. 67-95, February.

Siegrist J (1996) 'Adverse Health Effects of High Effort—Low Reward Conditions at Work', *Journal of Occupational Health Psychology*, Vol. 1, pp. 27-43.

Siegrist, J., Siegrist, K., and Weber, I. (1986) 'Sociological Concepts in the Etiology of Chronic Disease: The Case of Ischemic Heart Disease', *Social Science and Medicine*, Vol. 22, pp. 247- 253.

Singer, J. D. (1993) 'Are Special Educators' Career Paths Special ? : Results from a 13-year Longitudinal Study', *Exceptional Children,* Vol. 59, No. 3, pp. 262-279.

Singh, A. and Sharma,T.R. (1999) *'Manual for Job Satisfaction Scale'*, National Psychological Corporation, Agra.

Singh, D. (2003) *'Emotional Intelligence at Work : A Professional Guide'*, 2nd ed., Sage Publications, New Delhi.

Singh, D. (2006) *'Emotional Intelligence at Work : A Professional Guide'*, 3rd ed., Response Books - A Division of Sage Publications, New Delhi.

Singh, G. (2007) 'Job Satisfaction of Teacher Educators in Relation to Their Attitude Towards Teaching', *Journal of All India Association for Educational Research,* Vol. 19, No. 3 and 4, pp. 86-87, Sep. and Dec.

Singh, K. and Billingsley, B.S. (1996) 'Intent to Stay in Teaching : Teachers of Students with Emotional Disorders Versus Other Special Educators', *Remedial and Special Education,* Vol. 17, No.1, pp. 37-47.

Singh, K. and Billingsley, B.S. (1998) 'Professional Support and Its Effects on Teacher's Commitment', *The Journal of Educational Research,* Vol. 91, No. 4, pp. 229-239, Mar. - Apr.

Singh, S. and Koteswari, V.B. (2006) 'Emotional Intelligence and Coping Resources of Stress Among Project Managers', *EduTracks,* Vol. 5, No. 12, pp. 33-36, August.

Singhal, S. (2004) *'Stress in Education : Indian Experience'*, Rawat Publications, New Delhi.

Sinha, A.K. and Jain, A. K. (2004) 'Emotional Intelligence : Imperative for the Organizationally Relevant Outcomes', *Psychological Studies,* Vol. 49, No. 2 & 3, pp. 81-96, April –July.

Slaski, M. and Cartwright, S. (2002) 'Health, Performance and EI: An Exploratory Study of Retail Managers', *Stress and Health,* Vol. 18, No. 2, pp. 63- 68.

Slaski, M. and Cartwright, S. (2003) 'EI Training and Its Implications for Stress, Health and Performance', *Stress and Health,* Vol. 19, No. 4, pp. 233-239.

Smith T. M. and Ingersoll R. M. (2004) 'What are the Effects of Induction and Mentoring on Beginning Teacher Turnover ?', *American Educational Research Journal, Vol. 41,* pp. 681-714.

Smith, E., Anderson, J. L., and Lovrich, N. P. (1995) 'The Multiple Sources of Workplace Stress Among Land-grant University Faculty', *Research in Higher Education,* Vol. 36, pp. 261-282.

Smith, J. and Cline, D. (1980) 'Quality Programmes', *Pointer*, Vol. 24 No.2, pp. 80-87.

Smith, P.C., Kendall, L.M. and Hulin, C.L. (1969) *'Measurement of Satisfaction in Work and Retirement'*, Rand McNally- Chicago, IL.

Snelgrove, S.R. (1998) 'Occupationalstress and Job Satisfaction: A Comparative Study of Health Visitors, Districts Nurses and Community Psychiatric Nurses', *Journal of Nursing Management*, Vol. 6, No. 2, pp. 97-104.

Solman, R. and Feld, M. (1989) 'Occupational Stress: Perceptions of Teachers in Catholic Schools', *Journal of Educational Administration*, Vol. 27, No. 3, pp. 55-68.

Sparks, D.C. (1979) 'A Biased Look at Teacher Job Satisfaction', *Clearing House*, Vol. 52, No. 9. pp. 447-449.

Sparks, D.C. and Hammond, J. (1981) *'Managing Teacher Stress and Burnout'*, Educational Information Research, Educational Information Research Center, No. 200252, Washington, DC.

Spector, P. E. (1997) *'Job Satisfaction: Application, Assessment, Causes, and Consequences'*, Sage Publications, Inc, Thousand Oaks, California.

Spector, P.E. (2000) *'Industrial and Organizational Psychology : Research and Practice'*, 2nd ed., John Wiley & Sons, New York,

Spector, P.E. (1994) *'Job Satisfaction Survey'*, Department of Psychology, University of South Florida, Tampa, FL.

Spector, P.E. and Goh, A. (2001) *'The Role of Emotions in the Occupational Stress Process'*, In P. L. Perrewe and D. C. Ganster (eds.), Exploring Theoretical Mechanisms and Perspectives, JAI, New York, pp. 195-232.

Spielberger, C.D. (1979) *'Understanding Stress and Anxiety'*, Harper & Row, New York.

Spielberger, C.D. and Vagg, P.R. (1999) *'Job Stress Survey: Professional Manual'*, Psychological Assessment Resources, Lutz, Florida.

Sreedevi, P. and Saradaa Devi, M. (2008) 'Stress and Coping Among Parents of Children with Learning Disabilities', *Journal of Community Guidance and Research*, Vol. 25, No.3, pp. 333-339, November.

Srivastava, A.K. and Krishna, A. (1991) 'Development of a Functional Role Stress Scale', *Advances in Psychology*, Vol. 6, pp. 11 - 17.

Srivastava, A.K. and Krishna, A. (1994) 'Work Motivation and Job Involvement of Male and Female Teachers: A Comparative Study', *Journal of Psychological Researches*, Vol.38, No. 1 & 2, pp. 55-59.

Srivastava, A.K. and Singh, A.P. (1981) 'Construction and Standardization of an Occupational Stress Index : A Pilot Study', *Indian Journal of Clinical Psychology*, Vol. 8, pp. 8-12.

Stamps, P.L. and Piedmonte, E.B. (1986) *'Nurses and Work Satisfaction: An Index for Measurement'*, Health Administration Press Perspectives, Ann Arbor, MI.

Starnaman, S.M. and Miller, K.I. (1992) 'A Test of a Causal Model of Communication and Burnout in the Teaching Profession', *Communication Education*, Vol. 41, No.1, pp. 40-55.

Steinberg, A. and Ritzmann, R. F. (1990) 'A Living Systems Approach to Understanding the Concept of Stress', *Behavioral Sciences*, Vol. 35, pp. 138-146.

Stempien, L.R. and Loeb, R.C. (2002) 'Differences in Job Satisfaction Between General Education and Special Education Teachers: Implications for Retention', *Remedial and Special Education*, Vol. 23, No. 5, pp. 258-267.

Sternberg, R. J. (1996) *'Successful Intelligence: How Practical and Creative Intelligence Determine Success in Life'*, Simon & Schuster, New York.

Stress Report (1999) *'Study on stress : The cause of stress for teachers, its effects, and suggested approaches to reduce it'*, Education International (EI)/ European Trade Union Committee for Education (ETUCE) in collaboration with the World Health Organisation (WHO).

Sud, A. and Malik, A.K. (1999) 'Job Related Stress, Social Support and Trait Anxiety Among School Teachers', *Journal of the Indian Academy of Applied Psychology*, Vol. 25, No. 1 & 2, pp. 25-33.

Sultana, A. (1995) *'Role Stress in Special Groups'*, In D.M. Pestonjee (ed.), Stress and Coping : The Indian experience (2nd ed. - pp.137-215), New Delhi, Sage Publications.

Sumangala, V. and Ushadevi, V.K. (2009) 'Role Conflict, Attitude Towards Teaching Profession and Job Satisfaction as Predictors of success in Teaching', *EduTracks*, Vol. 8, No. 9, pp. 25-30, May 2009.

Suresh, K. and Rao, D.B. (2009) *'Social Intelligence of Student Teachers'* Discovery Publishing House, New Delhi.

Suresh, K.J. and Joshith, V.P. (2008) *'Emotional Intelligence as a Correlate of Stress of Student Teachers'*, EduTracks, Vol. 7, No. 12, pp. 26-32.

Suryanarayana, N.V.S., Himabindu, G. and Sarma, G.M.S.S. (2009) *'Teachers Stress in Relation to Job Satisfaction'*, Retrieved from http:// www.articlesbase.com /education-articles/teachers-stress-in-relation-to-job satisfaction- 1295058.html on 12.01.10.

Sutherland, V.J. and Cooper, C.L. (1991) *'Understanding Stress : A Psychological Perspective for Health Professionals'*, Chapman and Hall, London.

Swani, P. (2008) 'The Impact of Emotions on Health and Well-being', *Journal of Community Guidance and Research*, Vol. 25, No. 1, pp. 98-105, March.

Swanson, V., Power, K. and Simpson, R. (1998) 'A Comparison of Stress and Job Satisfaction in Female and Male GPs and Consultants', *Stress Medicine*, Vol. 12, No. 1, pp. 17-26.

Sweeney, J. (1981) 'Professional Discretion and Teacher Satisfaction', *High School Journal*, Vol. 65, pp. 1-6.

Sy, T., Tram, S. and O'Hara, L.A. (2006) 'Relation of Employee and Manager Emotional Intelligence to Job Satisfaction and Performance', *Journal of Vocational Behaviour*, Vol. 68, No. 3, pp. 461-473.

Talmor R., Reiter S. and Feigin N. (2005) 'Factors Relating to Regular Education Teacher Burnout in Inclusive Education', *European Journal of Special Needs Education, Vol. 20*, pp. 215-229.

Talmor R., Reiter S. and Feigin N. (2005a) 'Erratum: Factors relating to regular education teacher burnout in inclusive education', *European Journal of Special Needs Education, Vol. 20, pp.* 455.

Tasnim, S. (2006) *'Job Satisfaction Among Female Teachers: A Study on Primary Schools in Bangladesh'*, M.Phil. Thesis Submitted to the University of Bergen, Norway, Retrieved form www.masteropgave.tasnim.pdf.html. On 05.08.10.

Tatar, M. and Horenczyk, G. (2003) 'Diversity-related Burnout Among Teachers', *Teaching and Teacher Education*, Vol. 19, pp. 397-408.

Tellenbeck, S., Brenner, S.O. and Lofgren, H. (1983) 'Teacher Stress : Exploratory Model Building', *Journal of Occupational Psychology*, Vol. 56, pp. 19-33.

Thiebaut, E., Breton, A., Lambolez, E. and Richoux, V. (2005) 'Study of Relations Between the Bar-On Emotional Intelligence EQ-I Scores and Self-reports of Job Satisfaction', *Psychologie du Travail et des Organisations*, Vol. 11, No. 1, pp. 35-45.

Thomas, N., Clarke, V. and Lavery, J. (2003) 'Self-reported Work and Family Stress of Female Primary Teachers', *Australian Journal of Education*, Vol. 41, No.1, pp. 40-55.

Thompson, C. J. and Dey, E. L. (1998) 'Pushed to the Margins: Sources of Stress for African American College and University Faculty', *Journal of Higher Education*, Vol. 69, pp. 324-345.

Thorndike, E.L. (1920) *'Intelligence and Its Uses'*, Harper's Magazine, Vol. 140, pp. 227-235.

Toni, E. (2005) *'The Relationship of Occupational Stress, Psychological Strain, Satisfaction with Job, Commitment to the Profession, Age, and Resilience to the Turnover Intentions of Special Education Teachers'*, Thesis Submitted to Virginia Polytechnic Institute and State University.

Tosi, H. L., Mero, N. P. and Rizzo, J. R. (2000) *'Managing Organizational Behaviour'*, 4th ed., Blackwell Business, Cambridge, Mass.

Travers C. J. and Cooper, C. L. (1996) *'Teachers Under Pressure: Stress in the Teaching Profession'*, Routledge, London.

Trendall, C. (1989) 'Stress in Teaching and Teacher Effectiveness: A Study of Teachers Across Mainstream and Special Education', *Educational Research*, Vol. 31, pp. 52-58.

Troman, G. (2000) 'Teachers Stress in Low Trust Society', *British Journal of Sociology of Education*, Vol. 21, No. 3, pp. 331-353.

Tsai, E., Fung, L. and Chow, L. (2006) 'Sources and Manifestations of Stress in Female Kindergarten Teachers', *International Education Journal*, Vol. 7, No. 3, pp. 364-370, Retrieved from http://iej.com.au *364* on 02.03.08.

Umadevi, M.R. (2009) 'Relationship Between Emotional Intelligence, Achievement Motivation and Academic Achievement', *EduTracks*, Vol. 8, No. 12, pp. 31-35, August.

United Kingdom Health and Safety Commission, London, (1999) *'Stress at Work'*, NIOSH Publication No. 99-101, NIOSH, Cincinnati, Retrieved from http://www.cdc.gov/niosh on 13.08.09.

Usha Rao, (2008) 'Emotional Maturity and Role of the Teacher', *EduTracks*, Vol. 7, No. 8, pp. 12, April.

Ushasree, S. and Jamuna, D. (1990) *'Role Conflict and Job Stress Among Special and General School Teachers'*, Paper Presented at the 27th Annual Conference of IAAP, Aligarh Muslim University, Aligarh.

Usmani, S.N., Pandey, S.N. and Ahmad, J. (2006) 'Teacher Job Satisfaction in Relation to Their Personality Type and Type of School', *EduTracks*, Vol. 5, No. 6.

Vaijayanthi, R. and Sunny, J. (2010) 'Stress Among Student Teachers in Coimbatore City', *Research Highlights*, Vol. 20, No.1, pp. 51-57.

Vijayalakshmi, G. (2005) 'Teacher Effectiveness and Job Satisfaction of Women Teachers', *EduTracks*, Vol. 4, No. 7, pp.29-30, March.

Vijesh, P.V. and Sukumaran, P.S. (2007) 'Stress Among Mothers of Children with Cerebral Palsy Attending Special Schools', *Asia Pacific Disability Rehabilitation Journal*, Vol. 18, No. 1, pp. 76-92.

Vinokur-Kaplan J.X. (1991) 'Job Satisfaction Among Social Workers in Public and Voluntary Child Welfare Agencies', *Child Welfare*, Vol. 155, pp.81-91.

Vroom, V.H. (1960) *'Some Personality Determinants of the Effects of Participation'*, Englewood Cliffs, Prentice-Hall, New Jersey.

Vroom, V.H. (1964) *'Work and Motivation'*, John Wiley, New York.

Wanberg, E.G. (1984) 'The Complex Issue of Teacher Stress and Job Dissatisfaction', *Contemporary Education*, Vol. 56, No. 1, pp. 11-15.

Wanous, J.P. and Lawler, E.E. (1972) 'Measurement and Meaning of Job Satisfaction', *Journal of Applied Psychology*, Vol. 56, No. 2, pp. 95-105.

Warr, P., Cook, J. and Wall, T. (1979) 'Scales for the Measurement of Some Work Attitudes and Aspects of Psychological Well-being', *Journal of Occupational Psychology*, Vol. 52, pp.129-148.

Weisinger, H. (1998) *'Emotional Intelligence at Work'*, Jossey-Bass, San Francisco, pp. 45-51.

Weiskopf, P.E. (1980) 'Burnout Among Teachers of Exceptional Children', *Exceptional Children*, Vol. 47, pp. 18-23.

Weiss, D.J., Davis, R.V., England, G.W. and Lofquist, L.H. (1967) *'Manual for the Minnesota Satisfaction Questionnaire'*, The University of Minnesota Press, Minneapolis, MN.

Wetzel, C.M., Kneebone, R.L., Woloshynowych, M., Moorthy, K. and Darsy, A.D. (2006) 'The Effects of Stress on Surgical Performance', *The American Journal of Surgery*, Vol. 191, No. 1, pp. 5-10.

Wheeler, K., Gurman, R. and Tarnoweiski, D. (1972) *'The Four-Day Week'*, American Management Association, New York.

Whitehead, A.J. and Ryba, K. (1995) 'New Zealand Teacher's Perceptions of Occupational Stress and Coping Strategies', *New Zealand Journal of Educational Studies*, Vol. 30, No. 2, pp.177-188.

Wiener, R.M. (1987) 'Ten Steps to Implement a Special Education Microcomputer Curriculum', *Closing the Gap*, Vol. 6, No. 1, pp. 8.

Wiley, C. (2000) 'A Synthesis of Research on the Causes, Effects, and Reduction Strategies of Teacher Stress', *Journal of Instructional Psychology*, Vol. 27, pp. 80-87.

Williams, H. W. (2008) 'Characteristics that Distinguish Outstanding Urban Principals: Emotional Intelligence, Social Intelligence and Environ-mental Adaptation', *Journal of Management Development*, Vol. 27, No. 1, pp. 36-54.

Williams, K., and Poel, E.W. (2006) 'Stress Management for Special Educators: The Self Administered Tool for Awareness and Relaxation

(STAR)', *Teaching Exceptional Children Plus*, Vol. 3, No. 1, Retrieved from http://escholarship.bc.edu/education/tecplus/vol3/iss1/art2 on 04.12.09.

Williams, M. and Gersch, I. (2004) 'Teaching in Mainstream and Special Schools: Are the Stresses Similar or Different ?', *British Journal of Special Education*, Vol. 31, No. 3, pp. 157-162, September.

Wilson, V. and Hall, J. (2002) 'Running Twice as Fast ?: A Review of Literature on Teachers' Stress', *Scottish Educational Review*, Vol. 34, No. 2, pp. 175-187, November.

Winefield, A.H., Gillespie, N., Stough, C., Dua, J. and Hapuararchchi, J. (2002) '*Occupational Stress in Australian Universities: A National Survey 2002*', National Tertiary Education Union, South Melbourne.

Wisniewski, L. and Gargiulo, R.M. (1997) 'Occupational Stress and Burnout Among Special Educators : A Review of the Literature', *The Journal of Special Education*, Vol. 31, No.3, pp. 325 -346.

Wong, C.S., Wong, P.M. and Peng, K.Z. (2010) 'Effect of Middle-level Leader and Teacher Emotional Intelligence on School Teacher's Job Satisfaction'. *Educational Management, Administration & Leadership*, Vol. 38, No. 1, pp. 59-70.

World Health Organization (WHO) (2005) 'Mental Health and Working Life', *WHO European Ministerial Conference on Mental Health: Facing the Challenges, Building Solutions*, Retrieved from www.euro.who.int/document/mnh/ebrief06 .pdf on 19.06.2007.

Wu, S., Li, J., Wang, M., Wang, Z. and Li, H. (2006) 'Intervention on Occupational Stress Among Teachers in the Middle Schools in China', *Stress and Health*, Vol. 22, No. 5, pp. 329 - 336.

Yate, M. (1977) '*Career Smarts, Jobs with a Future*', Ballantine Books, New York

Yee, S. M. (1990) '*Careers in the Classroom: When Teaching is More Than a Job*', Teacher's College Press, New York.

Yezzi, J. and Lester, D. (2000) 'Job satisfaction in teachers', *Psychological Reports*, Vol. 87, No. 1, pp. 776.

Yoon J. S. (2008) 'Teacher Characteristics as Predictors of Teacher-student Relationships: Stress, Negative Affect and Self-efficacy', *Social Behaviour and Personality, Vol. 30,* pp. 485-494.

Zabel, R. H. and Zabel, M. K. (1982) 'Factors in Burnout Among Teachers of Exceptional Children', *Exceptional Children*, Vol. 49, pp. 261-263.

Zabel, R.H., Boomer, L.W. and King, T.R. (1984) 'A Model of Stress and Burnout Among Teachers of Behavioural Disordered Students', *Behavioural Disorders*, Vol. 9, pp. 215-221.

Zembylas, M. and Papanastasiou, E. (2004) 'Job Satisfaction Among School Teachers in Cyprus', *Journal of Educational Administration*, Vol. 42, No. 3, pp. 357-374.

Zhihong, L., Xuming, R., Lin, L. and Kan, S. (2008) 'Stressors, Teaching Efficacy and Burnout Among Secondary School Teachers', *Psychological Science*, Retrieved form http://en.cnki.com.cn/Article_en/CJFDTOTALXLKX 20080 1050.htm on 05.04.09.

Zhong, F., Yano, E., Lan, Y., Wang, M., Wang, Z., & Wang, X. (2006) 'Mental Ability and Psychological Work Performance in Chinese Workers' *Industrial Health*, Vol. 44, pp. 598-603.

Index

S